# Writing for a Reason

# Writing for a Reason

## William H. Barnwell
University of New Orleans

Houghton Mifflin Company   Boston

Dallas   Geneva, Illinois   Hopewell, New Jersey   Palo Alto   London

... and report cards I was always
Afraid to show
Mama'd come to school
And, as I'd sit there softly crying
Teacher'd say he's just not trying
He's got a good head if he'd apply it
But you know yourself
It's always somewhere else

I built me a castle
With dragons and kings
And I'd ride off with them
As I stood by my window
And looked out on those
Brooklyn roads ...

—Neil Diamond, "Brooklyn Roads"

**To my students, with love.**

## Acknowledgments

Part opening photographs by Thomas Wedell/Skolos, Wedell & Raynor.

ANGELOU, MAYA   From AND STILL I RISE, by Maya Angelou. Copyright © 1978 by Maya Angelou. Reprinted by permission of Random House, Inc.

DIAMOND, NEIL   From BROOKLYN ROADS by Neil Diamond. © 1968 Stonebridge Music. All rights reserved. Used by permission.

GIPE, GEORGE   The following article is reprinted courtesy of SPORTS ILLUSTRATED from the September 15, 1975 issue. © 1975 Time Inc. Yesterday by George Gipe. "Did The Crash Of A Stanley Steamer in 1907 Influence U. S. Foreign Policy?"

GROSS, SUZANNE   "Dateline Death" by Suzanne Gross was first published by *The Beloit Poetry Journal* in *TERN'S BONE: A CHAPBOOK OF POEMS BY SUZANNE GROSS.*

WRIGHT, RICHARD   Specified excerpts (pp. 14–16, 218–219) from BLACK BOY by Richard Wright. Copyright, 1937, 1942, 1944, 1945, by Richard Wright. Reprinted by permission of Harper & Row, Publishers, Inc.

In addition, the author would like to thank those students who contributed essays to the book.

Library of Congress Catalog Card Number: 82-83174

ISBN: 0-395-32597-8

# Contents

# To the Instructor

This text is intended for beginning writers. It is based on the premise that these students have something to say in their writing and have the ability to say it. I have tried to make the text as comprehensive as possible so that you will find what you need—whatever your teaching style—as you plan for a particular class of students.

## Approach

In the text I attempt to reinforce strengths students already have and, at the same time, teach organization, style, and the mechanics of English. I believe that beginning writers can best improve their writing by completing short essays on topics that are important to them. This way they see that writing is not just an exercise but that it adds to their lives: they learn that there is a reason for writing.

A few years ago I asked my beginning students to write about an experience they would like to forget and to say what they learned from the experience. I showed them samples of student writing on the same assignment, made suggestions on how to organize their papers, and urged them to tell their stories as though they were talking to other members of the class. I then asked the students to read their papers aloud to small groups that were led by more advanced writing students who had done well in their English courses. Over the next few days I went from group to group, sitting in, listening to the papers that were read and to the discussion that followed. The advanced students had completed the same assignment and were also reading their papers to the groups.

To my surprise, it was hard to tell, just from listening to the papers, which had been written by beginning students and which had been written by more advanced students. The beginning students used vivid detail, usually told their stories in a coherent way, and seemed to give good variety to their sentences. Later, after I had heard the papers read aloud, I collected them to edit and grade. Some of the papers that had sounded quite good were not only full of errors but were written in handwriting that was at times hard to decipher. What had sounded like interesting compound and complex sentences often turned out to be fragments and run-on sentences. This time there was no doubt as to which papers had been written by the beginning students and which had been written by the advanced students.

I came to realize from that experience and others like it that even though beginning students may need practice with the mechanics of English, they do have the capacity to express their thoughts in writing. I realized further that as their instructor I needed to give them encouragement, suggestions for organization and style, and practice both in writing essays and in the mechanics of English. *I did not need to impose on them a whole new way of speaking in their writing.* My hope is that this text will help students identify strengths they already have and will supplement, not replace, those strengths.

## Organization

Part One, "Writing with Style" (Chapters 1 through 4), is designed to lead students one step at a time to the point where they can write well-structured essays of 300 or more words. Chapter 1, "You and Your Audience," should help students get to know one another and to relax when they write, through use of in-class group assignments. By the time they finish the chapter, they should have a good sense of audience, of writing *to* someone.

In Chapter 2, "Resources for Writing," students are encouraged to use their own thoughts, feelings, observations, and experiences in writing. Suggestions are also offered on how to use reading material, classroom lectures, and the library as resources for writing. Prewriting is emphasized in this chapter. But students are asked to learn the skills of prewriting by *writing*—paragraphs and short essays. (The sections in this chapter on reading, note-taking and using the library can be used at any point during the course, as well as in their present sequence.)

Chapter 3, "The Writing Method," introduces a six-step writing method, the first step being information gathering, which is based on the prewriting of Chapter 2. I devote special attention to the thesis (or purpose statement, as it is called in this text) and to the plan for the essay. A method for revising papers (separate from the six-step method) is included in this chapter. The revision checklist on the inside of the front cover is based on this material. It should assist the student with organization and style. The editing checklist on the inside of the back cover assists with mechanics.

Chapter 4, "Specialized Writing Assignments," contains a discussion of seven types of writing: description, narrative, process, example, comparison and contrast, classification, and argument. Each of these is illustrated by the six-step method described in Chapter 3. In Chapter 4, students move from writing about their own experiences to writing on topics outside of their immediate experience. More suggestions are offered on how to write an argument essay than any of the other essays because writing an effective argument is such a difficult skill for most beginning writers to learn.

Throughout Part One extensive use is made of student samples. In my experience students respond well to carefully chosen student writing models because the content is usually interesting to them and the quality of the writing is within their reach; in fact, they sometimes turn in better essays than the models themselves. As a teacher I like to use student writing models because they can be made to illustrate particular points I am making.

You will find that I suggest many times that students read their writing aloud in small groups, though I realize some instructors prefer not to use small groups in their classes. You will also note that at times I indicate alternative writing assignments. My hope is that by my offering a variety of material, you, as instructor, will find what you need.

Part Two, "Writing in Standard English" (Chapters 5 through 11), is devoted to the mechanics of English. Explanations of the various rules are brief, and numerous practice exercises are given in which the students apply the rules they are learning. When possible, I have used student writing (both sentences and essays) in the exercises. The individual sections of each chapter in Part Two are designated by a decimal for easy reference (e.g., 5.0, 5.1, 5.2). Answers for the exercises are provided in the Instructor's Manual.

Part Two is designed to be used *while* the students are learning the process of writing in Part One. Some instructors may spend two days a week on process and one day a week on mechanics, or vice versa. Other instructors may prefer to have students work on their own in Part Two, in the areas in which they need more practice. Frequent cross-references, discussion of the mechanics of the student samples, and specific suggestions for editing the papers assigned in Chapters 3 and 4 all help to relate Parts One and Two of *Writing for a Reason* in a practical manner.

Chapter 5 is devoted to identifying the parts of speech and includes an exercise in distinguishing between adjectives and adverbs.

Chapter 6, "Writing Whole Sentences," deals with simple, complex, and compound sentences. Students first see that writing sentences is a natural process since we most often express ourselves in sentences. Then they learn how to combine simple sentences and clauses to make complex and compound sentences. Throughout the chapter, I give suggestions and practice on avoiding fragments and run-on sentences. And finally, I introduce six comma rules, which come up for discussion naturally as the students are learning sentence structure. (These rules are explained more fully in the section on commas, Chapter 11.4.)

Chapter 7 is devoted to verb agreement and Chapter 8 to other verb forms. Extra emphasis is placed on verbs to give students a thorough explanation of how verbs function and a great deal of practice in which they apply the various rules concerning verbs. Students whose first language is either a nonstandard dialect of English or a language other than English often must learn all of the conjugations before they can master verbs.

Chapter 9 is on spelling. Included in this chapter—besides the usual discussion of homonyms and a spelling list—are explanations on how to form plurals, make contractions, and use hyphens. Chapter 10 consists of explanations and exercises on avoiding pronoun errors, with a special section on gender confusion.

Chapter 11, on capitalization and punctuation, appears at the end of the text so that students can use it more easily as a reference while editing their essays.

## Features

In addition to student samples, *Writing for a Reason* contains a number of other features that assist the student in learning. Many student samples in Part One are accompanied by sections called Questions for Discussion and Word and Sentence Use. Questions for Discussion direct the student to thematic and structural aspects of the sample, often including questions about the sample's effectiveness. The Word and Sentence Use section includes questions and brief exercises on the mechanics of the sample.

Throughout Part One, students will find specific suggestions on structure, style, and mechanics in material called Learning Notes. The Learning Notes are boxed so that students will be able to refer back to them easily later in the course as well as use them in the sections of the text in which they appear. All Learning Notes are listed in the Contents, and cross-referenced throughout the text.

Exercises are found throughout the book, integrated with the text and Learning Notes in Part One, and as practice in the mechanics of writing in Part Two. Writing assignments, of course, appear throughout and additional exercises of all types are found in the Instructor's Manual.

In spite of all the emphasis I put on the mechanics of English both in the text and in the Instructor's Manual, I nevertheless ask the students who use this text always to remember that learning the mechanics of writing is a way to reach their goal, but that the goal itself is for them to say what they want to say in writing.

## Acknowledgments

This text has evolved over the last eight years. Various instructors with different teaching styles contributed their ideas and at times provided me with exercises, many of which I used after testing them in the classroom. I wish to thank, especially, Byrd Gibbens, now of the University of New Mexico; Nancy Regalado of New York University; and David Shroyer, Julie Price, and Robert Thigpen of the University of New Orleans. To the other members of the English Department and the College Life Department of the University of New Orleans I also give my thanks. Tamara Bally was a fine typist. My family—my wife, Corinne, and children, Ben, Janet, Mary Royall, and Abigail— were all patient and supportive.

The following reviewers were most helpful in their examination of the manuscript in its later stages: Mary K. Croft, University of Wisconsin; Nancy C. DeSombre, Wilbur Wright College; Loisjean Komai, Malcolm X College; Ben W. McClelland, Rhode Island College; and Elisabeth McPherson.

But it is to my students that I owe my greatest thanks. Not only did they contribute the fifty or so samples of writing that I used in the text, but they also taught me, along the way, a lot about writing and a lot about life.

William H. Barnwell
University of New Orleans

I was sitting at my desk with only my desk lamp on; my fingers were racing across the typewriter keys.

# Part One

## Writing with Style

# Chapter 1
## You and Your Audience

## 1. The Personal Letter

August 15, 1982

Dear Students,

The primary goal of this course is to help you say in writing what *you* want to say, with style and with accuracy. The assumption is that you have a great deal to say that is worth saying. During the semester your instructor will lead you through various activities and exercises that are designed to help you relax in your writing and bring forth your strengths.

An important objective of this chapter is that you begin to know your classmates. They, along with your instructor, will be your audience for most of the writing assignments. In Chapter 2 you will discover and develop new resources for writing. By the time you complete Chapter 2, you should never have to worry about having something to say when you are asked to write an essay. Then, in Chapter 3, you will learn a step-by-step writing method that should be helpful to you in all of your college writing. Finally, in Chapter 4 you will write more specialized papers, as you describe a relative, tell a story, show how to make or do something, and argue for a belief. Most of the writing assignments in the text are accompanied by one or more samples of student writing. I offer these not because they are perfect but, rather, because they will give you ideas for your own writing. Throughout Part One, you will find learning notes, which you will not only refer to during each chapter, but which you may easily refer to later on. (The first learning notes, entitled "The Personal Letter," appears on page 9.)

Part Two (Chapters 5–11) is a handbook that provides instructions and practice in the mechanics of writing: how to write in complete sentences, how to use verbs and pronouns correctly, how to spell, how to punctuate, and, finally, how to edit your own papers. For college writing and for most careers, it is essential that you learn to write in correct standard English. But you should never forget that learning the mechanics of writing is a way to reach your goal, not the goal itself.

I hope you enjoy this course and learn to enjoy writing. I would appreciate it if you would fill out the student response form at the end of the text and send it to me, so that I can know how well this text worked for you. Also, I would like to see some of your writing. Perhaps I will be able to use an essay of yours as a student sample in the future.

Sincerely yours,

William H. Barnwell

The following exercise will give you practice in writing a personal letter and will help you get to know your classmates. They, along with your instructor, will be your audience for most of the writing assignments in this text. The better you get to know them, the more you will have a sense of writing *to* someone.

Here, and in all the writing assignments, follow the step-by-step procedure for writing. When you finish this assignment, you should have a 150- to 300-word letter about yourself in which you have said what you wanted to say to your classmates.

**Step One.**   Read the student letters below to get ideas for your letter.

**A**                                                                 August 28, 1982

Dear Classmates,

Hi! My name is Karen, and I have attended two high schools. First there was Grace King, then Slidell High, and then I quit and enrolled in John Jay Beauty College. I loved beauty college because I could relate so well to everyone there. A few of us became good friends and would go everywhere together. There was a college atmosphere. In other words, you could do as you pleased. The teachers took a special interest in everyone. If you weren't sure of a cut or the solution for coloring hair, they came running to your aid. While I liked John Jay, I thought I should get a couple of years of regular college while I still had the chance.

I picked this community college because I've always heard it was a hard but good school. My family warned me that it would be unsociable, and it is. People will look you right in the eye and not even speak, as if you weren't even there. Yesterday, when I said hello to a girl about my age, she didn't even look at me. I hope this class will be different, and we will get to know each other.

I hope to be a teacher when I finish school because I love kids. I can't wait. Good luck to everyone.

Sincerely yours,

Karen

**B**                                                                January 28, 1982

Dear Classmates,

It all started on December 14, 1961, and is still going on. I know you are wondering *what* started, so I'll ease your curiosity and tell you that I was born, me, Will Myles. I grew up in a middle size city of about 50,000 people, where I went to a good high school, Greenwood High. At Greenwood, I played basketball for a while but could never be as good as I wanted. There were five other guys who kept me on the bench. So I went on to boxing and was given the name "Windmill" because people said that I swung my arms like a windmill.

Now that I've graduated from high school, I want to pursue bigger and better things. Everything as of this moment is just great as far as my studies go, but the dorm where I stay is too noisy. My roommate is a jazz lover and is the noisiest of all. He constantly plays his music, and it really annoys me. I suppose he doesn't know he's rooming with Windmill Will.

In the year 1984, I hope to have graduated and to be on my way to become another Walter Cronkite. You see, classmates, my intended major is communications, and being the best is all I want. I want to excel in my work and feel that if I don't have a condominium, drive a Mercedes, and have a Swiss bank account, I will be a failure. Maybe I'm setting my standard of living too high, but if I don't, I may not work hard to get it. Classmates, I hope that each of you can one day turn on your television set and see my smiling face in your living room.

Sincerely yours,

Will Myles

**C**                                                                January 24, 1982

Dear Class,

I am thirty-three years old and probably the senior member of this class. I am a single parent with two main interests in life, to be a good mother to my seven-year-old son and to succeed in my work.

As a single parent, I have to play the role of mother and father and set down all the rules for my son. He must keep clean because to me cleanliness is next to godliness. He must be well behaved and treat adults with respect. And finally, he must work hard at school because education is the most important means to a productive future. In order for my son to become successful, he must know who he is and where he is going.

Presently, I am employed as a licensed practical nurse in the recovery room at West Jefferson General Hospital. After working as a practical nurse for three years, I discovered that there is no upward mobility in this job. So I decided to further my education and become a registered nurse with a B.S. degree. I love people, and I love helping them, especially the ones who cannot help themselves. In addition to the good feeling nursing gives you, the salary is excellent.

My future and my son's future will depend on a positive attitude towards education and personal success. I'm looking forward to getting to know everyone in the class.

Sincerely,

Gustavia Pritchard

**Step Two.** Fill out *one* of the two worksheets below to use as a guide for your letter.

**A**

_____
(date)

Dear Classmates,

When and where did you last go to school (or work)? _____

_____

_____

First paragraph (past)

What did you like best (or least) about your school or job, and why?

_____

_____

_____

Give an example of what you liked best (or least). _____

_____

When and why did you decide to come to this college or university?

_____

_____

How do you feel about your decision now? _____

Second paragraph
(present)

_____

Name one particular thing that makes you feel this way and explain why.

_____

_____

_____

_____

What do you hope to do when you finish school? _____

_____

_____

Third paragraph
(future)

What has influenced you in your career choice? _____

_____

_____

_____

Add anything else you would like to say to your classmates. _____

_____

Fourth paragraph
(optional)

_____

_____

Sincerely yours,

_____

B

_____
(date)

Dear Classmates,

Describe the things that most people know about you. _____

First paragraph {
_____

_____

_____
}

Second paragraph {
Describe some things that very few people know about you. _____

_____

_____

_____
}

Third paragraph {
What would you like people to know about you, and why? _____

_____

_____

_____
}

Fourth paragraph
(optional) {
Add anything else you would like to say to your classmates. _____

_____

_____

_____
}

Sincerely yours,

_____

**Step Three.** Follow the suggestions in the learning notes on page 9, "The Personal Letter," and write your letter. If the worksheet you filled out does not fit what you want to say, don't use it. But before you write, make sure you know what you want to say and in what order you want to say it. The student who wrote sample C used her own plan in preparing the letter.

## THE PERSONAL LETTER

On occasion you will want to write someone you know too well for a formal business letter, but you will want your personal letter to be just right. Such a person could be a good friend or a high school teacher whom you are writing for a letter of recommendation. The suggestions below for the personal letter are fairly standard and should be helpful to you. (The letter written to you on page 3 is a personal letter. Refer back to it to see what goes where.)

1. Place the date at the top right-hand corner of your paper.
2. Begin the letter with "Dear" and the person's name followed by a comma. (You should begin this greeting on the left-hand margin a couple of lines below the date.)
3. Group your main thoughts by paragraphs. Here are two examples:
   a. What have you done in the past
   b. What you are doing in the present
   c. What you hope to do in the future

   *or* (to a teacher for a recommendation)

   a. What you have been doing since you saw him or her last
   b. Why you are writing to request a letter of recommendation
   c. Where and when to send the letter
   d. An expression of thanks
4. When writing by hand, indent your paragraphs about an inch and a half; when typing, indent five spaces.
5. In your closing, capitalize the first word only, for example, "Very truly yours," "Love always." (Begin your closing on the right-hand side of the paper, a few lines below your last sentence.)

**Step Four.**   Read your letter in a small group of four to seven people. After each person reads his or her letter, take turns summarizing what the letter said and answer the following questions:

1. What interested you most?
2. What, if anything, could you identify with? Explain.
3. What would you like to know more about?

*Try to give equal time to each member of the group.* If your group should bog down, call on your instructor for help.

## 2. The Classroom Interview

A good writer must have a keen ear for what people say. The better you listen, the more you will have to write about. Much of the skill of active listening is simply deciding to concentrate on what other people are saying. In the next exercise you will practice active listening as you interview one of your classmates for five to ten minutes. After the interview, write a paragraph of about 150 words introducing your classmate to the rest of the class.

Before moving into the exercise, list as many characteristics of a good listener as you can think of.

_____          _____

_____          _____

_____          _____

Check your list against the observer checklist at the end of *step one* below.

**Writing Assignment**

**Step One.**   Form into groups of three, preferably with students you do not yet know well. Each person in the group will function in turn as a speaker, a listener (an interviewer), and an observer. The listener will ask questions and try to help the speaker say just what he or she wants to say. At the end of the interview, the observer will use the observer checklist to evaluate how helpful the listener was to the speaker. As listener, you will want to learn enough about the person you are interviewing to write a full paragraph introducing that person to the class. Here are three suggestions for the listener:

1. Don't take notes *while* you are interviewing, but wait until the interview is over.
2. Invite the speaker to answer in some detail each question you ask, but don't push the speaker on any question. The object of the exercise is not to embarrass anyone but, rather, to help others say what they want to say.
3. Summarize from time to time what you have heard the speaker say. Your summary will show that you were listening and will give the speaker a chance to correct anything you misunderstood.

You may want to ask the speaker some of the following questions, but don't feel that you must ask them in order:

1. What are some of the nicknames you have had in the past? What did you think of them?
2. What are your hobbies?
3. What is your Zodiac sign? Does it have any significance for you?
4. What feature of your personality are you most proud of?
5. How important is religion in your life?
6. What is your favorite television program?
7. What emotions do you find most difficult to control?
8. Do you consider yourself a political liberal or a conservative?
9. What are your favorite jokes or expressions?
10. What sorts of jobs have you had in the past? Which did you like the most (the least)?
11. What is your intended career? Are you having second thoughts about it?
12. What things frighten you the most?
13. How are you enjoying this college (or university) now?
14. What are some things you haven't mentioned so far that very few people know about you?

After the interview, the observer should evaluate how helpful the listener was to the speaker. The following checklist will assist the observer:

1. Did the listener seem interested?
2. Did the listener ask too many questions, not enough questions, or just the right amount of questions?
3. Did the listener summarize what the speaker said in a helpful way?
4. Did the listener seem relaxed?
5. Did the listener maintain good eye contact?
6. In short, did the listener help the speaker say what the speaker wanted to say?

Before leaving your three-person group, jot down as much as you can remember of what the person you interviewed said. These notes will serve as the raw material for your paragraph.

Someone from each group should report to the rest of the class on how well the interviews went.

**Step Two.** Read the following student samples for ideas on how to use the notes from your interview in writing the assigned paragraph. The learning notes that follow on pages 12 and 14 will help you to write transition sentences as you need them and will help you plan your paragraph.

**A**    GREGORY NUNN

I interviewed Gregory Nunn who believes nicknames tell a lot about a person. With this being the case, let me tell you some of his nicknames. Some call him "Lover Man" because he's *always* flirting. Others call him "Bleep-Man," because he's good at basketball. Bleep is just a term used when the ball goes through the hoop. Most call him "Beach Bum," because during the summer he spends more time in Florida than at home. But there is a lot more to Greg than just nicknames. He's eighteen, a graduate of St. Mark's High School, and his hobbies are tennis, woodwork, and cracking bad jokes. (He managed to get off a couple of these in the interview.) He wants to be a lawyer when he finishes school but is not looking to be a millionaire. He mainly wants to be surrounded with good friends who enjoy a good time. Someday he would like to have a wife, two kids, and a great big dog, but he says he's not going to rush into that kind of life.

**B**    DAWN HUBBARD

Dawn wants us to know two things about her. First, she wants to make a career of music. She has been singing with a band for the last three years and practices many hours a week. She is taking music at the university and is thinking of majoring in it. The band she sings with is called Pryntz. They have written and composed ten songs on their own and hope to record some soon. Dawn herself wrote the lyrics for seven of the ten songs. The second thing she wants us to know about her is that she is very interested in psychology. She spends many hours with her family and friends talking about the ways people relate to each other. Psychology catches her attention because she enjoys helping people with the different problems they face. I enjoyed talking to Dawn and was particularly interested in her background in music.

## TRANSITION SENTENCES: WITHIN PARAGRAPHS

The word *transition* means a passage or movement from one thing to another. You made a transition from high school (or whatever you were doing) to college. If the transition seems an easy change, it is a *smooth* transition; if not, it is a *rough* transition. In your writing you will learn to use smooth transition sentences to help your reader move from one thought to another. Sometimes these transitions will help your reader move easily from one paragraph to another (see page 109), sometimes from one thought to another within the same paragraph.

In student sample A above, the writer was telling us about Gregory Nunn's nicknames and then switched to giving us other information about him. To make the switch smooth, she used the transition sentence, "But there is a lot more to Greg than just nicknames."

### SUGGESTIONS FOR WRITING TRANSITION SENTENCES

1. Follow your instincts. As we talk to one another, moving from point to point, we naturally use transitions. Use those same kinds of transitions in your writing.

2. Refer to the last thing you have discussed. The reference to nicknames in the example above refers to the first part of the paragraph on Gregory Nunn: "But there is a lot more to Greg than just nicknames." Also, direct your reader to what you will discuss next. The statement "But there's a lot more to Greg" directs the reader's attention to other things the writer will say about Greg.

3. Sometimes, you will use two or more transition sentences in the same paragraph. For the sake of clarity, you may want to make them *parallel* to each other; that is, write the same kinds of sentences to introduce each point. In student sample B above, the writer used two transition sentences that are generally parallel to each other:

> ► First, she wants to make a career of music.

> ► The second thing she wants us to know about her is that she is very interested in psychology.

These sentences are generally parallel because they contain the following similar elements:

| *First sentence* | *Second sentence* |
| --- | --- |
| The word *first* | The words *the second thing* |
| What she wants us to know—that she wants to make a career of music | What she wants us to know—that she is very interested in psychology |

Transitions and parallelism in writing will be discussed throughout this text.

**C**        TRACY FRIEDLER

During my interview with Tracy, I found out that she and I are alike in many ways. One thing we both enjoy is laughing. As I interviewed her, I found that she laughs at just about anything, and it's hard for her to stop sometimes. Each time she began to laugh, I started to laugh as well. I also found out that we are both shy, but I am a little more shy than she is. It's too bad that we're shy because we both like meeting people. We have problems making conservation, even though we are friendly to almost everyone. As we continued talking, I found out that we also have our differences. I found out, for example, that Tracy is quick tempered but cools down easily. I'm the opposite. I don't get mad often, but when I do, it takes me a long time to get over it. I also found out that her favorite hobby is eating and that she does not gain a lot of weight. You can look at me and tell that when I eat I gain weight. In my opinion Tracy is a very nice person and would make a great friend to anyone. Even though we both may be shy, we talked as though we had known each other for years.

### Questions for Discussion

1. Was the student successful in helping you get to know Tracy? In your own words, describe Tracy. Do you know anyone like her? Explain.
2. What are the transition sentences? Underline them. Do they succeed in helping you move from one point to the next *smoothly?*

**Step Three.** Write a paragraph of about 150 words introducing the person you interviewed to the class. Emphasize what stood out for you in the interview; you will not be able to tell everything. Introduce the paragraph with one sentence that names the person you interviewed and says generally what the paragraph will be about. (See the student samples for ideas.) In the rest of the paragraph, tell at least two things about the person that seem important. Back up each item with enough information for your reader to understand the points you want to convey. Before writing the paragraph, study the following learning notes on the single paragraph. The title for your paragraph can simply be the full name of the person you are introducing.

## THE SINGLE PARAGRAPH

A paragraph expresses some thought or point that is complete in itself; it may consist of a single sentence, although usually it contains several sentences. In your college writing, you will sometimes want to write single paragraphs to answer certain discussion questions on exams, for example. At other times, you will want to write several paragraphs on one topic. (See page 226 for a discussion of the paragraph written as part of a several paragraph essay.) Throughout this text the expression *organizing principle* will be used to describe the main idea of a paragraph. Many instructors refer to the first sentence of a paragraph as the *topic sentence.*

Most paragraphs in books and magazines run from 50 to 200 words. Paragraphs in newspapers are typically shorter. In this chapter and the next, you will be asked to write several single paragraphs, which should run about 150 words. In Chapters 3 and 4, you will be asked to write essays of about four to six paragraphs: the paragraphs in the body of these essays should run about 100 words each, although the introductory and concluding paragraphs may be a good deal shorter.

### SUGGESTIONS FOR WRITING A SINGLE PARAGRAPH

1. Begin with a sentence that points your reader towards the subject matter of the paragraph. The student sample interviews began with such sentences:

   ▶ I interviewed Gregory Nunn, who believes nicknames tell a lot about a person.

   ▶ Dawn wants us to know two important things about her.

   ▶ During my interview with Tracy, I found out that she and I are alike in many ways.

2. Support each point you make in your paragraph with enough information so that your reader will understand what you are saying. The details you give in support of your points will excite your reader's interest and make your points believable. Readers are convinced by details and examples, not by general, abstract statements. Instead of just making the statement that Gregory Nunn believes nicknames tell a lot about a person, the student who wrote the paragraph gave three examples of Gregory's nicknames: "Lover-Man," "Bleep-Man," and "Beach Bum."

3. If you make more than one point in your paragraph, be sure your reader can move from point to point *smoothly.* (See the learning notes on the transition sentence.) Here are two examples of transition sentences within a paragraph:

First sentence ▶   American political parties are unique among the world's democracies.

    ▶ First, the members of American parties do not have to pay dues. (The writer then explains how this is different from political parties in countries such as England and France.)

    ▶ Second, the members may switch easily from one party to another. (The writer explains that changing parties is fairly common in the United States but seldom done in other countries.)

    ▶ Third, the members do not have to support the party's leader. (The writer explains how in the United States the members of Congress can vote against the wishes of the president, even when the president belongs to their party.)

First sentence ▶   Each of us should make an effort to cut down on our use of fuel.

    ▶ One way we can reduce our fuel consumption is by driving less. (The writer explains.)

    ▶ Another way we can reduce our use of fuel is by insulating our homes. (The writer explains.)

    ▶ A third way we can cut down on fuel is by using less hot water. (The writer explains.)

Other ways of tagging several points within a paragraph include:

| First, | One example of | The first reason |
|---|---|---|
| Next, | A second example of | The second reason |
| Finally, | A third example of | The third reason |

4. End your paragraph with a statement that lets your reader know you are through. Think of the ending as the end of a conversation, and let your conclusion flow naturally from what you have just said. And be brief. The student who introduced Dawn Hubbard in example B concluded this way:

    ▶ I enjoyed talking to Dawn and was particularly interested in her career in music.

Notice how much more natural that sounds than this:

► In conclusion, Dawn wants us to know first that she is going into music and second she wants us to know that she is very interested in psychology.

Here are two other examples of to-the-point endings:

► Only in America do members of political parties have so much freedom.

► There is much each of us can do to reduce fuel consumption in this country.

5. Make your title brief (usually three to six words, seldom a whole sentence) and closely related to what the paragraph is about. See pages 52–54 for ideas and rules on writing titles.

## SOME NOTES ON FORM

1. When writing by hand, indent the first line of each paragraph about 1½ inches from the left; when typing, indent the first line 5 spaces.
2. Keep your left-hand margin straight. (If you use lined paper, begin your lines at the red vertical line. If you use unlined paper, set your left-hand margin about 1½ inches from the edge.)
3. Do not divide a word at the end of a line if you can help it (your right-hand margin need not be straight) but, if it is necessary, divide the word between syllables as follows:

                                        . . . with these qualifi-
cations.
                                . . . a government that is central-
ized.

   Consult a dictionary to see how to break the word into syllables.
4. Do not end a line with an opening quotation mark.
5. Do not begin a line with a comma, a semicolon, or any end punctuation mark.

**Step Four.**  Read your paragraph either in a small group or to the whole class. Your classmates, along with your instructor, will be your audience for most of your writing assignments. (See page 19 on "Writing to an Audience.")

Donald M. Murray, a teacher of writing at the University of New

Hampshire, wrote the following on the importance of sharing your writing with your classmates: "When students read their papers [to each other] aloud they hear the voices of their classmates without the interference of mechanical problems, misspellings, poor penmanship. . . . They laugh with the author, grieve with the author, nod in understanding, lean forward to try to learn more. That's how the writing class begins, and that is what carries it forward." As you read your paper and hear others read to you, you will discover that writing papers is not just an exercise but also a way of communicating ideas that are important to you.

After you have read your paragraph, first ask yourself if it sounded like your voice, like you talking. When others have read theirs, address the following questions:

1. Did the writing sound natural?
2. Was it clear? If not, what was confusing?
3. Was the writing convincing?
4. What more would you like to know about the person described in the paragraph?

**Step Five.**   Rewrite your paragraph, making use of what you learned in the small group discussion. Consult the person you are writing about if you need more information.

## 3. The Outside Interview

Following the steps outlined above for the classroom interview, choose one of the following people for a second interview and write a paragraph of about 150 words on that person.

1. Your oldest relative or the oldest person on your block
2. Your priest, minister, or rabbi
3. Your college dean
4. A high school or college teacher
5. A police officer or mail carrier you know
6. A coach
7. A foreign student
8. A student of the opposite sex (from outside this class) you would like to know

As you write, be aware that you are writing *to* someone.

## WRITING TO AN AUDIENCE

For most of your writing in this course, you will write to your class-mates and your instructor. Since they will be your audience, keep them in mind as you write. It is much easier to write to someone than to write to no one in particular. In a few assignments, how-ever, you will be addressing persons other than your classmates—public officials in an argument paper, an instructor in another course as you practice essay writing for exams, and, in the next section of this chapter, yourself as you begin a journal. Whenever you write, analyze the particular audience you are addressing. Who are they? What are they like? What will it take to convince them that your point is valid?

### KEEP THE FOLLOWING IN MIND AS YOU WRITE TO AN AUDIENCE:

1. *Be yourself.* Read your papers out loud when possible to make sure you hear yourself talking. It is true that you may need to change certain constructions and certain words you use in your everyday speech, but the paper should nevertheless sound like you; the words, phrases, and emphasis should be your own.
2. *Be clear.* Imagine that you are reading your paper aloud in a small group and that someone is going to summarize what you have written. Will you have made your point clearly enough so that what you hear repeated back is what you intended to say? To write consistently clear papers, begin by asking yourself if what you are writing is completely clear *to you.*
3. *Be convincing.* Ask yourself what it will really take to convince your classmates of the point you are trying to make. In the para-graph on Gregory Nunn in Section 2, the writer had to convince the reader that nicknames did tell us a lot about Gregory. The writer sought to convince us by giving examples of Gregory's nicknames and what they meant. In the paragraph on Dawn, the writer had to give enough information about Dawn's inter-ests to convince the reader that music and psychology really are important to her.
4. *Keep to the point.* Say what you mean to say as briefly and directly as possible. If you have written a clear sentence, you will not have to restate it in another way. Concrete examples and details persuade; simple repetition of one idea does not. In

writing to a classroom audience, use *I* and *you* when these pronouns help you say what you want to say. In later writing, such
as a research paper, you may be asked to keep *I* and *you* to a
minimum.

## 4. The Personal Journal

One of the best ways to learn how to write effectively is simply to do
a lot of it. What is true of an artist, a musician, or an athlete is also
true of you as a writer—you become skilled through practice. Keeping
a diary or personal journal is perhaps the best single way to practice
your writing. Take the time at the end of each day to write about
something that was important to you or something that at least caught
your attention. Besides giving you practice, keeping a journal will give
you an abundant supply of material for the various essays you will
write.

The following essay from a second-semester freshman student describes her struggle with herself as she tries to write. The person she
calls Hilary is the part of herself that demands perfection but also
keeps her from expressing her best thoughts. The student makes a
strong case for free, uninhibited writing, and that is the kind of writing
you can practice in a journal.

### THE TREATY WITH HILARY

It was this past summer when I first began to acknowledge Hilary.
I was sitting at my desk with only my desk lamp on; my fingers were racing
across the typewriter keys. Thoughts were coming to me so quickly that I
could hardly type fast enough to write them all down. It was well into the
middle of the night when she made herself known. When she did appear,
I recognized a mirror image of myself, but without any blemish or imper-
fection. She was like Mary Poppins, "perfect in every way." Dressed in
white, she held a dictionary and a thesaurus in her left arm and clutched
two sharpened number two pencils with erasers in her right hand.

"You're typing too fast," she said coolly. "If you go slower, you'll
find that you will type much more neatly. Besides, you don't know how to
type very well, anyway, and you're tired. Why don't you go to bed?" Without hesitation, I went to bed. And I never did finish that particular paper.

Hilary is always telling me that it is better not to write anything at all than to write something with so many run-on sentences and misspellings in it. I always become very intolerant and suggest that she just go read her dictionary and leave me alone. Anytime I have difficulty with my writing, I hear the same things: "Why don't you clean this place? Your room is just as messy as your writing. Perhaps if the surroundings were more refined, your writing would be more refined, too. Perhaps if you knew exactly what you wanted to write about, your writing would sound more polished."

I don't know why I allow such abuse; however, I do know it is time for a change. No matter how much I'm bothered by her, Hilary and I must be friends. We need to make a treaty, with equal rights. She must agree to leave the room at times and let me write as fast and as messy as I like, whenever I like. And I guess I have to agree to let her have twice as much time to proofread and revise the writing I am going to turn in. Yes, she can even use her dictionary and thesaurus. As difficult as it is to live with Hilary, I know in my heart that I need her; I just don't need her all the time.

### Questions for Discussion

1. Who is Hilary?
2. How does she interfere with the creative process?
3. Can you identify with the student? Explain.
4. What blocks you from saying what you want to say in writing? What helps?
5. How does Hilary help?

The student's conflict with Hilary is common not just to freshman English students but to everyone, even the most distinguished professional writers. One of our great poets, Edwin Arlington Robinson, described one full day's worth of writing as follows: "This morning I took the hyphen out of hell-hound and this afternoon I put it back." How can you, on the one hand, be creative and write down thoughts as they come to you, saying what you want to say? On the other hand, how can you be precise, careful, and correct in your writing? Every writer needs to answer both questions. There are many exercises in this text designed to help you say what you want to say in writing, but keeping a journal will be a good beginning. You too can banish the critical Hilary from the room and experience the joys of uninhibited, free writing. But as the student pointed out, Hilary has her rights too. Part Two of this text, for example, belongs to her.

**Beginning Your Journal**    **Step One.**    Read the following excerpts from students' journals to get some ideas about what you might want to write in yours.

**A**

This morning was another gloomy Saturday morning. It began about 8:00 A.M. when I felt a cold hand around my ankle jerking my tired body up and down in bed. It was my mother. Frowning and fussing, she said, "I told you not to stay out too late after that dance, didn't I?" I gave a huge yawn and ignored her unpleasant voice. I rolled over in my soft, warm bed and went back to sleep, but I dreamed that it was already nine o'clock and I had just shown up for work in my nightgown, stale make-up, and hair standing straight up on my head. So this time, I woke up for good and began hurrying through my routine so that I wouldn't be late for work. Suddenly, I realized I felt bad, so with a mouth full of toothpaste, I hollered, "Ma, will you call work for me and tell them that I'm sick and can't come in today?" "No!" she yelled back. "Because if I call, I'm going to tell them just why you don't want to go in." With that I dried my mouth and began searching for the car keys. . . .

**B**

I spent most of the afternoon in the hospital waiting room waiting for Granny. The room was dimly lit, and I could sense the sickness through-out the hospital by breathing the clean, cold air that smelled like rubbing alcohol. Sitting on the blue and red cloth-covered couch, I began to won-der what I would do if I became sick and actually had to come to this place. Opposite me were pictures on the wall that honored the founders of the hospital. They all looked the same, dressed in black or dull gray suits with white shirts and black ties. I tried to imagine what kinds of people they were and what kinds of lives they led. An artificial green plant and medi-cal magazines were on a low table under the pictures. For some reason they depressed me. Off to my right was the receptionist's desk with her sign, "Give me your name and the patient you want to see." I finally got tired of sitting and took a walk up and down the pale gray floors that had been expertly mopped and waxed. I could see my shadow on the floor and little designs in the tile that looked like clouds on a clear day. . . .

**C**

Today was a very interesting day in my Drama and Communica-tions 1000 class. The class usually starts at eleven o'clock, but today it didn't. No teacher. At twenty after eleven I was about to leave when our teacher came storming in the door. She was sweating, out of breath, and looking very tired. She said, "Class, I'm sorry for being late, but I just had a car accident." She was still out of breath but managed to continue, "I was planning on giving you a pop quiz, but I left the test in my car. I was going to give you a lecture, but I left the notes in my car. I guess I'll have to give the lecture off the top of my head." I could tell she was emotionally upset and not prepared to teach a class.

I admire her because even though she had just been through a bad experience she was committed to doing her job. Other teachers would have just dismissed their classes. But Instructor Anne Collins is a real professional. After she took a moment to compose herself, she began her lecture. She discussed theater from the 6th century B.C. to the year 1520. She talked about the Romans and Greeks and the church in medieval times. What I liked most was the part about a Greek god named Dionysus. She said Dionysus was god of fertility and wine and that people honored this god with rituals of sex and wine. Later today I told my girlfriend that she and I should go worship Dionysus, but she didn't know what I meant.

D                                                          NOVEMBER 1, 1981

My father is a person I hardly even know. Whenever I want to talk about something important, he's too busy to listen. I don't hate my father. I just want him to be with me more often. Is that too much to ask someone you love? Sometimes I want to tell him all kinds of things, like what I did on the weekend. But it's the same old response—"I'm too busy now," or "I'll be back tomorrow. We'll talk then." *Then* never comes.

Today I finally got my father to talk to me, but I was very disappointed. It was like talking to a stranger. I hope that when I have children, I will be a good listener and not say I'm busy right now. Too many kids have problems with their lives because of not enough love from their parents. I hope my father will some day learn what it would mean to me to just hear him say, "I understand." I mean understand the joy, tears, mistakes, and love that I want to share with him. Maybe when I'm old I'll think about how much I really loved him.

The following student essay is a fine example of the kind of writing you may want to strive for in your journal writing. It is a description of life in Harlem.*

In the midst of this decay there are children between the ages of five and ten playing with plenty of vitality. As they toss the football around,

*I am indebted to Mina P. Shaughnessy of the City University of New York for this example. It comes from her book *Errors and Expectations* (New York: Oxford University Press, 1979), p. 278.

their bodies full of energy, their clothes look like rainbows. The colors mix together and one is given the impression of being in a psychedelic dream, beautiful, active, and alive with unity. They yell to each other increasing their morale. They have the sound of an organized alto section. At the sidelines are the girls who are shy, with the shyness that belongs to the very young. They are embarrassed when their dresses are raised by the wind. As their feet rise above pavement, they cheer for their boyfriends. In the midst of decay, children will continue to play.

Besides helping you with your writing, your journal will be an excellent way to remember the little—but significant—events of your life. Some day you may want to pass on your journal, or some of it, to your children and your children's children. Think how helpful it would be for the young woman who wrote sample D to share that journal entry with her own teen-age children.

**Step Two.** Study the suggestions for keeping a journal in the learning notes below.

**Step Three.** Clear your desk or table of everything except your journal and a pen or pencil. Let yourself become completely relaxed, taking several deep breaths, inhaling and exhaling slowly. Write as quickly as you can. Do not censor your thoughts.

After you have kept your journal for a while, you may want to share some of it or all of it with your instructor or other members of your class. But when you write, don't worry about what others might think: You are writing for yourself.

---

## THE PERSONAL JOURNAL

1. Imagine that you are on a magic carpet that is taking you to the most peaceful place you can think of. When you arrive, you find yourself talking to the one person you feel most comfortable with. For some students, that person is simply themselves.
2. Start telling this person all about one thing that happened in the last day or so that was important to you. Often it is difficult to recall just exactly what was important. If nothing comes to mind, simply begin with, "I got up and then." Tell just what happened

as you went through the day, but when you come to something that captures your attention, begin writing about it. If you find that you have little to say about this topic, move on, recalling in chronological order other things that happened until you come to something you can write quite a lot about.

3. The following are some things to look out for as you decide what to write about:

   a. What you dreamed the night before. What were the details of the dream? What was your dream trying to say to you? (*Hint*: Make notes on your dream as soon as you wake up.)

   b. An unusual conversation. Who said what? What were the exact words?

   c. A particular object that captured your attention, such as a brown leaf on a tree that was otherwise completely green, a cloud that looked exactly like your collie's face, or a hat that was two sizes too big. (Make a point from time to time to write about things like these that are completely outside yourself. Giving variety to the entries in your journal will help keep you interested in it).

   d. A particular person who captured your attention, such as a professor whose shirttail hung out under his coat, a police officer who was laughing so hard that he was slapping his knee, a woman across from you on the bus who was holding her baby in a loving way.

   e. A difficult situation you found yourself in. First, tell as objectively as you can what happened (that is, just give the facts), then explain how you felt at the time of the situation, and finally describe the feelings you have about it now. Maybe your difficult situation was a time you felt out of place, or a time you found yourself in conflict with someone else, or a time you had to make a hard decision.

   f. A time when you felt completely on top of things, a mountaintop experience when the heavens and earth seemed to touch.

   g. A time you set out to write but found yourself blocked. Let that side of you that prevents you from writing talk to that side of you that is trying to write. (See the Hilary paper for ideas.)

4. To give your journal variety, try the following "newspaper" entries:

   a. Write a letter to Dear Abby or Ann Landers. (Abby and Ann are columnists to whom many people write for advice on

tricky problems. Many daily papers carry their columns.)
Once you have written Abby or Ann, play her part and write
yourself back, giving the advice you requested.

b. Write the news headline you would most like to see in tomorrow's newspaper and an article to go with it.

c. Write your own obituary (death notice), praising yourself for
your accomplishments.

# Chapter 2
## Resources for Writing

"What am I going to write about?" "What can I possibly say for 200, 300, or 400 words?" These questions are very common among freshman English students. This chapter is an attempt to give you so much to write about that you will begin to worry not about what to say but, rather, about what to leave out. First you will learn in this chapter how to use yourself as a resource for writing. Then you will learn how to use dialogue (what people say), reading, lecture material, and the library as other resources for writing. Your instructor may want to postpone the reading, lecture, and library assignments and move directly from the section on dialogue to the writing method described in Chapter 3.

## 1. Yourself

*You* are by far the best resource for writing. What you feel, your ideas, your perception of the world around you, and your memories are all excellent resources.

One definition of the word *experience* is "the act of living through an event." Thus, anything you have seen, heard, touched, smelled, or tasted you have experienced. The word *awareness,* on the other hand, means "knowing or being conscious of what is happening." In this section you will become more conscious of your experience, more in touch with your ideas and feelings—in short, more aware, and therefore more able to write interestingly and precisely. Awareness can be developed. You can choose to become aware, to observe closely, to notice fine details.

**Awareness of Feeling: Responding to Poetry**

In this assignment, you will be asked to respond to three poems that were chosen to bring forth strong feelings. You will then be asked to write your response to one or more of the poems. As you write the various essays assigned in this text, it is important to reflect on how you feel about the subject matter and, at times, to explain your feelings to your readers. Responding to these poems should be a good beginning. Feelings are the stuff poetry is made of. But notice, as you read the poems, that the authors' feelings are conveyed without mentioning such "feeling" words as *hate, happiness,* or *sadness.*

James Dickey, a well-known poet, has written this about poetry: "The first thing to understand about poetry is that it comes to you from outside you, in books or in words, but that for it to live, something from within you must come to it and meet it and complete it. Your response with your own mind and body and memory and emotions gives the poem its ability to work its magic; if you give to it, it will give to you, and give plenty."

**Step One.**   Read the following poems carefully and name the feeling or feelings each poem evokes in you. *Look up any words you do not understand.*

This poem, although said to be written by a high school student, is anonymous. In it and the two poems that follow you will notice that the standard grammatical rules are sometimes broken. Poets claim the right to use nonstandard constructions, such as fragments, in their writing.

He always wanted to explain things.
But no one cared.
So he drew.
Sometimes he would draw and it wasn't anything.

He wanted to carve it in stone or write it in the sky.
He would lie out in the grass and look up in the sky.
And it would be only him and the sky
and the things inside him that needed saying.
And it was after that he drew the picture.
It was a beautiful picture.
He kept it under his pillow and would let no one see it.
And he would look at it every night and think about it.

And when it was dark, and his eyes were closed he could still
　　see it.
And it was all of him.
And he loved it.
When he started school he brought it with him.
Not to show to anyone, but just to have it with him like a
　　friend.

It was funny about school.
He sat in a square, brown desk.
Like all the other square, brown desks.
And he thought it should be red.
And his room was a square, brown room.
Like all the other rooms.
And it was tight and close.
And stiff.
He hated to hold the pencil and chalk.
With his arm stiff and his feet flat on the floor.
Stiff.
With the teacher watching and watching.
The teacher came and spoke to him.
She told him to wear a tie like all the other boys.
He said he didn't like them.
And she said it didn't matter!

After that they drew.
And he drew all yellow and it was the way he felt about
　　Morning.
And it was beautiful.
The teacher came and smiled at him.
"What is this?" she said, "Why don't you draw something like
　　Ken's drawing? Isn't it beautiful?"
After that his mother bought him a tie.
And he always drew airplanes and rocket ships like everyone
　　else.
And he threw the old picture away.

And then he lay alone looking at the sky.
It was big and blue and all of everything.
But he wasn't any more.
He was square inside.
And brown.
And his hands were stiff.
And he was like everyone else.

And the thing inside him that needed saying didn't need it any
   more.
It had stopped pushing.
It was crushed.
Stiff.
Like everything else.

The next poem is based on a newspaper story. Notice how the
author sets the mood in the first verse as she imagines herself drown-
ing. Beginning with the second verse, the poem follows the newspaper account very closely and switches from the first person ("I") to
the third person ("they"). The newspaper said, "She could not have
known the thing she chose." What is it the girl "could not have
known"? What would you like to say to her?

### DATELINE: DEATH

The paper told where
it happened of course.
I have forgotten
the place now. It could
have been the corn-green
town where I was born
and the trestle curves
a little west to
cross the power dam:
there where I stood once,
stricken on the bank
above the rainbow,
and let explosions
in the water spin
me down and drown me.

The paper said three
children walked across
a trestle tall as
mine was. They were one
boy nine years old, one
girl of six, and one
thirteen, who was her
sister. When they had
come halfway across,
the water running

louder under them,
glittering more now
into their squinting,
they heard the diesel
horn behind them blow.
Silently all three
began to run. Then
the youngest fell, caught
her ankle hard, down
between the shaking
ties. The others leaped,
before they missed her,
safe from the roadbed.
Then, only then, one
saw her sister held
before the train, who
turned again, ran back
again, and tore at
the shackled foot. Then
she knelt on the ties
and took her sister
in her arms, blinding
her against her breast,
and said to her see,
I am here with you,
there is nothing to
be frightened of.
And the train struck them.

It may have taken
five minutes at the
most, the newspaper
said. She could not have
known the thing she chose.
She could not have known.

Suzanne Gross

As you read the following, ask yourself if the poem is primarily about blacks rising out of oppression. Or could it be about any minority group or any individual person? On the other hand, could it be mostly about women? Is it human nature to begrudge other people their victories?

### STILL I RISE

You may write me down in history
With your bitter, twisted lies,
You may trod me in the very dirt
But still, like dust, I'll rise.

Does my sassiness upset you?
Why are you beset with gloom?
'Cause I walk like I've got oil wells
Pumping in my living room.

Just like moons and like suns,
With the certainty of tides,
Just like hopes springing high,
Still I'll rise.

Did you want to see me broken?
Bowed head and lowered eyes?
Shoulders falling down like teardrops,
Weakened by my soulful cries.

Does my haughtiness offend you?
Don't you take it awful hard
'Cause I laugh like I've got gold mines
Diggin' in my own back yard.

You may shoot me with your words,
You may cut me with your eyes,
You may kill me with your hatefulness,
But still, like air, I'll rise.

Does my sexiness upset you?
Does it come as a surprise
That I dance like I've got diamonds
At the meeting of my thighs?

Out of the huts of history's shame
I rise
Up from a past that's rooted in pain
I rise
I'm a black ocean, leaping and wide,
Welling and swelling I bear in the tide.

Leaving behind nights of terror and fear
I rise
Into a daybreak that's wondrously clear
I rise

Bringing the gifts that my ancestors gave,
I am the dream and the hope of the slave.
I rise
I rise
I rise.

Maya Angelou

**Step Two.** In small groups, discuss one or more of the poems. The following suggestions may be helpful. (Give each group member equal time.)

1. Reread the poem you are discussing. Perhaps someone will agree to read it aloud.
2. Discuss what the author is trying to say to you in the poem. For the time being, withhold your response to the poem.
   What lines best capture the meaning of the poem?
   What is the message of the poem?
   What feeling does the author convey? Anger? Sadness? Hate? Happiness? Arrogance? Hopelessness?
3. Talk back to the poem.
   What colors does the poem remind you of?
   What piece of music?
   What would you like to say back to the author of the poem, or to any of the people in the poem?
   What one word best describes how you felt as you read it?
4. Try to relate the poem to your own life. Explain the relationship to the group.
   What situation does the poem remind you of? Why?
   Can you find yourself in the poem? Explain.
   Does the poem remind you of someone you know?

**Step Three.** Write a two-paragraph paper on one of the poems, using the following as organizing principles for each paragraph. Make your transition from the first paragraph to the second as smooth as possible.

1. *Paragraph one:* What is the author trying to say in the poem? How does he or she say it? What images or pictures does the author want you to see? What feeling is conveyed? What line says it best?
2. *Paragraph two:* What would you like to say to the author or any of the people in the poem, and why? How does the poem make you feel? Does the poem relate to your own experience or the experience of someone you know? Explain.

**Awareness of Thoughts: The Brainstorm**

For this assignment you will first practice a technique called *brainstorming,* which will help you collect ideas for writing papers. You will then be asked to write a paragraph using some of the ideas you have collected.

All of us have more ideas and know more information than we are willing to express. Before writing anything at all, students often start worrying about what others will think of their thoughts. Will they sound stupid to the instructor, to other students, or even to themselves? As a result of their worry, many of these students sit back and say only what is "safe"—things that will not be criticized or laughed at. But what you do not say is sometimes the best thing that you are thinking.

The poet W. H. Auden called the internal force that keeps us from expressing ourselves freely "the Watcher at the gate." The Watcher always wants to make sure that we do not say the wrong things, always wants us to say things perfectly, and is thus always ready to close the gate on what we are capable of saying. The Watcher performs a valuable service when it comes time to proofread and revise. But if the Watcher is allowed to close the gate too soon on what we could say, we may find that we have very little to write about. A second-semester freshman wrote the following essay explaining how the Watcher at the gate prevents him from writing what he wants to write:

> My Watcher at the gate is a built-in critic who is tougher on the writer than Rex Reed is on movie producers. I often picture my Watcher as a duplicate of my 11th grade English teacher, a slightly balding man in his early thirties, always wearing a doorman's uniform. He sits in a straight back chair in front of a heavy wooden door and lets nothing escape his discriminating eyes.
>
> I believe that deep inside me is a writer, as well as a Watcher, who is waiting to surface. This writer is very small compared to my Watcher. The writer strives to be original and let the thoughts flow from my mind to the paper without stopping at the gate. Only at certain times, however, can my Watcher be caught off guard. One of these times is at three o'clock in the morning. While my Watcher is dreaming away, I am left alone, free to express myself. The Watcher can also be caught off guard in the closing moments of a deadline. At this point in time, the Watcher becomes frantic about making the deadline, so he becomes less critical and allows free thought to flow.
>
> My Watcher hates to take chances. He would rather block my thoughts and copy the style of another than risk failure. Because of this fact,

most of my writing sounds as if it were taken from the pages of an English text instead of from my own mind. When all is taken into account, however, the Watcher at the gate is necessary in the writing of proper English. He does make me look up words in the dictionary and insists that each of my "sentences" is a sentence. Who knows? He may even have helped me in this essay about him.

Brainstorming is a technique that helps a writer open the gate, allowing all the thoughts—perfect, imperfect, silly, beautiful, or ugly—to flow freely from the brain to the paper, without stopping at the gate. The technique asks simply that the writer make a decision to open the gate and to jot down as many thoughts as possible on paper. Later, once all the thoughts are written down, the writer can pick and choose which ones to use. Here is how one student brainstormed when asked to describe the ideal mate. The student made her first list in the left-hand column and then, once she could think of nothing else, went back to see if any of her items reminded her of other characteristics of the ideal mate. These she wrote in the right-hand column.

| | |
|---|---|
| - six feet tall, dark hair | ← big dreamy eyes that melt my heart |
| - good sense of humor | ← likes practical jokes played on him |
| - sensitive to problems I bring to him | ← willing to do anything for me and others as well |
| - jogs every morning | ← muscular, lean, great shape |
| - doesn't mind doing dishes | ← willing to sweep, dust, scrub, etc. |
| - a little crazy + wild at times | — in short, just like |
| - has style and grace. | my Harry |

**Writing Assignment (Brainstorm #1)**

**Step One.**   Imagine that you are being given a brand new car with everything on it you could possibly want. As quickly as you can, without stopping to think twice, write down *everything* you could possibly want on or in this car. *Don't censor your thoughts!* Express them all—

creative, silly, brilliant, stupid, beautiful, ugly—everything. If you bog down, see if any of the items you listed remind you of other items.

_____     _____

_____     _____

_____     _____

_____     _____

_____     _____

_____     _____

_____     _____

_____     _____

Since brainstorming usually works better when done with others because one thought inspires another, share your most original ideas with the rest of the class. Someone should volunteer to write the ideas on the blackboard. As you hear the ideas of others, you will get new ideas. Write those down as well.

_____     _____

_____     _____

_____     _____

_____     _____

_____     _____

**Step Two.** Read the following paragraph for ideas on how you might use _your_ brainstorm items in a similar paragraph.

### MY CADILLAC 999xxx

Let me introduce you to my new Cadillac 999 Triple X. This car can hit fifty miles per hour in 2.3 seconds. For that reason and many others, it has been my dream car for quite a while. The outside is black with gold racing stripes flowing across both sides of the car. They match the fourteen carat gold spoke wheels that cost me a considerable amount of money. All of the windows on my car are tinted light blue. Let's move on to the best part, the inside of the car. The first thing you notice is the tilt steering wheel. The second thing is the cruise control, which is located on the turn signal collar. The dash contains the usual gauges and also an altimeter to let me know how high I am above sea level, an AM-FM cassette stereo, a two-inch built-in television, and four vents for airconditioning. Both seats are upholstered in soft light gold leather. The floors are covered with a one-inch thick carpet. But the fanciest thing about my car is the computerized remote control. By punching the right button, I can make virtually anything happen.

**Questions for Discussion**

1. Does the first sentence effectively introduce the paragraph?
2. The writer first describes the outside of the car. What transition sentence does he use to move the reader to the next part of the paragraph? Is the transition smooth?
3. The writer collected most of the details of his paragraph in a brainstorm session. How successful is he in using the details? Can you get a good picture of the car in your mind's eye?

**Step Three.** Using your own brainstorm ideas, write a paragraph of a least 150 words describing your ideal car. Before you begin, make sure you have a plan that introduces your reader to your car in a logical way. In your mind's eye, place yourself outside the car but close enough to see inside. From this position, describe the car. Here are some possible methods of developing your paragraph:

1. Describe the outside and then the inside of the car.
2. Describe five eye-catching features of the car.
3. Describe the car from front to back.

See the discussion of transition sentences on page 12 and of the paragraph on page 14.

**Writing Assignment**
**(Brainstorm #2)**

**Step One.**    Imagine that you are looking down from a helicopter on an ideal town or a section of an ideal city. As quickly as you can, list everything you see in the left-hand column. Be as specific as possible. What buildings, street scenes, vegetation, or open spaces do you see? What little things catch your eye?

| | |
|---|---|
| _____ | _____ |
| _____ | _____ |
| _____ | _____ |
| _____ | _____ |
| _____ | _____ |
| _____ | _____ |
| _____ | _____ |
| _____ | _____ |

**Step Two.**    Now go back and, in the right-hand column, describe each item more specifically. If, for example, you listed "church" in the left-hand column, describe what it looks like and what denomination it might be. If you listed "athletic field," describe what kind it is and what people are doing on the field at the moment. Brainstorming often brings general ideas to the surface that should be made more specific as you use them in your writing. The more precise your writing is, the more your readers will appreciate it and profit from it. Share your most vivid "sights" of the ideal city or town with the class.

**Step Three.**    Study the following student example for ideas on how you might use your brainstorm notes in a paragraph.

#### THE MOST BEAUTIFUL CITY

I am now flying over the most beautiful city in the world. What stands out the most are the gold sidewalks and the tops of the large oak trees that look like the tops of green umbrellas from where I am. What I notice next are the houses, each with a different shape. Some are sky-scrapers, some are dome shaped, and some are like Wilt Chamberlain's house. (Wilt's house has a tinted glass roof so that from above you can see everything inside.) The next thing I notice is that there are no manufacturing plants in the city, and that means no pollution. Everything looks scrubbed. The last sights that catch my eye are the many athletic fields. People are playing everything from football to horseshoes. Through my handy tele-scope, I can see a chart outside of one of the recreational buildings an-nouncing the upcoming events. On Saturday, there's going to be a dance, and I am going to be there, dancing away in my ideal city.

**Questions for Discussion**

1. Is the first sentence an effective beginning? For practice, write an-other first sentence to introduce this paragraph.
2. What four transition sentences does the writer use in his para-graph? Do they help you move from point to point smoothly?

**Step Four.**   Write a paragraph of at least 150 words describing your ideal town or city. You may want to focus on just a block or two. When you write, write as an artist paints, emphasizing the most im-portant things. You need not describe everything that a camera would pick up. But what you do describe, describe in some detail, writing as precisely as possible.

Before you begin, make sure you have a good plan for your paper. Here are two suggestions for ordering your material:

1. Describe what you see, moving from the left side of the scene to the right.
2. Describe four or five things that stand out, beginning with the most eye-catching.

**Other Writing Assignments**

Here are some other writing assignments in which you can make good use of the brainstorming technique:

1. Describe the ideal home (or the garden outside of the ideal home).
2. Describe the ideal mate.
3. Describe the ideal English teacher.
4. Describe the ideal coach.
5. Describe the ideal church or religious center.
6. Describe the ideal five-course meal.

For each assignment, begin with a brainstorm, making a long list of all the ideal features. Then make a plan that will help you say what you want to say as clearly as possible as you use your brainstorm list. And then write a paragraph of 150 or more words.

**Awareness of Surroundings**

There are two ways of making a trip from one place to another. You can walk or ride with your eyes open, noticing the details of your surroundings, or you can, like most of us, just get there. Likewise, there are two ways of looking at a room or an object. You can look at it and really see it—its colors, its unique features, and so forth—or, again like most of us, you can just look at it without concentrating on the details. In the writing assignments below, practice looking at and *seeing* the details of your surroundings. Your observation of fine details is an important preliminary step to your writing. The more details you describe in your writing, the more you will help your reader to "see" the scene you create.

**Writing Assignment #1**

**Step One.** Get a mental picture of your room at home, your dormitory room, or some other room you have strong feelings about. Make a brainstorm list of all the details of the room you can possibly think of. What furniture is in it? What colors do you see? What little items catch your eye? What is out of place?

**Step Two.** Study the example below for ideas on how you might use your brainstorm list in writing a paragraph on a room.

> My room is usually clean, but when I left this morning, it had gotten so messy that my dog wouldn't come in. My pink silk robe and pajamas were thrown across my unmade bed. My slippers were lying there in the middle of the floor, and I hate to admit it, but the floor was covered with big gobs of lint. Off to the right, my bureau top was piled high with caps from lotions, old empty bottles, hair curlers, deodorant, and many purses. And finally, my closet was overflowing with dirty clothes left over from last week and maybe the week before. When I think of my room, it makes me glad I'm not there.

**Questions for Discussion**

1. Is the first sentence effective? For practice, write another sentence to introduce the paragraph.
2. How is this description organized? Right to left? Left to right? Could the organization have been made clearer? How?
3. Name five particular things that the student described.

**Step Three.**   Plan your paragraph. Here are some suggestions:

1. In your first sentence, say when you were last in the room and in one or two words summarize its general appearance.
2. Decide on at least five things that stand out as you think of the room.
3. Decide on some method for ordering what you will write about. Will you describe the room from left to right, right to left, from the most eye-catching features to the least eye-catching ones? You may want to place yourself in the doorway as you view the room.

**Step Four.**   Write a paragraph of at least 100 words, describing the details of the room as precisely as possible. In your last sentence, give the one word or expression that best describes how the room makes you feel.

**Writing Assignment #2**

**Step One.**   On your next trip to or from class, try to concentrate on what you see along the way. While you are making the trip or soon afterwards, take notes on what you have seen.

**Step Two.**   After you have made up a long list of things you have seen, pick the most important to write about. Be sure you have a plan for your paragraph. You may simply want to write what you saw in the order that you saw it.

**Step Three.**   Write a paragraph of at least 150 words describing your trip. In your last sentence tell your readers what it was like to go to class (or return home) with your eyes "open."

**Writing Assignment #3**

Write a paragraph of no less than 100 words saying at least five things about an object without ever naming it. Pick something that is not too big, preferably something you can get your arms or perhaps your hands around. Your description should be so exact that your audience can guess what it is you are describing. (Don't make it too obvious, though. If you are describing teeth, for example, don't describe them as something you bite with.) Study the following two student examples:

**A**

It is huge, dark brown, inexpensive, and weighs a ton. It is also at times the family joke. Everyone cannot get over the fact that it contains so many different items and is so heavy to carry around. Often my husband has said that if our country were bombed, our family would survive due to the contents of my object. It contains headache pills, stomachache pills, and back-ache ointments, and if you dig deep enough, you can even find dental floss for those once-in-a-year emergencies. It contains chewing gum, a date-book, a mini-umbrella, a check book, and several other things I can't tell you about because then my object would be a dead giveaway.

**B**     I am to be admired for what I am. I grow and I die along with the seeds of life. People love me and those who give me. I bring life to dull and shady corners. I bring warmth and smiles to the hearts of my owners. I dress up many major dinners and decorate great celebrations. I am the color of a fair lady's blush and contrast with the blue in the eyes of the one who wears me. I must be seen only, for if I am touched, I'll fall to pieces. What am I?

When you finish your paragraph, read it to the class to see if they can guess your object.

**Other Writing Assignments**     In preparing for your paragraphs on the following topics, either visit the place you are describing and make a list of all the details that stand out for you, or get a good picture of the place in your mind's eye and brainstorm for as many details as you can see. Once you have a long list, write a paragraph of 150 words or more.

1. Describe the most peaceful place you can think of.
2. Describe the most unusual person (or people) you saw on the bus today.
3. Describe your English classroom.
4. Describe a farm scene—cows in a pasture, a farmer broadcasting his seed, an old barn, or your favorite sight on a farm.
5. Describe a scene from nature—a mountaintop, a beach, a desert (help people who are unfamiliar with deserts to see some of the things that untrained eyes would miss), or your favorite sight.
6. Describe a busy intersection.

**Awareness of Past Experience**     In the writing assignments that follow, you will become aware of past experiences that you may not have thought of in a long time. Besides giving you an important resource for writing, the act of recalling past experiences will help you gain more control over your life. Your past is you: the more you know and understand the past—the hard times and the good times—the better you will know yourself.

So far in this chapter, you have gathered information for your writing assignments from class discussion, from brainstorming, and from making notes on your surroundings. In the assignments that follow, you will gather information for your writing through yet another method—*freewriting*. In freewriting, you write as fast as you can without worrying about spelling, punctuation, or using the most precise word, although you should try to write in whole sentences instead of just jotting down notes as you did in the brainstorming exercises. As you write, one thought will lead you to another. Instead of debating whether or not to use any particular thought, simply write them all down, as fast as they come to you. The freewriting will serve as the raw material for a paper of several paragraphs.

**Writing Assignment #1**

**Step One.**   This assignment calls for your instructor to read the following, which is designed to take you on a fantasy trip into a kind of twilight zone. As your instructor reads, close your eyes and listen closely. Clear your desk of everything except paper and pen or pencil so that you will not be disturbed.

It is early morning, just after sunrise. You find yourself alone, relaxed, happy, walking along a winding country road (or a street in the city with lots of trees on it). You are walking in the general direction of the sun, which is still not too bright but is trying to shine through the early morning haze or fog. On either side of you are tall green trees. Try to get a picture of what they look like. *(Pause)* Dew is still on the grass and the leaves.

You begin to notice everything around you, becoming aware of the slightly damp morning breeze, the feel of your feet as you walk along, the birds' singing, the fresh smells, the sun's warmth on your face. *(Pause)*

As you walk along, you begin to have a sense that something rare and special is going to happen. *(Pause)* Up ahead to the right of the road, you see a large clearing, an open field. As you walk closer, you see at the far end of the clearing, a living creature. Moving closer still, you see that the living creature is a small child, about six years old, quietly playing in its own private world.

You are irresistibly drawn to this child. *(Pause)* There is something familiar. You are tuned in to the child's movements and expressions. You recognize the clothing the child is wearing. The child is playing the way you used to play, smiling the way you used to smile. Try to get a picture of the child at play. *(Pause)* Suddenly, you realize that the child in the clearing is you! You are flooded with memories from age six: how large everything seemed, how much you liked and cared for certain things, what you wore, the games you played.

Take yourself back to age six. Become aware of yourself at

that age. *(Pause)* Now let yourself and the child have a conversation. Keep your eyes closed for another two or three minutes. *(Pause)* In a moment I will ask you to open your eyes. Begin to write as fast as you can about what happened from the time you first found yourself alone on the road until you met yourself at age six. When you write, include the following:

► What you saw, heard, and felt along the road

► What you saw as you looked at the child: the clothes, the facial expressions, the movements

► What you saw the child doing

► What you and the child said to each other

► How you felt encountering yourself at age six

Now slowly open your eyes and write as fast as you can.

**Step Two.**   Read your freewriting aloud in a small group, and address the following questions as you hear other papers read:

1. What do you like best about the paper?
2. What details stand out the most?
3. What descriptions could be made more precise? How?
4. What else would you like to know about the child?

**Step Three.**   Read the following student samples for ideas on how you might use your freewriting to write a more finished paper.

A        THE ROAD OF MY LIFE

I am walking down the road of my life. Its sights are very vivid as my mind wanders aimlessly. It is quite cold. A light mist brings on the appearance of another world. As I walk along the edge of the road, the crunch of the pebbles beneath my feet is barely audible. A slight breeze whispers through the tall pines causing the needles and the tall grass beneath the trees to sway in rhythmic motion. The sun is a brilliant orange as it clears the horizon. I know the cool moisture in the air will soon disappear. The birds sing in unison but with different calls, letting me know that they are seeking breakfast. The road is like a tunnel of serenity because all is so peaceful here. Because of the upgrade of the road, I am taking my time, breathing deeply of this dream. The fragrance of the pines and the green grass give off an aroma unmatched by any man-made perfume.

As I walk further along the road, I notice a clearing to the right. As I near it, I see a little boy standing beside the road as if he is waiting for someone, but he doesn't look my way. I am only a short distance from the boy now, and I can see that the clearing is paved with concrete. The little boy is wearing old clothes, like I used to wear when I was a kid, mostly hand-me-downs. Then he turns around with a blank expression on his face, and suddenly it hits me; he looks exactly like me in every detail. He reaches out his hand in a begging gesture. Because my senses were trained on him, I had not noticed what was to my right. It was a ghetto! What a trip. I kept walking fast.

### Questions for Discussion

1. What are three pictures or details that stand out for you in this essay?
2. What was the six-year-old trying to say when he held out his hand in a begging gesture? What unnamed feeling was being expressed?
3. Why did the author keep "walking fast"? What feeling was being expressed?
4. What more would you like to know about the boy or the adult?
5. What tense (present time or past) did the author use for most of his story? Why did he choose that tense?
6. Locate the point near the end of the essay where the author switched to the past tense. Was that change necessary? For practice rewrite that portion of the essay in the present tense.

**B**     The Child in Me

As I was walking along a country road, I looked up and saw lonely birds, flying high, flapping their wings, against an early morning pink sky that looked like soft and sweet cotton candy. I continued my walk down the road until out of nowhere a little girl appeared.

The little girl had two long ponytails with blue barrettes at the end of each. She had glowing white teeth, except for the one that was missing in the front. She was a skinny little girl and had on a pair of blue shorts and a white blouse. I smiled at the little girl, asking her her name. She answered by saying, "You should know my name." The little girl said to follow her, and she would help me find out her name. She then took my hand and led me to a playground where I used to play. There were lots of kids playing games: jump rope, jacks, dolls and hopscotch. The little girl joined the other children as I sat on the bench. I watched the child closely and suddenly saw her fall. When I ran over to help, she began to cry and the other kids called out, "Crybaby, crybaby, ha, ha, ha." At that moment, I realized that the child was me, the one who cried over everything and got teased for it. As I picked her up and carried her over to the bench, she said with a sad face, "Now you know who I am." I looked at her and smiled. "You got that right, good buddy," I said. We both gave each other a big hug and laughed. The little girl said that when we met again, she hoped I would not forget who she was.

This was an important exercise for me. I realized that the nice things in life and the bad things will always be a part of my thoughts and dreams. I knew when I saw the child that I could never be alone no matter what I was doing, no matter where I was. She would always be with me, and from now on, I will know her name.

### An Exercise

1. Sample A was written almost entirely in the present tense. Rewrite it so that all of it is in the past tense. You should begin as follows:

   ▶ I *was* walking down the road of my life. Its sights *were* very vivid as my mind *wandered*. . . .

2. Sample B was written in the past tense. Rewrite the first two paragraphs in the present tense. You should begin like this:

   ▶ As I *am* walking along a country road, I *look* up and *see* lonely birds. . . .

*Note:* Ordinarily *will* and *can* are used with present-tense verbs and *would* and *could* are used with past-tense verbs. See Chapter 8.2.

**Step Four.** Using your freewriting, write a two- or three-paragraph paper of 200 to 300 words. Make use of the small group discussion. In the next chapter you will learn more complete techniques for revising your papers. But for now here are some suggestions:

1. Be ready to add to, delete, or change any of your freewriting.
2. Plan your paper in a logical way, letting your paragraphs express whole thoughts. In the first paragraph, you may want to describe your experience on the road before meeting the child. In the second, you may want to describe your encounter with the child. In the last sentence of the second paragraph (or in a short third paragraph), you may want to tell your readers how you felt about the experience.

3. Make sure you move from paragraph to paragraph with smooth transitions. Notice how the students in the samples above began their second and third paragraphs.
4. There are two mechanical errors you should try especially to avoid in this assignment: the run-on sentence and confusion of tense. When you are writing something in the past tense, as when you are telling a story, it is very easy to join sentences incorrectly because they are often so closely related in content. Study the rules for preventing run-on sentences in Chapter 6.8. Also, when you are writing something in the past tense, make sure you end your regular verbs with *d* or *ed* and use the correct verb form for irregular verbs. Study Chapter 8.0 and 8.3.
5. Give your paper a title. See the learning notes on page 52.

## SIMILES AND METAPHORS

In describing people, things, or actions, you can sometimes strengthen your writing by saying what they remind you of. In the first student sample above, the writer spoke of his road as being like a "tunnel of serenity." The image of the tunnel makes the reader imagine trees that grow up on either side of the road, their branches touching in the middle. Another student spoke of early morning noises as being like "a symphony, nature's orchestra." In another assignment, one student described a relative as short and chubby and shaped like a "loosely rolled sleeping bag." When you say one thing is like another thing, you are using what is called a *simile*. What is the simile in the first paragraph of sample B above?

### AN EXERCISE

Make up your own similes for the following:

1. The rising sun was like ⸺⸺⸺⸺⸺⸺⸺⸺

2. The green pasture looked like ⸺⸺⸺⸺⸺⸺

3. The child was as skinny as ⸺⸺⸺⸺⸺⸺⸺

While a simile says one thing is *like* another, a *metaphor,* to stir the imagination, says that one thing *is* another. Instead of saying that the road was *like* a tunnel of serenity, the writer of the first sample above could have used a metaphor and said that the road *was* a tunnel of serenity. Instead of saying that his grandfather's nose looked like a ''cherry tomato'' (a simile), one student wrote that his grandfather had a ''cherry tomato of a nose'' (a metaphor).

## AN EXERCISE

This time make metaphors by completing the sentences:

1. The rising sun was _____

2. The green pasture was _____

3. The child was a(an) _____

_____

**Writing Assignment #2**

**Step One.**   For this assignment, write a paper of several paragraphs (300 words or more) in which you recall an event from your past that you would like to forget. As an introduction to this assignment, read the following folktale:

Once upon a time a handsome young prince offended the King and Queen of his land. They condemned him to be beheaded. When he pleaded to be forgiven, they offered him an alternative. They said that if within fourteen days he could find the answer to a very complicated riddle, he could not only have his freedom but their beautiful daughter as well.

The young prince went out and searched everywhere for the answer to the riddle, but by the fourteenth day he still had no answer. Worn out and depressed, he headed back to the castle. Near the gate, however, he met a bent, shriveled up old hag. She motioned to him with her bony, crooked fingers and whispered in a croaking voice that she could tell him the answer to the riddle, but in return he must promise to grant her request if she ever needed a favor. Desperate, he agreed.

To the surprise and delight of everyone, the young prince returned to the court with the answer to the complicated riddle. True to their word, the King and Queen gave him both his freedom and also their daughter.

Just before the wedding ceremony was about to take place, the old hag appeared and said she was ready to make her request. She pointed her finger at the prince. ''I want you to marry me,'' she said and then cackled. The prince was horrified, but being a noble young man, he did as he had promised and married the old hag.

On their wedding night, though, he was so repulsed by the old hag's grotesque appearance that he lay in bed with his back to her, keeping as far away as possible. But she nudged him with her bony fingers and insisted that he embrace and kiss her.

The prince gathered all his courage, turned to the hag, took her in his arms, and—taking a deep breath—kissed her on the lips. At that very moment, to his sheer amazement, the prince felt her body grow soft and graceful. He saw that the person in his arms was no longer a loathsome old hag, but the beautiful young princess, the woman of his dreams.

**Step Two.** The storytellers who passed this story down from one generation to another thought that *life* was like the story of the prince and the loathsome lady. They believed that what seemed ugly and loathsome was often the very thing that would turn into a beautiful source of growth and life *if* it were embraced.

In your own life, surely you can think of some loathsome ladies, sad or unpleasant experiences you would like to forget forever. In this assignment, you will recall one or more of them as you write on the topic "What I Would Most Like to Forget." Perhaps you too will find that your loathsome lady is a fine source of growth.

Brainstorm for a long list of the things you would most like to forget. Use the following headings:

1. My saddest experiences

2. My most embarrassing moments

_____

_____

_____

_____

_____

_____

3. My greatest goofs

_____

_____

_____

_____

_____

_____

Now choose the experience you would most like to write about.

**Step Three.**   In your freewriting, first determine when your story really begins. If you are telling about the death of a loved one, perhaps you should begin with the moment when you first heard the news. If you are telling about the time you showed up for a party in shorts when everyone else was in a dress or in a coat and tie, perhaps you should begin your story when you first received the invitation and tell how excited you were about going.

Now tell your story from beginning to end, writing as fast as you can. Try to write in whole sentences, but don't worry about grammar and punctuation for this draft. If you get sidetracked, don't worry about it; you may be uncovering important parts of your story.

**Step Four.**   Read the student samples that follow for ideas on how you might write your finished paper.

A           I would most like to forget the time my godfather died. I was seven years old when it happened, and it was my first experience with death. We had a very close relationship. He used to joke about how I was his princess and he was my knight in shining armor.

The one morning I will never forget is September 22, 1970. It was on this morning that I found out he had died. When my mother told me, I began to cry. Questions seemed to pour out of me. I wanted to know why he died and what was going to happen to him. Mother told me that God does not like to see people suffer and that he had suffered enough from his illness. She said he was going to heaven. I then asked her what he was going to do there. She took a long pause, and then her answer was brief. She told me he was going to be my guardian angel. As fast as the questions began. they stopped. I stood there looking at my mother with a feeling of emptiness. I did not believe her.

The next thing that happened was when I went to the wake. As we walked into the funeral home, I could see the coffin from a distance. Tears began to fill my eyes, and I started to shake. My mother put her arm around me and led me into the room. Everything from that point on was a blurred vision. The only thing I can remember is my godmother taking me to the coffin. While I was looking at him, memories began to fill my mind: how he used to let me "ride the horsey" on his knee, how he always "dunked" his bread in his milk, how he called me Ba-ba-hop-along-too because I was always running after my sister. I was hoping that he would wake up, but I knew it wasn't going to happen.

The funeral the next day was the worst part. The sun was hidden by dark clouds, rain came down in sprinkles, and cold breezes passed through me. Everybody was standing in a circle. The priest said a few words, and we bowed our heads to pray. The next thing I saw was my four cousins picking up the coffin and placing it in a big hole in the ground. I knew that this was the end.

By bringing back this experience, I understand a little better the meaning of death. It is becoming clear to me that we are born to serve a purpose. After our purpose is fulfilled, we die. But just because a person dies doesn't mean that he is forgotten.

### Questions for Discussion

1. What did the student learn by recalling this childhood experience?
2. What is the organizing principle (the controlling idea) of each paragraph?
3. Beginning with the second paragraph, look at the first sentence of each paragraph. Is each an effective transition sentence; that is, does it help you move from one paragraph to the other smoothly?
4. What would be a good title for this paper? See the learning notes on pages 52–54.

**B**    I would most like to forget the basketball game we lost to Abita Springs. Our problems started the week before the game. We didn't give ourselves enough time to practice. Only two days before the game, there were new faces on the team. On seeing the new faces, I realized we were going to be in trouble.

When the game started, everyone felt butterflies, but soon we began to feel shame. We fell behind several points only three minutes into the game. When our leader called time out, we got ourselves together somewhat, but we still trailed at the half by four points.

In the second half, we gradually caught up. With only two minutes left in the game, we actually moved ahead by one point. The lead then changed several times, and every shot was a crucial one. I was amazed at the caliber of my teammates and was beginning to think I was wrong and that we would win after all. Then with about sixteen seconds left, Abita Springs got the ball and was playing for the last shot. The clock continued to click down. The crowd was going wild. We were again ahead by one point. One of their men was about to make a lay-up, so we fouled him. It was just our luck to foul the best free-throw shooter on their team. He went to the line and sank the first shot. He got the ball again and sank the second shot. We immediately called time because we were now losing by one point.

With nine seconds left on the clock, we took the ball in. I can remember Chip, our point guard, shouting, "Get your tails down court and set up," our coach, David, yelling, "Shoot it," myself screaming, "Pass the damn ball. I have a shot." "Don't shoot." "Shoot," came the voices from the stands. Finally, I got the ball in the middle of all this confusion. The clock went off, but the ball didn't. It stayed right there in my hands.

In the locker room there was total silence. No one had anything to say. The only sound we heard came from the toilet. Bringing back this experience made me realize that winning isn't the most important thing; it is the only thing.

### Questions for Discussion

1. What did the student learn by bringing back his loathsome lady?
2. What is the organizing principle of each paragraph?
3. In the last paragraph how does the writer make you aware of his feelings without naming feelings?
4. What would be a good title for this essay?

**Step Five.**   Using your freewriting as the basis for your paper, write an essay of 300 or more words on your loathsome-lady experience. Most students need three to six paragraphs for this assignment. The suggestions below are similar to the revision strategies discussed in the next chapter.

1. Be willing to add to, delete, or change any of your freewriting.
2. Plan your paper in a logical way. In deciding how to form paragraphs, refer back to the student samples to see how those writers set up their paragraphs. Have an organizing principle in mind for each paragraph.
3. In your first paragraph, move your reader into the story as quickly as possible. You may want to begin your paper with "I would most like to forget. . . ."
4. Use smooth transition sentences to begin your second paragraph and those following.
5. In your last paragraph, tell your readers what you learned by bringing back your experiences.
6. Give your paper a title. See the learning notes below for rules and suggestions concerning titles.

## TITLES

Unless your instructor gives other instructions, practice giving titles to all your papers, even the ones that are just one paragraph long.

## Suggestions for Composing Titles

1. Make your title relate to the main idea of your paper.
2. Try to pick a title that stimulates interest.
3. If possible, keep your title short: three to six words. Usually the title should not be a whole sentence.

## Rules for Writing Titles

1. Do not underline or put quotation marks around your title when it appears at the top of your paper.
2. Always capitalize the first and last words of your title and every other word of five or more letters.
3. Capitalize all other words except the following:

   Articles: *a, an, the*
   Short conjunctions, such as *and, but, or, when, if*
   Short prepositions, such as *in, on, of, to, with, but,*
      *by, up, upon, over, into, at, from*

   ▸ The Ghost of the Plantation

4. Skip two or three lines between your title and the first line of your paper.

## Two Exercises

**A.**   Using the rules above, capitalize the appropriate words in the following titles:

1. the room that can't breathe
2. my room in Tubman Hall
3. an experience on the road
4. the little boy who couldn't speak
5. when I was very young
6. the trip that took me home

**B.**   The titles below were written as full sentences. Shorten them to a few words (three to six if possible). Follow the rules of capitalization.

1. Sex education should be taught to young people in high school.
2. Only in very rare circumstances should abortion be allowed.

3. If we don't begin to reduce nuclear weapons soon, we may not survive the century.
4. The Gay Fellowship should be allowed to operate as an official campus organization.
5. Atticus Finch in *To Kill a Mockingbird* is a man of great courage and gentleness.

**Other Freewriting Assignments**

Begin your writing with one of the following statements and let your imagination take you wherever it wants to go.

1. I found myself at age twenty on the outskirts of Chicago with no money in my pockets and no relatives or friends to turn to. It was getting dark, and I was chilly in the early fall air. I was hungry, I didn't know what to do, but I knew I had to do something fast, so I. . . .
2. I have always believed that somewhere in the world there lives the perfect mate for me. I was at this small party the other night, and when I happened to look up towards the door, I saw him (or her) standing there alone. I knew, as I have never known anything so definitely before, that this was the right person for me. I gathered my courage and I. . . .
3. I was walking along the beach last summer and happened to see an old bottle with barnacles growing all over it. As I approached, I saw there was a piece of paper, a letter, inside the bottle. I had to break off the end of the bottle to get the letter, and then I read these words: . . .
4. I am a sick man . . . I am a spiteful man. I am an unpleasant man. I think my liver is diseased. However, I don't know beans about my disease, and I am not sure what is bothering me. I don't treat it and never have. Yesterday on the way home from work I fell down on the sidewalk and a little boy offered to help me up and. . . . (These lines, except for the last sentence, are the first words of *Notes from Underground* by Fyodor Dostoyevsky. Feel free to substitute "woman" for "man.")

## 2. Dialogue

**Introduction**

A second resource for your writing is dialogue, which is simply conversation between two or more people. In the writing assignments that follow, you will become more aware of the way you speak and the way others speak and will learn how to record spoken language in your essays. There are at least three reasons for learning to use dialogue in your writing. First, dialogue can give life to your writing. When you let people speak for themselves, you make your writing exact, specific, and interesting—always important goals in writing. The following excerpt from a student's paper demonstrates how dialogue can give life to a paper. Entitled "Jailbird," this story is about a time the author was arrested for being in the wrong place at the wrong time.

There were cops coming from every direction, shouting, "Against the wall, hands high." There was screaming, pushing, and shoving. About twenty of us were taken to Central Lockup.

When we arrived, we were allowed one phone call. Showanda and Sylvia made their calls first, and their parents agreed to come get them right away. I then called home. Of all the people in the house, my mother had to answer the phone. The conversation went something like this:

"Hello, Mama."
"Bernetta, what happened?"
"I'm in Central Lockup."
"Oh my God! My child is in jail."
"Come and get me out before it's too late and I have to spend the night."
"Child, how did you get arrested?"
"The discotheque got raided."
"You told me that you were going to a party."
"I lied."
"Well since you lied to me, Honey, I'm going to lie to you and say I'm coming to get you out."
"But Ma!"

The phone hung up and I thought the world was coming to an end.

The next morning I returned home. There was no conversation all the way home until I opened the door and then . . .

Mama: "You are the first one to bring the family down."
Brothers: "What kind of birds don't fly?"
Sisters: "Jailbirds."

A second reason for learning to use dialogue is that with this skill you can employ community dialects, often rich in their rhythms and expressiveness, in your writing. One goal of this course is to help you write in standard English, since most of your writing in college and on the job will have to be in standard English. (Standard written English is used in magazines, newspapers, and most books and should be learned by all college students. It is a common ground for communication in a society of great diversity.)

But the emphasis on standard English does not mean that spoken dialects have no place in your writing. Just about everyone in this country speaks some kind of dialect. Any group that has a special identity develops over the years special ways of speaking English. (Examples are blacks, Hispanics, Orientals; also Native Americans, Irish-Americans, Polish-Americans, Italian-Americans, southern Americans, and others.) Some of the dialects are more pronounced, with greater variations from the norm, than others. People are, to some degree, what they speak, and from time to time in your writing you will need to let them speak for themselves in their own dialects.

One of our great American novelists, Mark Twain, said that he worked "painstakingly" to record accurately the dialects that he put into the mouths of his characters. Listen to one of the characters, Huckleberry Finn, describe his ne'er-do-well father, whom he had not seen in some time:

He was most fifty, and he looked it. His hair was long and tangled and greasy, and hung down, and you could see his eyes shining through like he was behind vines. It was all black, no gray; so was his long mixed-up whiskers. There warn't no color in his face, where his face showed; it was white; not like another man's white, but a white to make a body sick, a white to make a body's flesh crawl—a tree-toad white, a fish-belly white. As for his clothes—just rags, that was all. He had one ankle resting on t'other knee; the boot on that foot was busted, and two of his toes stuck through, and he worked them now and then. His hat was laying on the floor—an old black slouch with the top caved in, like a lid.

This description would have lost much of its power if Huck had been writing about his father in standard English. Now listen to Huck's father speak to him, complaining about Huck's going to school:

"Well, I'll learn her [the widow who had been taking care of Huck] how to meddle. And looky here—you drop that school, you hear? I'll learn people to bring up a boy to put on airs over his own father and let on to be better'n what *he* is. You lemme catch you fooling around that school again, you hear? Your mother couldn't read, and she couldn't write, nuther, before she died. None of the family couldn't before *they* died. I can't; and here you're a-swelling yourself up like this. I ain't the man to stand it—you hear? Say, lemme hear you read."

So, if you are familiar with a nonstandard English dialect, hold on to it—it can be a rich resource for you in your writing. When you want to use nonstandard English, simply let it come from the mouths of the people you are writing about. Here is an example of how one student recorded her own expressive dialect in a *standard* English essay. (Notice how she mixes the comic with the tragic as she records this conversation.)

### A CONVERSATION AT CHARITY HOSPITAL

Today, at about 3:30 P.M., I was sitting in the waiting room at Charity Hospital, and I heard a conversation that was a little bit funny and a little bit sad. Two middle-aged women were talking about someone they knew in common. It was noisy as usual in the waiting room, and I couldn't hear everything, but I did hear most of what they were saying. Lady A didn't seem too sick, but she did seem glad to see Lady B. Here is what they said:

Lady A: "Girl, what you doin' here?"
Lady B: "Gorl, em in year with my sista."
"What's wrong with ha?"
"Gorl, I donno. She been complainin' about ha side, but with a man like the one she got she lucky that's all that's hortin' ha."
"You mean to tell me that she still takin' ass whippins off that man!"
"Gorl, it ain't ever stopped. Em so sick of this stuff."
"Well all I can tell ya is to pray, Hunnay. Ask the Lord to look down on ha."
"Oh yeah. That's all I can do."
"Yeah."
"Well, how the folks in the country? What is Gertrude doin'?"
"Girl, that's what I wanta tell ya. Gertrude done got herself thrown in jail."
"What! Gorl, ya lyin'. What in the world did she do? Gool Lord!"
"Girl, the woman shot her man twice before, but this time she done it for good. You ain't heard about it?"
"You know em always busy, ain't got time fa myself. I don't hear nothin' any more, but I sure sorry to hear 'bout them gettin' along like that."
"Ya know my niece gettin' married, hah?"
"What ha name? Geraldine?"
"Huh, ain' nobody goina marry that lil' hoe. No, Girl, it's Kathleen that's gettin married."

Then my name was called. The conversation made me feel empathy for both women.

A third reason for learning how to use dialogue in your writing is that this skill will help you as you learn how to quote written material in your essays. Instructions on how to use quotations are presented in the next section of this chapter.

**Writing Assignment #1**

**Step One.** Two people need to volunteer for each of the following skits. *After* each skit, write down as much of the conversation as you can recall, as quickly as you can.

*Situation #1.* It is late afternoon. Player A has just finished the last class of the day and is about ready to take the bus home but discovers that he (or she) has no money. To make matters worse, a dark rain cloud is forming overhead. Everyone seems to have gone home except an English teacher, Player B. Players A and B have a two- or three-minute conversation, in which Player A asks Player B for the bus fare.

*Situation #2.* Same situation, except Player B is another student, someone of the opposite sex, and a stranger to Player A.

*Situation #3.* Same situation, except now Player B is an old friend of Player A.

**Step Two.** Several people from the class should read aloud what they have written. Did they record the exact words that were spoken, or did they substitute their own words? What did they leave out? Fill in any significant part of the conversation that you missed.

**Step Three.** Rewrite one of the conversations using Method #1 described in the learning notes below. Make use of your notes, the class discussion, and the following student sample. (In this conversation Player A was an Hispanic student, for whom English was a second language.)

> Speaker A: "Hey, man, how you doin'?"
> Speaker B: "Well, thank you."
> "I'm glad. Hey, I have a little problem. You see, I spent all my money for lunch, you know. And I forgot to save any. So could you lend me some money for the bus fare. I'll pay you back, man."
> "I'm afraid I'm not in the habit of lending money out."
> "Man, come on! I'll pay you back. Say listen you're an English teacher, huh?"
> "Yes, I am."
> "Say, man, English is a beautiful language."
> "Okay, you win. Here's a token."

## RECORDING A CONVERSATION: METHOD #1

In recording a conversation that contains several exchanges, the following method is useful if you simply want to record the conversation itself. If, however, you want to make the conversation into more of a story, use Method #2 described in the learning notes that follow Writing Assignment #2.

### SOME SUGGESTIONS ON FORM

1. Give the names of the people who are speaking to one another:

   I heard this conversation between Maria, Mrs. Shell, and Mrs. Fox in the laundromat yesterday.
   In our English class today, I heard this conversation between Player A and Player B.

2. Use a new paragraph for each speaker, like this:

   Maria: "I'm sorry I'm late with your clothes."
   Mrs. Shell: "I don't understand the young people of today. They are always late."
   Mrs. Fox: "Things aren't like they used to be. When I was a girl, we were never late with our work."

3. Use a colon (:) after the names of the speakers, as shown above.
4. Use quotation marks at the beginning and end of each speaker's statements, but *not* after each sentence. Mrs. Shell and Mrs. Fox both spoke two sentences, but quotation marks were not used after the first sentences.
5. Always place your periods *inside* the quotation marks, as shown above.
6. If you drop a letter to make a word sound the way it was pronounced, use an apostrophe to show the omission:

   How you doin'?

7. If there are only two people talking and it is clear which one is speaking, drop the names before each speech. See the student

sample in *step three* above. If three or more people are speaking, name the speaker each time. See Chapter 11.7 for more on the use of quotation marks.

**Writing Assignment #2**

Rewrite the same conversation, or another one you heard in the class skits, making it into more of a story. Read the sample below and study the learning notes that follow.

> Speaker A walked up to Speaker B, an English teacher, outside of the Language Arts Building and said, "Hey, how you doin'?"
>
> "Very well, thank you," the teacher responded, as she looked up from her book.
>
> "I'm glad," Speaker A continued, looking away. "You see, I spent all my money for lunch, you know. And I forgot to save any. So could you lend me some money for the bus fare? I'll pay you back."
>
> But the English teacher was not moved. "I'm afraid I'm not in the habit of lending money out," she said. She began reading her book again.
>
> Player A was not about to give up, however. "Man," he said, "come on! I'll pay you back. Listen, you're an English teacher, huh?"
>
> "Yes, I am," the teacher answered.
>
> "Say, man, English is a beautiful language."
>
> "Okay, you win. Here's a token."

## RECORDING A CONVERSATION: METHOD #2

The following method is useful when you want to make a conversation into a story. Compare the samples in the above Writing Assignments #1 (a straight conversation) and #2 (a story).

### SOME SUGGESTIONS ON FORM

1. Use speaker tags like those underlined below as one person speaks to another:

   He said, "Hey, man, how you doin'?"

   "Very well, thank you," the English teacher responded.

   "Yes I am," the teacher answered.

Usually the best speaker tags are the most direct ones: *said, asked, answered, replied,* and so on.

2. Use a comma (or commas) with each speaker tag:

   After: <u>He said,</u> "Hey, man."
   Before: "Yes, I am," <u>the teacher responded.</u>

   If the speaker tag comes in the middle of a sentence, use commas on both sides of it:

   "Man," <u>he said,</u> "come on! I'll pay you back."

3. A direct quotation is often a complete sentence. Begin it with a capital:

   He said, "**M**ay I have some money for the bus?"

   But the speaker tag is not capitalized unless it begins a sentence:

   "I will think about it," **t**<u>he teacher responded.</u>

4. In a conversation with several exchanges, use a new paragraph each time the speaker shifts.
5. Place both commas and periods inside the quotation marks:

   "Man," he said . . .
   "Yes I am," the teacher answered. . . . a beautiful language."

   Place a question mark inside the quotation marks when a whole question is quoted:

   "May I have some money for the bus fare**?**" he asked.

   But place the question mark outside quotation marks when they are used to set off only part of the sentence, such as the title of a poem: Have you read the poem "Dover Beach"**?**

6. If it is completely clear who is speaking, you may drop the speaker tags if you choose. In the last two lines of the student sample in Writing Assignment #2, the speaker tags were dropped because it was completely clear who was speaking.

See Chapter 11.7 for more on the use of quotation marks.

**Writing Assignment #3**

**Step One.**   Position yourself near two or more people who appear to be having an interesting conversation: in the campus coffee shop, in the halls, outside the library, on the bus going home, or somewhere in your neighborhood. Write down as much of the conversation as you can. Be sure to use the speakers' words and not your own. If you object to listening in on such a conversation, record a recent conversation in which you yourself participated, or record a conversation from a radio or television talk show.

**Step Two.**   Study the two student samples in the introduction to this section on dialogue and the learning notes on the two methods for recording a conversation.

**Step Three.**   Write a 200- to 300-word paper reporting the conversation. Here are some suggestions:

1. Begin your paper something like this:

   Yesterday, I was sitting _____,

   and I heard a very _____ conversation.

   Choose the most exact word to describe the conversation, such as *stimulating, funny, emotional, disgusting,* or the like.
2. Include in the first paragraph a brief description of each speaker (a sentence or two).
3. Use either the first or second method, described in the learning notes above, to record the conversation. Be sure to use a different paragraph for each shift of speaker because your conversation will have several exchanges.

**Step Four.**   Read your writing in a small group. After each person reads, answer the following questions:

1. Did the dialogue really sound like people talking? Explain.
2. What more would you like to know about the people or the conversation itself?

Exchange your paper with someone else to check for proper paragraphing, punctuation, and capitalization. Before making any changes, however, check with your instructor.

## 3. Reading

**Introduction**    A third source for your writing is what you read—your texts, magazine and newspaper articles, and fiction and nonfiction books. The further you progress in college the more you will need to incorporate material from your reading into your writing. This text does not have enough room to offer many reading assignments, but it is nevertheless true that how much you read will determine, in the long run, how well you write. Read as much as you can. Here are some suggestions: find newspapers, magazines, and books *that you enjoy reading*; make sure the vocabulary is not so difficult that you will get discouraged; and finally, pick out articles and books that you will finish. If you have not been in the habit of reading for pleasure, don't start on a 500-page novel; start instead on a shorter work. College students usually enjoy the following: *Black Boy*, by Richard Wright; *Catcher in the Rye*, by J. D. Salinger; *Flowers for Algernon*, by Daniel Keyes; *Of Mice and Men*, by John Steinbeck; *One Flew over the Cuckoo's Nest*, by Ken Kesey; *The Outsiders*, by S. E. Hinton; and *To Kill a Mockingbird*, by Harper Lee. Ask your instructor for additional suggestions for particular titles.

When Richard Wright, in his book *Black Boy*, told his story of growing up in the midst of poverty and oppression in the first part of this century, he said over and over again that what enabled him to free himself from the bondage of his youth was, more than anything else, *reading*. Reading novels, especially, allowed him to enter new worlds and transcend the crippling everyday world into which he had been born:

Reading grew into a passion. My first serious novel was Sinclair Lewis's *Main Street*. It made me see my boss, Mr. Gerald, and identify him as an American type. I would smile when I saw him lugging his golf bags into the office. I had always felt a vast distance separating me from the boss, and now I felt closer to him, though still distant. I felt now that I knew him, that I could feel the very limits of his narrow life. And this had happened because I had read a novel about a mythical man called George F. Babbitt.

Although you may not face the same difficulties Wright faced in growing up, reading for pleasure can be just as liberating for you.

In this section you will work at developing reading skills that you can apply when careful reading is required. Then you will learn how to use reading material in your writing. First, study the reading method described in the learning notes that follow.

# A READING METHOD: SRR (SKIM, READ, REVIEW)

Any time you must read something that requires maximum comprehension, such as when you read something you will be tested on or something you will use as the basis for a writing assignment, the following method should be helpful. Once you become used to this method, you will find that it takes only a little bit longer than ordinary reading. Most students find the extra time well worth the trouble.

## FIRST, SKIM THE MATERIAL

1. Try to pick out the main idea of the piece you are reading. Often you can find it in the title or first paragraph.
2. Look out for definitions and difficult words at the beginning that you must understand before you can understand what follows. Look them up in the dictionary if necessary.
3. Read all subheadings. They will help give you an overview of the material.
4. Read the first (and sometimes second) sentences of enough paragraphs so that you will know, generally, what the subject matter is.
5. If something confuses you, stop and see if you can figure it out. If you still don't understand, move on.
6. Read the last paragraph or two.

## SECOND, READ THE MATERIAL THOROUGHLY

1. Underline the main ideas. When possible summarize the main points in the margin. (If you own the book, write all over it if it will help you learn.)
2. Relate the material to your own experience when possible. Make notes naming the experience the reading material reminds you of.
3. Write down questions to ask your instructor or another student on any important points that you don't understand.
4. Look up words that you don't understand in a dictionary. Keep a list of new words and their definitions.

THIRD, REVIEW BRIEFLY THE MATERIAL YOU HAVE READ

1. Without looking back, ask yourself: What was the main point of the material? What ideas and facts were presented to back up the main point?
2. If you can't remember, look back at the material and read over your notes.
3. If you were the instructor, what might you ask about the material on a quiz?

**Writing Assignment #1**

*Stanley Steamer — a car operated by steam*

**Step One.**   After studying the suggestions in the learning note for underlining, defining words, and summarizing main points in the margin, read the article below from an issue of *Sports Illustrated*. Make use of each step of the reading method.

*Did the crash of a Stanley steamer in 1907 influence U.S. foreign policy?*

*It is entirely possible that a little gully on a Florida beach 68 years ago had a weighty influence on America's current foreign policy and environment. As of January 25, 1907, the American people were still undecided about what kind of automobile they wanted. the industry was in its* formative *stages, with a variety of models on the market, including cars powered by gasoline, steam and electricity. From the beginning, the limitations of the electric automobile were all too apparent, but advocates of steam and gasoline vehicles debated, sometimes genially and often furiously, the merits of their favorites.*

*formative means "pertaining to growth"*

*In 1907, the Am. people were trying to decide between steam and gasoline engines.*

*steam versus gasoline*

YESTERDAY

Did the crash of a Stanley steamer in 1907 influence U.S. foreign policy?

It is entirely possible that a little gully on a Florida beach 68 years ago had a weighty influence on America's current foreign policy and environment. As of Jan. 25, 1907 the American people were still undecided about what kind of automobile they wanted. The industry was in its formative stages, with a variety of models on the market, including cars powered by gasoline, steam and electricity. From the beginning, the limitations of the electric automobile were all too apparent, but advocates of steam and gasoline vehicles debated, sometimes genially and often furiously, the merits of their favorites.

Both engines had advantages. Perfected by twin brothers, F.E. and F.O. Stanley, the steamer was a quiet and smooth-running automobile. It also was capable of extraordinary speed and acceleration. To the astonishment of a large crowd at a race in Detroit on Oct. 11, 1901, a steamer hit 30 mph and won the five- and 10-mile events. Thereafter, steamers won so regularly that they were sometimes banned from races with gasoline cars, despite the fact that competition was supposedly open to all autos of the same price range. (The ban was unofficial and inconsistent. Racing drivers had learned that Stanleys did less well when the distance was more than five miles. They were at their best in short distances.)

After establishing several speed records with their passenger machines, the Stanley brothers designed and built a car specifically for racing. Shaped like an inverted canoe, painted red and dubbed "Wogglebug" by the press, the racer made history in January 1906 by covering a mile in 28⅕ seconds—an average speed of 127.659 mph.

In addition to being fast, the steamer was a simple machine. "Our present car is composed of but 32 moving parts," the Stanleys said in their 1916 catalog, "which number includes front and rear wheels, steering gear, and everything moving on the car, as well as the power plant. This is about the number of parts contained in a first-class self-starter. We use no clutch, nor gear shifts, nor fly wheels, nor carburetors, nor magnetos, nor spark plugs, nor timers, nor distributors, nor self-starters, nor any of the marvelously ingenious complications which inventors have added in order to overcome the difficulties inherent in the internal-explosive engine and adapt it to a use for which it is not normally fitted."

The Stanleys also could have stressed the nonpolluting nature of their steamer. Not only did it not foul the air with unburned hydrocarbons, but it produced little or no noise. And it was capable of using fuels, such as kerosene, alcohol, coal gas and even coal, that were much cheaper than gasoline and more readily available.

On the other hand, operation of the steamer often could be troublesome, especially before the addition as standard equipment of a condenser permitting the vehicle to re-use its water supply. Until that step was taken, steamer owners had to carry a hose with them in order to raid horse troughs every 40 or 50 miles.

The biggest problem that confronted steamer manufacturers was fear. Americans had been through nearly a century of boiler explosions on boats and locomotives, and were extremely wary of high-pressure steam systems. The fact that early steamers trailed a light vapor as they moved along, giving the impression that the vehicles were already on fire or were smoldering preparatory to a massive explosion, did not build public confidence. Nevertheless, by 1907 the steamer had become a favorite of President Teddy Roosevelt and was making steady if not spectacular headway in the safety department. So close was it to winning acceptance that even the most avid partisans of internal-combustion engines would not have dared to predict its imminent demise.

Then came the international speed trials at Ormond Beach, Fla. on Jan. 25, 1907. Expecting a new record, an unusually large crowd turned out to view such vehicles as the first Rolls-Royce entered in a U.S. race and, of course, the Wogglebug with ace driver Fred Marriott at the tiller.

Gradually warming up his car for the record run, Marriott made two dashes along a mile section of beach, the first in 32 seconds, the second in 29⅗, less than a second and a half slower than his world record.

On his third run, Marriott hit the starting line at full throttle and shot up the beach. Although running against the wind, the steamer's speed was approaching 150 mph when the accident occurred. "He was nearly out of sight, being almost at the end of the mile, when the machine upset," wrote a reporter in *The New York Times.*

No one knew exactly what had happened. Those nearest the car agreed that the hood appeared to come loose—"seemingly lifted by the wind while the front wheels were so tilted upward that they did not strike the sand of the beach by several inches. . . . The tubing broke and the car was enveloped in a cloud of steam."

By the time spectators had raced up the beach to the scene of the accident, a Rolls-Royce had arrived and Marriott had been picked up, "his face covered with blood and lying insensible across the laps of two men in the rear seat. . . . He was found well up on the beach, while the round boiler, four or five times the size of a cheese box, was rescued rolling around in the ocean. When the car broke in two it dropped the boiler as it did Marriott. . . . The debris was thrown into two piles, over which hundreds of amateur photographers hovered like seagulls and many souvenirs were carried away. . . ."

The Stanleys later argued that a gully in the sandy beach caused the racer to rise, but they accepted blame for their flat-bottomed design, which, even if the gully was responsible for the steamer's take-off, contributed greatly to its becoming airborne.

Although Fred Marriott survived the accident by more than half a century, the American public and the Stanley brothers were greatly discouraged. The twins never again used their automobiles for racing. The public, its fear of steam propulsion revived, leaned more and more to the gasoline engine, a preference that was clearly established within a decade. Although the Stanleys continued producing cars until 1927, those ripples in the sand at Ormond Beach effectively ended their dream of a steam-powered society that might have left us today with an environment relatively free of noise and air pollution and a foreign policy less vulnerable to the pressures of oil-producing countries.

George Gipe

**Step Two.** Make a list, drawing on your notes, your memory, and the article itself, of everything that relates to the questions, "How might the wreck of a Stanley Steamer have influenced our foreign policy?" (This is simply a way of summarizing the article.)

_____

_____

_____

_____

_____

_____

_____

_____

_____

**Step Three.** Using the information you have gathered, write a paragraph of about 150 words in response to the question above. Here are some suggestions:

1. Begin your paragraph with a summary statement as follows: "The wreck of a Stanley steamer in 1907 might have influenced our current foreign policy. The wreck was significant because . . ." Complete the statement _with your own words_.
2. Explain the attitude in this country before the wreck toward using the steam engine for automobiles. Be sure to include some of the advantages.
3. Describe the wreck in one or two sentences.

4. Explain how the wreck changed attitudes toward the steam engine and how that might have influenced our foreign policy today.

**Step Four.**   Rewrite your paragraph, this time including at least one short direct quotation from the article itself to help illustrate your point. See the learning notes that follow.

## QUOTING READING MATERIAL

In quoting from reading material, observe the following key rule: Use quotations to back up or further explain *your* points, but don't depend on them too heavily. Quotations are generally used to give an expert's opinion or to pass on to your reader a particularly important or well-written phrase or sentence. In short papers, quotations should be kept short. Experiment with using quotations from time to time until you master the art. When you do quote, give the author's full name and the source of the quotation, such as the name of the magazine or the title of the book from which the quotation was taken. If you use the author's name a second or third time, you only have to give his or her last name.

### FOUR WAYS OF QUOTING READING MATERIAL

**Method #1.**   You can make the quotation part of the grammar of your sentence. Here you complete *your* sentence with the exact words of the author, as follows:

In his article "Yesterday" in *Sports Illustrated* (September 15, 1975), George Gipe shows how "a little gully on a Florida beach 68 years ago had a weighty influence on America's current foreign policy and environment."

If we had adopted the steam engine for automobiles, argues Gipe, "that might have left us today with an environment relatively free of noise and air pollution and a foreign policy less vulnerable to pressures of oil-producing countries."

### Rules on Form

1. When the quotation is part of the grammar of your sentence, do not capitalize the first word of the quote, unless of course the first word would be capitalized anyway. The beginning

words *a* and *that* in the quotations above are not capitalized because they do not begin whole sentences.
2. Use quotations marks only if you quote the *exact* words of the author.

**Method #2.**　You can make the quotation stand by itself as at least one full sentence, as follows:

In his article, "Yesterday," George Gipe wrote, "It is entirely possible that a little gully on a Florida beach 68 years ago had a weighty influence on America's current foreign policy and environment."

### Rules on Form

1. If the quotation can stand by itself as a full sentence or more, capitalize the first word of the quotation.
2. Use quotation marks.
3. When introducing a direct quotation with a verb, such as *said, wrote,* or *stated,* use a comma after the verb:

▶ George Gipe wrote, "It is entirely possible . . ."

4. When introducing a direct quotation with an expression, like one of the following, that is not a verb, use a colon:

▶ Gipe wrote the following: "It is entirely possible . . ."

▶ Gipe made this argument: "It is entirely possible . . ."

Note that in both of these examples the quotations are introduced by statements that are, grammatically speaking, complete sentences.

**Method #3.**　For quotations of five or more lines, you should indent as follows:

Gipe described how the driver of the steamer, Fred Marriott, crashed. He then went on to describe the results of the accident and the possible loss to our nation:

> Although Fred Marriott survived the accident by more than half a century, the American public and the Stanley brothers were greatly discouraged. . . . Although the Stanleys continued producing cars until 1927, those ripples in the sand at Ormond Beach

> effectively ended their dream of a steam-powered society that might have left us today with an environment relatively free of noise and air pollution and a foreign policy less vulnerable to the pressures of oil-producing countries.

Gipe makes a good point. One cannot help but wonder what would have happened if the steamer had not crashed.

### Rules on Form

1. When you use a long quotation of five or more lines, set it off by indention (as shown above) and not quotation marks. Indent the entire quotation five spaces from the left-hand margin if you are typing, or an inch if you are writing by hand.
2. Skip an extra line both above and below the indented quotation. If you are typing, single-space the quotation.
3. Do not further indent to show the beginning of *any* paragraph. But if you quote two or more paragraphs, skip an extra line between them.
4. Introduce quotations such as the one above with a colon.
5. Use *ellipsis points* ( . . . ) to show omitted material. If you use ellipsis points, make sure the quoted material reads smoothly. The reader should be able to move from the last words before the ellipses to the first words after them without pausing. See the ellipsis points in the quotation above. (The first dot there is the period at the end of the sentence.)

**Method #4.** You can make the quotation indirect and not exact, as follows:

In his article "Yesterday," George Gipe explains that an accident sixty-eight years ago caused our automobile industry to reject the steam engine as a means for powering automobiles.

Gipe said that because we rejected the steam engine for automobiles we were left with only the gasoline engine, which has contributed to noise and air pollution and to oil shortages.

Here you are *paraphrasing,* that is, rewriting the author's statement in your own words. The advantage of using indirect quotations is that you have much more flexibility. Often your quote can be a lot shorter as you sum up the author's point of view. Compare the second quotation above with the long quotation in Method #3.

### Rules on Form

1. Do not use quotation marks for a paraphrase or indirect quotation, but if you use any of the *exact* language of the author, you should use quotation marks for those words. See *Method #1* above.
2. Indirect quotations are often introduced by the word *that,* as in the samples above.

See Chapter 11.7 for more on the use of direct and indirect quotations.

### Other Rules on Form

1. Give the full name of the author of the piece you are quoting the first time you quote, but only give the last name after that:

   George Gipe wrote in an article . . . Gipe went on to say . . .

2. Give the source of the quotation the first time only. Put quotation marks around the titles of short pieces, such as articles, essays, poems, songs, and television programs. Underline the titles of longer works, such as magazines, books, plays, and movies.
3. A convenient way to show the date of the magazine you are quoting from is to place it in parentheses immediately following the magazine title:

   ▶ . . . in *Sports Illustrated* (September 15, 1975) . . .

4. Try to avoid quotations within quotations (they can be very awkward), but if you must use a quotation that contains a quotation, use a single quotation mark (') at the beginning and end of the inside quotation, as follows:

   Gipe described the accident as follows: "Although running against the wind, the steamer's speed was approaching 150 mph when the accident occurred. 'He was nearly out of sight, being almost at the end of the mile, when the machine upset,' wrote a reporter in *The New York Times*."

**Writing Assignment #2**  The following reading selection comes from the "My Turn" column in the January 18, 1982, issue of *Newsweek*. It was written by Vicki

Williams, a factory worker in Huntington, Indiana. In this article Williams demonstrates the practical value of learning to express oneself in writing. Although she is not a professional writer, she is able, through writing, to express her point of view on a subject most important to her—taxes.

Read the selection carefully, using the reading method described on page 64, and then write a two-paragraph paper of about 200 words in response. Begin your paper with one or two sentences stating the author's point of view. In the first paragraph summarize her arguments. In the second paragraph give your personal response to the article and say why you hold this point of view. If you have not yet struggled over paying taxes yourself, consult friends, parents, or other relatives who have. You may want to show them the article and see how they react. It may be helpful to think of your essay as a letter to the editor of *Newsweek,* written in response to the Williams essay.

In your first paragraph use at least one direct quotation from the selection, making use of the learning notes on pages 69–72.

### The View from $204 a Week

I consider myself the classic "poor overburdened taxpayer" that you hear so much about these days. I work for an electronics company and make $6.58 an hour which translates into $204 per week after deductions, $30.21 of which are Federal withholding taxes. I have a husband, laid off, whose unemployment compensation has run out, and a 13-year-old son who thinks he should have a leather coat, a P.K. Ripper motocross bike, a Pioneer stereo and an Asteroids game. It bothers me a lot that I can't afford to buy him any of these things. It also bothers me that I'm not sure how we're going to fill up the fuel tank often enough to stay warm this winter.

There is something else that bothers me, though not to the same extent as my son's unfulfilled desires or the ever-hungry fuel tank, and that is that every single politician and editorialist is positive he knows exactly what I think. Everyone seems to be wildly anxious to be my spokesman. Yet these people don't know a damn thing about how the "poor overburdened taxpayer" thinks or lives. I imagine it's been quite some time since most politicians or well-known journalists lived on $204 per week, though I've read plenty of complaints from congressmen about their meager salaries. One even said he had to sleep in his office because he couldn't afford to buy a house. Do you know how much pity I can spare for a senator who can't live on $60,000 a year?

**Tired.**  I know I'm not as articulate as the people who write the editorials for newspapers and the speeches for politicians, but just once I'd like to have on the record the thoughts of an average taxpayer. I'm tired of these people putting their words in my mouth and their thoughts in my head.

One of the statements I read and hear most often is how fed up I'm supposed to be with the amount of my taxes that goes toward welfare, food stamps, programs for the elderly, subsidized school lunches and other supportive social services. Wrong! What the people "up there" don't understand is that I identify with the beneficiaries of these programs much more than I do with the politicians and the media people. "There, but for the grace of God, go I." So far, I have never had to rely on welfare, free lunches or Medicaid, but I very well might someday. When I was divorced, I could have qualified for welfare. Fortunately, I had parents who were in a position to help, but if I hadn't, you can believe I would have swallowed my pride rather than watch my son go hungry. People like me, who live only a hairbreadth from economic disaster, are glad those programs are out there, though we pray we'll never have to use them. We feel sympathy for the ones who do.

In 1977 my sister-in-law was abandoned by her husband. Her health did not permit her to work full time, so she drew $194 per month from the welfare department to support herself and her child. I doubt that anyone can think she lived extravagantly on $194 per month.

I think it's possible that at least one of the very same politicians who are now complaining about welfare recipients might have taken a political junket during one of the months that my sister-in-law and her son lived on $194. Believe me, I resent that junket at my expense much, much more than I resent helping an ADC mother, or buying eyeglasses for an elderly person or free lunches for a ghetto child. . . .

If there is even one child in this country who is hungry or one old person who needs medical care, then I want my $1,570.92 in taxes to go toward helping that child or that old person. I think this country is based on the philosophy that when that $1,570.92 is gone, we will find more to take its place, as long as the need is there.

I know about the cheaters. There are always cheaters. They are a part of life as surely as death and taxes. Certainly, if they are caught, they should be punished and denied aid, but I know we'll always support some cheaters along with the "truly needy." If we have to give a free lunch to one child whose parents could afford to pay in order to give free lunches to nine children who genuinely deserve them, so be it.

**Benefits.**    The much-touted tax cut doesn't make sense to me. Perhaps there's a complicated economic formula that explains the logic of a tax cut at the same time we're slashing Federal programs because of lack of funds, but if so, I missed it. I pay $30.21 per week to the Federal government. As I understand it, when all the tax cuts are in effect, I will only pay $22.66, giving me $7.55 extra to save or spend. Well, I could do a few things with $7.55 a week but, had I been consulted, I would have just as soon paid it and kept the food-stamp program or veterans' benefits intact. I suspect that the government will give it to me with one hand and take it away with the other.

You see, I really believe that most politicians and media people think that those of us out here in America who work in the factories and offices are ignorant. I believe that they think we will never catch on to their sleights of hand. I believe that they think they can tell us the grass is black one day and white the next and we'll never trust ourselves enough to look down and say, "Why, that grass isn't black or white—it's green!" Well, we know the grass is green. We just don't know what to do about it.

We don't really believe that 56 oil companies recorded 98 percent of the increase in all corporate profits from 1978 through 1980 for *our* benefit. We don't believe the tobacco subsidy is for *our* benefit. We don't believe that congressmen who were violently anti-AWACS magically changed their minds for *our* benefit. We know it's always us who pay the bills that result from the politicians' machinations.

I wish a politician would come along who'd tell me that the grass is green.

Vicki Williams*

What is the main point of this article?

_____

_____

# 4. Classroom Lectures

**Introduction**    A fourth resource for your writing is the classroom lecture. During your years in college you will probably have many classes that are primarily lectures. Some of the tests on these lectures will be in the form of essay questions. In this assignment you will first learn a method of taking notes and then you will practice note taking as you listen to (or read) an actual classroom lecture. Then you will practice writing two short essays based on your lecture notes, the kinds of essays that might be asked for on tests. Finally, you will practice writing definitions and identifications that come from the lecture.

## TAKING LECTURE NOTES

There is no right or wrong way of taking lecture notes. What works for you is the right method. Some students like to make long, elaborate outlines; others like to take their notes in full sentences, using paragraphs. The important thing is to get a full, legible record of what was said in class, so that when you are studying for a test or an exam you will have everything you need right before you. Most students forget over 80 percent of what they hear in class in just a few weeks. Thus, good note taking is essential. It is possible to take so many notes that you do not understand what the lecturer is saying, but most students have the opposite problem: they don't take enough notes! As a very rough guide, for a fifty-minute lecture class you should probably take at least three full pages of notes, assuming your handwriting is of average size.

### SUGGESTIONS FOR NOTE TAKING

1. Before class, always read the material that has been assigned. If you have a general idea of where the lecturer is going and already understand some of the most important terms, your note taking will be much easier.
2. During the class
   a. Pay particular attention to the lecturer's introduction and to any summary remarks. This way you can figure out where the lecturer is going and, at the end, what you should have learned.
   b. Write down all major points. Be on the lookout for words tagging these points, such as "The first cause . . . The second cause . . . ," or "Today we will first talk about . . . And then we will talk about . . . And finally, we will talk about . . ."
   c. Make sure you understand each major point and write down enough information on it so that, at exam time, you will be able to explain that point in your own words. Write down examples and details, such as names and dates, that the lec-

turer uses to explain the major points. Ask your instructor to explain any point you don't understand. If you are reluctant to ask your instructor in class, put a question mark in the margin so that you will remember to find out the answer later.

d. Write down anything that the instructor writes on the board or repeats. Often, instructors will write important names, dates, events, and definitions on the board. You should have good notes on all of these.

3. After class, as soon as possible, review your notes and compare them to the relevant reading material. Make sure you understand all the major points that were presented. From the reading material, fill in gaps in your notes *and* supplement your notes with pertinent information not mentioned in class. (Some students leave very wide margins for this purpose or leave the back side of each notebook page blank.)

**Writing Assignment #1**

**Step One**    Take notes on the following lecture that was actually given in a freshman political science class. (It took about thirty minutes to deliver.) Make use of the note-taking suggestions described above. Your instructor may choose to present this lecture him- or herself or may simply ask you to read it. The underlined words and phrases were written on the board as the lecturer came to them.

### POLITICAL PARTIES IN DEMOCRACIES

I. Introduction

II. Functions of political parties in general

III. Unique features of American political parties

It is not easy for us Americans to understand political parties in other countries, because our political parties are weak compared to those in other democracies, such as England, France, and other countries of Western Europe. Even our two large political parties, the Republican and Democratic parties, are weak compared to those of Western Europe. In Europe, being a member of a political party is more like joining a club. There are frequently dues to be paid, meetings to be attended, and duties to be carried out, such as campaigning for the parties' candidates in elections.

In the U.S., we ordinarily consider a person to be a member of a political party if he or she simply identifies with a party when registering to vote. But there are no dues to be paid, no meetings one must attend, and no duties one must perform. It is hard to point to the real party leaders because those with the highest titles often have little influence. For example, the national chairperson of the Republican or Democratic party has relatively little influence within the party.

Today, we will first talk about the functions of political parties in general; that is, we will talk about how political parties operate in democratic countries around the world. Then, we will talk about the unique features of American political parties.

There are seven basic functions of all political parties in democratic countries. First, political parties try to win votes for candidates in elections. In a representative government, the people choose government officials in elections. Political parties developed historically when the masses of people won the right to vote. This was not so long ago. The United States was the first country in the modern world to permit large numbers of its citizens to vote. But even here, during the early years of our history, the only persons who could vote were white, male property owners. Those who were not property owners gained the right to vote by the 1830s. Women won the right to vote through the 19th Amendment to the Constitution in 1920. Blacks achieved the constitutional right to vote in 1870, with the passage of the 15th Amendment, but it was not until the Voting Rights Act of 1965 that large numbers of blacks were actually permitted to vote in southern states. Once large numbers of people won the right to vote, political parties developed as organizations that attempted to win enough votes for candidates to get them elected.

A second function of political parties is to serve as a source of government personnel. The parties run candidates for elective office, candidates that are recruited from the party organization. Once elected, the candidates appoint other executive officials and sometimes judges as well. The American president, for example, appoints the top U.S. executive officials and federal judges. (Those officials and judges are almost all chosen from within the party of the president.)

A third function of political parties is to serve as a source of government policy. The parties propose general goals and specific programs as solutions to problems that face the nation. Those candidates who are elected try to make the goals and programs of their party the official policy of government. [The instructor asked if there were any questions on this point.]

A fourth function of political parties is to educate the public on political matters. As a party campaigns in elections, it tries to convince voters to choose its goals and programs over those of the other parties. To persuade the voters, a party must show why its goals and programs provide better solutions to the country's problems. Competition between parties develops interest in political issues and helps the voters to decide which policy alternatives they prefer.

A fifth function of political parties is to simplify voter choice. Because a party exists over a long period of time, from one election to another, voters come to associate certain goals and programs with each party. And they can identify themselves with the party whose goals and programs they most prefer. The choices of voters in elections are thus simplified. Voters do not have to make a choice between candidates running for every office. They can simply vote the party ticket; that is, they can vote for every candidate of their party. The party ticket is also called the party slate.

Sixth, parties help the public to hold public officials accountable for their actions. Since a candidate is chosen because the people prefer the goals and programs of the candidate's party, public officials are expected to enact those goals and programs into law. If they do not do so, the public can refuse to support these officials when they run for reelection.

Seventh, parties function to bring social unity. A major party is a coalition of many diverse groups, for a coalition is necessary if a party is to have a reasonable chance to elect its candidates to office. The diverse groups that are brought together within a party learn to cooperate and compromise, thus unifying the country to some degree. For example, in the U.S., the Democratic Party is a coalition of blacks, of labor and professional groups, of northerners and southerners, of the poor and the well-off.

So far we have been talking about the general functions political parties can perform. Now we turn to the unique features of American political parties. In the U.S., parties are relatively uncentralized and undisciplined and therefore are nonprogrammatic, in comparison to parties in other democracies.

U.S. parties are uncentralized because the real power in the parties lies at the local and state levels, not at the central or national level. [The instructor asked if there were any questions at this point.]

They are undisciplined because elected officials do not always support the party programs, even if the leader of the party is president. This contrasts sharply with England, which has centralized, disciplined parties. Power in English parties is centralized because the national party leaders have more power than local leaders. English parties are disciplined, as well, for the members of the parties in the legislature (called Parliament or the House of Commons) vote together in support of the parties' goals and programs. This insures that the programs of the majority party will pass the legislature intact. But

American parties are undisciplined. Party members in Congress will even vote against the president on particular issues. [Any questions at this point?]

American parties are also nonprogrammatic. This means that they do not formulate a set of clearly distinguishable programs that the party is committed to enact into law if its candidates are elected. The parties do write a party platform before national presidential elections, and this platform is supposedly a statement of the goals and programs the party favors. But, because the parties are not centralized and disciplined, much of the platform cannot be enacted into law. Since party leaders realize the platform will not necessarily become public policy, they have little incentive to draw up a platform that is clearly distinguishable from the platform of the other principal party. [Any questions?]

Finally, we need to show *why* American parties are uncentralized, undisciplined and nonprogrammatic. Although the reasons are quite complicated, we can single out two. One reason is the federal system in the U.S. that gives substantial power to the individual states. Because state and local officials have important powers, these officials can be more independent of national party leaders than if there were no federal system. [Any questions?]

A more important reason for the uniqueness of American political parties is the voting habits and expectations of the people. In the U.S., voters decide which *person* they most prefer for a given office. The candidate's personal leadership abilities and positions on the issues are carefully considered. In some countries, such as England, voters decide which party they prefer, based on their assessment of the parties' goals and programs and the qualifications of the parties' *general* leadership. In England the persons who are running for each government position may not receive much attention as individuals, since these persons are simply expected to carry out the party goals and programs. In contrast, in the U.S. people often say, "I vote for the person, not the party." The result is that American politics tends to be personal politics rather than party politics. Political parties, therefore, tend to function quite differently in the U.S. than in other western democracies.

Robert Thigpen
The University of New Orleans

**Step Two.** Check your notes with your instructor. Did you write down everything you needed? Be sure to ask questions on any point that you don't understand. Fill in the gaps in your notes. Look up words you did not understand in a dictionary.

**Step Three.**   Using your lecture notes, write a one-paragraph essay of about 150 words on the following exam topic: "What in your view are the most important functions of political parties in democratic countries? Describe at least four functions." (*Hint:* The most important functions may not have been presented first in the lecture.)

1. Begin with a sentence that gets right to the point, such as "The most important functions of political parties are the following."
2. Tag each point clearly, something like this:

▸ First, they . . .

▸ Second, political parties . . .

▸ Third, they . . .

▸ Fourth, political parties . . .

   Notice the pronoun *they* is substituted for *political parties* to give the essay variety. What *they* refers to in the context of the essay must be perfectly clear, though.
3. For each point, state the function in your own words, as clearly and as briefly as possible, and then write a sentence explaining the function, something like this:

▸ First, they get out the vote for their candidates. Political parties, in fact, only came into being when large numbers of people got the right to vote. Second, political parties . . .

   See the learning notes on transition sentences within paragraphs, pages 12–13.

**Writing Assignment #2**

Write an essay of about 150 words on the following exam topic: "Show how American political parties are unique and explain why." Here are some suggestions:

1. Begin with a sentence that appropriately introduces the paragraph, such as the following:
   American political parties are (fill in the best word) compared to political parties of other democracies.
2. Explain the three key words the lecturer used in describing American political parties.
3. Use a second paragraph to explain *why* American political parties are unique.

**Definitions and Identifications**   Define each of the following *in a whole sentence.* See the learning notes on page 83.

Example ▶ Define <u>party slate</u>.

<u>A party slate is a list of candidates that a political party has recommended for election to various offices.</u>

1. <u>15th Amendment</u>

_____

_____

2. <u>Voting Rights Acts of 1965</u>

_____

_____

3. <u>19th Amendment</u>

_____

_____

4. <u>House of Commons</u>

_____

_____

_____

5. <u>Party platform</u>

_____

_____

_____

## DEFINITIONS AND IDENTIFICATIONS

Many of your tests and exams in college will contain questions that ask you to define certain words and identify particular dates, people, events, and places. You should answer the questions as clearly and as briefly as possible, including as much relevant information as you can. Your instructors may have somewhat different ideas on how much information you should include and how long your answers should be. If you are in any doubt, *ask*.

### SUGGESTIONS FOR WRITING DEFINITIONS AND IDENTIFICATIONS

1. Most of the time you will probably be able to say what you need to say in one or two sentences. Observe how the following information can be given in two sentences:

   Robert E. Lee was a famous military general for the South in the Civil War. He was born in 1807 and died in 1870. He was the commander of the Confederate forces. He surrendered at Appomattox in 1865. He later served as president of Washington College, which was named Washington and Lee after his death. (5 sentences)

   *Shorten to:*

   Robert E. Lee (1807–1870) was the famous commanding military general for the South in the Civil War. He surrendered at Appomattox in 1865 and went on to become president of Washington College, which was named Washington and Lee after his death. (2 sentences)

2. In your first sentence, define or identify your subject by first giving a noun that says what (or who) the word, event, date, place, or person is, and then give an adjective clause that further identifies your subject. Here are two examples:

   a. Ulysses S. Grant (1822–1885) was a president of the United States who made a name for himself as the victorious commander of the Union armies during the Civil War.

   The noun that identifies Grant is *president*. The writer is saying that Grant's being president is the most significant thing about him. The adjective clause beginning with *who made a name for himself* further identifies Grant. Note that a convenient way to give the dates of an individual's life is to put them in parentheses immediately following the name, as shown above.

    b. <u>Photosynthesis</u> is a food-making process that occurs in green plants when energy from light combines with water and carbon dioxide.

The noun that best identifies the word *photosynthesis* is *process*; but *process* is such a general word that it is appropriate to define it further with the adjective phrase *food-making,* and then to define it even further with the adjective clause that begins with the words *that occurs in green plants.* Note that when words are defined in a sentence, the words themselves are underlined. In print, though, italics replace underlining.

3. Give examples when appropriate.

    a. A *preposition* is a part of speech that connects a noun or pronoun (the object of the preposition) to another word in the sentence. Some examples of commonly used prepositions are *of, on, in, to, from,* and *with.*

    b. *Personification* is a figure of speech in which an inanimate object or abstract word is treated as a person, for example, "Mother Earth," "the whispering wind," "Love is patient and kind."

Note that in *a* above a separate sentence is used to give the examples; in *b* the examples are connected to the sentence with the words *for example.* Note also how commas are used.

## EXERCISE

Use the information below to write a definition or identification in one or two complete sentences. (You may want to complete the sentence-combining exercises on pages 280, 289, 293, 302, and 305 before proceding.)

1. Identify the Taft Hartley Act.

An act of Congress. Passed in 1947. Very controversial. Forbids unions to require all workers in a plant or place of business to be members of the union.

_____

_____

_____

2. Define *polynomial.*

A term used in algebra. Two or more symbols connected by addition or subtraction signs. Examples: $x - y + z$ or $2B + C - A$.

_____

_____

_____

3. Identify Martin Luther King, Jr.

Dates are 1929–1968. Eloquent pleas for racial justice won wide support. Baptist minister. Preached "nonviolent resistance." Won the Nobel peace prize in 1964. James Earl Ray was convicted of murdering King.

_____

_____

_____

## 5. The Library

A fifth source for your writing is your college or university library. One of the main objectives of this section is to help you feel at home in the library so that you will begin to use it not just as a resource for writing, but also as a place to study and a place to find enjoyable and informative reading material in newspapers, magazines, and books.

In this section you will first learn how to find your way around the library, then you will practice finding various kinds of information in the library, and finally you will write a response to an article in a magazine that was written the week you were born.

## USING THE LIBRARY

The library belongs to you. Get to know it—where everything is—as soon as possible. Library staff are there to answer your questions and help you find what you cannot find on your own. *Use them.* Check at the main desk to see if brochures on the library are available and if the staff gives tours of the library. Take advantage of such resources.

### WHAT YOU NEED TO LEARN ABOUT FIRST

**1. The Card Catalog.**   This is the main index of all the books in the library. It is a large cabinet full of many tray-like drawers and is usually located near the main desk. In many card catalogs, there is a separate index for titles, authors, and subjects of books. If you know the exact title of a book or the name of an author, simply look up the book in the title or author index. (Books are not alphabetized by *A, An,* or *The.* Look up the next word in the title. For example, *The Moon and the Sixpence* would be filed under *M.*) If you are trying to find a book on a particular subject, like magic, sleep, civil rights, prehistoric man, or abortion, use the subject index.

When you are looking for information in the subject index, you will often find cards that read "See" or "See also." For example, if you look up *Negro* in the subject index, the card may say, "See Afro-Americans," or "See Blacks." If you look up *prehistoric man,* the card may say, "See also Man, Prehistoric." ("See also" means that you will find cards under both subject headings.) Often students look up a common-language word like *car,* which will be listed in the card catalog as "Automobile." If you cannot find any card on your subject, ask your librarian for help. Sometimes the author and title indexes in the card catalog will be combined; sometimes all three indexes will be combined.

When you find the card for the book you want, write down the entire *call number* (the number printed in the top left-hand corner). The number will look something like this:

F                                        191.9
279                 *or this*            S233
.C49N4

The *F* designation is from the Library of Congress Classification system. (The call number in this system always begins with a letter.)

The 191 designation is from the Dewey decimal system. (The call number in this system always begins with a number, 000 to 999.) The library directory or a diagram of the floor plan will show you where to find both the *F* bookshelves (or stacks, as they are called) and the 191 bookshelves. The.books will be shelved alphabetically and numerically. Once you find the *F* stacks, for example, you then look for the shelves labeled 279. Next you look for the books designated .*C*. And finally, you look for the particular book with the designation .C49N4. If you have trouble finding your book, ask the library staff for help.

**2. Periodicals (Magazines, Newspapers, and Journals).** Often you will want the very latest information about a particular subject, such as astronauts, ecology, or birth control. Recent magazines are a good source for this information. You can find the latest edition of many magazines in the magazine section of your library. Browse around until you become familiar with the various magazines your library subscribes to.

Periodicals from previous years are bound together in book covers and shelved in order by year. The best way to find particular articles is to consult *The Readers' Guide to Periodical Literature.* (You will see it near the main desk.) It is bound in separate volumes by year and contains listings of articles from about two hundred magazines. The articles are listed by both subject and author. Here is a sample entry:

ASTROLOGY
All the stars came out for the astrologer
Carroll Righter. il pors People
3:112 F 18 '80

This tells you the following:

a. The article title: "All the Stars Came Out for the Astrologer"
b. The author: Carroll Righter
c. The magazine in which the article appears: *People*
d. Art work: illustrated (il) with portraits (pors)
e. Location: volume 3, page 112 of *People,* which was dated February 18, 1980

If any abbreviations confuse you, check the list of abbreviations and what they stand for at the beginning of *The Readers' Guide.* The magazine abbreviations are listed together. If you cannot find your subject listed, perhaps you are using a different term from the one used by *The Readers' Guide.* Ask for assistance if necessary.

Now, consult the *Serials Index* (also near the main desk) for the call number of the magazine you need to find. (Sometimes the *Serials Index* is a loose-leaf book with listings of periodicals; sometimes it is in trays like the card catalog.) Once you have the call number of the magazine, consult the general plan of the library to see where the back issues of the magazine are located.

Newspapers are also a good source of current information, especially newspapers like *The New York Times* and *The Wall Street Journal* that contain lengthy coverage on a wide variety of news items. Browse through the newspapers and find one, other than your local newspaper, that you enjoy reading.

**3. The Reference Shelves.** Here you will find full-length dictionaries that will help you to learn the meaning of any word you don't understand. You will also find encyclopedias, such as *Encyclopaedia Britannica* and *Encyclopedia Americana,* that will give you excellent background and statistical information for many of the essays you will be assigned. Your instructors will probably ask you to go beyond what you can find in an encyclopedia to develop your papers, but an encyclopedia is a good place to begin, especially if you are unfamiliar with your topic.

**4. Publications on Reserve.** Some instructors put certain books and periodicals "on reserve"; that is, they ask the library staff to make these publications available to students only for short periods of time. This way the whole class has access to the books and articles. Consult the library floor plan to find the location of the reserve section.

**Orientation Exercise**    Answer the following questions:

1. Give the hours when the library is open. _____

_____

2. Check out a novel that you think you will enjoy reading. Give the following information about your book:

   a. The call number _____

   b. The title _____

c. The author _____

d. When the book is due _____

e. The amount of the fine each day the book is late _____

3. Who is the author of *The Brothers Karamazov?*

   _____

4. If your name were in the card catalog, what name would come just before it?

   _____

5. How many books are in your library on the subject of jazz musicians (or jazz, if there is no subject card for jazz musicians)? List the title and author of one of these books.

   _____

6. How many books are in your library on the subject of alcoholism? List the title and author of one of these books.

   _____

7. Exactly where is *The Readers' Guide to Periodical Literature* located in your library?

   _____

8. Exactly where is the *Serials Index* (the index of magazines with their call numbers) located?

   _____

9. Locate an article on nursing that is listed in one of the latest five volumes of *The Readers' Guide.* Give the name of the article, the author, the magazine it appeared in, and the call number of the magazine (if your library subscribes to it).

   _____

   _____

10. In which volume of the most recent edition of the *Encyclopedia Americana* will you find an entry on Harriet Tubman? What is the page number?

    _____

    _____

11. In which volume of the most recent edition of the *Encyclopaedia Britannica* will you find an entry on capital punishment? What is the page number?

_____

12. How would you address a letter to the editor of *The New York Times*?

_____

_____

13. Of all the magazines your library carries, which is your favorite?

_____

**Writing Assignment**   Locate the issue of *Newsweek, Time, Ebony,* or *U.S. News & World Report* that came out the week you were born. Find a news article that particularly interests you (anything from international news to sports) and write a two-paragraph essay (about 200 words) on it. Here are some suggestions:

1. In the first paragraph, summarize the news article, giving the most important information. Begin the paragraph with a one-sentence statement of what the article is about. Be sure to include the name and date of the publication, and since it is a magazine, underline the title. If you use the title of the article itself, enclose it in quotation marks but do not underline.
2. In the second paragraph, say why you chose that particular news article to write on. Why did it interest you? What from your own experience made you interested? If, for example, you chose an article on the Beatles, you may want to explain your particular interest in popular music. If possible, relate the news article to today's news.

# Chapter 3
# The Writing Method

In the process of developing a sense of audience in Chapter 1 and resources for your writing in Chapter 2, you have been learning a writing method. In most of the assignments, you gathered information on what to write about, you read student samples, you made a plan for your writing, and you may have read your writing in a small group. But in this chapter you will concentrate on the writing method itself, a method that should help you in all your college writing.

First you will learn how the method works; then you will practice using it in two writing assignments; and finally you will learn a procedure for revising your essays. The learning notes are devoted to teaching skills in organizing and developing a paper—how to plan a paper, how to join paragraphs with transition sentences, how to state your purpose or thesis, and finally how to write an introduction and conclusion.

Instead of cramping your writing style, the suggestions on how to organize and develop your paper should give you an opportunity to express yourself more freely and clearly. Once you fully understand the structure of an essay, you can then concentrate on other things—using the most precise word, writing a strong sentence, making a careful observation, developing a logical argument, letting your imagination flow into your writing, and so on.

# 1. The Method Described

Suppose a campus organization you belong to is planning a picnic to begin the new school year. The president might ask the members to make as many suggestions as they possibly can about what they would like to do, while a recorder writes them down. When the list is complete, the president asks the recorder to read the list aloud and then asks the group members, "What do you think?" As you analyze the various suggestions, you realize that some seem better than others. Some are probably repeated. Perhaps several people have suggested that the picnic include some kind of sports activity, like volleyball or softball. The group members probably have different views on where to have the picnic and what food and drink to take.

Your president then says, "Tell me now, just what is the purpose of this picnic? What exactly do you want to happen?" There might be several suggestions until someone says the thing that is just right, a perfect way to describe what the group wants to happen, something like this: "The picnic should be fun and should help the new members to feel included." The next step is for the organization to plan the details of the picnic—where you will go, what you want to happen hour by hour, what you will take, and who will do what to prepare for it. You then go on the picnic, and at your next meeting your president asks, "Well, how'd it go? Was the picnic what you hoped it would be?"

The writing method used throughout this text is very similar to this procedure. There are six steps to it.

Step One: Gather Information
Step Two: Analyze the Information
Step Three: State Your Purpose
Step Four: Make Your Plan
Step Five: Write
Step Six: Evaluate and Edit Your Paper

**Step One: Gather Information**

When an instructor gives you a general topic to write on, the first thing you should do is collect as much information about it as you can. In Chapter 2 you practiced several ways of gathering information—brainstorming, freewriting, taking notes during classroom discussions and lectures, taking notes on reading material, and finding source material in the library. Make a *long* list of information and ideas relating to the topic. This step is like the first step the organization took when it planned its picnic. You will be like the recorder, writing as many ideas as you can think of on a sheet of paper.

**Step Two: Analyze the Information**

After you have gathered your ideas and information on the subject, the next step is for you to sit back and ask yourself what things on the list stand out. This step is like the president asking the organization, after the recorder read back the suggestions, "What do you think?" Here you begin to narrow down the information and to make your general topic more specific. What are the most important things on the list? What items could be omitted? Which are closely related? How might you order the material?

**Step Three: State Your Purpose**

After analyzing the information, you now need to say *in one sentence* what you hope to prove in your paper. The purpose statement (often called a thesis) is a statement of what you hope will "happen" in your paper. The purpose statement for the picnic was "The picnic should be fun and should help new members to feel included." Ordinarily you should include the purpose or thesis statement in your first paragraph. Think of your preparation and writing as sand running through an hourglass.

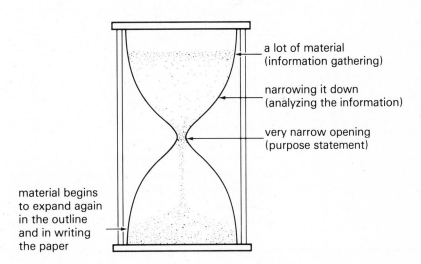

a lot of material
(information gathering)

narrowing it down
(analyzing the information)

very narrow opening
(purpose statement)

material begins
to expand again
in the outline
and in writing
the paper

**Step Four: Make Your Plan**

Just as the picnic needed considerable planning, so will your paper. You have gathered and analyzed information and stated your purpose; now you must figure out the best way to accomplish your purpose, to prove your point. In this step you will need to make a plan that helps you accomplish your purpose. Your plan should contain not just your general points but a list of the details and examples that you will use in supporting your points. The list you made in *step one* should be a rich source for your details and examples. While it is important to have a carefully made plan, you should be willing to change it as you write, if you see that you can best accomplish your purpose in some other way. Plans for papers, like plans for activities, sometimes do *and should* change.

**Step Five: Write**

Look at your purpose statement—perhaps you will want to write it at the beginning of your first paragraph—look at your plan, and begin to write. New thoughts will come to you as you write, some of which you will certainly want to use.

**Step Six: Evaluate and Edit Your Paper**

After the organization returned from the picnic, the president asked for an evaluation: "Was the picnic what you hoped it would be?" When you finish your paper, evaluate it. Were you able to carry out your purpose? Did you accomplish in your paper what you set out to do? Did each paragraph have an organizing principle? Did you have smooth transitions from paragraph to paragraph? Did you give enough examples and details to support the points you made? Did you bring the paper to a clear ending?

At the end of this chapter you will learn a procedure for revising essays (rewriting them afresh) and will find that the evaluation of your paper leads right into the revision process. Even when you don't have time to revise a paper, such as when you write one in class, you can still evaluate it to learn from its strengths and weaknesses. As you evaluate an essay, make use of the revision checklist on the front inside cover of this book and make whatever minor changes you can.

Part of the sixth step is to edit or proofread your paper to correct as many mechanical errors as possible. Since it is difficult to look out for all possible errors in just one or two readings, you probably should read your paper at least three times: once to evaluate it; a second time to look out for any particular problems you are having, such as sentence, verb, or pronoun errors; and a third time to catch any other errors. Many students complain that they can't catch errors in their essays because the writing is so familiar, especially if they have read a paper over several times. If you have this problem, try the following: for your second or third reading, proofread your paper a sentence at a time starting with the last sentence, and moving backward to the first sentence. Proofreading in this way will force you to look at each sentence by itself. Make use of the editing checklist on the back inside cover of this book.

A student wrote this paper while carefully following the six steps of the writing method. The questions at the end are designed to help you understand how to use the writing method.

### MY HOME IN THE COUNTRY

When I think of the sights, sounds, and smells of our place in the country, it makes me wish I were there right now. You see, I have been living in the high-rise student dormitory for the last few months and have heard nothing but the screaming sirens, screeching tires, roaring motors, and other boisterous sounds of the city.

There are many beautiful things to see around my home, for instance, blue and white cranes wading in ponds and dipping their heads in the water to catch fish, frogs, and other things to eat. In the spring, when the farmers are beginning to prepare the ground, white egrets swoop down behind the tractors preying on bugs and insects harmful to crops. These egrets along with white cranes, water turkeys, and various other birds come each spring and nest in large cypress trees.

If one is lucky, he can probably see deer running across the fields with their tails sticking up and the whiteness of the hide underneath shining brightly. Also, squirrels can readily be seen jumping and playing games in the tip-tops of the trees. There is a large red squirrel with his half-rust, half-fire color and big fuzzy tail. On the other hand, there is the elite gray squirrel, who must think he is a smart little rascal because each time you try to get a look at him, he moves around to the other side of the tree.

One can experience the seasons of the year by watching what happens to the lush green crops and the green woods around them. When the crops ripen and the fall steals the life from the trees, there is a beautiful blending of brown, gold, and rust colors. An old shack nearby hardly seems to notice the death and rebirth of the crops.

Many different sounds can be heard around my home. To begin with, one can hear all those birds I have been describing, cawing and chirping, making you wonder if they have a distinct language of their own. Oil wells can be heard in the distance, with their "pop-pop-pop-pow" repeated over and over. It seems as though that sound will go on indefinitely for eternity. At nightfall, when the crickets produce their chirping sound, which combines with the deep bellowing and croaks of the bullfrogs, it is like beautiful sweet music to someone who has heard these sounds all his life.

Finally, there are distinctive smells around my home. My favorite smell is the indescribable smell of rain as it beats down on the raw earth after the soil has been plowed. There are also the bad smells, such as trash

burning or a skunk that has emitted his device of self-defense. But when I    37
get homesick, I miss those smells too.    38

    My father tells me I should learn to like the city as much as I like    39
the country, but I have a long way to go.    40

**Questions for Discussion**

1. The student gathered a lot of detail for his paper. Did he use too much of it? What particular detail stood out for you?
2. What is the purpose statement (the one sentence that says what the essay will be about)? Did the student accomplish his purpose in the essay? Explain.
3. In developing his paper, the student tried to build each paragraph on a controlling idea, an organizing principle. The organizing principle for the second paragraph, for example, was the birds he can see around his home. What is the organizing principle of the other paragraphs in the body of the essay? (The *body* is simply the main part of the essay; it is the essay less the introduction and conclusion.)

*Par. 1:* Introduction (includes purpose statement)

*Par. 2:* *Things to see, especially birds*

*Par. 3:* _____

Body *Par. 4:* _____

*Par. 5:* _____

*Par. 6:* _____

*Par. 7:* Conclusion

4. Would you prefer to live in the city or the country? Why?

**Word and Sentence Use**

1. In paragraph 5, the student used the phrase "indefinitely for eternity." But *indefinitely* and *for eternity* mean almost the same thing. His paper would have been stronger if he had used only one of the two expressions. Try not to use words that are redundant, that is, words that repeat what you have already said. Redundancies

are designated S-1 in the revision checklist on the inside front cover.

2. The student has a way of overusing the passive voice. For example, in paragraph 3 he says, "Also, squirrels can readily be seen jumping and playing games in the tip-tops of trees." The verb *can be seen* is passive because the subject, squirrels, does not act but is acted upon. The sentence would be stronger if the student wrote it in the active voice, in the same manner that he wrote the previous sentence:

> If one is lucky, he *can* probably *see.* . . . Also, one *can see* squirrels jumping and playing games in the tip-tops of trees.

*Try not to overuse the passive voice.* As a general rule, if you can say what you want to say in the active voice (in order to make the subject act), choose it instead. (See Chapter 8.5.)

| *Choose* | *Instead of* |
| --- | --- |
| Johnson read *Moby Dick.* | *Moby Dick* was read by Johnson. |
| She deposited the check. | The check was deposited by her. |
| One can smell bean soup. | Bean soup can be smelled. |

Overuse of the passive voice is designated S-6 in the revision checklist.

## 2. The Neighborhood Paper

Write a paper of 300 or more words on your own neighborhood or another one with which you are very familiar. Use each of the six steps in the writing method as carefully as possible. The more you use the method, the easier it will come to you. Near the end of this section are two samples of student writing. Before writing your paper, read those essays and the learning notes on planning your paper (page 102) and on writing transition sentences to join paragraphs (page 109).

**Step One: Gather Information**

In this step you will first brainstorm to gather information about your neighborhood. (Later you can fill in any gaps by closely observing your neighborhood with a pad and pencil in hand.) So that you will not be distracted, clear your desk of everything except this text, a couple of sheets of paper to take notes on, and a pen or pencil. Take several deep breaths, inhaling and exhaling slowly. Get comfortable, relax.

1. Imagine yourself across the street from your house or some place where you can get a good view of everything going on. Conjure up a vivid picture of your neighborhood. Become aware of every detail before you. In the left-hand column below write down *every* detail that you see. Do not censor your thoughts. Take about five minutes.

_____    _____

_____    _____

_____    _____

_____    _____

_____    _____

_____    _____

_____    _____

2. To test just how precise your details are, try out some of them on the class or with the instructor. Now go back and make your more general observations as exact as possible, this time writing in the right-hand column, for example:

| | |
|---|---|
| *blue car parked in front* | *baby-blue '52 Cadillac with 2 flat front tires, rusty fenders, for sale* |
| *green hedge* | *10' high green hedge hiding fr. porc* |
| *yellow cat* | *yellow and white striped cat prowling over turf as if he was somebody* |

3. You are still at the spot where you saw everything in your neighborhood. Only now, imagine that you cannot see but have a keen sense of hearing. Become aware of everything you might hear over the course of a day—horns honking, mothers calling their children (What are their exact words?), boys arguing over a baseball, and so on. Make use of your skill in recording a conversation. Again, use the left-hand column.

_____     _____

_____     _____

_____     _____

_____     _____

_____     _____

_____     _____

_____     _____

_____     _____

4. Share some of your list with the class or check it with your instructor. In the right-hand column, make your observations even more precise, for example:

*Mother calling son to dinner*          *Mrs. Sims bellowing, "Charles get in here right now before I come after you with the cattle prod."*

*church bells*          *church bells ringing every hour*

5. Imagine that you now have a superior sense of smell. You are still at the same place. Write down everything you might smell in your neighborhood in the course of a week—fumes from automobiles, your neighbor's cooking, trash burning, garbage, and so on. Make your observations as precise as possible.

_____     _____

_____     _____

_____     _____

_____     _____

_____     _____

_____     _____

6. If someone were to ask you how you felt about your neighborhood, how would you answer that person?

_____

_____

_____

_____

**Step Two: Analyze the Information**

Sit back, with pen in hand, and read over the information you have gathered so far and ask yourself what you think. What detail is most interesting to you? Which items are closely related? Which items will you probably not want to use? How might you order the material? Write notes to yourself. Now might be a good time to read the student samples at the end of this section for ideas on how you might use your information. Be ready to add to your list if you notice any gaps.

**Step Three: State Your Purpose**

Try to say in one sentence what you really want to tell your reader about your neighborhood. It usually takes several tries and misses before one can write an effective purpose statement. In the next section of this chapter, a learning notes box is devoted to the purpose statement. But for this essay, keep the following suggestions in mind as you try to come up with a good purpose statement:

1. Does it include *your opinion* about the neighborhood?
2. Is it narrow enough in scope so that you will not have to write about *everything*?
3. Is it at the same time broad enough so that you will have enough material to write 300 or more words?

Here are some examples of purpose statements from successful papers:

▸ My neighborhood is so noisy it disturbs the dogs. (In this paper, the student used each paragraph in the body to discuss a different type of noise.)

▸ Only in swampy St. Bernard could there be a neighborhood like mine. (The student showed what it was like living on the edge of a swamp and showed just how unique her neighborhood was.)

▸ My neighborhood is fun-loving. (This student focused on three different ways people had fun in his neighborhood.)

▸ The neighborhood I live in is plain, but the people in it aren't. (In the first paragraph, the student described just how plain everything looked, but in the paragraphs in the body of the essay he described four individuals who appeared on the sidewalk during the day and showed how unique each one was.)

▸ My neighborhood is a nightmare; it has everything to terrify you: junkies, police, child abuse, adult abuse, pistol shots at night. (The student described what she had actually seen and heard in her neighborhood at various times and showed how these things did indeed terrify her.)

Experiment with your purpose statement until you get it just right, and then write it here.

_____

_____

_____

**Step Four: Make Your Plan**   Study the learning notes on planning an essay and then make an informal outline for your neighborhood paper in the space provided.

# PLANNING AN ESSAY

You should write a plan for each of your essays. Your plan is a kind of outline, but it need not be rigid in form. The best plan is the one that helps you say what you want to say. You may need to change it once you begin to write your essay.

## SUGGESTIONS FOR PLANNING AN ESSAY

1. Your plan should help you accomplish your purpose. For that reason, it should not be written until after you have stated your purpose. Which of the following abbreviated outlines does not carry out the purpose statement?

    ▶ *Purpose statement:* My neighborhood is so noisy it disturbs the dogs.

    *Point 1:* It is noisy in the morning.

    *Point 2:* It is noisy in the afternoon.

    *Point 3:* It is noisy at night.

    ▶ *Purpose statement:* Many things keep my street from being a community.

    *Point 1:* There are no sidewalks, and the houses are far apart.

    *Point 2:* People don't seem to care about one another.

    *Point 3:* No one spends any time out of doors. There are no children, no one working on cars, no one working on lawns.

    ▶ *Purpose statement:* My neighborhood is overrun by children, but I enjoy them all.

    *Point 1:* The five Read children are always in and out of everyone's house.

    *Point 2:* The eleven- and twelve-year-old set play ball in the street every afternoon.

    *Point 3:* Each yard on our block is very well kept.

    *Point 4:* Last year a terrible fire burned down the house next door.

2. Your outline should be consistent; that is, each major point should *fit in with* the other major points. Here are two examples of abbreviated outlines whose points do fit together:

| | |
|---|---|
| 1. Introduction | 1. Introduction |
| 2. Sights in the neighborhood | 2. Neighborhood in the morning |
| 3. Sounds in the neighborhood | 3. Neighborhood in the afternoon |
| 4. Smells in the neighborhood | 4. Neighborhood at night |
| 5. Conclusion | 5. Conclusion |

Which, if any, of the following abbreviated outlines are not consistent? Apply the "Sesame Street" test: Which of the things (organizing principles) is not like the others?

| | | |
|---|---|---|
| 1. Introduction | 1. Introduction | 1. Introduction |
| 2. Most eye-catching features | 2. Neighborhood as viewed from the left | 2. One example that illustrates the purpose |
| 3. Next most eye-catching features | 3. As viewed straight ahead | 3. A second example that illustrates it |
| 4. Crime in the neighborhood | 4. The best things about the neighborhood | 4. A third example that illustrates it |
| 5. Conclusion | 5. Conclusion | 5. Conclusion |

3. Your outline should reflect the paragraph division in your paper. Name the organizing principle of each paragraph in the outline itself. The student who wrote the paper on his country home set up his outline as follows:

*Par. 1:*  Introduction _____

*Par. 2:*  Things to see, especially birds _____

*Par. 3:*  Things to see, especially animals _____

*Par. 4:*  Things to see, especially vegetation _____

*Par. 5:*  Things to hear _____

*Par. 6:*    Things to smell

*Par. 7:*    Conclusion

In deciding how to divide your paper into paragraphs, be sure you have enough information to make a paragraph. In an essay of 300 to 350 words, the paragraphs in the body of your essay should probably run between 50 and 100 words. In the outline above, the student divided "things to see" into three paragraphs, each of which turned out to be over 50 words, but he described "things to hear" in one paragraph, which turned out to be about 100 words.

4. The introduction and conclusion should be designated in the outline as separate paragraphs, even though they may be short (fewer than 50 words).

5. Under each major point in your outline, include enough notes so that you will have before you, as you sit down to write, the detail and information necessary to support your point. If you can't think of enough detail, perhaps you need to rework your outline, changing your major points. The student who wrote the paper on his home in the country wrote detail into his outline in the following way:

Organizing Principle ▸ *Par. 1:*    Introduction

Detail ▸ purpose statement, how long in the city,

contrast with the country

Organizing Principle ▸ *Par. 2:*    Things to see, especially birds

Detail ▸ cranes in pond, white egrets behind tractors,

nests, birds eating bugs harmful to crops

Paragraph development is explained more fully on page 226.

Write your outline in the space provided on the next page. If you limit your paper to 350 words, you will probably not need more than five paragraphs, but space is provided for an extra paragraph just in case. Include in your introduction where you live, how long you have

lived there, your purpose statement, and anything else that will capture the reader's attention. If you can't think of a conclusion in the
outline step, don't worry about it; the best conclusions will often come
to you after you have written the rest of the paper.

_____
                              (title)

**Organizing Principle ▸** _Par. 1:_    Introduction _____

         **Detail ▸** _____

_____

**Organizing Principle ▸** _Par. 2:_    _____

         **Detail ▸** _____

_____

**Organizing Principle ▸** _Par. 3:_    _____

         **Detail ▸** _____

_____

**Organizing Principle ▸** _Par. 4:_    _____

         **Detail ▸** _____

_____

**Organizing Principle ▸** _Par. 5:_    _____

         **Detail ▸** _____

_____

**Organizing Principle ▸** _Par. 6:_    Conclusion _____

         **Detail ▸** _____

_____

Check your outline with your instructor before going on to the next step.

**Step Five: Write**

As you write, keep in mind the following suggestions:

1. Use smooth transition sentences to connect your paragraphs. (See the learning notes on transitions to join paragraphs on page 109.)
2. Avoid words that are redundant, that is, words that repeat what you have already said.
3. Avoid the passive voice.
4. If you have stated a point clearly in one sentence, you need not repeat the same idea in another sentence.
5. Let your conclusion flow naturally from what you have said. Make sure your reader knows you are through. (See the learning notes on conclusions on page 128.)

**Step Six: Evaluate and Edit**

Evaluate your paper.

1. Did the purpose statement meet the criteria given on page 102?
2. Did each paragraph help to carry out the purpose statement?
3. Was there enough information to support each major point?
4. Did you repeat yourself unnecessarily at any time?
5. Did the conclusion effectively bring the essay to a close?

Now edit your paper, using the checklist on the back inside cover of this book. Two errors that often appear on this assignment are verb-agreement and fragment errors. (See Chapter 7 for verb agreement and Chapter 6.7 for avoiding fragments.)

**Share Your Writing**

Read your papers in a small group and discuss the questions listed in step six above after each person reads. How close do the group answers come to the answers you gave yourself when you were doing your own evaluating?

**Other Student ►
Samples**

**A**

**MY HOME IN THE PROJECT**

When I think of the sights, sounds, and smells of my neighborhood, 1
it makes me wish that I were living somewhere else instead of the Bradley 2
Housing Project. I have lived in my neighborhood all my life. When 3
my family first moved there, they said that the area was very pleasant 4
and the apartments were recently built. During that time the lawn was 5
nice, and the environment was clean. But things have changed in my 6
neighborhood. 7

There are no beautiful things to see. The project consists of brick 8
apartments, which have faded in color. Outside, there is only a limited 9
amount of grass. The grounds consist mostly of dirt. The streets have large 10
holes and a lot of glass. If you are trying to avoid getting a flat tire, please 11
do not visit. Many people pile up trash on the sidewalk, which is a sight to 12
see. You can see paper flying all around on very windy days. 13

There are no nice sounds to hear. You may hear gunshots when 14
people are fighting. Obscene language is used frequently, such as 15
"bitch," "ass," etc. Children are constantly playing and making noise with 16
their big wheels, skates, and also noise is heard when the baseball game 17
is going on. Most of the parents call their children without using their names. 18
They say, "Come here, you little bitch," words I don't enjoy hearing. At 19
night and during the day, it is very disturbing hearing police sirens and 20
trains passing across the tracks. I really wish my neighborhood would quiet 21
down. 22

There are no pleasant things to smell. What you smell is mostly 23
weed scent. Guys walk the street and stand in hallways smoking grass. At 24
times there are foul odors from trash burning and from urine, and some- 25
times there is no smell at all. 26

What I like most about my neighborhood is that the people in my 27
building and I get along well. Even though I'm not satisfied with the area 28
in which I live, I'm very comfortable inside my own home. I feel as though 29
I have most of the things I want inside my home, regardless of what is seen, 30
heard, and smelled outside. 31

### Questions for Discussion

1. What details stand out for you the most? What else would you like to know?
2. What information does the student include in the introduction besides the purpose statement? Is it effective? Why?
3. In her conclusion, the student makes a different point from what she has been saying. What is it?
4. The first sentences in paragraphs 2, 3, 4, and 5 are transition sentences. They are meant to join the paragraphs. Are they effective?
5. If you were describing this neighborhood to someone else, what would you say about it?

B    AT HOME IN THE CITY

Peaceful is the word that best describes my neighborhood. My 1
neighborhood is named Kennedy Heights, and it is located on the west 2
bank of the Mississippi River. 3

I see pleasant things in my neighborhood, such as beautifully kept  4
brick houses. These houses have white iron bars covering the doors and  5
windows. On the roofs of the houses, there are blue jays and red robins  6
picking food that has fallen from the large mimosa trees that line the block.  7
These trees have pink flowers and shade the entire fronts of the houses. The  8
driveways, which are curved, are neatly trimmed. In front of my house there  9
are three little girls with jump suits on playing jump rope, while four others  10
play hopscotch. I can also see a Trans Am with a white vinyl top and a  11
gold Mercedes parked right down from my house.  12

What I hear in my neighborhood may sound noisy to others, but to  13
me the sounds are peaceful. There is music coming from car radios and  14
stereos inside the houses, everything from Rick James to Beethoven. Moth-  15
ers call their children inside to do homework or to get ready for bed. A  16
mother will say, "Billy, it's time for you to come inside and get your bath for  17
tomorrow." He will answer. "Ah, Ma, can I please stay out for just five more  18
minutes?" Also there are freight and passenger trains that make noise  19
when they pass by in the distance. I guess those are peaceful sounds to  20
me because I've heard them all my life.  21

My neighborhood has few smells. On Sundays the usual smell is  22
that of barbequed chicken coming from a neighbor's backyard. On Sat-  23
urdays there is the smell of grass being cut. Sometimes there's the smell of  24
marijuana in my neighborhood, but not often.  25

I have lived in my neighborhood for nineteen years, and I appre-  26
ciate all of its sights, sounds, and smells.  27

### Questions for Discussion

1. Does the student successfully carry out her purpose statement in the body of her paper?
2. Could any of the transition sentences joining paragraphs together be improved? How?
3. What detail stood out for you the most?
4. Was the dialogue in paragraph 3 effective? Did it sound real? Why or why not?

### Word and Sentence Use

1. The student who wrote sample B has a way of overusing expletive expressions *(it is, there is, there are)*. In paragraph 2 she says, ". . . there are blue jays and red robins picking food that has fallen from the large mimosa trees . . ." The same sentence could be written more simply, more directly, like this:

▶ . . . blue jays and red robins pick food that has fallen from large mimosa trees . . .

Change the following two expletive expressions to sentences with active verbs.

▶ . . . there are three little girls with jump suits on playing jump rope . . .

▶ Also, there are freight and passenger trains that make noise when they pass by.

(The overuse of expletives is designated S-5 in the revision checklist.)

2. In paragraph 2, the student writes, "The driveways, which are curved . . ." She could say the same thing, with fewer words and one less *are*, simply by saying "The curved driveways . . ." (Wordy sentences are designated S-4 in the revision checklist.)

3. Note that the student correctly underlined the word *peaceful* in paragraph 1 because she used a word as a word. However, you should seldom underline words to show emphasis. It is better to show emphasis through the way you write, rather than by underlining or using exclamation points. (Overuse of emphasis is designated S-11 in the revision checklist.)

## TRANSITION SENTENCES TO JOIN PARAGRAPHS

All of your paragraphs should be connected as smoothly as possible by transition sentences, as shown in the diagram on page 110.

Transition sentences that join paragraphs have three functions: (1) to connect a paragraph with the previous paragraph, (2) to point to the content of the new paragraph, and (3) to help carry out the purpose statement. Keep these functions in mind, but remember the main purpose of the transition is to help the reader move from point to point *smoothly*. You will often come up with the best transition sentence when you revise your paper. (Review the notes on transition sentences *within* paragraphs on page 12.)

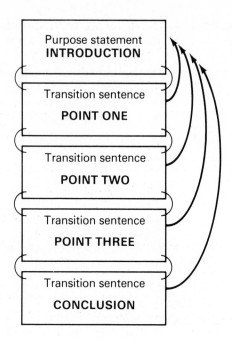

## TWO TYPES OF TRANSITION SENTENCES THAT JOIN PARAGRAPHS

1. *Parallel:* Sometimes you will want to make your transition sentences parallel to each other, that is, similar in form. The transition sentences in "My Home in the Project" (page 106) are closely parallel:

Purpose Statement ▶ When I think of the sights, sounds, and smells of my neighborhood, it makes me wish that I were living somewhere else besides the Bradley Housing Project.

Transition Sentences ▶ There are no beautiful things to see.

▶ There are no nice sounds to hear.

▶ There are no pleasant things to smell.

In this paper, the transition sentence repeats itself not unlike the refrain of a song. See page 209 for more on parallel sentences.

2. *Nonparallel:* Sometimes you will want your transition sentences to contain variety and connect your paragraphs loosely, as in the paper "My Home in the Country" (page 95):

Purpose Statement ▶   When I think of the <u>sights</u>, <u>sounds</u>, and <u>smells</u> of our place in the country, it makes me wish I was there right now.

Transition Sentences   ▶ There are many beautiful things to <u>see</u> around my home.

▶ If one is lucky, he can probably <u>see</u> deer running across . . .

▶ One can experience the seasons of the year <u>by watching</u> . . .

▶ Many different sounds can <u>be heard</u> around my home.

▶ Finally, there are distinctive <u>smells</u> around my home.

Notice how the underlined words in the purpose statement connect with the underlined words in the transition sentences.

## 3. The "Those-Were-the-Days" Paper

The assignment is to write a paper of 300 or more words on the general topic "Those Were the Days," again using each step of the writing method described earlier in this chapter. Before writing your paper, read the samples of student writing and the learning notes on the purpose statement, on introductions, and on conclusions. There is an alternative (or additional) assignment on page 130.

**Step One: Gather Information**   In this step, you will brainstorm, bringing back past memories from the years you were between six and eleven or twelve—your elementary school years. Before you actually write your paper, you may want to ask your parents or others who knew you in those years to help you fill in any information gaps.

1. As you think about yourself when you were in elementary school, what comes to mind when you hear the word *home*? Do not censor your thoughts. Write down everything!

_____

_____

_____

_____

2. What comes to mind when you think of the schools you attended during those years?

_____

_____

_____

_____

_____

3. Who were your best friends over those years? Write down one or two things that stand out about each of them.

_____

_____

_____

_____

_____

_____

4. What setbacks (accidents, illnesses, deaths, parents' divorces, and the like) did you experience in those years?

_____

_____

_____

_____

5. What special times do you remember (birthdays, awards, victories, vacations, and the like)?

_____

_____

_____

_____

_____

**Step Two: Analyze the Information**

One of the tasks of this step is to narrow down the information you have gathered. Of the five categories above, pick the one that you would find the most meaningful (or fun) to write about. Look at the information you listed under the other headings and see if any of it relates to the category you have chosen. If so, add that information to the list, and add any other information you can think of. Use the blanks below.

_____

_____

_____

_____

_____

_____

Sit back and look at this revised list. What stands out? Which things relate to each other? How can you begin to give an even more narrow focus to your topic? Which things can be eliminated from the list? What information gaps can your parents or someone you knew during those years help you fill in? At this point it may be helpful to read the student samples near the end of this section.

**Step Three: State Your Purpose**

You began with a very large topic, your elementary school years, you narrowed it down to one of five subtopics—home, school, friends, setbacks, or special times—and you have begun to give a more narrow focus to the subtopic. Now you will need to narrow down the subtopic even more and say in _one sentence_ what you will try to prove in your paper.

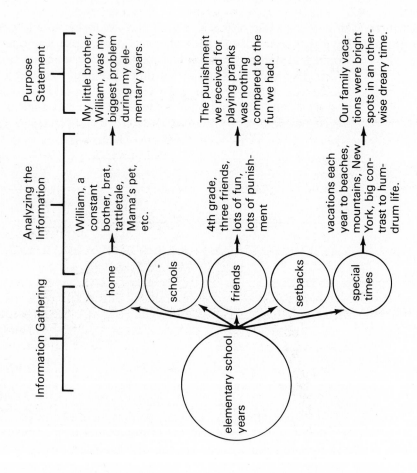

The purpose (or thesis) statement should not be simply a statement of your subject, as the following purpose statements are:

▶ In this paper I will write about my three best friends from the fourth grade.

▶ This paper is about the various vacations my family and I went on when I was in elementary school.

Instead, include within your purpose statement something you will have to convince your reader of—an opinion, something that will challenge you to be persuasive. The two purpose statements above could be revised as follows:

▶ The punishment we received for playing pranks was nothing compared to the fun we had.

▶ Our family vacations were bright spots in an otherwise dreary time.

Now you have to write convincingly to persuade your reader that the fun you had with your friends really was worth the punishment, or that the vacations you and your family had really were bright spots in years that really were otherwise dreary.

The illustration on page 114 shows how you can move from your information gathering to your purpose statement. See also the learning notes, "The Purpose (or Thesis) Statement," on page 116.

Here are some more examples of effective purpose statements for this assignment. In each, the writer must convince the reader of something.

▶ The hard times of my youth were also times of great learning. (The writer must not only describe the hard times but show *why* they were occasions of great learning.)

▶ The hobbies I became interested in when I was ten years old changed my life. (The writer must both describe the hobbies and show *how* they changed her life.)

▶ Whenever Mike, Tommy, Bean, and I are together, we get to talking and long for the good old days at Libson Elementary. (The writer must show just *why* he and his friends long for the good old days. What made them so memorable?)

▶ Even though we had our bad times as well as our good times, I'll never forget Curtis Johnson as long as I live. (The writer must not only describe the good and bad times but also *make the reader believe* that the relationship with Curtis Johnson is unforgettable.)

Write your own purpose statement and check it with your instructor.

_____

_____

_____

## THE PURPOSE (OR THESIS) STATEMENT

A purpose statement, often called a *thesis statement* in college, is a short, to-the-point declaration of what you will try to convince the reader of in your paper. Unless your teacher gives you different instructions, include your purpose statement in the first paragraph, except in narratives (see page 155).

Sometimes it takes a very long time to come up with just the right purpose statement. Students will often write an entire essay before they know what they really want to write about and will then write a fine purpose statement in their conclusion. That's okay if you are going to revise your paper, for you can simply begin the new draft with the purpose statement. But ordinarily, try to come up with the purpose statement that is just right before you make your plan.

### SUGGESTIONS FOR WRITING AN EFFECTIVE PURPOSE STATEMENT

1. The purpose statement should be narrow enough in focus, specific enough, so that you don't have to write about everything related to your topic:

Weak ▶ Aunt Kathleen was a very interesting person.

Strong ▶ Aunt Kathleen was poor but proud.

Weak  ▸  *To Kill a Mockingbird* is an enjoyable book.

Strong  ▸  *To Kill a Mockingbird* is a story of both tenderness and courage.

    2.  But it should be broad enough so that you will have *enough* to write about. Sometimes you will not know if your purpose statement gives you enough to write about until you get to the planning step. If you find that you cannot think of enough points to write a good outline, perhaps you need to find another purpose statement.

    3.  It should express an opinion, a position, something you will have to convince your reader of. The following "tell-them-what-you-are-going-to-tell them" statements are *not* strong purpose statements:

Weak  ▸  In this paper I will write about three ways to improve study habits.

Weak  ▸  In this essay I will discuss the times that Dr. Eugene Woods, my dentist, lectured to me on politics while I sat helplessly in the chair.

    If used at all, these kinds of sentences should be revised so that the *I will* is taken out. They should then be placed *after* the purpose statement, as follows:

Strong  ▸  Developing good study habits is simply a matter of self-discipline. There are a number of things you can do to improve your study habits, and you can begin now.

Strong  ▸  Dr. Eugene Woods, my dentist, should have been a politician. On several occasions he has lectured to me on politics while I sat helplessly in the chair.

    4.  It should state just one thing, the one point you will need to prove. A good paper will often have secondary purposes, but they should not compete with the main point, the thrust of your essay. The student in the second example above may want to explain how Dr. Woods is a fine dentist, but the main point that must be kept before the readers is that the doctor lectures to his patients on politics when they are in no position to respond. Here is another example:

Weak    ▸ The federal government should take steps to make cigarette smoking illegal and should actively seek nuclear disarmament.

Strong   ▸ The federal government should take steps to make cigarette smoking illegal.

*or*

Strong   ▸ The federal government should actively seek nuclear disarmament.

Both ideas could be combined in a sentence like the following:

Strong   ▸ The first two priorities of the federal government should be to make cigarette smoking illegal and to seek nuclear disarmament.

## An Exercise

Mark the following sentences *W* for weak purpose statement or *S* for strong purpose statement. Be able to say why. Instructors as well as students may differ on a couple of them.

_____ 1. The reading texts we used in my elementary schools taught us to dislike reading.

_____ 2. Capital punishment should be abolished and long jail sentences should be shortened.

_____ 3. John Steinbeck's *Of Mice and Men* is a story of hopeless hope.

_____ 4. In this paper I will describe three types of high school teachers.

_____ 5. The drivers in Washington, D.C., must be the worst in the nation.

_____ 6. My bridge partner, Donella, is nice.

_____ 7. Learning to write well is largely a matter of developing self-confidence, and the same thing is true of reading.

_____ 8. My two pets are as different as you can imagine any pets to be.

_____ 9. I will describe discrimination against women, first in
the United States and then in Russia.

_____ 10. The only difference between my pet and me is that
she has four legs and I have two.

Rewrite the weak purpose statements to make them stronger.

**Step Four: Make Your Plan**

In the space provided, write an informal outline that effectively carries out your purpose statement. If you have difficulty making enough points and filling in enough detail, perhaps you need to rewrite your purpose statement. Your paper should probably consist of four to six paragraphs. See the learning notes on pages 128 and 129 on introductions and conclusions.

_____
(your title)

Organizing Principle ▸ *Par. 1*      Introduction (include purpose statement) _____

Detail ▸ _____

_____

Organizing Principle ▸ *Par. 2*      _____

Detail ▸ _____

_____

Organizing Principle ▸ *Par. 3*      _____

Detail ▸ _____

_____

Organizing Principle ▸ *Par. 4*      _____

Detail ▸ _____

_____

Organizing Principle ▸ *Par. 5* _____

Detail ▸ _____

_____

Organizing Principle ▸ *Par. 6*   Conclusion _____

Detail ▸ _____

_____

Before moving to the next step, check your outline with your instructor.

**Step Five: Write**   As you write, keep in mind the following suggestions:

1. Most of your paper will probably be written in the past tense. If you switch to the present tense, make sure you have a legitimate reason for doing so.
2. Let your sentences flow into each other as smoothly as possible.
3. Give your sentences variety. Write some as compound, some as complex, and some as simple sentences. (See Chapter 6.)
4. If you have stated a point clearly in one sentence, do not repeat the idea in another sentence that says just about the same thing, unless you are doing so for emphasis.

**Step Six: Evaluate and Edit**   Evaluate your paper:

1. Did the purpose statement meet the criteria given on page 116?
2. Did the introduction meet the criteria given on page 127?
3. Did the conclusion effectively bring to a close what you wanted to say?
4. Was there enough information to support each major point?
5. Did you use any examples to develop your paragraphs? If you did, what were they?
6. Did you use dialogue? If so, was it effective?
7. Did you repeat yourself unnecessarily at any time? If so, how would you change what you wrote if you were rewriting the paper?

Now edit your paper, using the checklist on the back inside cover of this book. Two errors that often appear on this assignment are verb-tense errors and run-on-sentence errors.

**Verb Tense.** Be careful to give regular verbs a -d or an -ed ending when they refer to action in the past. Watch out especially for those verbs whose endings are hard to hear:

► She look<u>ed</u> very pretty for the party.

► He help<u>ed</u> us all more than he knew.

If you have any problem at all with irregular past-tense endings, check all irregular verbs against the list in Chapter 8.0. Watch out especially for those that are often missed, such as:

► He <u>began</u> his work on time that day.

► He <u>laid</u> his pen on the table and refused to write.

► It <u>cost</u> more last year than it costs this year.

**Run-on Sentences.** Be careful not to run your sentences together. In telling of events in the past, many of your sentences will be closely related in content. The more closely related they are, the easier it is to run them together. (See Chapter 6.8.)

Incorrect ► I was finally admitted by the nurse, she X-rayed my arm in different positions.

Correct ► When I was finally admitted by the nurse, she X-rayed my arm in different positions.

Incorrect ► A friend of the family from across the street came over, he saw what had happened and rushed me to the hospital.

Correct ► A friend of the family from across the street came over. He saw what had happened and rushed me to the hospital.

**Share Your Writing** Read your paper in a small group and make use of the evaluation questions in *step six* above as each paper is read. Next, exchange papers with one other person and proofread the paper you receive. Be sure to check with the student before writing any changes on the paper.

This is the last time the suggestion will be made to share your writing. Your instructor, however, may ask you to read your papers in small groups for the assignments in Chapter 4. If class time does not permit small group discussions, share your paper with a classmate outside of class when possible. It makes good sense to read your paper to the people for whom it was written and to listen to their papers as well. It is also a good practice to exchange papers for proofreading and editing.

Other Student ▶ Samples

**A**

### Those Were the Days

The friend I can remember best from my childhood is Curtis Johnson. I met Curtis Johnson in Children's Hospital when I was there in 1969, but I haven't seen him since. Even though we had our bad times as well as our good times, I'll never forget Curtis as long as I live.

I entered Children's Hospital a year after my family moved to this country from Cuba. Curtis used to come up to me and talk about many things. At first I would never talk back because I didn't speak English. I learned how to speak English in the hospital. There was a school room in the hospital, and every day the teacher, Mr. Manuel, would show me flash cards with different letters and words on them. Pretty soon I began to speak a little English. I started communicating with Curtis, and he would talk to me as though I were a native-born American. I think that's why I picked up English so fast. Curtis and I started hanging around each other. It was as though I depended on him and he depended on me. As you know, I can't use my legs, and he doesn't have arms.

Curtis and I did everything imaginable together. We played games, went to parties, chased all the female volunteers, hunted blue jays in the yard with sling shots, set up squirrel traps, and played tricks on people. The best times we had were when we tried to talk to pretty volunteers. I mean here were a couple of young punks, one ten and the other eleven, trying to make it big with girls seventeen and older. Curtis had a line that would get them every time. It went something like this: "Hi, my name is Curtis; I'm from Turtle Creek. Have you ever heard of it?" Then Curtis would drop something on the floor on purpose knowing that the girl would feel sorry for him and pick it up. When she reached down, Curtis would stand near her and the moment she stood up would kiss her smack on the lips. Can you imagine that? He tried to get me to do it a few times, but I didn't have the nerve. With my luck, the girl would probably have slapped me. We did many things that were fun and sometimes got into trouble doing them.

Every now and then Curtis and I would get into fights. Our worst brawl happened one day when I had a visitor who brought me some chocolate-chip cookies. When my visitor was leaving, I escorted her out. When I returned, all my cookies were gone. Curtis had cookie crumbs on his lips, so I asked him, "Curtis, did you eat my cookies?" He said no. Then I said, "You're lying!" He answered, "You calling me a liar, Rudolfo?" I said "Yeah, you are a liar." That started feet kicking and fists swinging. Well, to

1
2
3
4
5
6
7
8
9
10
11
12
13
14
15
16
17
18
19
20
21
22
23
24
25
26
27
28
29
30
31
32
33
34
35
36

make a long story short, Curtis gave me a good beating with his feet. It      37
was a real back-alley brawl with flying books, flying toys, and flying peo-   38
ple (mainly me). We both got punished for three weeks.                        39

      During that time we made up and became good friends once    40
again. I often wonder what Curtis is doing now.                               41

### Questions for Discussion

1. What is the purpose statement? Is it effective? Is the student successful in carrying it out?
2. What is the organizing principle of each paragraph?
3. Look at the transition sentences that introduce the second, third, and fourth paragraphs. Could any of them have been written more effectively?
4. One of the best ways to develop your paragraphs is by giving examples. What examples does this writer give? What points do they illustrate?
5. Does the student give enough background information in the introduction for you to put his paper in some context?
6. Is the conclusion effective? Should he have summarized what he said? Would you like him to say more? If so, what?
7. What might be a more exact title for this essay than the one the student used?

### Word and Sentence Use

1. The student described his experiences with Curtis in the past tense, but on several occasions had to switch to the present tense because he was making a comment in the present time:

   ► Line 1: The friend I can remember best from my childhood is Curtis Johnson. (Although the writer will tell about Curtis in the past tense, he is remembering him in the present.)

   ► Line 28: Can you imagine that? (Here the writer is asking a question of the reader in the present time.)

   ► Line 41: I often wonder what Curtis is doing now. (The writer makes this comment about what he is thinking *now*.)

   Misuse of tense is designated ST (shift in tense) in the editing checklist on the back inside cover.
2. For the most part, the sentences in this essay flow into each other

smoothly, but there are a few places where the sentences are choppy. In line 8, for example, the student writes:

▶ At first I would not talk back to him because I didn't speak English. I learned how to speak English in the hospital.

The student probably would not speak like that. More than likely he would join those two sentences, something like this:

▶ At first I would not talk back to him because I didn't speak English, but later I learned how to speak . . .

Choppy sentences are designated S-8 in the revision checklist.

3. On several occasions the student used unnecessary words. Here are two examples:

▶ Line 14: It was as though I depended on him and he depended on me. (*It was as though* doesn't add anything to the meaning and could be omitted.)

▶ Line 21: I mean here we were a couple of young punks . . . (*I mean* doesn't add anything to the meaning, and it too could be omitted. *Well,* when used as "Well, let me tell you," is similar to *I mean* and can often be omitted.)

The use of unnecessary words is designated S-1 in the revision checklist.

**B**     ### THOSE WERE THE DAYS

I was twelve years old when my father died. On November 23, 1972, I came home from the store on a Sunday morning about 10:00 A.M. and got the news. I had lost someone I loved, my father.

When I walked up to our front door, I saw plenty of people standing around our house. I wondered what was going on at this time of morning. Everyone was crying and whispering. I just knew something had happened. My mother's best friend told me that my father had died. I cried and cried. At first it was hard for me to believe. Mrs. Rose (my mother's best friend) told me he had a heart attack. When they brought him out to the car to go to the hospital, he died.

That day was one of the worst days of my life. Everybody in the house was crying. I remember how all of my aunts, uncles, and friends

gave us their sympathy. It was late that night before everyone seemed to   13
have left. I cried the whole night. I wondered how much I was going to   14
miss my father.   15

    The funeral was at Illinois Funeral Home on North Claiborne Ave-   16
nue, November 25, 1972. All the family was ready for the funeral, except   17
me. I did not want to go. I was frightened knowing this was the last time I   18
was going to see him. I was late. Everyone waited for me so that they could   19
close the casket. Mother and I said a prayer together. After we finished   20
praying over my father's body, they closed the casket. The chauffeur drove   21
us to the cemetery. The preacher prayed over my father's body. After all   22
the family and friends had left, I picked a rose from the basket of roses   23
and I dropped it on the casket. I told this to him: "Good-bye, Daddy. I will   24
miss you. I love you very much."   25

    Adjusting to life without him was not easy. I was too fright-   26
ened to go to sleep in my bed at night, so I slept at my friend's house   27
as much as I could. I did anything not to sleep in my bed at home.   28
About six months after he died, I finally started to sleep in my bed but   29
often woke up screaming. It was hard as I grew up without my father   30
in my younger teens. I had no one to help me with my homework,   31
nobody's back to jump on. Now that I am older I have accepted his   32
death, and I am going to try to make my daddy proud of his   33
daughter.   34

### Questions for Discussion

1. The student is writing about an event that was very sad for her. Was she able to convey her sadness without sounding too emotional in her writing? Do you feel the sadness with her? If so, what did she say that made you feel that way?
2. What examples did the student give as she developed each paragraph?

### Word and Sentence Use

1. The beauty of this essay is its simplicity: it moves forward in short, straightforward, uncomplicated sentences. But still, the writing would be even more effective if the student joined some of her sentences to give her writing variety. Here are two examples:

▶ Line 5: I wondered what was going on at this time of morning. Everyone was crying and whispering. I just knew something had happened. (She could join the first two sentences and keep the last sentence as it is, something like this: "I wondered what was going on at this time of morning because everyone was crying and whispering. I just knew something had happened.")

► Line 7: My mother's best friend told me that my father had died. I cried and cried. (These two sentences could be joined as follows: "When my mother's best friend told me that my father had died, I cried and cried.")

Rewrite the fourth paragraph joining some sentences to help the flow of the story. Rely on your ear: if you were speaking the words, how would you say them?

*Give your sentences variety.* Write some as compound sentences, some as complex sentences, and some as short simple sentences. (Choppy sentences are designated S-8 in the revision checklist.) See Chapter 6 for more on joining sentences.

2. In line 13, the student wrote, ". . . before everyone seemed to have left." The words *seemed to have* add nothing to the meaning. Omit them. Wordy sentences are designated S-4 in the revision checklist.

3. On at least one occasion the student repeated what she said in one sentence in another sentence:

► Line 7: My mother's best friend told me that my father had died. . . . Mrs. Rose (my mother's best friend) told me that he had a heart attack.

The second sentence would not be necessary if the student had included the necessary information in the first sentence:

► My mother's best friend, Mrs. Rose, told me that my father had died of a heart attack.

*Do not repeat what you have said in one sentence when writing another sentence.* Include enough information in the first sentence so that you do not need to repeat yourself. Repetitive sentences are designated S-10 in the revision checklist.

**An Alternative (or Additional) Writing Assignment**

Write a paper of 300 or more words on the same topic, "Those Were the Days"; only this time focus on your high school years (or some other four-year period in your life). Make use of all the learning notes, the student samples, and the tips to improve your style.

# INTRODUCTIONS TO ESSAYS

You can usually introduce a one-paragraph paper effectively with one or two sentences, but when you are writing a paper consisting of several paragraphs, you will probably need a separate paragraph for the introduction. Writing a good introduction is often the most difficult and time-consuming part of writing an essay. While preparing for an in-class essay, it is wise to write out your introduction as well as your outline ahead of time so that you will know exactly how to begin your essay when you sit down to write in class. The introduction is usually—though not always—shorter than the paragraphs in the body of your paper.

## WHAT TO INCLUDE IN AN INTRODUCTION

1. Unless your instructor gives other directions, include your purpose statement. Place it at the point where it is most effective. If it is a catchy purpose statement, like "My neighborhood is so noisy it disturbs the dogs" or "My Cousin Cassandra has freaked out over religion," use it as the first sentence.
2. Include enough background information so that your reader will be able to put your essay in some context. For the neighborhood paper, you were asked to say in your introduction where your neighborhood was and how long you lived there. In the "Those-Were-the-Days" paper you might tell which of the early years you are talking about, where you were living at the time, and perhaps what school or schools you were attending. In Chapter 4, when you are writing an argument, you should say why the particular issue you are taking a stand on is important.
3. Include a summary statement only if you believe it will help your readers understand what you want to accomplish in the paper. This statement is often the last sentence of the first paragraph. It should always come after the purpose statement. Keep it brief.

Weak ▸ In this essay, I will write about three ways to improve your study habits. First, I will write about how important it is to plan your study time carefully. Second, I will write about how important it is to use the library. Third, I will write about how important it is to keep up with all of your assignments.

Strong ▶    There are a number of things you can do to improve your study habits, and you can begin now.

In other words, when you are writing summary sentences, don't overdo it. Your transition sentences at the beginning of each paragraph should make your individual points clear.

4. Include anything else that will stimulate your reader to read on. One effective way to begin a paper is with an example. If you were writing about how a student's life is a difficult one, you might begin with a short example that illustrates your point. (See the example essay on page 186.)

## CONCLUSIONS TO ESSAYS

In each essay you write, you must make sure your reader knows you have come to the end of what you want to say. Like the introduction, the conclusion is usually—but not always—shorter than the paragraphs in the body of the paper. If it is just one sentence long, you may want to hook it onto the last paragraph.

Your concluding statements will usually come naturally to you, much like ending a telephone conversation:

▶ And so you see, everybody gossips.

▶ If I had my way, I would live in this house at 42 Legare Street the rest of my life.

▶ The "good old days" weren't so good after all.

▶ Thus, television should be outlawed.

### OTHER IDEAS FOR YOUR CONCLUSIONS

Besides bringing your essay to an end, you may want to include in your last paragraph one of the following:

1. *A contrasting idea.* The student who wrote the paper on the Bradley Housing Project (page 106) used the conclusion to show what she *did* like about her home after writing the rest of

the paper about what she did not like about it. If you are writing about sad or difficult times in the "Those-Were-the-Days" paper, you may want to use your last paragraph to note that not *everything* was bad, beginning perhaps with a sentence like "But not everything was disappointing during those years."

2. *A statement of the significance.* When you finish making your points about why something is true, you may want to bring your reader up to date, saying what it all means. One student described the highlights of her fifth-grade year in her essay and then wrote the following conclusion, explaining the significance of what had happened to her that year:

> ▸ These experiences were important to me then, and they are still important to me. I continue to play the trumpet, first chair in concerts, and in the school marching band. Mary and I are still best friends. And would you believe, I still play baseball *every* chance I get?

> If you were writing a paper about why sex education should be taught in high schools, you might conclude with a statement on the difference it would make to young people if your ideas were accepted.

3. *A call to action.* If you are arguing for a belief, you may want to ask your reader to join with you in trying to remedy a certain problem, for example:

> ▸ The best way for us to conserve energy is to make a decision— right now—that we will cut down on our driving, we will use less heat in our homes, and we will learn to take cold showers.

> ▸ If you agree that capital punishment should be abolished, write your state and congressional representatives today.

4. *A summary.* Beware of this one. You will not need to repeat *each* point that you made in a separate sentence. Summary endings are useful if each point can be expressed in a word or two and the summary takes only a single sentence, for example:

> ▸ Whether male or female, young or old, everyone likes to gossip.

> ▸ A young person will not go wrong if he or she goes into banking, computer science, or nursing.

## 4. Revising Papers

Revision is more than rewriting; the word, *re-vision,* means "re-seeing," that is, looking at your paper with fresh eyes to see how it can be improved. Once you have written your first draft, let it sit for a day or two, evaluate and edit the paper (*step six* of the writing method), and *then* rewrite, incorporating your new ideas into the revised essay.

Some students are disappointed when teachers ask them to revise a paper; they think that means they have somehow failed in writing the first draft. But remember, writing is a kind of art form; it takes a lot of practice and sometimes several drafts of a paper before you can say what you really want to say. Portions of this text, for example, were revised ten, even twelve times.

When you revise a paper, you have an excellent opportunity to work on improving your style, which is the *way* something is said or done, as opposed to its content or substance. Read the following learning notes, which describe the procedure you should follow in revising your papers.

## REVISION OF PAPERS

Revise your papers before handing them in. Revising an essay will help you not only on the particular paper on which you are working; it will also help you a great deal in mastering the principles of organization, the elements of style, and the rules of grammar. Although this text does not specifically ask you to revise papers in Chapter 4, it will be assumed from now on that you will revise papers when you can.

When you do revise a paper, be willing to change, delete, and add to material you have already written. If you see that your paper is not working and probably can't be made to work, be willing to start over, perhaps with a different topic. There are three steps to revising a paper: first, read your paper through a couple of times; second, write notes on your paper about exactly what needs to be revised (make use of the checklist below, or the abbreviated form of it on the front inside cover, and of the editing checklist on the back inside cover); third, rewrite the paper incorporating the changes. When you are making notes on your paper about what needs to be changed, use a different color ink to highlight the changes.

## A Revision Checklist

A. General ▶

_____ **G-1.** Did you choose the right topic? Is it a topic you know enough about to write on? Is it a topic you care about? Is the topic too broad, too narrow? Should you start over with another topic?

_____ **G-2.** In rereading your paper, does it sound like you talking? If not, what sentences might you change so that they do sound like you?

_____ **G-3.** Is the tone of your paper appropriate for the audience you are addressing? (See the learning notes on page 19.)

_____ **G-4.** Is the title appropriate for the content? (See the learning notes on page 52.)

B. Organization ▶ _____ **O-1.** Is the purpose statement effective? Does it meet the criteria given on page 116? Look at your conclusion. Can you use it to write an even more effective purpose statement in your next draft?

_____ **O-2.** Does the overall structure enable you to carry out your purpose? Do you at times stray too far away from your purpose? (See the learning notes on planning a paper on page 102.)

_____ **O-3.** Does each paragraph have an identifiable organizing principle? Is each a suitable length? (See the learning notes on page 102.)

_____ **O-4.** Is each paragraph properly developed, with enough details, examples, arguments, and the like? (See the learning notes on page 226.)

_____ **O-5.** Are the transition sentences *within* paragraphs smooth? (See the learning notes on page 12.)

_____ **O-6.** Are the transitions sentences *between* paragraphs smooth? Do they meet the criteria given in the learning notes on page 109?

_____ **O-7.** Does the introduction give the necessary background information and announce the purpose? Could you add anything to it to catch your reader's attention? (See the learning notes on page 127.)

_____ **O-8.** Does the conclusion effectively bring the essay to an end? Is there anything else you might write about in your conclusion? (See the learning notes on page 128.)

**C. Style ▶** _____ **S-1.** Do you use any words that are redundant (that is, that repeat what you have already said) or words that are unnecessary? See if you can omit any of the following: *in today's society, well, plus, seem, it could be said, so, and so, in conclusion.*

_____ **S-2.** Do you use the same word (or another form of that word) too many times?

_____ **S-3.** Do you use the most exact word or words to say what you mean? Be careful not to use too many general words like *good, bad, nice, interesting.* And be careful not to use inexact words: words like *aspects* and *factors* are often misused. Make use of a dictionary or thesaurus if you are having trouble finding the best word. (See the learning notes on finding the most exact word on page 152.)

_____ **S-4.** Can you write any of your sentences more concisely, that is, more to the point, with fewer words?

_____ **S-5.** Do you use too many expletive expressions *(there is, there are, it is)*? (See page 108).

_____ **S-6.** Do you overuse the passive voice? (See page 97 and Chapter 8.5)

_____ **S-7.** Are any of your sentences awkward, hard to understand?

_____ **S-8.** Do you give enough variety to your sentences? Should you join some of your sentences? Do you use an appropriate balance of simple, compound, and complex sentences? (See Chapter 6.)

_____ **S-9.** Do you use parallel constructions (constructions that are similar in form) for parallel thoughts? (See the learning notes on page 209.)

_____ **S-10.** Can you delete any of your sentences without taking away from what you want to say in your essay?

_____ **S-11.** Do you overuse underlining or exclamation points to show emphasis?

(S-12 and S-13 are left blank for your instructor to fill in if he or she has special stylistic concerns that are not covered in the checklist.)

_____ **S-12.** _____

_____

_____ **S-13.** _____

_____

**D. Mechanics**    Make use of the editing checklist on the back inside cover of this book.

**Revision Exercise #1**    **Step One.** Study the essay below and the instructor's comments carefully, and then read the revised version. Look up the abbreviations in the revision and editing checklists.

*Center title* ↴

**THE PEOPLE WHO MEAN THE MOST**    *change one (S-2)*

*unnecessary expletive (S-5)* → There are [a lot of] people who mean [a lot] to me, but I have chosen only three of them to write about.

*purpose statement too broad (O-1)*    The person who means the most to me is my mother, Violet. [She means the most because] she is always there when I *Ca.* need her. As long as I can remember, she has been there, and I'm sure

*see conclusion for ideas*    she will continue being there. [She means the most because] she has *← omit - wordy (S-4)*

*omit - wordy (S-4)*    been a mother [plus] a father for me as well as for my sisters and *Ca* brother. She has made me the person that I am today, and I am very

*and (S-3)*    pleased with myself. She was never at any time overprotective or too *because I have always done what I was told to do*

*Omit and use information in sentence above (S-10)*    strict. She has confidence in me to do the things (that's) right. [She has *VA* never been too strict because I have always done what I was told to

*Paragraph too general - needs detail example (O-4)*    do with very little or no opposition.] My (mother) is a very understand- *S-2* ing (mother) and I would never want anyone else to take her place.

My Aunt Caroline means a great deal to me also. She is my

*awkward - reword (s-7)*

A mother(s) sister and [she's] like a second mother to me. If someone had

*omit - wordy (s-4)* to take my mother's place when I was a child, I would have (choosen) *s*

her. [I would have choosen her because,] as a child, I spent a great *ca*

*omit - wordy (s-4)* deal of time [by] her house when my mother went over there to visit.

She and my mother are very close because they live in the same city

*ww* and can see and talk to each other every day. [Because they see each

*omit - wordy (s-4)* other so much] they do things in a similar way [and that makes my *ca*

aunt similar to my mother in so many ways.] [This is why I say that my

aunt is like a second mother to me and could take her place if anyone

*omit - wordy (s-4)* had to.] *Paragraph too general - needs detail, examples (0-4)*

*omit - wordy (s-4)* My Aunt Susan, who is also my mother's sister, is a third

person who means a lot to me. As a child I didn't get to see her much

because she usually only came to visit for holidays. Her ways aren't

similar to my mother's or Aunt Caroline's because she isn't around

them enough to adopt their ways. She means a lot because I know

*omit - wordy (s-4)* that she will [make it a point to] be there for me if I should ever

need her. *Paragraph too general - needs detail, examples (0-4)*

*unnecessary expletive* [There are] many others [who] mean a lot to me and would do

anything for me, [but there are just too many to write about.]

*Expand conclusion - What does this mean for you (0-8)*

Revised Version ▶        THE PEOPLE WHO MEAN THE MOST

Many people mean a lot to me, but I have chosen only three of    1
them to write on. I can count on all three to do anything for me.    2
    The person who means the most of the three is my mother, Violet.    3
She is always there when I need her. As long as I can remember she has    4
been there, and I'm sure she will continue being there. She has been a    5
mother and a father for me, as well as for my sisters and brother. She    6
worked hard at her job to give us what we wanted, and she always kept    7
a nice house. She has made me the person I am today, and I am very    8
pleased with myself. I am in college right now because she helped me    9
with my homework almost every night. She was never at any time overpro-    10
tective or too strict because I have always done what I was told to do. She    11
has confidence in me to do the things that are right. She never made me    12

come in at a particular time because she knew that I would show good    13
judgment. My mother is very understanding, and I would never want any-    14
one else to take her place.    15

My Aunt Caroline means a great deal to me also. She is my moth-    16
er's sister and like a second mother to me. If my mother had died when I    17
was a child, I would have chosen Caroline to take my mother's place. As    18
a child I spent a great deal of time at her house when my mother went    19
over there to visit. She and my mother are so close because they live in the    20
same city and can see and talk to each other every day. Because they    21
do things in a similar way, I feel comfortable with Aunt Caroline. Once    22
when my mother went on a trip for two weeks, I stayed with Aunt Caroline.    23
I missed my mother but didn't have to do anything differently because my    24
aunt and my mother live the same kinds of lives.    25

My Aunt Susan, who is also my mother's sister, is a third person who    26
means a lot to me. As a child I didn't see her much because she usually    27
only came to visit for holidays. Her ways aren't similar to my mother's or    28
Aunt Caroline's because she isn't around them enough to adopt their ways.    29
But she still means a lot to me because I know that she will be there for me    30
if I should ever need her. She is helping to pay my way through college    31
and once told me that if I ever needed any money to write her and she    32
would help.    33

Besides my mother and my aunts, many others mean a lot to me    34
and would do anything for me. I am very lucky to have such a nice family    35
and set of friends.    36

**Step Two.**    Underline everything in the revised version that has been added or changed. Make sure you know why each change was made. If you are in doubt, ask your instructor.

**Step Three.**    What changes might you make to the *revised version* to make it a more effective paper? In the second paragraph, for example, seven sentences begin with *she*. How might you give some of these sentences more variety?

**Revision Exercise #2**    **Step One.**    Read the next essay and the teacher's comments very carefully. If you do not understand any of the comments or corrections, ask your instructor to explain. In *step two* you will rewrite the essay incorporating the suggestions.

*Find a more exact title (6-4)* ⟶ THREE PEOPLE WHO MEAN THE MOST TO ME

*5-5* ⟶ There are many of my relatives and friends who mean a lot to me, but I am going to focus on three individuals who mean the most to me. *(0-1) Make more exact. The conclusion gives a more narrow focus.*

One individual who means a lot to me is my mother. If it weren't for her and the Lord, I wouldn't be here today. Although my *Give example or two (0-4)* mother died when I was twelve years old, I can still remember the good times we had together. My mother taught me a lot of things *(s-8) Join with "but"* while she was living. She also whipped me when I was wrong. The sad thing about any mother-daughter relationship is that the daughter *Why not just "person"? (s-3)* doesn't realize the significance of her mother until she is grown. My mother was and still is an important [factor] in my life. [One of the main things that makes her important to me now is that she taught me how to be responsible.] *s-10*

*s-2* Another individual who means a lot to me is my grandmother. [My grandmother] is very important to me because she picked up where my mother left off. After my mother died, my grandmother took me to live with her. My grandmother took on my mother's re-*ww "by"* sponsibilities (in) raising and caring for me until this day, and she has *v — (did)* a very good job. She's not like the ordinary grandmother. My grandmother will go out of her way to make things pleasant for me. *(s-8) Join with "but". Omit "My grandmother"* For example, every morning when I wake up, breakfast is waiting for me, and every evening when I come home from school, dinner is ready. I will always cherish and honor her because she is really like my own mother!! *← s-11*

*Omit (s-5)* Third, [there is] my boyfriend. [He] really means a lot to me. We are both young, but I am glad I can say that we are helpers (of) one *ww* another. Whenever I have a problem or just need someone to talk to, *A good place for an example* I can depend on him. He goes out of his way to make me happy. [He has shown me love outside of the family, and that is very impor-*s-10* tant.]

*These*

The three people [I mentioned above] have been most helpful to me, but I won't make a crutch out of them.  *S-4*

**Step Two.**   Rewrite the paper making the corrections and incorporating the suggestions. You will, of course, have to make up examples in paragraphs 2 and 4. Don't stop at the suggested changes; make any other changes that you believe will help the writing.

**Revision Exercise #3**   Using what you have learned from the exercises above, write your own paper on the three most important people in your life. After you finish the first draft, let the paper sit for a day or two and then revise it, using the entire revision checklist.

**Revision Exercise #4**   Revise either your neighborhood paper or your "Those-Were-the-Days" paper, using both the revision and editing checklists. Even if you have already rewritten your paper once, the revision process will be worthwhile. You will think of more details and examples and can always improve your style.

# Chapter 4
## Specialized Writing Assignments

In Chapter 3, you learned a general method for developing and writing an essay. As the need arises, refer back to the learning notes in Chapter 3 on the purpose statement, outline, transitions between paragraphs, introduction, conclusion, and methods of revising a paper. This chapter teaches special techniques for particular assignments you may receive in both English classes and other courses that require essays. It contains learning notes and step-by-step instructions on how to write the following kinds of essays:

► The description essay (how to convey your dominant impression of a person, place, object, or event)

► The narrative essay (how to tell a story about something that is important to you)

► The process essay (how to explain the best way to do or make something you are good at)

► The example essay (how to illustrate your purpose statement by giving examples)

▶ The comparison and contrast essay (how to show the ways in which two people or things are both alike and different)

▶ The classification essay (how to describe three or more classes or categories of something)

▶ The argument essay (how to argue persuasively for a personal belief)

This chapter also contains learning notes on using the most exact word, writing numbers, using comparative and superlative adjectives, writing parallel sentences, and developing support for the main point of a paragraph.

When possible, read your papers to one another and exchange them for editing.

## 1. The Description Essay

To describe something is to tell about it in detail. A description essay should help the reader *see* the person, place, object, or event you are describing; but it should do more—it should also help the reader *know* the person or thing you are describing. When you were describing your neighborhood in Chapter 3, the task was to help your reader know something of what it is like to live where you live, to know your neighborhood from the inside. If you are describing a person, the task is to help your reader get to know that person. If you are describing a sunset, the task is not only to help your reader see as a camera "sees," but also to experience with you *what it is like* to see the sunset.

In the assignment that follows you will need to draw on these skills: seeing clearly, hearing with open ears, and recalling particular events that help explain the point you are making. Remember, no one sees and hears exactly like you. Don't ever give in and simply say what you think others want you to say. Your descriptions should come from *your* perceptions.

Learning to write descriptions will help you in other courses. In a literature class you may be asked to describe George and Lennie's dream in *Of Mice and Men* by John Steinbeck. In a history class you may be asked to describe the reign of Louis XIV. In a philosophy class you may be asked to describe Plato's symbolic cave. Moreover, your skill in describing people and things will be a most useful tool in paragraph development in all of your papers.

# THE DESCRIPTION ESSAY

Objective ▸ To convey to your reader your dominant impression of the person, place, object, or event you are describing.

## SUGGESTIONS FOR THE ESSAY

1. Stress details. Your paper can be only as strong as the details in it. Whether you are telling your reader what you see or what you hear, describe the details as precisely as you can. If, for example, you are describing a room, ask yourself the following kinds of questions to produce a detailed description:

What is the size of the room?
What small items does one see?
Do they smell?
Do they have rough edges? smooth?
Are they rusty? shiny?
Is the air dank and musty, or fresh?
Are there cracks in the walls and old wax stains around the edges of the floor?
Is the wallpaper bright and colorful?

2. Let yourself become involved with the person or thing you are describing. To a casual observer, the oak tree in the back yard may be just an oak. But when you are writing a descriptive essay, you are no longer a casual observer. Look at the tree closely and perhaps you will see ancient initials carved in the trunk—the bark where they were carved long ago now bulging like scar tissue. Listen carefully. Does the wind really whistle through the leaves, or is it more of a broom-sweeping sound? And try to remember what the tree meant for you in the past. When you were very young, did you and your friends have tea parties in the shade of the great oak on hot, dry summer days? Did you ever build a tree house in the arms of the oak? If so, can you still see the nails? What memories come back to you when you think of that tree house you built (or always wanted to build)?

3. Don't feel that you have to conjure up spectacular people or things to write about. The ordinary, the everyday will do just as well. But always look for meaning in the ordinary. The grass that grows in the cracks of a downtown sidewalk need not be

just grass; it can be a reminder that while people pollute, build pavement everywhere, even bomb cities into wastelands, they can't kill life altogether; it keeps coming back, like grass in the cracks of a downtown sidewalk.

4. When describing people, let them speak for themselves when you can. A single parent, the mother of six, reveals pages about herself when she tells her children, "The Lord makes the back to bear the burden." The old man who sits in front of the television set every day watching the same programs, and who every day makes the same one-word comment—"Stupid!"—at the conclusion of each program tells us quite a bit about himself, if not about television.

5. Tell stories a paragraph in length, or even shorter, to help convey your main point, your dominant impression. If you are writing about how your son Ernesto is cranky, tell a short story to help illustrate his crankiness. If you are describing a typical midwinter day in your icy climate, tell a short story about what you did once to protect yourself from the cold.

6. Make use of similes and metaphors (see page 47). The description essay is an ideal time to say what something reminds you of. And don't settle for the similes and metaphors you always hear, like "He was as thin as a rail." Ask yourself what really looks thin to you and make up your own simile. One student wrote, "He was thin as capital I." Another wrote, "The frozen ice pond looked like grandmother's cloudy, cracked bureau mirror." Still another wrote, "Her hair was like a jungle with a narrow road cut through the middle."

Read this essay in preparation for writing a description essay on one of your relatives or friends. How effective is the student in helping you get to know her grandmother?

### MOLLY

If you ever bump into my grandmother, you'd probably say she's    1
the perfect picture of a mean, old, grouchy grandmother. But really deep    2
down inside she isn't that way at all. I'll give you a complete description of    3
her, so you can get to know her better.    4

Her name is Molly, and that's what she's called by everyone. Her    5
hair is gray with white streaks and is usually combed into braids. She al-    6
ways walks with a cane, which she carries for protection. You can rarely    7
understand what she's saying because she has very few teeth in her mouth.    8

And when you only have a few teeth, it's mighty hard to get those words     9
out. I guess you could say Molly is a small-framed woman. She weighs only   10
one hundred and ten pounds. But even though she's little, she's a woman     11
that gets around.     12

    An important thing for Molly is her routine of walking from the back     13
of the house to the front. Molly makes this little journey at least five times     14
daily. When she makes this trip in the late afternoon, she goes out the front     15
door and sits on the porch. She is stationed there for the rest of the evening.     16
As night falls, everyone comes out to greet a friend or visit a neighbor.     17
People who pass in front of Molly's know to speak to her. If you don't hap-     18
pen to speak, you get a big argument from her and a lot of name calling.     19

    It's not a good idea to do or say anything to offend Molly. If you     20
do, there's a guarantee you won't hear the end of it. I remember one inci-     21
dent. I was combing my hair, and I accidently left my comb and brush on     22
her dresser. When I finally remembered where I had left my belongings, I     23
hastily went back to get them. But when I got there, to my surprise, every-     24
thing was on the floor. There was a note on the dresser which read, "Don't     25
ever leave your mess on my dresser again or your things won't be the     26
same." When I finished reading the note, I was so angry I tore it up and     27
threw it into the fireplace. But I should never have done that because Molly     28
was standing right behind me. She politely made me go to her study and     29
write another note and tear it into small pieces. Then she made me pick     30
up the pieces and put them together like a puzzle. Boy! That was the last     31
time I made a mistake like that.     32

    Molly isn't always a mean person. Usually on Sundays she is in a     33
good state of mind. Early in the morning she attends church service and     34
then returns home to finish cooking dinner. After the dinner is eaten, we all     35
sit down and peacefully talk. The evening ends with one of Molly's favorite     36
desserts. Molly is really a wonderful person. You just have to understand     37
her. She is now ninety-one years old. That's a lot of years of sweet grouchi-     38
ness.     39

### Questions for Discussion

1. What is the purpose statement? Does the student succeed in helping you get to know Molly? How? What else would you like to know about her? Does the student seem personally involved in her description?
2. What is the organizing principle of each paragraph?
3. Does paragraph 2 help carry out the purpose statement?
4. Look at the transition sentences that join the paragraphs. Are they effective? Could they be improved? How?
5. What particular use does the student make of the concluding par-

agraph? Does the example she uses in that paragraph effectively illustrate her point?

### Word and Sentence Use

1. In the first paragraph, the student used four contractions: *you'd, she's, isn't,* and *I'll.* Try to avoid so many contractions. In more formal writing, you should use them seldom, if at all. What contractions could you change in the rest of the essay without hurting the writer's style?
2. In the first sentence, the student used the present-tense verb *bump* with *you'd say* (for *you would say*). However, *would* usually goes with past-tense verbs. The sentence should be written as follows:

   ▸ If you ever *bumped* into my grandmother, you *would* probably say she *was* the perfect picture of a mean, old, grouchy grandmother.

   To put the sentence in the present time, you would write it:

   ▸ If you ever *bump* into my grandmother, you *will* probably say she is the perfect picture of a mean, old, grouchy grandmother.

   See Chapter 8.2 for a further discussion of *will* and *would.*
3. In line 3, *inside* can be omitted: it adds nothing to the meaning of the sentence (S-1).
4. The sentence that begins with *When* in line 15 and the sentence that begins with *She* in line 16 should probably be joined (S-8). What would be the best way to join them?
5. The sentence that begins with *I remember* in line 21 can be omitted (S-10). What word or words would you then need to add to the next sentence to provide a smooth transition into the short story?

**Writing Assignment**   The task is to write a paper of 300 or more words on a relative or friend. First, choose the person to write on and then follow the six steps of the writing method as you write the paper. A second sample essay is presented after the writing assignment.

**Choose the Topic.**   List some of your relatives (living or dead) or friends that you could *possibly* write about.

_____  _____  _____

_____  _____  _____

_____  _____  _____

_____  _____  _____

Look over the list and pick a person who is especially interesting to you, someone you know well enough to write about. (Don't be too quick to pick your mother, father, boyfriend, girlfriend, or spouse. The people who are closest to you are often the most difficult to write about.)

▸ Your choice: _____

**Step One: Gather Information.**

1. Using the brainstorm method, write out in the left-hand column exactly what you see when you look at your friend or relative. What would a camera with color film pick up? What are the physical characteristics? What kinds of clothes does the person typically wear?

   _____        _____

   _____        _____

   _____        _____

   _____        _____

   _____        _____

   _____        _____

   _____        _____

2. In the right-hand column, make your description more precise, as in the following examples (from different papers):

| | |
|---|---|
| *always smoking* | *always smoking a long, thin cigarette* |
| *bald head* | *shining dome of a head with bushy hair around the ears* |
| *white hair* | *snow white hair that matches the teeth he takes out at night* |
| *short and chubby* | *shaped like a loosely rolled sleeping bag* |
| *limps* | *has a hernia that forces him to tilt to the left when he walks* |
| *always bundled up* | *wears two black, ankle-length coats buttoned to his chin* |
| *red nose* | *a cherry tomato of a nose* |

3. How does your relative or friend spend time? Think in terms of what he or she does in a typical day or a typical week.

_____

_____

_____

4. What are some of your relative's or friend's favorite expressions? Here are a few examples to get you started:

▶ "It jes' ain' no use tryin' to please everybody."

▶ "Whereya at, man?"

▶ "If I ever die, don't cry over me."

▶ "When one door closes, another opens."

▶ "I can't tell you how strongly I feel about that."

▶ "Tommydamnrot"    "Horsefeathers"    "Fiddlesticks"

_____

_____

_____

Think of as many incidents (events of short duration) as you can that would tell the reader something significant about your relative or friend. Use the fourth paragraph of the Molly paper as an example. Identify these events in just a few words.

_____

_____

_____

6. Consult with someone who also knows your relative or friend and see what information that person can add to your lists.

**Step Two: Analyze the Information.**   Read over the information you have gathered and check the items that seem most significant. At this point you may want to read the student sample on page 150 for ideas on how you might use the information you have gathered. Write down three or four of the most significant things about your relative or friend. (For this step, the author of the Molly paper wrote, "old, grouchy, loving, determined.")

_____

_____

_____

**Step Three: State Your Purpose.**   State in one sentence exactly what you would like to say about your relative or friend. (Review the criteria for the purpose statement on page 115.)

_____

_____

Here are some examples from successful papers:

▸ I have a hustler for a cousin.

▸ My Aunt Birdie is a rare species of aunt that will soon become extinct; she cares more for her family than for herself.

> ► Aunt Gerdie Mae "don't take nuttin' from nobody."

> ► Mr. Terry takes care of anything that's homeless—from dogs to human beings.

> ► Though Lloyd's life was short, the time we had with him was special.

**Step Four: Make Your Plan.** You will probably need four to six paragraphs to carry out your purpose statement. In your outline, include details you will write about. Brainstorm for more details, more examples for each paragraph, if you find yourself short. You may want to include the physical description in the introductory paragraph or, like the author of the Molly paper, you may want to use a separate paragraph for it. Use the space provided below for your outline.

Here is an example of part of an outline from one student's paper:

Organizing Principle ► *Par. 3*    Mr. Terry takes care of dogs _____

Detail ► his four well-kept dogs (describe), people bring him dogs, finds _____

homes for them, the time my dog was hurt _____

_____

(your title)

Organizing Principle ► *Par. 1*    Introduction (include purpose statement) _____

Detail ► _____

_____

Organizing Principle ► *Par. 2*    _____

Detail ► _____

_____

Organizing Principle ► *Par. 3*    _____

Detail ▸ _____

_____

Organizing Principle ▸ *Par. 4*    _____

Detail ▸ _____

_____

Organizing Principle ▸ *Par. 5*    _____

Detail ▸ _____

_____

Organizing Principle ▸ *Par. 6*    Conclusion _____

Detail ▸ _____

_____

Before moving to the next step, check your outline with your instructor.

**Step Five: Write.**   Here are some suggestions to keep in mind as you write. First, pay attention to detail. Remember, the word *describe* means to tell about something *in detail.* Use the information you have gathered. You will think of more as you write. Second, let yourself become involved with the person you are writing about. Show your reader through your writing why this person is important to you in either a positive or negative sense. Third, read over the learning notes on the conclusion (page 128) and use your conclusion to make a contrasting statement or a statement about the significance of the person for you.

**Step Six: Evaluate and Edit.**   Evaluate your paper, making use of the revision checklist. Pay particular attention to the following questions:

1. Did each of your paragraphs help carry out your purpose statement? If not, did you have a valid reason for using each paragraph the way you did?

2. Did most of your detail relate directly to your purpose statement? Did you use too little or too much detail?
3. Did you use dialogue? If so, did it sound like your relative or friend talking?
4. Can any of your sentences be omitted altogether? Can any be shortened?

Edit your paper, using the editing checklist. Errors that often appear on this assignment are errors in verb agreement, verb spelling, and punctuation of dialogue.

1. *Verb agreement.* In writing about what your relative or friend does each day, you probably need to use third-person singular, present-tense verbs. (*See* Chapter 7.1.) This form calls for using the *-s* or *-es* ending for regular verbs, *has* instead of *have,* and *is* instead of *are*:

| Correct | Incorrect |
|---|---|
| She acts as if . . . | She act as if . . . |
| George has a nice . . . | George have a nice . . . |

2. *Verb spelling.* When you add *-s* or *-es* to verbs that end in *-y,* follow the rules given in Chapter 7.1. The following forms are correct:

► Ricky *flies* around the house . . .

► She *tries* her best to please . . .

3. *Punctuation of dialogue.* Follow the rules given on page 60 and in Chapter 11.7.

### PIE

**Student Sample ►**

If you ever go to visit Woodville, Kansas, you probably will meet  1
up with my grandfather. He is a very respected man in the town of  2
Woodville. The people say, "Pie was a working man, and he still works  3
when he can."  4

His real name is Johnson Tolliver, but he is known by everyone as  5
Pie. The top of his head looks like a crystal ball, except for the hair on the  6
side. Pie has a hard time getting his words out because he stutters and has  7
very few teeth. Pie is a medium-framed man and weighs about 180  8
pounds. Even though he's eighty, he can move as fast as any twelve-year-  9
old.  10

Let me tell you a little about my grandfather's past. As a boy, he 11
was alone. He had to work all the time because his mother was ill. He 12
could not attend school because of working in the field. Other little children 13
used to play as Pie worked. They would make fun of how he worked and 14
hardly ever played. 15

When Pie's mother passed away, he left home to make his own life. 16
He moved on a white man's farm. Soon after that, he married. Years 17
passed, and he had "nine head of children," as they say in those parts. As 18
soon as the children were able to walk, they were working in the field. Pie 19
worked harder than anyone else on the farm. He started out at six in the 20
morning and ended at eight at night, always trying to pay his debts to the 21
white man and make extra profits for himself. His children never had time 22
to play. My mother told me one day, "Mary, my daddy worked me so hard 23
at the age of four; you just don't know how lucky you are." He raised extra 24
corn, cattle, hogs, and chickens and was able to pay his way off the farm 25
and have enough money to buy land. 26

On this new land was a shack that was about to fall down. That's 27
where Pie and his family lived. They planted crops and worked from sunup 28
to sundown. The rest of the black people were still on the white man's land, 29
saying, "I wish I would have worked as hard as Pie and his family. Maybe 30
I would have been off this white man's land." Pie's first wife passed away 31
when she was giving birth to a child. Pie was sad but kept on with his 32
work. 33

Pie finally did remarry. Now he has a home and acres of land. He 34
bought this on his own and doesn't owe a soul. At the age of eighty, he 35
rides around in his car, with other people saying, "Pie has it real good. He 36
has a house, land, and very good children. Pie was a working man and 37
still works when he can." In Woodville, most of the blacks are still poor and 38
uneducated. To see a black man with luxuries is like seeing a king. Pie is 39
helping out some of the blacks in Woodville, but he has always said, "Peo- 40
ple, you have to work hard for what you want and make the best of it." 41

**Questions for Discussion**

1. How effective was the student in helping you get to know Pie? If
   you were "introducing" Pie to someone else, what might you say
   about him?
2. What is the purpose statement? Could it have been written more
   precisely? How? Was the student successful in carrying it out?
3. Read aloud all of the dialogue in the paper. Does it sound like real
   people talking? Was it used effectively?
4. What use did the student make of the conclusion?
5. What are the similes in paragraphs 2 and 6? Are they effective?

### An Exercise

Write a paragraph introducing Pie to others. Use your words, not the words of the student.

### Word and Sentence Use

1. What two words could be omitted in the first sentence (S-1)?
2. Can the sentence that begins in line 11 be deleted (S-10)?
3. Beginning in line 18, the student writes:

   ▶ As soon as the children were able to walk, they were working in the field.

   What other form of *work* might be substituted for *were working*?
4. Look at the sentence that begins with *He* in line 20 and ends with *himself* in line 22. In the first draft the student had written:

   ▶ He started out at six in the morning and ended up at eight at night. He always tried to pay his debts to the white man and make extra profits for himself.

   In the revised draft, the student joined the second sentence to the first by dropping the *He* and changing the verb *tried* to the participle *trying* (S-8).
5. In line 36, the words *with other people saying* are a bit awkward (S-7). How could they be changed?

## FINDING THE MOST EXACT WORD (S-3)

While you are in the process of writing your first draft, you probably should not spend too much time looking for just the right word. But as you proofread and then revise your paper, look at each word separately to see if you have chosen your words well and are saying what you want to say.

When in doubt, consult a dictionary or thesaurus. Besides giving the definition of a word, a good dictionary will also give synonyms (words of similar meanings) for many words. A thesaurus is a reference book consisting entirely of synonyms and antonyms (words of opposite meaning). Ask your instructor to recommend a complete dictionary and perhaps a thesaurus.

### SUGGESTIONS FOR USING THE MOST EXACT WORD

1. Do not use a general word like *good, bad,* or *interesting* when you can think of a more precise word. Instead of *good friend,* maybe you want to say *dependable friend, close friend, fun-loving friend.* Of course, maybe you do want to say *good friend.* If so, say it. The important thing is to make a decision about the words you use.
2. Avoid inexact words. Words like *aspects, factors,* and *things* have their uses, but all too often they are used casually and, thus, misused.
3. Do not use a slang word unless it really is the best word to say what you mean. In writing about his cousin, one student used the slang expression *freaked out:* his cousin was freaked out over religion. He was looking for an expression that was negative but not too belittling, an expression that was not overly serious. Perhaps *freaked out* was his best choice. Ordinarily, however, avoid slang words. Later in the paper the student spoke of women who were *into* religion. Certainly, he could have found a word that was not slang that could replace *into,* as used in that way.
4. It is important to try out new words from time to time, even though you will not always use them correctly. But be careful. Everyday words are usually better than high-sounding words:

| *Choose* | *Instead of* |
|---|---|
| spit | expectorate |
| his death | his demise |
| opening | aperture |

**Other Writing Assignments**

Look once again at the assignments for writing a one-paragraph description (page 142), but this time write a four- to six-paragraph paper of 300 or more words on one of the topics. Here are some other possibilities for a description essay:

1. Describe two animals fighting.
2. Describe the salesclerks who work in your favorite or least favorite store.

3. Describe people in busy shopping areas who are either selling things, preaching, or begging.
4. Describe the night before a battle.
5. Describe the worst storm you were ever in.
6. Describe the most beautiful scene in the world.
7. Describe a street corner and the group that gathers there each day.
8. Describe a jog in the park (or wherever else you jog).
9. Describe an automobile wreck that you either were in or witnessed.
10. Describe a particular tree (or any other plant) that is special to you.

## 2. The Narrative Essay

For this assignment you will write a narrative (which is simply a story) that will tell of a time when you learned something important to you. At the end of this section are suggested topics for writing other narratives.

Many students respond to this assignment by saying that they can think of nothing to write about. They are convinced that they have no story to tell. By the time you complete this assignment, however, you should find that you have in your memory many stories worth telling, worth writing down. You will discover that in its own way, your life is full of drama, not necessarily the kind you see on television, but a kind that grows out of situations that are *important to you*. The single best thing you can do in writing a narrative is to prod yourself to tell the whole story: give all the important details, report all the important dialogue, tell all the significant events within the main event.

One of our great American writers, Flannery O'Connor, has written about telling stories, "There is a certain embarrassment about being a storyteller in these times when stories are considered not quite as satisfying as statements and statements not quite as satisfying as statistics; but in the long run, a people is known, not by its statements or its statistics, but by the stories it tells"(*Mystery and Manners*). We know about Jews and Christians primarily from the stories they told, which were eventually written down to make one long story, the Bible. We know about the beginnings of Greek, and thus Western, culture from the stories the early Greeks told and Homer retold in the *Iliad* and the *Odyssey*. In your English class, you will learn more about each other and more about yourself if you will do the hard work of prodding yourself to recall some of your story so that you can tell it in detail.

Learning to write narratives will help you in other courses in college, especially when you are given such questions as the following:

1. In a history course: "Trace the events leading up to the Bolshevik Revolution."
2. In an economics course: "Tell what happened when the stock market crashed in October, 1929."
3. In a literature course: "Tell what happened when Odysseus returned home after years of trying to find his way."

## The Narrative Essay

Objective ▶   To tell in detail a story that has one main point to it.

### Suggestions for the Essay

1. Make sure you write a story, not reflections on a story. If you were in an automobile accident and went to see a lawyer about it, your lawyer would ask you to tell exactly what happened, not give your views on reckless driving or your views on how right you were and how wrong the other driver was (there would be time for that later). When you write your story, it is appropriate to use your introduction to give background information and your conclusion to write about the significance of the story for you, but most of your paper should be an account of exactly what happened.
2. For short essays choose events of short duration to write about, events that take place in an hour, half a day, a day at the most. Don't tell your reader what happened last summer or during the three weeks you worked at Sammy's Salmon Camp. Pick *one* event from last summer or one event from your work at the camp that illustrates what it was like.
3. In narrative writing one often discovers the main point of the story as one writes. Be willing to revise your essay until you make the point you really want to make. In the final draft, however, you should have a main point or purpose in mind, although you may decide not to state it outright anywhere in the essay.

4. When possible, develop conflict in your story. Conflict is the stuff powerful stories are made of. Here are three kinds of conflict you can write about:

   a. *Conflict between people.* If you are describing a disastrous canoe trip, in which you and your friends argued heatedly about whether to stop and make camp or whether to paddle on to the next campsite, describe the argument.

   b. *Conflict between an individual and the environment.* Perhaps one of the reasons the canoe trip was a disaster was because it rained and turned much colder. Write about the conflict between the canoe party and the forces of nature.

   c. *Conflict within yourself.* Perhaps you really did not want to go on the canoe trip in the first place knowing that there would be bad weather, but your friends put a lot of pressure on you. You were torn between doing what they wanted you to do and what you wanted to do yourself. Write about the conflict within yourself.

5. Make use of your skills in presenting detail and, when it helps your story to come alive, recording dialogue.

---

The following is taken from Richard Wright's famous book, *Black Boy*. As you read it, ask yourself what the main point of the story is.

One evening my mother told me that thereafter I would have to do the shopping for the food. She took me to the corner store to show me the way. I was proud; I felt like a grownup. The next afternoon I looped the basket over my arm and went down the pavement toward the store. When I reached the corner, a gang of boys grabbed me, knocked me down, snatched the money, took the basket, and sent me running home in panic. That evening I told my mother what had happened, but she made no comment; she sat down at once, wrote another note, gave me more money, and sent me out to the grocery again. I crept down the steps and saw the same gang of boys playing down the street. I ran back into the house.

"What's the matter?" my mother asked.

"It's those same boys," I said. "They'll beat me."

"You've got to get over that," she said. "Now go on."

"I'm scared," I said.

"Go on and don't pay any attention to them," she said.

I went out of the door and walked briskly down the sidewalk, praying that the gang would not molest me. But when I came abreast of them someone shouted.

"There he is!"

They came toward me and I broke into a wild run toward home. They overtook me and flung me to the pavement. I yelled, pleaded, kicked, but they wrenched the money out of my hand. They yanked me to my feet, gave me a few slaps, and sent me home sobbing. My mother met me at the door.

"They b-b-beat me," I gasped. "They t-t-took the m-m-money."

I started up the steps, seeking the shelter of the house.

"Don't you come in here," my mother warned me.

I froze in my tracks and stared at her.

"But they're coming after me," I said.

"You just stay right where you are," she said in a deadly tone. "I'm going to teach you this night to stand up and fight for yourself."

She went into the house and I waited, terrified, wondering what she was about. Presently she returned with more money and another note; she also had a long heavy stick.

"Take this money, this note, and this stick," she said. "Go to the store and buy those groceries. If those boys bother you, then fight."

I was baffled. My mother was telling me to fight, a thing she had never done before.

"But, I'm scared," I said.

"Don't you come into this house until you've gotten those groceries," she said.

"They'll beat me; they'll beat me," I said.

"Then stay in the streets; don't come back here!"

I ran up the steps and tried to force my way past her into the house. A stinging slap came on my jaw. I stood on the sidewalk, crying.

"Please let me wait until tomorrow," I begged.

"No," she said, "go now! If you come back into this house without those groceries, I'll whip you!"

She slammed the door and I heard the key turn in the lock. I shook with fright. I was alone upon the dark, hostile streets and gangs were after me. I had the choice of being beaten at home or away from home. I clutched the stick, crying, trying to reason. If I were beaten at home, there was absolutely nothing that I could do about it, but if I were beaten in the streets, I had a chance to fight and defend myself. I walked slowly down the sidewalk, coming closer to the gang of boys, holding the stick tightly. I was so full of fear that I could scarcely breathe. I was almost upon them now.

"There he is again!" the cry went up.

They surrounded me quickly and began to grab for my hand.

"I'll kill you!" I threatened.

They closed in. In blind fear I let the stick fly, feeling it crack against a boy's skull. I swung again, lamming another skull then another. Realizing that they would retaliate if I let up for but a second, I fought to lay them low, to knock them cold, to kill them so that they could not strike back at me. I flayed with tears in my eyes, teeth clenched, stark fear making me throw every ounce of my strength behind each blow. I hit again and again, dropping the money and the grocery list. The boys scattered, yelling, nursing their heads, staring at me in utter disbelief. They had never seen such a frenzy. I stood panting, egging them on, taunting them to come on and fight. When they refused, I ran after them and they tore out for their homes, screaming. The parents of the boys rushed into the streets and threatened me, and for the first time in my life I shouted at grown-ups, telling them that I would give them the same if they bothered me. I finally found my grocery list and the money and went to the store. On the way back I kept my stick poised for instant use, but there was not a single boy in sight. That night I won the right to the streets of Memphis.

### Questions for Discussion

1. What is the main point of the story? How would you write a purpose statement for it?
2. Was Richard's mother acting responsibly in making Richard fight? Have you ever had a similar experience? Must violence always be met with violence?
3. Where is the conflict in the story?
4. How did Wright develop suspense in the story? What did he do in telling the story that made you want to read on?
5. Read some of the dialogue aloud. Does it sound real to you? Can you actually hear Richard and his mother talking?
6. Did you like the story? Why? Why not?

### An Exercise

Name, in order, the events that made up the story. (You should be able to identify six to eight events *within* the story.)

1. *Richard's mother showed him how to shop.*      3. _____

2. _____      4. _____

5. _____    7. _____

6. _____    8. _____

**Writing Assignment**    Tell a story of 300 words or more about a time you learned something important to you. First, choose a particular event, and then follow the six steps of the writing method as you write your paper. Two
student samples follow.

**Choose the Topic.**    Using the brainstorm method, name as many
events from your past as you can think of in which you learned something important. The categories below should help you think of such
events.

1. Times you learned that not all promises should be kept:

_____

_____

_____

2. Times you learned a bitter lesson:

_____

_____

_____

3. Times you learned something important about the opposite sex:

_____

_____

_____

4. Times you learned not to _____ ever
again:

_____

_____

_____

5. Times you learned to take care of yourself:

_____

_____

_____

6. Times you learned that mothers (or fathers) are not always right (or wrong):

_____

_____

_____

7. Times you learned what the police are like:

_____

_____

_____

8. Times you learned to grin and bear it:

_____

_____

_____

9. Other times you learned something important to you:

_____

_____

_____

Now is a good time to read the student samples for ideas. Pick one of the above events to write about. Ask yourself if you can write at least 300 words on that particular event. Write the name of the event here:

_____

**Step One: Gather Information.**    Write down at least four episodes within the main event. Use the exercise following the Wright story as a guide.

1. _____

2. _____

3. _____

4. _____

5. _____

6. _____

Prepare the worksheet below, filling out as much of it as you can. Follow this order for each episode.

episode within the main event _____    who did what _____

who said what _____

what you felt _____

_____    _____
(first episode)

_____

_____

_____    _____
(second episode)

_____

_____

_____    _____
(third episode)

_____

_____
(fourth episode)

_____
(fifth episode)

_____
(sixth episode)

**Step Two: Analyze the Information.**   Ask yourself the following questions:

1.  Where is the conflict in the story? How can you develop it?
2.  Where is the story going? What is it really about?
3.  What dialogue might you use in your narrative? (Although dialogue is not essential, it often helps make a story come alive for the reader.)

**Step Three: State the Purpose.**   The narrative is one kind of writing in which the purpose statement is often concealed until the middle or the end of the paper, or even left out altogether. But you should know where you are headed in your narrative and what you want to accomplish. Thus, you should have a purpose statement in mind, even though it may not be expressed. Look over your work so far and write your purpose statement.

_____

_____

_____

One way to prepare your purpose statement for this assignment is simply to fill in the blanks in the following sentence:

▶ I learned _____ the time _____

_____.

A purpose statement for Wright's story could be "Richard Wright learned how to take care of himself the time his mother forced him to fight." (As pointed out above, once you begin to write you may find that you need to change your purpose statement and begin again.)

**Step Four: Make Your Plan.** Write an informal outline that will help you to accomplish your purpose. If you quote a conversation with several exchanges, you may not be able to set up your outline in the usual paragraph form since you will have to begin new paragraphs each time the speaker shifts. Instead, let each episode within the event you are writing about constitute one of the main points in the body of your outline. You will of course want to make use of the information-gathering worksheet as you write your outline, but remember the outline itself is not information gathering; it is rather *a plan to help you carry out your purpose.*

You may want to use the introduction to place the event you are writing about in a larger context by mentioning other events that led up to it. And you may want to use the conclusion to show the significance of the event for you.

**Step Five: Write.** As you write, make sure you are telling the whole story: your narrative should have a beginning, a middle, and an end. Also, make sure you are not going off in directions that take you away from your purpose. If you can build suspense into your narrative, do so. Emphasize the conflict as defined in the learning notes. Concentrate on using detail and, when it seems helpful, dialogue. Finally, be careful to give your sentences variety. (Avoid using too many *ands* and *thens* to join sentences or clauses.)

**Step Six: Evaluate and Edit.** Evaluate your paper.

1. Did you tell what happened, or is your story mostly reflections on what happened or what could have happened?
2. Did you keep the main point of the story before you the whole time? If not, where did you go off in another direction?
3. Did your story take place within a short period of time? If not, what was the time span of your story?
4. Do your sentences flow smoothly into each other, or are they choppy? Did you use too many *ands* and *thens* to connect sentences and clauses?

Edit your paper, using the checklist on the back inside cover. Watch out especially for the following errors: run-on sentences, tense confusion, and errors in punctuating dialogue.

**Student Samples ►**
**A**

|  |  |
|---|---|
| The streets were crowded with people. They were bumping, shoving, and stabbing each other with their packages, which were huge in size and numerous in quantity. I was staggering down Broad Street, a part of those shoving people that day. And I was gasping for fresh air, not air polluted with cheap perfume, donuts, and the sickening smell of new clothes. I was searching for the advertisement with the famous Icee Cola Bear so that I could quench the sizzling fire that was burning in my aching throat. I saw it! The sign was up ahead at the next shop. I made a mad dash for the door. | 1 2 3 4 5 6 7 8 9 |

It was inside this store that I first learned something important to me about the opposite sex. During the mad dash to the store I collided with a handsome young man and sprayed my packages here and there. So, like a real gentleman, he helped me collect my packages. He apologized for bumping into me, and we introduced ourselves. His name was Anthony Gaines, and he was a teacher of karate at some school or other. I don't remember now, and I didn't take it in then because I was too busy gazing attentively at his tantalizing brown eyes, his sensuous lips, his protruding muscles, and his gorgeous brown legs, which showed beneath his tan shorts. He was just a well put-together dude.

Neither of us was in a hurry, so we shared an Icee Cola and a pretty conversation while he waited for his chicken and french fries to be delivered. It was then that he started his fast talking, letting his charm and arrogance go to work for him. He talked about how he fell in love with me when we bumped into each other and how he would like to know me better, and he asked me what my phone number was and where I lived, etc. Not succumbing to his vicious charms, I gave him a fake phone number and address and promised to think about him until he came to pick me up that night to go to a drive-in movie.

"Ha! Ha! Ha!" I laughed when I left the store. I laughed long and hard. The handsome young man thought he was using me. I knew I had used him. I laughed because I wondered how he would accept defeat when he dialed the wrong number. I laughed more; I was the victor.

10 11 12 13 14 15 16 17 18 19

20 21 22 23 24 25 26 27 28

29 30 31 32

**Questions for Discussion**

1. The student said in line 11 that this was the time she learned something about the opposite sex. But is this story really about what she learned from the handsome young man? If not, what is it about? What did she learn? What would be a good title?

2. Does the story read smoothly all the way through? If not, where are the rough places?
3. Except for her laughing in line 29, the student used no dialogue. Would dialogue have improved the paper? How could it have been used?
4. Were you surprised by the ending?
5. What did you like best about the essay?

### Word and Sentence Use

1. In line 4, the student began a sentence with *and*. It is perfectly legitimate to begin a sentence with *and*—occasionally—if you want to give emphasis to the sentence *and* introduces.
2. The student said in line 10 that she went into a *store*. But from what she told us, the place she entered does not sound like a store. What would be a more exact word to use (S-3)?
3. In line 13, the student began a sentence with *so*. Does *so* add anything to the quality of the writing (S-1)?
4. In lines 16 and 17, the student speaks of being "too busy gazing attentively at his tantalizing brown eyes . . ." The wording is somewhat redundant (S-1). How could it be changed?
5. Is the last sentence in the second paragraph the best way to bring that paragraph to an end? How might you rewrite it?

### An Exercise

The student uses quite a few adjectives to "dress up" her nouns. Some of them follow. Are they effective? Do they help you experience what she experienced?

| | |
|---|---|
| line   7—sizzling fire | line 17—protruding muscles |
| line   7—aching throat | line 18—gorgeous brown legs |
| line   8—mad dash | line 21—pretty conversation |
| line 17—tantalizing brown eyes | line 26—vicious charm |

Replace each of the above adjectives with one of your own.

This student went beyond the instructions and used a week or so as the setting for this narrative, but in telling the story she concentrated on just two events within the week.

**B**      THE TIME I LEARNED TO STAY AWAY FROM DRUGS

    One summer afternoon while I was sitting in my living room read-    1
ing, a friend knocked on the door. "Who is it?" I said. "Jackie," she re-    2

sponded. "What's happening, Jackie? You don't look good." "I know," she  3
said, "Can I bring some drugs in here for awhile?" As she entered, the  4
police drove up to the edge of the project with sirens screaming. "Slam  5
the door," Jackie said, and I did. "Where can I put this at?" "Here," I an-  6
swered, "under my carpet. They'll never find it."  7

In the meantime, the police had found my apartment and were  8
banging and kicking the door. "Open, or we'll break it down," they  9
shouted. I ran to the door and opened it. Pushing me aside, the police  10
entered my house.  11

"Here's the little bitch," one of the police officers said, grabbing  12
Jackie by the arm. "Where are the drugs?" he asked her. "What drugs?"  13
she said. "We saw you pick them up, and we followed you here." The other  14
police officer began to search the house when I said, "You have a search  15
warrant?" "Who the hell is this smart bitch?" was the answer. More officers  16
came in. One started hitting at the bar with a hatchet, then at the sofa and  17
chair. Another was upstairs emptying the drawers and taking the clothes  18
out of the closet. When they finished, everything was destroyed, totally. The  19
icebox was empty, meat and food were on the kitchen floor, the furniture  20
was smashed and chopped to pieces, clothes were in the bathtub in wa-  21
ter, and glass was all over the place. But no drugs. "Take that Miss Lady  22
out of her house," one officer said.  23

As I sat down on the sofa crying, one officer grabbed me and said,  24
"Where are the drugs?" When I didn't answer, he handcuffed me. Out the  25
door Jackie and I went, into the police car. People were everywhere, look-  26
ing and whispering. They knew we were being arrested by narcotic agents.  27

Upon arriving at Central Lockup, I was booked as an accessory  28
and for having drugs with the intent to distribute. Jackie was booked with  29
having drugs, armed robbery, and for the simple reason that she was a  30
junkie.  31

I stayed in jail about a week, where I was questioned and con-  32
stantly asked where the uncut heroin was. Constantly, I said, "I don't know."  33
My lawyer was trying to get me out of jail, but they placed me on $10,000  34
bail, so there I sat.  35

In the meantime, Jackie had broken and needed heroin bad. The  36
officers kept telling her that if she would tell them where the heroin was  37
they would fix her up. Jackie, whose cell was right next to mine, was very  38
sick. She screamed often. "I need some stuff bad," she said over and over  39
again. "Someone please help me."  40

All I could do was cry and remember the great friendship we had,  41
knowing that if Jackie told where the drugs were I was going to get fifteen  42
years in jail. Suddenly, maybe for the first time, my life began to be impor-  43
tant to me. I thought about going back to college, studying hard to be an  44
RN. At the time I was twenty years old and just beginning to have fun.  45

Jackie, lying in the jail cell next to me, suffering and looking at me said, "Daphne, you're a good friend and I love you with all my heart. You helped me when no one else would. You fed me, gave me money for drugs when my parents wouldn't. Sometimes, I used to think you were doing me great harm by giving me the money, but I knew you loved me." 46 47 48 49 50

"Jackie," I said, "I didn't know what to do. I was all upset worrying about you. I was afraid if I didn't give you the money, you would steal something or break into a store or even shoot someone. One side of me said to give you the money; one side said not to. I knew I was doing you great harm, but your mother couldn't tell you anything and who was I? Just a friend with tears in my eyes." 51 52 53 54 55 56

Jackie said something I'll never forget. "I'm going to die in here because I am never going to tell them where the drugs are at because I want you to have a beautiful life, the one I didn't have." Laughing, I said, "Girl, you're not going to die. Stop saying that." 57 58 59 60

While sweating out what the police call "cold turkey," Jackie died. For a while I just stared at her, and then I began to scream uncontrollably, "Someone please help her." A police officer, who was one of them who arrested us, came to the cell and said, "I'm going to help her if you tell me where the drugs are." For a full minute, I looked at him with tears in my eyes, knowing she was dead. I just sat on the concrete floor and looked at him. 61 62 63 64 65 66 67

Someone came and removed her body. I fell into deep thought for a long time. Then I was released because they never found the drugs. 68 69

### Questions for Discussion

1. What is the story about? Does the title capture the most important meaning of the story?
2. Describe the conflict in the story.
3. In line 43, the student says that for the first time her life began to be important to her. What did the story have to do with that insight?
4. Does the story seem real to you? Why or why not? Do you think the writer exaggerated at any point in the narrative? Explain.

**Additional Writing Assignments**

Using the suggestions for the narrative described above, write an essay of 300 words or more on one of the following topics.

1. A mountaintop experience (a time that was so perfect, so meaningful that the heavens and earth seemed to touch).
2. Your most embarrassing experience.
3. The funniest thing that ever happened to you.

4. The strangest (most unexplainable) thing you ever experienced or witnessed.
5. A turning point in your life.
6. An event that marked your passage from adolescence to adulthood (a time that you were forced to grow up).
7. A story from your life that could have as its main point the quotation from Shakespeare's *Hamlet,* "To thine own self be true."
8. A time you should have kept your mouth shut.

## 3. The Process (or How to) Essay

A process paper is often called a "how to" paper because it tells you how to do or make a particular thing. The explanation of the six-step writing method (page 92) is an example of process writing. You might be asked to write several process papers in college. In a political science class, for example, you could be asked to tell how a bill becomes a law. Here you would begin with the legislator or private citizen who first formulates a bill that he or she would like to see enacted into law, and then you would tell step-by-step what must be done until the president finally signs the bill and it becomes the law of the land. In a biology class you could be asked to show how photosynthesis works. In an education class you could be asked to explain how you would teach a blind person—step by step—to ride a bus.

The key point to remember in writing a process paper is that you tell how to do or make something a step at a time, from beginning to end. The form of a process paper is much like the form of a narrative, and that is why it comes after the narrative in this text. Both essays are based on a chronological sequence: one thing leads to another, and then to another, and then to another.

Some students ask why they should write a process essay at all. Why not just make a list of instructions, such as a recipe in a cookbook? If the main point is to show how to do or make something, why does the paper have to be in essay form? The answer to this question lies in the meaning of the word *essay.* In this text an essay is being defined as a short literary composition on a single subject presenting the personal views of the author. Thus, in a process paper, you should make your views known and say *why* one should do or make the thing you are describing. As you write the essay, help your readers learn from your experience. You can't do that just by making a list.

The assignment is to write a paper of 300 or more words in which you tell how to do or make something that you do well. Once you have learned the form of a process paper, you will be able to use it in writing process papers on quite different assignments, such as those mentioned above.

# THE PROCESS (OR HOW TO) ESSAY

Objective ▶ To explain clearly, step-by-step, how to do or make something.

### SUGGESTIONS FOR THE ESSAY

1. Be clear. Keep in mind the audience you are writing to, and ask yourself if the people reading your paper could actually do what you are showing them how to do. In order to be clear, write your process essay in steps and define all terms that might be unclear to your particular audience. If, for example, you are writing to your class telling them how to master the skill of editing, you will need to define *editing* if the class has not yet talked about what editing is. If the class has already discussed the term, you will not need to define it.

2. In your first paragraph, in addition to including your purpose statement, you may want to tell *why* it is important to do or make the thing you are explaining and you may also want to tell how you happened to learn this skill. One student began her paper as follows:

> If you want to decorate your living room for a special occasion, try making a flower arrangement. I've worked at a florist shop for the last three years and have discovered what a nice touch a flower arrangement can add to a room. In this paper, you will see just how easy it is to arrange flowers.

3. In your purpose statement you should both state what you are going to explain how to do and also say one thing about the process of doing it. In the example above the student not only stated that her paper would show how to make a flower arrangement, but also that arranging flowers was *easy*. Thus, she must accomplish two things in her paper: first, she must explain the steps of flower arranging; and second, she must persuade the reader to accept her point of view, namely, that it is *easy*. If she had a different point of view, she would need to state her purpose differently, perhaps as follows:

▶ Making a flower arrangement can be fun.

▶ Arranging flowers is good therapy.

▶ To me, arranging flowers is an art.

4. If you need materials to do or make the thing you are explaining list everything that is needed, as your first step. If you are explaining how to make your favorite dish, for example, you should list the necessary ingredients first. But use common sense. In explaining how to shoot free throws in basketball, you don't have to tell your readers that they need a basketball and a basketball court.

5. Group your steps into logical units. There might be fifteen actual steps to changing a tire, but you don't need fifteen paragraphs to explain how to do it. You might want one paragraph on gathering the necessary equipment, another on jacking up the car, another on actually changing the tire, and a final paragraph on lowering the car from the jack and putting on the hubcap. Three to five paragraphs should be enough for the body of most process papers. Remember, you are writing an essay, not simply writing a list of instructions as you would in a recipe book.

6. Use smooth transition sentences to connect your paragraphs. If you have three paragraphs in the body of your paper, you may want to begin your transition sentences as follows:

▶ First, you . . .

▶ And then you . . .

▶ Finally, you . . .

(Note that a comma follows *first* and *finally* but not *and then.*) If you have four or more paragraphs in the body of your paper, you may want to use numbers—*first, second, third, fourth,* and so on—to introduce the paragraphs, perhaps substituting *finally* for the last number.

7. In the body of the paper, when you are giving instructions, address your audience in the second person: "First, gather all of the necessary equipment . . . Second, let your engine . . . Third, crawl under . . . ." In each sentence *you* is understood.

As you read the following essay, ask yourself if you could change the oil in an automobile from these instructions. You may even want to try doing it.

### HOW TO CHANGE OIL

With prices as they are today, people are trying to figure out ways  1
to economize. Americans are wising up and wanting to learn how to do  2
simple and easy maintenance on their cars. Changing your own oil is one  3
way you can save plenty of money. If you were to bring your car to a  4
garage for an oil change, you would find that he would charge you about  5
$15.00 and maybe take a whole day. What many people don't realize is  6
that you can change the oil yourself for about $5.00 and fifteen minutes of  7
your time. So for those who don't know how to change their oil, this is how  8
it is done.  9

First, gather all of the necessary equipment. You will need a jack,  10
a blanket to lie on or a creeper, a wrench to fit the nut on the oil pan, an  11
oil filter wrench, a bucket to catch the oil, an oil filter, and new oil. Ask a  12
salesman at an auto supply store to help you pick out the right wrenches,  13
oil filter, and oil.  14

Second, let your engine run for about five minutes to get the oil  15
hot. Turn the motor off and put the emergency brake on. Then jack the car  16
up just high enough so that you can fit under it without any trouble. Before  17
you get under the car, make sure that the bucket, the wrenches for the oil  18
pan nut, and the oil filter are all close by. If you have a creeper, use it to  19
slide under the car, but, if you do not, throw an old blanket on the ground  20
to prevent your clothes from getting dirty.  21

Third, crawl under the car and look for the oil pan, behind the  22
radiator, under the engine block. At the corner of the oil pan there will be  23
a nut about a half inch wide. Put the bucket under the nut and loosen it.  24
Be careful, because the oil may be hot. After the nut is off, let the oil drain  25
into the bucket for about five minutes. Put the nut back on and make sure  26
it is very tight.  27

Fourth, look for the oil filter. It is next to the oil pan and is about the  28
size of a man's wrist. It should be only hand tight, but if not, use the oil filter  29
wrench to take it off. Some oil will still be in the filter; let it drain. Now you  30
have the option of either keeping the old filter or using the new one. (You  31
should change the filter at least every other oil change.) If you decide to  32
put on the new filter, take a little of the old oil and rub it on the rubber  33
gasket around the filter to make a better seal. Tighten the filter only hand  34
tight as you screw it in.  35

Fifth, to put fresh oil in the engine, raise the hood and look on the  36

side of your engine for a cap that screws into the engine block. It usually 37
says "oil." Take the cap off and put the right amount of oil in your engine, 38
usually four or five quarts. After the oil is in the car, run the engine for a few 39
minutes and examine the nut and the oil filter to see if any leaks formed. If 40
not, lower your car from the jack and put the equipment away. 41

You see, changing your oil wasn't hard, and it saved you $10.00. 42

### Questions for Discussion

1. Could you actually change the oil in your car from these instructions? Are any steps not clear? Is any step left out?
2. What is the purpose statement?
3. What is the organizing principle of each paragraph?
4. Did the author overuse transition words like *then, now,* or *next*?
5. Should the author have defined any terms? If so, what?

### Word and Sentence Use

1. In line 2 the student uses a slang expression *wising up.* How could
   he say the same thing without using slang (S-3)?
2. In line 3, he speaks of *simple and easy* maintenance. Why is it
   incorrect to use these two adjectives together (S-1)?
3. In line 5, he uses the pronoun *he* incorrectly; it has no clear antecedent (PA). How could he correct the mistake?

**Writing Assignment**    **Choose the Topic.**   Brainstorm for as many specific topics as you can
think of under the following general headings:

1. How to do something relating to automobiles:

   *(how to change oil)* _____    _____

   _____    _____

2. How to do or make something relating to music or art:

   _____    _____

   _____    _____

3. How to do something relating to sports:

   _____    _____

_____   _____

4. How to do or make something relating to homemaking:

_____   _____

_____   _____

5. How to do something relating to pets:

_____   _____

_____   _____

6. How to do something relating to study skills:

_____   _____

_____   _____

7. How to do something relating to raising children:

_____   _____

_____   _____

Or, consider writing on one of these topics:

8. How to succeed (or not succeed) in the military

9. How to win over the opposite sex

10. How to survive in college

11. How to make your first million

12. How to spend a rainy weekend

13. How to catch a big fish

14. How to plan a party

15. How to plan a trip

Now choose a topic that you would enjoy writing on and that you know enough about. Make sure that your topic is not too technical, on the one hand, or too general in scope, on the other. Write your topic here:

_____

**Step One: Gather Information.**   In a process paper, information gathering is a short but important process. In the left-hand column below, list the steps that your reader must follow to do or make the thing you are explaining.

_____    _____

_____    _____

_____    _____

_____    _____

_____    _____

_____    _____

_____    _____

Now look at each step carefully and see if you need to include additional steps, steps within steps, steps between steps. Write these in the right-hand column. Remember, your directions must be perfectly clear.

Look over your lists and see what equipment or materials, if any, your reader will need to gather before beginning. Write them below.

_____    _____

_____    _____

_____    _____

**Step Two: Analyze the Information.**   See what steps you can group together in a logical way, so that you will not have too many paragraphs in the body of your paper. Remember, you are writing an essay, not making a list. What terms will you need to define? What steps will be particularly hard to explain? Is there anything you can leave out and still be clear in what you have to say?

**Step Three: State Your Purpose.**   What word or words best describe the process you are explaining? Choose words like easy, difficult, fun, dangerous, important, relaxing.

---

Such descriptive words can help you construct a purpose statement. (But note that you need not use the descriptive word itself.)

  a.  *Descriptive word:* fun
      *Purpose statement:* Preparing for a trip is almost as much fun as the trip itself.
  b.  *Descriptive word:* difficult
      *Purpose statement:* Giving your dog a bath is more complicated than you might think.
  c.  *Descriptive word:* dangerous
      *Purpose statement:* In charging a battery with jumper cables, you must be very careful.
  d.  *Descriptive word:* easy (if motivated)
      *Purpose statement:* If you like to clap your hands and stomp your feet, you can learn to play the drums.

Keeping your descriptive word (or words) in mind, state your purpose.

---

---

**Step Four: Make Your Plan.**   Decide what you will include in your introduction, and then group the individual steps you are explaining in a logical way. (Three to five paragraphs in the body of your paper should be enough.) Instead of detail, under each of your paragraph headings list the individual steps. The student who wrote the paper on changing oil outlined his third paragraph this way:

Organizing Principle ▸ *Par. 3*   *Steps before you crawl under the car*

Steps ▸ *run engine, jack up car, get bucket ready, wrenches, blanket or creeper*

Write your outline in the space below. Try to use three to five paragraphs in the body.

_____
(title)

Organizing Principle ▸ *Par. 1*    Introduction _____

Organizing Principle ▸ *Par. 2*    _____

Steps ▸ _____

_____

Organizing Principle ▸ *Par. 3*    _____

Steps ▸ _____

_____

Organizing Principle ▸ *Par. 4*    _____

Steps ▸ _____

_____

Organizing Principle ▸ *Par. 5*    _____

Steps ▸ _____

_____

Organizing Principle ▸ *Par. 6*    _____

Steps ▸ _____

_____

Organizing Principle ▸ *Par. 7*    Conclusion _____

_____

_____

**Step Five: Write.**   As you write, try most of all to be perfectly clear. If your audience is the class, write to them: ask yourself if particular class members you have gotten to know will actually be able to do the thing you are describing. Be sure to define any terms that your audience is not likely to understand. Use numerals when appropriate. (See the learning notes on page 178.)

Also, try to give variety to your sentences. Avoid the following kind of writing:

First, you run around the track once. Then you do forty jumping jacks. Then you do thirty knee bends. Next, you do thirty back bends. Then you run around the track one more time. Finally, you catch your breath and relax.

One way to avoid such monotonous writing is to say *why* you should do the things you are writing about. The above passage could be written as follows:

First, jog around the track once slowly to loosen up your leg muscles and to increase the flow of adrenalin in your body. Then, to loosen up other muscles, do your warm-up exercises: forty jumping jacks, thirty sit ups, and thirty back-bends. You should be breathing hard by now, but you aren't quite through. Before you begin the race, run around the track one more time, at a slightly faster pace than before. Now catch your breath and relax completely.

**Step Six: Evaluate and Edit.**   Evaluate your paper.

1. Is *every* step of your essay clear: If not, where is it not clear? What can you do to make it clear?
2. Does your purpose statement meet the criteria set forth in *step three* on page 175?
3. Does your paper sound choppy when you read it aloud? At what point do you notice any choppiness? How might you change it?

Edit your paper using the checklist on the back inside cover of this book. Two kinds of errors that often appear in this essay are pronoun person shifts and run-on sentences.

1. *Pronoun person shifts* (PPS). Do not change the person of a pronoun within the same sentence unless you have a valid reason for doing so. (See Chapter 10.5.) What is the error in the following sentence?

   ▶ One has to walk very slowly, breathing deeply, if you are going to make it to the top.

2. *Run-on sentences* (RO). You cannot join two sentences (or independent clauses) with *then* or *next*, but you can join them with *and* or a semicolon. (See Chapter 11.5.) The following is a run-on sentence. Correct it.

▸ First, you make a white sauce, then you begin adding water slowly.

## WRITING NUMBERS

Numbers can be either spelled out or written as numerals. As a general rule, spell out numbers that can be written as one or two words: *forty, sixty-three, five hundred, two million, three-fourths.* Use numerals for all other numbers (*10,401, 325,* and so forth). Errors in writing numbers or numerals are designated N in the editing checklist.

### EXCEPTIONS

1. Spell out all numbers that begin sentences, for example:

▸ Two hundred and forty-one people are still missing.

2. Use numerals for the following:
   a. Most dates (October 12, 1938). But spell out *the twelfth of October.*
   b. Most dollar amounts ($10.51, $3.01, $17,00). But spell out numbers used to indicate general amounts (*a hundred dollars, five million dollars,* and so on).
   c. Street numbers *(42 Legare Street).*
   d. Percentage amounts *(20 percent of your earnings).*
   e. Times used with A.M. and P.M. *(8:00 A.M.).* But spell out *five o'clock* and *six-thirty* when used without A.M. and P.M.
   f. Page numbers and line numbers *(page 42, line 15).*
   g. Numbers in a list, set off by indention:

   ▸ You will need the following:
   | | |
   |---|---|
   | 5 lbs. of chicken | 3 onions |
   | 2 cups of cream | 1 lb. of bacon |
   | 1½ cups of flour | ½ lb. of mushrooms |

3. If you must write one number in a sentence as a numeral, write all the other numbers as numerals: "I caught 416 pounds of fish, 50 pounds of shrimp, and 91 dozen crabs last summer."

### HYPHENS

Use a hyphen (-) with all two-word numbers from twenty-one to ninety-nine and with all fractions (three-fourths, nine-tenths, and so forth).

### EXERCISE

Five of the following are incorrect. Correct them.

1. Nineteen hundred and one (a date)
2. Six o'clock
3. 5:30 P.M.
4. Five dollars and fourteen cents
5. Page sixteen
6  51 Canal Street
7. 8 o'clock
8. 56 percent
9. $10,550.00
10. Two-thirty P.M.

## 4. The Example Essay

An example essay is one in which you support your point of view on a particular topic simply by giving examples. Learning how to use examples in your writing will not only help you in writing an example essay but also in practically every essay you write. In writing about the civil rights battles in the 1960s, particular examples of the effects of segregation on black children will make your paper less abstract, more concrete, more real. In arguing against capital punishment, particular examples of people who were executed and then later proven innocent will certainly enhance your argument. In describing a particular character from a novel, examples of the character's actions in the story that illustrate your thesis (or point of view) will strengthen your essay.

Your readers will respond to examples because they make your writing interesting, easier to understand, and convincing. Notice how general—and how unconvincing—the following paragraph is:

My parents mean the most to me because without my mother and the help of my father, I would not be here today. My parents taught me how to conduct myself around others. They have given me all the things I need and most of the things I want.

The author has given no examples of *how* her parents have helped her, *what* they have taught her and given her. With examples, the same thoughts could be expanded and expressed as follows:

My parents mean the most to me because without my mother and the help of my father, I would not be here today. My mother stopped work when I was born just so that she could be with me. She made sure that I was held a lot, that I ate well, and that I got proper medical attention. My father taught me how to swim, ride a bicycle, take care of myself in the woods, and most important of all, he taught me how to do my school work. Together, my parents taught me how to conduct myself around others. They taught me to say "sir" and "ma'am" to adults. They taught me to do unto everyone as I would have them do unto me. They have always provided me with clothing, food, and enough money to buy the essentials. Though my parents are not wealthy, they did buy me a piano, knowing how much I love music, and they did manage to send me to this community college.

Your assignment is to make a statement about a particular group of people or a type of entertainment or activity and then defend your statement, in an essay of 300 or more words, by giving examples that illustrate your point of view.

## THE EXAMPLE ESSAY

Objective ▶ To support your point of view on a particular subject solely by giving examples.

### SUGGESTIONS FOR THE ESSAY

1. Offer at least three examples to illustrate your point of view. If you are making a particular point about children's television programs, give examples of at least three programs that prove your point. If you are making a general statement about high school teachers, give examples of at least three particular high school teachers who illustrate the point you are making.
2. Play fair with your reader. Don't make statements that are generally not true and then use unique examples to back them up. The statement "Teen-age marriages are usually successful" is statistically untrue. It is not playing fair for a writer to claim that the statement is true and then back up the claim by giving as

examples a few teen-age marriages that were successful. However, the same writer could state, and state fairly, "Contrary to popular belief, teen-age marriages are sometimes successful." And then the writer could use several examples to back up that position.

3. For emphasis, and to catch your reader's attention, place your most convincing example first.

4. Consider using an example to begin your paper. One way to attract your reader's attention in the introduction is by giving an example of the point you will illustrate in your essay. (See the student sample on page 186.)

5. Even though you are writing an example paper, avoid the expression *for example*. When you give an example, it is usually clear that that is what you are doing. The test is simply to read what you have written without *for example* and see if anything is lost by the omission.

### GOSSIPING ABOUT GOSSIP

**Student Sample ►**

There is something in today's society that everyone loves to do, and that is gossip. Everybody loves to gossip, whether standing on a street corner, sitting in a beauty salon, or even talking on the telephone. Everybody gossips.

On a bright sunny afternoon, you'll see a small group of young men standing on the corner talking. They are not just talking street talk, like "Hey man, what's happening?" They are gossiping. There is one person saying, "Hey man, did you hear what happened to Joe?" The other will say, "No man, what happened?" "Man, Joe got caught with dope last night. I heard he'll be spending a good while behind bars."

Next, visit a beauty salon on a Saturday morning when the weather is nice, and you'll hear everything from Bill changing jobs to Norman getting picked up for stealing the night before. One Saturday I was getting my hair fixed and suddenly others started coming in like crazy. After everyone got settled, the gossip started. One lady broke out with "Did you all hear about what happened to Janice last night?" The others replied, "No, tell us." The lady then started this long conversation about how Janice's husband found her sleeping with another man. What she said that for I don't know, but it surely started something. Everyone was shouting, "What did he do?" She said, "He called her mother and then kicked her and her man out." They seemed satisfied with the answer, but I wasn't. I am sick of gossip.

On any day of the week at any time, telephones stay busy with

gossip. Last summer I was working at a hospital on the switchboard with    24
an old lady. One day when we were receiving and putting through calls,    25
she ran across a "hot" line. Instead of plugging up the call and letting it    26
be, she decided to listen in on it. After a few minutes of listening, she was    27
dialing away to her friends telling them what she had heard. She said,    28
"Jerry, guess what I just heard?" Jerry replied, "What?" "Girl," she said,    29
"Patrona is coming in to have her baby, but Dan isn't the father." Jerry must    30
have asked fifty questions before they hung up. Later that afternoon I quit    31
because I didn't want to go there every day hearing that sort of thing.    32

So you see, everybody gossips. Whether it be men or women,    33
young or old, everybody does it. Gossip may be funny, but it can also be    34
very depressing.    35

### Questions for Discussion

1. What is the function of the second sentence of the first paragraph?
   How does it relate to the rest of the essay?
2. What three examples does the student give to illustrate her point?
   Are they effective? Do you think she exaggerates?
3. Read aloud the transition sentences that connect the paragraphs.
   How do they serve to carry out the purpose statement? What particular words in each of them make you think of gossip?
4. How does the student summarize the essay? How does the summary differ from the introduction?

### Word and Sentence Use

1. The word *about* in the title is a preposition, but it is nevertheless capitalized. Why? See pg. 53.
2. The first sentence contains an unnecessary expletive (S-5) and the unnecessary words *today's society* (S-1). How could you rewrite the sentence to avoid these problems?
3. The sentence beginning in line 8 contains another unnecessary expletive. How could you rewrite this sentence?

**Writing Assignment**    **Choose a Topic.** Complete the following sentences, selecting the most exact words you can think of:

1. A college student's life is _____.

2. Most of my jobs have been _____.

3. Soap operas are _____.

4. One thing everyone loves to do is _____.

5. Teen-age marriages are _____.

6. Children's television programs are _____.

7. Most college (or high school) teachers could be described as

_____

8. The military could be described as _____.

9. People in _____ drive like _____.
   (name your town or city)

10. _____ is _____.
    (name a sport)

Discuss the topics with the rest of the class to stimulate more ideas and then choose one topic to write on. (Remember that this is not the title of your paper.)

**Step One: Gather Information.**   In the left-hand column below, list as many examples as you can think of that will support your statement.

_____    _____

_____    _____

_____    _____

_____    _____

_____    _____

Now, in the right-hand column, write down as much supporting detail as you can think of to go with each example. If you are having difficulty, read the student essay on page 186 for ideas.

**Step Two: Analyze the Information.**   Which of your examples best *support your statement*? Can any of the examples be combined? Can any be omitted without taking away from what you want to say? Do you need more examples?

**Step Three: State Your Purpose.** The sentence you chose to write on could serve as your purpose statement, but now that you have gathered and analyzed information about your topic, you may find that you need to write a new purpose statement.

**Step Four: Make Your Plan.** This time when you write your outline, write out the transition sentences that will begin each paragraph in the body of your paper. See the student samples for ideas.

_____
(title)

*Par. 1*     Introduction _____

Detail ▶ _____

Transition Sentence ▶ *Par. 2*     _____

_____

_____

Detail ▶ _____

Transition Sentence ▶ *Par. 3*     _____

_____

_____

Detail ▶ _____

Transition Sentence ▶ *Par. 4*     _____

_____

_____

Detail ▶ _____

Transition Sentence ▸ *Par. 5*    _____

_____

_____

Detail ▸ _____

*Par. 6*    Conclusion _____

Detail ▸ _____

**Step Five: Write.**    As you write, make sure you go into enough detail to make each example convincing. If you are writing on gossip, don't just say someone is gossiping; give examples, preferably in dialogue, of the gossip. If you are writing on television programs, don't just say a particular program is violent; give particular examples that illustrate the violence. The more relevant detail you give the more convincing your example will be.

Also, as you write, be aware of the verb tense you are using. If the example you are reporting happened in the past, use the past tense. If the example is still going on, use the present tense. While using present-tense verbs, be sure to add *-s* or *-es* in regular third-person singular constructions. (Remember that in the third-person singular, present tense, the irregular verb *have* changes to *has* and that the correct form of the verb *be* is the verb *is*.)

**Step Six: Evaluate and Edit.**    Evaluate your paper.

1. Did you choose good examples to prove your point? Do you need more?
2. Did you go into enough detail with each example you gave? Which is your best-written example? Which is your least well-written example?

Edit your paper, using the checklist on the back inside cover. Be on the lookout for the following three errors: verb-tense confusion (*see* Chapter 8.3), verb-agreement problems (*see* Chapter 7), and errors in the use of *for example* or *for instance*.

*For example* errors ▸ When you need to introduce an example with *for example* or *for instance*, make sure you avoid a sentence error. If *for example* introduces an independent clause, either capitalize the *for* and write the clause as a sentence or use a semicolon before the *for example,* as follows:

▶ I enjoy reading novels about the sea. For example, I really love *Moby Dick* and *The Old Man and the Sea.*

*or*

▶ I enjoy reading novels about the sea; for example, I really love *Moby Dick* and *The Old Man and the Sea.*

If, however, *for example* introduces a word, phrase, or dependent clause (a word, phrase, or clause used as a noun and placed next to another word to explain it), connect it to the preceding sentence with a comma, as follows:

▶ I enjoy reading novels about the sea, for example, *Moby Dick* and *The Old Man and the Sea.*

Notice that in all of the above constructions, a comma comes after *for example.*

To give your sentences variety, try using *for example* following the example you give:

▶ I enjoy reading novels about the sea, *Moby Dick* and *The Old Man and the Sea,* for example.

### A STUDENT'S LIFE

**Student Sample** ▶

A student's life is a difficult one. My Aunt Mary has decided to go    1
back to school to get her degree. It would not be so hard on her if she    2
didn't have a house to clean, children to raise, and a family to feed. I do    3
not see how she has any time for homework. Can you imagine trying to    4
write an essay and yelling at children all at the same time? Sometimes she    5
has to make a choice of what is most important: the house, the family, or    6
the homework. Being a housewife, mother, and student are three major    7
jobs in themselves.    8

My friend Sue Laporte was complaining to me the other day about    9
her teachers. She said they expect too much of her. Sue is studying ac-    10
counting and therefore has a tremendous amount of homework. But to at-    11
tend school she must maintain her job. To add to her troubles, her mother    12
works, so after school Sue has to babysit for her younger brother and two    13

sisters. Her job is from six to ten-thirty, and by the time she arrives home and    14
showers, it is around eleven. She limits herself to four hours of studying a    15
night, which puts her to bed at about three in the morning. With the sched-    16
ule Sue has, there is very little or no time for herself. But she has decided to    17
commit herself to a few years of misery so that she can enjoy what she    18
calls "the laughs of luxury."    19

Speaking of having it rough, my friend José Rodriguez is attending    20
the University of Colorado on a scholarship, which means his grades must    21
stay at a certain average. He is majoring in chemical engineering, he car-    22
ries a total of seventeen credit hours, and he also plays baseball. Finding    23
himself low on money, José had to get a job. In one day he attends school,    24
practices for baseball, goes to work, and does homework. He wakes up    25
at six-thirty every morning and does not go to sleep until very late at night.    26
How he keeps his grade point average up is a mystery to me.    27

Sometimes teachers think that the only class you have is theirs. But    28
it is not really their fault. No one ever said life was easy, especially at    29
school!    30

### Questions for Discussion

1. Do you like the way the student began the paper? Should she have included any other material in the introduction? If so, what?
2. How do the transition sentences that begin the second and third paragraphs serve to carry out the purpose statement? What particular words in the transitions relate to the word *difficult* in the purpose statement?
3. Are the three examples the student gives effective in illustrating her point? Does she need to expand any example? Explain.
4. Is the conclusion a contrasting statement, a statement of significance, a call to action, or a summary?
5. Can you identify with any of the students she writes about?

### Word and Sentence Use

1. Note the use of *therefore* in line 11. Because it does not introduce an independent clause, it is not preceded by a semicolon.
2. The sentence that begins with *he* in line 22 contains three independent clauses. Semicolons are not used between them. Instead, they are treated as items in a series—independent clauses in a series—and are therefore correctly separated by commas.

## 5. The Comparison and Contrast Essay

Much of our thinking is based on comparison and contrast. When we say a house is big, we mean big in comparison to other houses. The same house is quite small when compared to a skyscraper or a large industrial plant. When we say a diamond is small, we mean small in comparison to large diamonds or perhaps other jewelry. The same diamond may be very large when compared to a truly small diamond, such as one used for the tip of a record player needle. The words we use to describe many things are meaningful only when those things are compared and contrasted with other things.

Your assignment is to compare and contrast two people, two places, or two things in an essay of 300 words or more. Many essays assigned in college call for comparison and contrast. In a sociology class, you might be asked to compare the political views of white-collar workers with those of blue-collar workers. In a political science class, you might be asked to compare communism as pràcticed in Russia with communism in Yugoslavia. In a biology class, you might be asked to compare meiosis with mitosis. The two methods presented in this section for writing a comparison and contrast paper should be helpful for any such essay you might be assigned in the future.

## THE COMPARISON AND CONTRAST ESSAY

### OBJECTIVE

To show how two people, two places, or two things are alike or different, or both.

### SUGGESTIONS FOR THE ESSAY

1. Compare and contrast two things only. Use the classification essay format (discussed in the next section) to compare and contrast three or more things.
2. In your purpose statement, give your views of the people, places, or things you are comparing. Don't just say that you will show in your paper how life in the suburbs is both similar to and different from life in the city. Offer an opinion as you compare the suburbs and the city. Here are several ways you could write your purpose statement:

▸ Life is easier (or more difficult) in the city than it is in the suburbs.

▸ The city is full of excitement, but the suburbs are boring.

▸ The suburbs are clean and carefree, but the city is dirty and dangerous.

▸ Life in the suburbs is surprisingly similar to life in the city.

Notice that in each of these purpose statements both units to be compared are mentioned.

3. In describing each of the two units, use your skill in giving examples, writing detail, and when helpful, recording dialogue.

### Two Methods of Planning the Essay

**Method A.** After your introduction, write one long paragraph about the first unit in your comparison, then one long paragraph about the second unit, and then give your conclusion. (If your paper is much longer than 300 words, you may want to subdivide each paragraph in the body into two or more paragraphs.) Here is an example of a Method A outline.

*Par. 1*      Introduction (include purpose statement)

Detail ▸ *my two most opposite friends from the airforce, how long I've known them, how they influenced me*

Organizing Principle ▸ *Par. 2*      *James Evans*

Detail ▸ *a. General Information: 6'7", thin, lives in Tombstone, AZ*

*b. Married Ella Kentuck, whose father owns an auto repair shop*

*c. Runs sports supply store*

*d. Odd habits: chews tobacco, always*

*e. Particular influence on me: convinced*

*me that there was a pot of gold*
*at the end of the rainbow*

Organizing Principle ▶ *Par. 3*    <u>Ted Spicer</u>

Detail ▶ *a. General Information:*    5'2", chubby, lives in
                                        *Cowan, Tennessee*

*b. Married to his fourth wife, Luella Writhe, whose*
*father left on a trip around the world when she was two*

*c. Works at odd jobs between marriages*

*d. Odd habits: dresses up on Sunday and sings*
*in the church choir (for him that's odd)*

*e. Particular influence on me: taught me how to*
*build a cabin*

*Par. 4*        Conclusion

Detail ▶ <u>*How both have influenced me*</u>

Note the following:

1. The particular items of detail (a.–e.) in paragraphs 2 and 3 are parallel to each other; that is, they follow the same pattern. If you use Method A, try to write your detail in a similarly parallel way. But not all of it has to be parallel. Perhaps you want to tell us that Ted Spicer has never voted but has nevertheless run for sheriff three times. Write this detail in your paragraph somewhere, even though you may not be able to think up parallel detail for James Evans.

2. When you are writing about the second unit in your comparison, try to refer back from time to time to the first unit so that your reader will be able to think of both units together. Otherwise, it may sound as though you are writing two separate essays. For example, you could introduce some of your detail describing Ted Spicer in the following way:

▸ While James has been married to the same woman for the last thirty years, Ted just got married for the fourth time to . . .

▸ James told me about the pot of gold, but Ted taught me how to saw a board.

When using these "reminders," don't overdo it. Rely on what sounds right to you, or your paper may sound contrived.

3. Be careful to write your sentences so that they flow into each other smoothly, or your detail will sound like a list. Again, rely on your ear, on what sounds smooth to you as you read your writing back to yourself.

4. Method A is a good choice for comparison and contrast essays that are not too long. The more you say about each unit the more difficult it becomes for your reader to think of the two units together.

**Method B.**  As the organizing principle for each paragraph in the body of your paper use the particular point of comparison or contrast. An outline for the James Evans, Ted Spicer paper might look like this:

*Par. 1*      Introduction (include purpose statement)

Detail ▸ *my two friends from the air force, how long I've known them*

Organizing Principle ▸ *Par. 2*    *General Information*

Detail ▸ *James Evans*

*Ted Spicer*

Organizing Principle ▸ *Par. 3*    *Marriages*

Detail ▸ *James*

*Ted*

Organizing Principle ▸ *Par. 4*    *Employment*

Detail ▸ *James*

*Ted*

Organizing Principle ▸ *Par. 5*    *Odd habits*

Detail ▸ *James*

*Ted*

Organizing Principle ▸ *Par. 6*    *Particular influences on me*

Detail ▸ *James*

*Ted*

▸ *Par. 7*    Conclusion

Detail ▸ *How they both have influenced me*

*Note the following:*

1. In each paragraph in the body of the outline, the first unit in the comparison (James) is presented first. This helps make the paragraphs parallel to each other.
2. You will need to use a transition sentence in the middle of each paragraph as you move from the first unit in the comparison to the second. Here is an example. The transition sentence is italicized.

> James married Ella Kentuck thirty years ago. She is also from Tombstone, and her father has run an automobile repair shop there for the last fifty years. Ella is a very traditional housewife and has raised four children with James. *Ted Spicer, on the other hand, has just married his fourth wife, Luella Writhe.* She's known mostly in Cowan, Tennessee, for being the woman whose father left home on a trip around the world when she was two and never came back. She doesn't like housework, but she has a good job in a neighboring town where she is a manager for Sears.

Here are two other ways the transition sentence could be written:

▸ But Ted Spicer has different ideas about marriage; he has just married his fourth wife, Luella Writhe.

▸ But Ted Spicer's wife is quite different.

Can you think of still other transitions? Try not to use the same transition words each time; instead give your writing variety.

3. Method B is a good choice for comparisons that are longer. But be careful not to write too many short paragraphs. You may need to combine two or more of your paragraphs with a new organizing principle. In the example above, paragraph 4 on employment might have been combined with other information in paragraph 2.

### TWO MEDICAL JOBS

**Student Sample ▸**
**(Method A)**

1  I have worked both as an X-ray technician in a hospital and as
2  an assistant in a private physician's office. Working in the hospital is more
3  fulfilling than working in a doctor's office.
4      In the hospital, where I am working now, there is never a dull mo-
5  ment. You work with a lot of people and many doctors. Since the hospital
6  is a non-profit organization, no one makes you hurry up, and I am able to
7  take my time with each patient. I talk with them and learn a lot of their
8  medical history. I don't feel like I'm the only one doing the work because
9  the staff is large enough to do all the work required. Also, the doctors are
10 nice and compliment us often on a job well done. Lunchtime is no prob-
11 lem, for the cafeteria is convenient and the prices are reasonable. Parking
12 costs employees only twenty cents a day. As long as I continue to work full
13 time, my hospitalization insurance is fully paid for. The best thing about the
14 work is that I'm not given a lot of extra work. All I am required to do is to X-
15 ray the patients and show a lot of interest in each of them.
16      But the doctor's office where I used to work was entirely different.
17 Many times the doctor wasn't in the office and everything was delayed.
18 Because the office was run to make a profit, the work was rushed, and I
19 was not able to take my time with each patient. It was like an assembly
20 line. "Get 'em in, and get 'em out," I was told. Lunchtime was a problem.
21 If I didn't bring my lunch, I had to go to a fast-food restaurant that was
22 expensive and poor. There was no parking for the employees and no in-
23 surance plan. The worst thing was that I not only had to do X-ray work but
24 almost everything else that came along, including bringing the doctor cof-
25 fee.

I am glad that I had the chance to experience both places of work    26
because now I know which is the most fulfilling.    27

### Questions for Discussion

1. Does the purpose statement meet the criteria given in the learning notes? Does the student successfully carry it out in the essay? For practice, write another purpose statement.
2. Read the essay aloud and comment on how smoothly it reads. Is the detail successfully incorporated into the essay, or does it sound like a list?
3. Is the transition sentence at the beginning of the third paragraph effective? Should there be other "reminders" of the work in the hospital in the third paragraph? Or, is the parallel structure sufficient for the reader to think of both jobs together?
4. What detail might the student have added to the introduction?

### Word and Sentence Use

1. In line 7, the pronoun *them* does not agree with its antecedent (PA). How should you change the antecedent to agree with *them?*
2. In line 8, *like* is not the best word choice (WW). *Like* properly introduces nouns or noun constructions, not dependent clauses. In place of *like,* use *as if, as though,* or *that.*
3. In line 14, the word *work* is used twice, unnecessarily (S-2). What word could you substitute?
4. In line 27, the word *most* is misused (WW). Read the learning notes on page 196 and explain why it is misused.

### An Exercise

Outline the detail in the second and third paragraphs and see if it is successfully presented in a parallel manner.

| *Paragraph 2* | *Paragraph 3* |
|---|---|
| a. _____ | a. _____ |
| b. _____ | b. _____ |
| c. _____ | c. _____ |
| d. _____ | d. _____ |
| e. _____ | e. _____ |

Compare your results with the suggestions made in Appendix D.

### THE CITY MOUSE

**Student Sample ►**
**(Method B)**

For over twenty-three years I lived in the city of Jefferson. City life 1
was all I knew as I was born and raised in the heart of the city. Thinking 2
that the grass was greener somewhere else, I moved to the suburbs seven 3
years ago. Only now do I appreciate the advantages of the city that I took 4
for granted when I lived there. 5

Residents of Jefferson enjoy many conveniences that people in 6
the suburbs miss out on. Bus service in the city is excellent. You can go just 7
about anywhere you want in the city if you are willing to change buses 8
once or twice. With buses stopping at every second street corner and 9
coming at intervals of every ten to fifteen minutes, city dwellers can de- 10
pend on the transit system as their chief means of transportation. Unfortu- 11
nately, bus service in the suburbs cannot compare to the city transit system. 12
Suburban bus routes are few and a wait at a bus stop can last thirty min- 13
utes. 14

The city of Jefferson is full of charm and beauty, which is lacking in 15
the suburbs. Huge oak trees line the avenues and boulevards of the city, 16
and the neutral grounds are decorated with blooming oleanders and aza- 17
leas. The city's two giant parks are a great asset to Jefferson. Many enjoy- 18
able Sunday afternoons can be spent feeding the ducks that swim lazily 19
on the ponds in the park. On the other hand, the suburbs have no real 20
parks. Small playgrounds are the most the suburbs have to offer. These 21
playgrounds are naked compared to the city's parks with their huge moss- 22
covered trees that the city is famous for. 23

Another advantage of the city is that city life is neighborhood ori- 24
ented. You can walk to a neighborhood grocery store in many parts of the 25
city. Children usually grow up together attending the same neighborhood 26
school. Unlike the city, life in the suburbs is not tight knit. Shopping is done 27
at large supermarkets. Children are bused all over the place to different 28
schools. Suburban neighbors seldom take time to get to know one another. 29

I find myself constantly returning to the city. I reside in the suburbs, 30
but my heart is in the city. 31

### Questions for Discussion

1. Why did the writer choose "The City Mouse" as the title?
2. Read the transition sentences *at the beginning* of each paragraph in the body of the paper, aloud. What words in these transitions relate back to the purpose statement?
3. Underline each transition sentence *in the middle* of paragraphs 2, 3, and 4. The author used these transitions to move from the first

unit in each comparison to the second. Are they effective? If not, how could they be improved?

4. What is the organizing principle of each paragraph?
5. Did the author give enough detail to support the three main points?

### Word and Sentence Use

1. The sentence that begins with *The city's* in line 18 contains an unnecessary phrase (S-4). What is it? Why is it wordy?
2. The sentence that begins with the word *Many* in line 18 is written in the passive voice (S-6). How would you change it to the active voice?
3. The word *city* is used nineteen times in the essay (S-2). See how many times you can omit the word or use another word or words in its place, without hurting the style of the paper.

## COMPARATIVE AND SUPERLATIVE ADJECTIVES

Adjectives change in form when the nouns they modify are compared and contrasted with other nouns. You may describe a farm scene as *lovely,* but if you think it is prettier than another farm scene, you say that it is *lovelier* than the other one, and if you think it is the prettiest farm scene anywhere, you say that it is the *loveliest* of them all. In comparing two nouns, use *comparative* adjectives; in comparing three or more nouns, use *superlative* adjectives.

### COMPARATIVE ADJECTIVES

1. For short adjectives, add *-er* to the ending. If the adjective ends in *-y,* change the *-y* to *-i* and then add *-er,* as follows:

   The work is hard.    The work is harder than it is
                     at the other place

   The work is easy.    The work is easier than it is
                     at the other place.

2. For longer adjectives (three or more syllables) use *more* before the adjective, but do not change the ending, as follows:

   ▶ The work is *more* fulfilling than the work at the other place.

### SUPERLATIVE ADJECTIVES

1. For short adjectives, add *-est* to the ending. If the adjective ends in *-y,* change the *-y* to *-i* and then add *-est,* as follows:

   My cat is smart.    My cat is the smart<u>est</u> cat on the block.

   My cat is lazy.    My cat is the laz<u>iest</u> cat on the block.

2. For longer adjectives (three or more syllables) use *most* before the adjective, but do not change the ending, as follows:

   ► My cat is the *most* unpredictable cat on the block.

### IRREGULAR FORMS

A few adjectives change in form completely when used as comparative or superlative adjectives:

| Basic form | Comparative form | Superlative form |
|---|---|---|
| bad | worse | worst |
| good | better | best |
| far | farther | farthest |
| little | less | least |
| much | more | most |

## COMPARATIVE AND SUPERLATIVE ADVERBS

1. One forms comparative and superlative adverbs in much the same way that one forms comparative and superlative adjectives:

   ► He walks fast<u>er</u> in the morning than in the afternoon, but he walks the fast<u>est</u> when he knows his lunch is waiting for him.

2. Adverbs that end in *-ly* are preceded by *more* in the comparison form and *most* is the superlative form.

   ► He spoke more angrily to us at half time than at the beginning of the game, but he spoke most angrily to us when we lost.

**Writing Assignment**   **Choose Your Topic.**   Fill in the blanks for as many of the following as you can:

1. Two jobs you could compare and contrast:

   _____        _____

2. Two relatives (two aunts, two cousins, or the like) you could compare and contrast:

   _____        _____

3. Two places you have lived:

   _____        _____

4. Two famous athletes (from the same sport):

   _____        _____

5. Two churches or religious centers:

   _____        _____

6. Two famous singers or musicians:

   _____        _____

7. Two opposing candidates:

   _____        _____

Choose one of the above or one of the following topics to compare and contrast:

8. Teaching methods in high school and college
9. Yourself and your pet
10. Yourself when you are glad and yourself when you are sad (or mad)
11. Your parents' (or children's) view of you and your view of you
12. Shopping with money and "shopping" without money
13. The Democratic and Republican parties
14. Soldiers and sailors
15. Officers and enlisted personnel
16. Hawks and doves
17. Foreign cars and American cars
18. Democracy and socialism

**Step One: Gather Information.**   In the left-hand column, using the brainstorm method, write down everything that comes to mind when you think about the first unit in your comparison. In the right-hand column, write down everything that comes to mind when you think about the second unit. (Think of particular examples as well as descriptive detail.)

| (first unit) | (second unit) |
|---|---|
| _____ | _____ |
| _____ | _____ |
| _____ | _____ |
| _____ | _____ |
| _____ | _____ |
| _____ | _____ |
| _____ | _____ |
| _____ | _____ |

Now draw lines connecting similar detail. In the brainstorm for the first student sample above, the student wrote the following and connected similar items in the comparison with lines, as shown:

*Work in the hospital*        *Work in the doctor's office*

lots of doctors ⟷ one doctor
good lunches                    had to do any jobs
time to work with patients      (bring coffee to doctor)
non-profit organization         no parking
hospitalization                 "Get 'em in and get 'em out."
good parking facilities
professional treatment

Go back over your lists and see what items were not connected. See if you can think of detail that corresponds to those unconnected items and add that detail to your lists. In the example above, three items in the left-hand column were not connected. The student added the following to the right-hand column to correspond to those items:

good lunches ←———→ poor lunches in fast-food restaurant
non-profit organization←→ everything for a profit
hospitalization←———→ no hospitalization

**Step Two: Analyze the Information.** Look over both lists and see what items are most important, what items might be grouped together, what items might be omitted. Which of the two units in your comparison do you prefer? Why? Has your preference changed any? If so, you may want to write about the reason for the change in your essay.

**Step Three: State Your Purpose.** Name both units of the comparison in your purpose statement and state your opinion of the two units when you think of them together.

---

Here are some examples:

▶ Shopping without money is more exciting than shopping with money.

▶ Except for the fact that my pet has four legs and I only have two, we are much alike.

▶ No twins could be more opposite than Joshanna and Jovanna.

▶ High school teaching related to our experience, but college teaching is abstract.

▶ Bill Walton was a good basketball player, but Wilt Chamberlain was great.

▶ My children see me as serious minded, but actually I am full of fun.

**Step Four: Make Your Plan.** Using the criteria given in the learning notes above, choose either Method A or Method B to outline your paper. (Use examples as well as descriptive detail to support your main points.)

Method A ▸ (Be sure to make your detail in paragraphs two and three parallel when you can.)

_____
(your title)

*Par. 1*      Introduction _____

Detail ▸ _____

Organizing Principle ▸ *Par. 2*    _____

Detail ▸ *a.*_____

      *b.*_____

      *c.*_____

      *d.*_____

      *e.*_____

      *f.*_____

Organizing Principle ▸ *Par. 3*    _____

Detail ▸ *a.*_____

      *b.*_____

      *c.*_____

      *d.*_____

      *e.*_____

      *f.*_____

*Par. 4*      Conclusion _____

Detail ▸ _____

Method B ▸ (Be careful not to use too many paragraphs in setting up your paper—three to five paragraphs in the body should be enough.)

_____
(title)

*Par. 1*          Introduction _____

Detail ▸ _____

Organizing Principle ▸ *Par. 2*          _____

Unit A ▸ _____

Detail ▸ _____

Unit B ▸ _____

Detail ▸ _____

Organizing Principle ▸ *Par. 3*          _____

Unit A ▸ _____

Detail ▸ _____

Unit B ▸ _____

Detail ▸ _____

Organizing Principle ▸ *Par. 4*          _____

Unit A ▸ _____

Detail ▸ _____

Unit B ▸ _____

Detail ▸ _____

Organizing Principle ▸ *Par. 5*          _____

Unit A ▸ _____

Detail ▸ _____

Unit B ▸ _____

Detail ▸ _____

Organizing Principle ▸ *Par. 6* _____

Unit A ▸ _____

Detail ▸ _____

Unit B ▸ _____

Detail ▸ _____

   *Par. 7*  Conclusion _____

Detail ▸ _____

**Step Five: Write.** A comparison and contrast paper is highly structured, but your writing does not have to sound rigid or contrived. Use the suggested structure, write clear transitions, and when possible make your constructions parallel, but remember, you are speaking to your readers through your writing, so make your writing sound like you talking.

**Step Six: Evaluate and Edit.** Evaluate your paper:

1. What opinion did you express in your purpose statement?
2. If you chose Method A, did you present your detail in a parallel manner?
3. If you chose Method B, check the transitions in the middle of the paragraphs in the body of your paper. Do they help the reader move easily from the first unit in your comparison to the second?
4. When you read your paper aloud, does it sound like you talking? If not, where in your essay does the writing not sound like you?

Edit your paper making use of the checklist on the inside back cover. Note the following. The phrase *on the other hand* functions as a conjunctive adverb and can begin a new sentence or follow a semi-colon in a compound sentence:

▶ The bank did not pay well. On the other hand, it did provide an excellent introduction to the business world.

▶ The bank did not pay well; on the other hand, it did provide an excellent introduction to the business world.

(See Chapter 6.5.)

Watch for fragments that begin with *while* or *whereas*. Correct these fragments, using commas to join them to the preceding sentences.

▶ My dog likes to be around people. While I like to go off by myself.

▶ Teachers in high school teach practical English. Whereas teachers in college teach egghead English.

(See Comma Rule 10 in Chapter 11.4.)

Watch out also for the misuse of *more* and *most* (see the learning notes above) and for the misspelling of *than*. (*Than* compares two things: One thing is better *than* another thing. *Then* is a time word, like *when*.)

**Additional Writing Assignments**

1. Pick another topic from the list on page 198. If you used Method A for structuring your first essay, use Method B for this one; if you used B, then this time use A.
2. Making use of the two outlines on James Evans and Ted Spicer, write a paper on them, inventing the necessary "facts" as you write.

## 6. The Classification Essay

*Classification* means the arranging or ordering of material. We make use of the principles of classification every day, for example, when we look up classified ads in the newspaper or use the "Yellow Pages" in the phone book. The other name for the "Yellow Pages" is, in fact, the *Classified Telephone Directory*. The items in the "Yellow Pages" are first classified alphabetically, but there are also classifications within some of the alphabetical listings. If you looked up churches under C in a large city directory, for example, you would see that the churches are classified by denomination. Under each denomination, particular churches are listed. If you kept reading, you would see that churches are also classified by where they are located in the city.

A common form of classification is the organizational flow chart, which shows, diagramatically, the particular functions within an organization. A community center, for example, classified the functions of its employees with the following flow chart shown below.

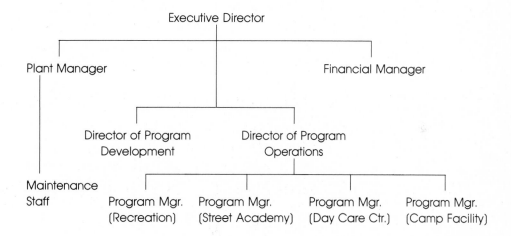

In a classification essay, your task is threefold: (1) to classify or arrange ideas and information on a particular subject in a logical way, whether the subject is contemporary music, college males or females, or the causes of the First World War; (2) to describe the classes or divisions within the subject area; and (3) to give your overall opinion of the subject area. If you were writing an evaluation of the Department of Program Operations for the community center shown in the diagram above, you would follow the same procedure. First, you would divide your evaluation into four parts: Recreation, Street Academy, Day Care Center, and Camp Facility. Second, you would describe how each of these programs is functioning. And third, you would give your overall view on how well the whole department of Program Operations is functioning, and why.

You have already been classifying material in your writing, especially in making outlines. In this assignment, however, you will concentrate on classification itself and write a paper of 300 words or more on one of several topics. The skills you learn will help you not only on many college essays, but also in practical writing required in many jobs. For example, some day you may be required to make a written report evaluating departments within an organization or divisions within a department.

# THE CLASSIFICATION ESSAY

Objective ▸ To divide a subject area into various classes, describe those classes, and state your overall view of the subject area.

## SUGGESTIONS FOR THE ESSAY

1. Make your classification as comprehensive as possible. If you are writing on contemporary music, try to group all of the music in one class or another. If you are writing on college males or females, try to place each individual within a certain class. If you are writing on soap operas and other television serials, try to include each program in your classification. A shortcoming of the classification essay is that many subject areas cannot be easily or rigidly divided into classes. The intent of the essay, however, is to give your reader a *general* idea of the types of music one might hear on the radio, the types of males or females one might discover on your campus, or the types of soap operas or other serials that play each week on television.

2. If possible, limit your classes or divisions to three or four. If several items do not fall into one of the classes, you may have to describe them under the category "Other," but avoid this category if you can.

3. Choose classes that fit together logically. You could classify college teachers logically in the following ways:
   a. Interested in students
      Indifferent to students
      Hostile to students
   b. Graduate assistants
      Instructors
      Professors
   c. Excellent teachers
      Average teachers
      Poor teachers
   d. Inexperienced teachers
      Moderately experienced teachers
      Highly experienced teachers

4. In your purpose statement, give your overall view of the individual classes *when considered together*. What is your dominant impression of the subject area? Here are some examples:

   ▸ Most of our teachers are interested in students, but some are indifferent and a few are even downright hostile to students.

▸ Teaching ability at our university has little to do with whether the teacher is a graduate assistant, an instructor, or a full professor.

▸ Most of our teachers are either too structured in their teaching or not structured enough, but some seem to use just the right amount of structure.

5. When possible, present detail for each class in a way that parallels the detail in other classes, as follows:

| Inexperienced teachers | Moderately experienced | Highly experienced |
|---|---|---|
| a. The way they lecture | a. The way they lecture | a. The way they lecture |
| b. The way they test | b. The way they test | b. The way they test |
| c. The way they deal with students | c. The way they deal with students | c. The way they deal with students |
| d. A particular example | d. A particular example | d. A particular example |

6. Write about the same length on each of the classes or divisions.
7. Try to make the transition sentences that introduce each paragraph in the body of the paper at least roughly parallel to each other. See the learning notes on parallel sentences on pp. 207–211.

### ROACHES AND SOCIAL CLASS

**Student Sample** ▸    The cockroach has a great deal to teach us about ourselves. Just ¹ as there are three social classes of human beings, there are three classes ² of roaches. ³

First of all, there is the affluent class of roach, which is like the rich ⁴ American businessman. This type of roach is a survivor of the fittest because ⁵ of its large size, which ranges anywhere from two to three inches. Roaches ⁶ of this class will have nothing but the best. For instance, it is the only kind ⁷ of roach daring enough to crawl over a delicious pot-roast, recently set on ⁸ the table, in broad daylight, right before a person's eyes. Like the rich ⁹ American businessman, this roach will go to any extremes to get what he ¹⁰ wants, and he cares less about the fate of others than any of the roaches. ¹¹ A good example is when one of these gross creatures is found digging ¹²

around the bottom of a sugar bowl on the kitchen table after everyone has 13
just finished eating. 14

Second, just as there is a division of Americans called the middle 15
class, there is also a middle class of roach, ranging from one to two inches 16
in size, that makes up the bulk of the roach population. This type of roach 17
is not as daring as the affluent class, and he usually settles for bread 18
crumbs and other scraps as a food source. Frequently, one would find this 19
roach propped up on one's toothbrush in the morning. This roach will stand 20
up for his rights, and the only way to get rid of him is to exterminate him. 21
However, by staying alert and moving very swiftly, this roach has become 22
highly resistant to being stomped on. 23

Third and last, there is the poverty class of roach. This type of 24
roach ranges from one-half to one inch in size. One startling characteristic 25
of this roach is that it is never seen in the daytime. Like bums and hobos, it 26
moves about in a dark and dreary world usually scavenging what it can 27
from garbage bags. This is the kind of roach that a person, lying in bed, 28
might find crawling up his neck. As long as this roach is in the dark, he is 29
very brave and courageous, but he becomes frightened and runs when 30
the light is flicked on. 31

Roaches, it seems, have social classes just as humans do. Many 32
people ponder on the theory of evolution. Just where have we, as humans, 33
been? Or, should I ask, where are we going? 34

### Questions for Discussion

1. What is the purpose statement? How does the student attempt to carry it out?
2. What particular examples does the student give in the three paragraphs in the body of his paper?
3. Would you say that the transition sentences introducing the second, third, and fourth paragraphs are closely parallel, roughly parallel, or not parallel at all? (See the learning notes on page 209.)
4. Does the writing meet all the criteria set forth in the learning notes on the classification essay? Explain.
5. The ending seems a bit weak. How might you write a stronger ending?
6. Is the roach analogy successful?

### Word and Sentence Use

1. Notice that in line 7, *for instance* begins a new sentence; it is not connected to the previous sentence with a comma. Why?
2. The student writes all of the third paragraph in the present tense

with one exception. What word in line 19 has he incorrectly written in the past tense (V)?
3. There is a redundant word in line 30 (S-1). What is it?

### An Exercise

Outline the detail as presented in paragraphs 2, 3, and 4 to see how closely parallel it is to the detail in the other two paragraphs in the body of the essay.

| *Affluent roach* | *Middle-class roach* | *Poverty-class roach* |
|---|---|---|
| a. _____ | a. _____ | a. _____ |
| b. _____ | b. _____ | b. _____ |
| c. _____ | c. _____ | c. _____ |
| d. _____ | d. _____ | d. _____ |
| e. _____ | e. _____ | e. _____ |

## PARALLEL SENTENCES

Parallel sentences consist of parallel grammatical elements. You will need to use parallel constructions in your sentences when you are writing two or more items in a series. You will also need to use parallel constructions at least some of the time in the transition sentences that connect paragraphs in the body of your essays. An error in parallel construction is designated S-9 in the revision checklist.

### ITEMS IN A SERIES

The sentence "I like swimming, hiking, and to collect things" is not parallel because *swimming* and *hiking* are both gerunds and *to collect* is an infinitive. (See Chapter 8.8.) In writing items in a series, use parallel grammatical constructions, as follows:

▸ I like swimming, hiking, and collecting things.

*or*

▸ I like to swim, hike, and collect things.

Here are some more examples of nonparallel and parallel constructions. (The nonparallel parts are underlined.)

Nonparallel ▶ I will argue that capital punishment deters crime, gets rid of dangerous people in our midst, and finally society should have a right to demand retribution. (The subject and verb society should is not parallel to the subject and verb capital punishment deters and [capital punishment] gets rid.)

Parallel ▶ I will argue that capital punishment deters crime, gets rid of dangerous people in our midst, and satisfies society's need for retribution.

Nonparallel ▶ When I finish at the university, I'm going to save some money, then I'm going to open my own business, and then sit back and get rich. (The subject-verb contraction I'm is omitted the third time.)

Parallel ▶ When I finish at the university, I'm going to save some money, then I'm going to open my own business, and then I'm going to sit back and get rich.

Parallel ▶ When I finish at the university, I'm going to save some money, open my own business, and sit back and get rich. (Note that this version is less wordy.)

Nonparallel ▶ You will need to gather the eggs, flour, the baking powder, honey, and the shortening ahead of time. (Use *the* before each item in the series; use it only once, at the beginning of the series; or omit it altogether.)

Parallel ▶ You will need to gather the eggs, flour, baking powder, honey, and shortening ahead of time.

### An Exercise

Make the following sentences parallel.

1. I will argue that capital punishment should be abolished because it does not deter crime, it is used only against the poor, and I think it is cruel and unusual punishment.
2. The neighbors on my block could be classified as friendly, indifferent, and some are mean.

3. The three classes of men on this campus are the intellectuals, the sports nuts, and then there are the women chasers.
4. He enjoys his nap in the afternoon, his bike ride in the early evening, and reading novels at night.
5. I watch the soaps in the morning, the news programs in the late afternoon, and television movies at night.
6. His responsibilities are to make the customers feel welcome, to show them to a table, and finding them a waiter.

## PARALLEL TRANSITIONS

As a general rule, write the transition sentences that introduce the paragraphs in the body of an essay so that they are at least roughly parallel to each other. But feel free to break this rule if the parallel constructions get in the way of what you want to say.

Here are examples of transition sentences that are closely parallel and roughly parallel to each other:

1. Closely parallel:

Purpose statement ▶ The fear of failing has caused me many problems.
    a. First, my fear of failing caused me to do poorly in reading when I was in elementary school.
    b. Second, my fear of failing made me unwilling to accept many simple challenges when I was in high school.
    c. And finally, my fear of failing caused me to put off going to college until I was twenty-five. (The construction *my fear of failing* + *a verb* is repeated and is followed by an infinitive.)
2. Roughly parallel:

Purpose statement ▶ The fear of failing has caused me many problems.
    a. When I was in elementary school, my fear of failing caused me to do poorly in reading.
    b. When I entered high school, my fear continued, and I did not accept many simple challenges.
    c. When it came time for me to go to college, I couldn't because of my fear of failing.

Transitions that are closely parallel to each other make your writing crisp and clear: they are particularly useful in writing essay questions on examinations. Transitions that are roughly parallel give you more flexibility in your writing, perhaps more of a chance to say what you want to say; generally, they are more interesting.

**Writing Assignment**    **Choose a Topic.**    Fill in three or four of the blanks for as many topics as you can. Choose classes that fit together.

1. Types of college males (or females):

   _____    _____

   _____    _____

2. Types of mothers (or fathers):

   _____    _____

   _____    _____

3. Types of teachers in your college (or high school):

   _____    _____

   _____    _____

4. Types of problems old people (or teen-agers) face:

   _____    _____

   _____    _____

5. Types of pitchers in baseball, quarterbacks in football, or (you name the position and the sport):

   _____    _____

   _____    _____

6. Types of social classes in America or your native country (try to focus on specific behaviors or traits, such as dress):

   _____    _____

   _____    _____

7. Types of television serials:

   _____    _____

   _____    _____

8. Types of people in your neighborhood:

_____    _____

_____    _____

9. Types of police officers, nurses, doctors, or (you name the profession):

_____    _____

_____    _____

10. Types of music played on AM (or FM) radio stations (or the types of music *within* a certain class, such as country music):

_____    _____

_____    _____

11. Types of bosses:

_____    _____

12. Types of sergeants or chiefs:

_____    _____

_____    _____

Discuss your classifications with the rest of the class or check them with the instructor to see if they meet the criteria given in the learning notes on page 206. Choose one topic to write on.

**Step One: Gather Information.** Brainstorm for details to describe and examples to illustrate each of the classes or divisions of the subject area you have chosen. In your brainstorm, include your opinions: what you like, what you don't like; what is most worthy of praise, least worthy; and so forth.

*Class one*                          *Class two*

_____    _____

_____    _____

_____    _____

_____    _____

_____    _____

_____    _____

_____    _____

_____    _____

*Class three*    *Class four (optional)*

_____    _____

_____    _____

_____    _____

_____    _____

_____    _____

_____    _____

*General brainstorm on the topic*

_____    _____

_____    _____

_____    _____

**Step Two: Analyze the Information.**   Have you chosen the best way to classify your material? Or do you need to rearrange your material in different classes? Check the information that is most important. What might you leave out?

**Step Three: State Your Purpose.**  In one sentence, state your views on all of the classes when considered together.

_____

_____

Here are some examples:

- ▶ All nurses perform valuable services.

- ▶ We sometimes forget about the many problems old people face.

- ▶ The most effective pitches in baseball are the curve, the fastball, and the change-up.

- ▶ Of all the music played on AM stations, I like country music the most.

- ▶ The chief petty officers run the Coast Guard.

- ▶ Each type of boss is a tyrant in his or her own way.

- ▶ The unusual teen-ager is the one who does not have serious problems.

**Step Four: Make Your Plan.**  In outlining your paper, first, try to make the transition sentences at least roughly parallel to each other; second, try to present the details and examples in each paragraph in the body of the essay so that they are parallel to the details and examples in the other paragraphs. Now might be a good time to read the other student sample.

_____
              (your title)

*Par. 1*        Introduction _____

Detail ▶ _____

Transition Sentence ▸ *Par. 2*    _____

_____

Detail and Examples ▸ a._____    d._____

b._____    e._____

c._____    f._____

Transition Sentence ▸ *Par. 3*    _____

_____

Detail and Examples ▸ a._____    d._____

b._____    e._____

c._____    f._____

Transition Sentence ▸ *Par. 4*    _____

_____

Detail and Examples ▸ a._____    d._____

b._____    e._____

c._____    f._____

Transition Sentence ▸ *Par. 5*    _____

_____

Detail and Examples ▸ a._____    d._____

b._____    e._____

c._____    f._____

*Par. 6*    Conclusion_____

Detail ▸ _____

**Step Five: Write.**   Like the comparison and contrast essay, the classification essay is highly structured. As you make use of the suggestions for parallel transitions and detail, be careful not to lose sight of the main task, which is to say what you want to say in your writing.

As you write, avoid sentences that begin

▸ There are three types of . . .

▸ The three types of problems are . . .

The trouble is that when you go to name the types, often your sentences become long and unwieldly, as follows:

▸ The three types of problems old people face are that their children often desert them, they live on a fixed income and every time the cost of living goes up they lose money, and many old people have illnesses or at least they can't get around very well.

Simply say in your introductory paragraph that old people face many problems. Each time you begin a new paragraph in the body of your essay, introduce one of the problems, something like this:

▸ . . . Old people face many problems.

▸   Many old people are lonely; often their children have deserted them.

▸   A second problem many old people have to deal with is that they live on a fixed income, and every time the cost of living goes up they lose money.

▸   A third problem that gets many old people down is that they sometimes can't get around very well.

**Step Six: Evaluate and Edit.**   Evaluate your paper.

1. Did you state your view in your purpose statement?
2. Did you present your detail and examples in at least a roughly parallel way?
3. Does the writing sound like you talking? If not, where in the essay does the writing not sound like you?
4. Did the classes of things you chose to write about fit together?

Edit your paper making use of the checklist on the back inside cover of this book. If you listed items in a series, make sure they are parallel to each other. Watch for verb-agreement errors, especially if you do use such constructions as *there are, three types are,* and the like. (As pointed out above, avoid these constructions if you can.) Finally, study Chapter 10.3–10.5 to avoid pronoun agreement errors, which are common in classsification essays.

**Student Sample ▶**

### BASEBALL PITCHERS

In major league baseball, each team is allowed at the most ten 1
pitchers on a team at one time. This means that there can be as many as 2
240 pitchers in the leagues. Even though this number is large, there are only 3
three types of pitchers. 4

One type is the kind who relies on his fastball. Fastball pitchers 5
throw the fastball an average of 85 percent of the time. The main reason 6
they throw this kind of pitch so often is that they are not skilled enough to 7
use any other. One prime example is J. R. Richard of the Houston Astros. 8
Richard is a relatively young man and has not yet learned how to throw 9
any other pitch especially well. But he is a very dangerous pitcher because 10
of his strong arm. When he is pitching in a game, he can throw the ball at 11
the speed of 100 miles an hour. 12

Another type of pitcher throws a curveball much of the time. Many 13
pitchers in the major leagues throw the curveball. The reason why a pitcher 14
will use this pitch is that he is not strong enough to throw an effective fast- 15
ball. Dan Quisenberry of the Kansas City Royals and Rollie Fingers of the 16
Milwaukee Brewers are two of the best pitchers of the curveball in all of 17
baseball. Quisenberry spins on his left foot and throws sidearm, and Fingers 18
throws a sort of looping pitch. 19

The last type of pitcher throws the screwball. One man is an expert 20
at throwing this kind of pitch, and he is the sensational Fernando Valen- 21
zuela. He is only twenty years old and has already perfected the most 22
difficult pitch to throw. This is an exceptional pitch to know how to throw 23
because the ball changes directions when the batter least expects it. 24

A pitcher can be great no matter what type of ball he pitches. But 25
I must admit that I like Valenzuela and his screwball most of all. 26

#### Questions for Discussion

1. Are the transition sentences that introduce the second, third, and fourth paragraphs closely parallel or roughly parallel?
2. Does the student present his details and examples in a parallel arrangement?

3. Does the essay read smoothly? Or is it made rigid or choppy by the structure?
4. Is the writer sufficiently clear in describing the various kinds of pitches? Does he need to explain his terms better for people who are not baseball fans?
5. Do you disagree with any of his descriptions of the baseball players? Explain.

### Word and Sentence Use

1. The writer begins his second paragraph with a wordy sentence: "One type is the kind who . . ." (S-4). He avoided this wordiness, however, in the transition sentences introducing his third and fourth paragraphs. Rewrite the sentence beginning in line 5.
2. The writer uses numerals three times in his essay. Should any of them be written out (N)? Why? (See the learning notes on page 178.)
3. The sentence that begins with the word *Many* in line 13 can be joined with the next sentence (S-8). How?
4. In the second and third paragraphs the student shifts from a singular subject in the transition sentence to a plural subject in the sentence that follows. The shift is legitimate because the student restates the subject the second time and does not use a pronoun (PA).

Correct ►   One type of pitcher relies on his fastball. Fastball pitchers usually throw . . .

Incorrect ►   One type of pitcher relies on his fastball. They usually throw . . . (In this case *they* is incorrect because it refers to the antecedent *pitcher,* which is singular.)

Correct ►   Another type of pitcher throws a curveball much of the time. Many pitchers in the major leagues throw . . .

Incorrect ►   Another type of pitcher throws a curveball much of the time. They throw . . . (Why is *they* used incorrectly?)

5. There are redundancies in the two sentences in line 23 (S-1). Correct them.
6. In the sentence that begins in line 25 the student uses the noun *pitcher* and the verb *pitches* (S-2). What word might be substituted for *pitches?*

## 7. The Argument Essay

The purpose of the argument essay is to convince your reader of the validity of your point of view on a particular subject. In a sense most of the papers you have written so far in this chapter have been argument papers, because you were asked to include your opinion in the purpose statements. But in the assignments in this section, you will concentrate on the argument itself. As you develop the essay, ask yourself what kinds of arguments would convince *you* of a certain point of view on the same subject. Probably you would not be convinced by emotional, screaming arguments or by general statements that were not soundly supported. Your reader is no doubt very much like you. State your opinion on the subject in the first paragraph and spend the rest of the essay defending it—with sound support—writing as persuasively as you can.

Many college essays—both in English and in other courses—are arguments. You may be asked to defend your point of view on why some historical event occurred, why the labor movement is or is not a constructive force in our economy today, why authors present the characters in their novels the way they do, why a poem is powerful, why Plato was a greater philosopher than Aristotle or vice versa.

But the skills you learn in writing an argument will also help you in a practical way when you leave college. Think of the many occasions when you might need to write a convincing argument. If you are concerned about a local issue, you can make your views known by writing your local newspaper, your city council representative, or your mayor. If you are concerned about a state or national issue, you can write your senators, congressional representative, or even the president. If you think your church, your club, or your children's school should do something differently, you can argue for your position in a letter to the appropriate official. And if you think you are entitled to a raise or promotion, you can state your argument in a letter to your employer.

There are three writing assignments in this section. The first calls for you to write an essay of 300 or more words in which you argue for a point of view on an issue of concern at your college, in your city or state, or throughout the nation. Your audience for this assignment will be either the readers of your school or local newspaper, or a policy-making official, real or imagined. The second assignment is to write a letter to the editor of a school newspaper answering another letter to the editor on the Equal Rights Amendment. The final assignment calls for you to argue for a point of view that is different from what most people think—something like, why fat is beautiful, why television should be banned, why all prisoners should be freed.

# THE ARGUMENT ESSAY

Objective ▸ To argue convincingly for a belief. If you choose your own topic, always pick one that is important to you so that you can make your essay a real argument.

## SUGGESTIONS FOR THE ESSAY

1. Emphasize arguments that are calm, rational, and not over-stated. Qualifying words and expressions like *maybe, perhaps,* and *it seems to me* are often appropriate, for example:

   ▸ In spite of the many sound arguments for The Equal Rights Amendment, it seems to me that . . .

2. Express your opinion in the purpose statement. Acknowledge the complexity of the issue if you like, but state a definite opinion. Think of yourself as a member of a jury. Consider the arguments on both sides of the issue, but then cast your vote— for or against.
3. Take advantage of all the information-gathering resources at your disposal: brainstorm, talk to others for ideas, and when appropriate, use the encyclopedia, periodicals, and books in the library. (See the suggestions for using the library on page 85.)
4. Address the arguments on the other side of the issue some-where in your essay. You want to avoid leaving your reader saying, "Yes, that sounds good, but . . ." If you address rea-sonable arguments made by the opposition, you will do much to reduce the "Yes, but . . ." response. Sometimes you can best address the arguments of the other side in your introduc-tion, sometimes as you make each of your own arguments, and at other times in a separate paragraph.
5. Make use of the different writing methods that you have studied in this chapter:
   a. *Description.* Your skill in observing detail and listening to dia-logue will help you support your arguments. Fine points and concrete details convince; the general and the abstract do not.
   b. *Narration.* Use your skill in telling a story to illustrate certain points in your essays. If you are arguing that sex education should be taught in high school, you may want to tell in one

paragraph what happened to someone you know who was not properly educated in this area.

c. *Examples.* Examples strengthen all arguments. In fact, many effective arguments are written as example essays: you state your point of view; then you back it up with three or four examples, using a paragraph or so for each one. You could write convincing essays on topics such as the following simply by giving examples:

▶ Capital punishment does take innocent lives.

▶ Disabled persons are often discriminated against.

▶ _____ has perhaps the worst drivers in the country.
   (Name a city)

d. *Comparison and contrast.* If you want to give full treatment to the other side of an issue, the comparison and contrast structure may work best for you. Here you would give the arguments for the other side of the issue in the second paragraph and then state your arguments in the third. (You may of course need to subdivide each of the two paragraphs in the body of the essay.) If you choose this structure, make your arguments parallel to the arguments of the opposition, when you can. For example:

| Par. 2 | Par. 3 |
|---|---|
| *For capital punishment* | *Against capital punishment* |
| deters crime, why | does not deter crime, why |
| ''an eye for an eye'' | ''To err is human, to forgive, divine.'' |
| now administered justly, examples | now administered unjustly, examples |

e. *Classification.* The most common method for writing an argument is to give three or more reasons why something is right or wrong. Your skills in classifying material will help you group your arguments together in a logical way.

6. For your introduction, consider telling why the issue under discussion is an important one. And consider ending your paper with a call-to-action conclusion (see page 128).

7. Support your main points with logical arguments and, when appropriate, with statistical facts, quotations from reading material, examples, descriptive detail, dialogue, and one-paragraph stories. See the learning notes on developing a paragraph that follow the student samples, especially point 8 on using logical arguments.

8. Throughout your essay keep your particular audience in mind. What will it take to persuade the particular reader or readers of your essay that you are right?

As you read these two essays, notice how the students have addressed the arguments of the opposition.

**A**         REASONS AGAINST CAPITAL PUNISHMENT

Capital punishment has been used since the beginning of man's      1
existence. In this century the number of people executed has been de-   2
creasing. In the 1930s, 1667 people were executed, compared to 717 in the   3
1950s. Since 1977, only four people have been executed. In spite of the   4
fact that a majority of Americans advocate keeping the death penalty, I   5
am glad it is being used less. In my view it should not be used at all.     6

The first reason why we should abolish capital punishment is be-   7
cause it is immoral and ethically unacceptable. "Thou shalt not kill" is the   8
fifth commandment that was given to us by God. An individual has no right   9
to kill, no matter what another person has done. Only God can create,   10
and he should be the only one to destroy.                  11

The second reason we should not have capital punishment is be-   12
cause it has failed in its purpose. Supporters of the death penalty argue   13
that the death penalty has a strong deterrent effect on people who could   14
be criminals. They use the theory that a person will weigh the amount of   15
the reward gained from killing someone against the pain of the punish-   16
ment. If the punishment is great enough, the person will not commit the   17
crime. But this is a false argument because most people who commit vio-   18
lent crimes are not rational at the time. A study by Dr. Grisby of the Univer-   19
sity of Florida showed that seventy-five percent of the males and more than   20
ninety percent of the females were under the influence of alcohol or drugs   21
and not rational when they committed violent crime.            22

The final reason we should do away with capital punishment is be-   23
cause it costs more than a life sentence. Most people think it is cheaper to   24
execute a criminal than it is to supply him or her with room, clothing, and   25
food, but they are wrong. The death penalty is very expensive because of   26
the long drawn-out jury selection, extended trials, maintenance of the pris-   27

oner on death row, and the long appeals process. For example, it cost the   28
State of Utah nearly a million dollars to try and execute Gary Gilmore.   29

    If you agree with me that capital punishment is not necessary and   30
that we would be better off without it, write your legislator about getting   31
our law changed.   32

### Questions for Discussion

1. Is the writing persuasive? If so, what in particular makes it persuasive? If not, what should be changed?
2. What logical argument does the writer use in paragraph 2 to support his position? (See point 8 in the learning notes that follow.)
3. How does the writer address the arguments of the opposition in paragraphs 3 and 4? Are you left saying, "Yes, but . . ."? If so, explain why.
4. The writer uses statistics in three of his five paragraphs. What are they? Are they effective?
5. Are the transition sentences in the body of the paragraphs closely parallel to each other or roughly parallel?
6. What kind of conclusion does the writer use?

### Word and Sentence Use

1. In line 2, the writer speaks of *man's existence*. More and more teachers and professional writers are avoiding exclusively male terms to refer to something that obviously pertains to females as well as males. While *man's existence* is technically correct, many teachers and writers prefer *humankind's existence*.
2. What is the redundancy in line 8 (S-1)? How can it be corrected?
3. The words *death penalty* are repeated unnecessarily in lines 13-15 (S-2). What pronoun could be substituted for them the second time?
4. In line 19, the student left off the first name of Dr. Grisby. The rule is to give the full name the first time and, if you like, only the last name in later references.
5. In line 28, the student used *for example* to introduce an example. See if the sentence would make just as much sense to you if the words *for example* were omitted.

B           A "YES" FOR CAPITAL PUNISHMENT

    Capital punishment is punishment by death, and it is some-   1
times given to people who are guilty of the most serious crimes. There   2
haven't been many people punished by death since the 1950s, but there   3

has been a terrible increase in crime in the United States in recent years. 4
If capital punishment were used more, surely crime would decrease signif- 5
icantly. 6

Some people argue against capital punishment because there 7
used to be so much racial prejudice against blacks, and it was mostly 8
blacks who were executed. There is no doubt that capital punishment was 9
used unjustly in many cases, but today there is not as much racial preju- 10
dice. Capital punishment could be given to all those who deserve such 11
punishment. The four men executed since 1977 have all been white. Speak- 12
ing as a black, I do not think the racial prejudice argument will stand any 13
more. 14

Some people argue that capital punishment does not deter crime, 15
but I disagree. Many people commit serious crimes because they know 16
that the law will not be enforced as it used to be. They know that they 17
could get a good lawyer to defend them, or they can plead insanity, or 18
they feel they can get out of jail early on probation or good behavior. If 19
capital punishment were enforced, people would know that if they were 20
found guilty of serious crimes, such as murder, they would be put to death. 21
This is not a way to control all crimes, but it is a way to control some of the 22
more serious ones. 23

Next, some people argue that capital punishment is immoral, but 24
the murders and rapes committed by criminals are also immoral. The law 25
cannot be totally moral when criminals in society aren't moral. As Walter 26
Berns said in his book *For Capital Punishment: Crime and the Morality of* 27
*the Death Penalty,* "The real issue is whether justice permits or even requires 28
the death penalty. I am aware that it is a terrible punishment, but there are 29
terrible crimes and terrible criminals." We can't let criminals take advan- 30
tage of the law but must stand up to them sternly. 31

The last argument against capital punishment is that it is too expen- 32
sive. The state spends millions of dollars on all types of programs which 33
don't always benefit people, so why shouldn't it spend money on enforcing 34
capital punishment? It is dangerous and a threat to innocent people to 35
have murderers and rapists in the streets. The state should realize the sig- 36
nificance of capital punishment and enforce it. Capital punishment should 37
be looked on as a necessity and should be enforced. 38

I hope you will join me in voting "yes" for capital punishment. 39

### Questions for Discussion

1. Is the writing persuasive? If so, what in particular makes it persuasive? If not, what should be added or changed?
2. The writer depends on logical arguments in making his points.
   What are they? Are they effective? (See point 8 in the learning
   notes that follow.)

3. How does the writer address the arguments of the opposition? Are you left saying, "Yes, but . . ."? If so, explain.
4. What statistics might the writer have used in the first and second paragraphs?
5. Is the quotation from an expert an effective one? Explain. (See page 69.)
6. Are the transition sentences in the body of the paragraph closely parallel to each other or roughly parallel?

**Word and Sentence Use**

1. In the sentence beginning with *They* in line 17, the student uses the verb *could* once and *can* twice. The same verb should be used each time. Which is correct? Why? (See Chapter 8.2.)
2. In line 26, the phrase *in society* can be omitted because it adds nothing to the meaning of the sentence (S-4).
3. There is a redundancy in the sentence beginning with *It is* in line 35 (S-1). What is it?
4. The sentence beginning with *Capital punishment* in line 37 repeats the meaning of the preceding sentence (S-10). Which should be deleted?

## PARAGRAPH DEVELOPMENT: A SUMMARY

These learning notes are devoted to the development of paragraphs within the body of an essay; the introduction of the essay is discussed on page 127 and the conclusion on page 128. Throughout the text suggestions have been made to help you develop your paragraphs with convincing information, examples, and logic. Often, for convenience, the ingredients of the paragraph have been referred to as *detail*. As you plan your supporting detail, ask yourself the following kinds of questions about the point you are making:

Why is it so?
What things demonstrate that it is so?
Who says it is so? Who says it is not so?
How long has it been so?
What feelings or responses does it evoke in you? Why?

What follows is a summary of what you may choose to include as you develop a paragraph.

**1. A Transition Sentence to Join Paragraphs.** This sentence is usually the first sentence in the paragraph, and it often has three functions:

a. To link the paragraph to the preceding paragraph
b. To point toward the content of the paragraph it begins
c. To help carry out the purpose statement

The transition sentence to join paragraphs is often made more effective when it is written in a way that is either closely parallel or roughly parallel to the other transition sentences that join paragraphs. (See pages 110 and 211.)

**2. Examples to Illustrate Your Point.** Clearly written, relevant examples always help to make a general statement believable. (See page 179.) If you were writing an argument paper explaining why foreign cars are disappointing, it would strengthen your argument if you gave examples of how several new or fairly new cars that you know of broke down.

**3. Short Stories.** The short narrative (a paragraph or less) is a kind of example and can be very convincing. In the essay on foreign cars, you may want to do more than just refer to examples of poorly made automobiles; you may instead want to tell about the car you bought in May and then drove across the country in June, and what happened to you and your family at various remote places as you drove that shiny new lemon. (See page 154.)

**4. Descriptive Detail.** Precisely written descriptions are more convincing than general statements. (See page 140.) Try to write so that your readers can *see* what you are describing. In writing a paper against those who contribute to air pollution, for example, describe in detail what it looks like on a humid morning in your city. Describe the black smog that overhangs the city like a witch's cape and the little flakes of ash that fall like black snow.

**5. Dialogue.** When you are describing people or giving their views on things, let them speak for themselves in their own words. (See page 154.) In an argument paper, you could refute a widely held belief by first letting someone voice that belief. For example, you might begin a paper against a huge defense budget in the following way:

▶ The president speaks for most Americans when he says, "If we aren't stronger militarily than the Russians, they may decide to attack one of our allies, or even us." But I disagree . . .

**6. Facts and Statistics.**   Reliable facts bring objectivity into writing and help convince readers. If you are writing a paper advocating more accessibility to public facilities for disabled persons in your city, give the number of disabled persons who reside in your city. If you are arguing in favor of banning all advertising for cigarettes, give the number of people who die each year of lung cancer, which the Surgeon General has linked to cigarette smoking. If you are arguing for more work-release programs for first offenders, give the number of people in the jails in your state and the expense of their maintenance to the taxpayers. Be careful, however, not to overuse statistics in your arguments: they should be relevant to the points you are making. The statistics you are looking for more than likely are written on some page somewhere in your library. You may need to give the source of your statistics in your essay, especially if anyone is likely to question their validity.

**7. Quotations from Reading Material.**   It is often helpful to quote from an authority—either directly or indirectly—in support of the point you are making. A direct quote is especially useful if it is clearly and convincingly worded. But use quotations sparingly and only to illustrate the point *you* are making. (See page 69.)

**8. Logical Arguments.**   Logic (clear, rational thinking) is a necessity in writing essays. Always ask if what you have written would be convincing *to you* if someone else had written it. If not, you know it will not convince other readers. Here are two logical statements that could be made about capital punishment:

▶ Capital punishment is not likely to deter others from committing crime. Stop and think about it. What person is going to make a rational decision about whether to kill on the basis of punishment by death or life imprisonment, if caught? Both fates are terrible.

▶ Capital punishment is bound to have some deterrent effect. Maybe it will stop only one person in a hundred from committing murder, but just think, one person's life is saved. In my view, that one person's life makes capital punishment morally right.

Qualifying words help to make each of these statements believable.

The expression *is not likely to deter* (rather than *will not deter*) qualifies the first statement. The word *maybe* qualifies the second statement.

**9. Transition Sentences Within the Paragraph.**   When a paragraph contains two or more points, transition sentences help the reader move from point to point smoothly. (See the learning notes on page 12.)

**10. A Concluding Statement.**   Sometimes it is helpful to bring a paragraph to an end with a clincher statement. Rely on your ear. What sounds right to you as you read your paper aloud? Be careful not to end your paragraphs with sentences that simply repeat what you have already said. The concluding statements in the second paper on capital punishment are effective clincher statements:

▸ Speaking as a black, I don't think the racial prejudice argument will stand any more.

▸ This is not a way to control all crimes, but it is a way to control some of the more serious ones.

▸ We can't let criminals take advantage of the law but must stand up to them sternly.

▸ Capital punishment should be looked on as a necessity and should be enforced.

**Writing Assignment #1**
Write an argument essay of 300 words or more on an issue of concern at your college, in your city or state, or throughout the nation. *Choose an issue that is important to you.* Your instructor may ask you to write your paper in the form of a letter addressed to an editor (of a school or local newspaper) or to a person who makes policy decisions in the area of your concern. It may be helpful to write your paper first in essay form and then to rewrite it as a business letter, which should probably be less than 300 words and thus shorter than your essay.

**Choose a Topic.**   Brainstorm for possible topics in the areas of concern listed on page 230. Examples are given to stimulate *your* ideas.

*Issues at your college or university:*

► We should (or should not) have a football team.

► We should fire the outfit that serves the food in our cafeteria. (Or: Contrary to popular opinion, I believe our food service is excellent.)

► The foreign language requirement should (or should not) be dropped.

► The Gay Fellowship should (or should not) be given official status as a campus organization.

_____

_____

_____

*Local and state issues:*

► Vote for _____. (Or: Vote against

_____.)

► Decriminalize marijuana. (Or: Keep the marijuana laws in effect.)

► Pass House Bill 1154, which provides for more work-release programs for first offenders.

► The city council should take steps right away to make public facilities more accessible to people in wheelchairs.

_____

_____

_____

*National issues:*

► Birth control pills should (or should not) be readily available to high school girls.

▶ We should decrease (or increase) our defense budget.

▶ In the next presidential election, vote for _____.

▶ Abortion is usually wrong (or always wrong). (Or: Each woman should be able to decide for herself on the issue of abortion.)

▶ The government should declare war on (pollution, or poverty, or

_____).

▶ Women are oppressed in our society (Or: Women are not oppressed in our society.)

_____

_____

_____

_____

Now check the issues (both the examples and the ones you wrote in) that are most important to you. Which of these do you feel most competent to write on? Choose your topic and write it here:

_____

_____

Next, decide to whom you will write—a real audience or imagined audience.

**Step One: Gather Information.**   Think of as many reasons as you can why your position on this issue is the right one, and write those reasons in the left-hand column below. Then think of all the arguments that could be made for other positions on the issue and write those in the right-hand column. (This is a difficult but very important step.) In addition to brainstorming, discuss the issue with others. When appropriate, research the issue in the library, using encyclopedias, periodicals, and books. Make notes on the relevant information and copy quotations you may want to use. Then include the notes and quotations in the information-gathering lists. Space is provided on page 232 for you to make your lists.

*Your position*                                      *Other positions*

_____

_____

_____

_____

_____

_____

_____

_____

*Write any statistics or quotations here*

_____

_____

_____

_____

_____

_____

_____

**Step Two: Analyze the Information.**    Looking at both sides of the issue, ask yourself which arguments are valid. Which are weak? Which do not make sense at all? Exactly where do you stand on the issue? Has your position changed any since you began to reflect on the issue?

**Step Three: State Your Purpose.**    In an argument essay the purpose statement is usually simply a statement of what you believe, such as the following:

► If you want progress in our city, vote for _____.

► Rights for gays should be supported by all Americans who love freedom.

► Abortion is wrong.

If you have reservations about your position, let your purpose statement reflect those reservations, for example:

► In spite of the strong arguments that can be made for sex education in high school, I am against it.

► The advantages of sex education in high school are greater than the disadvantages.

Write your purpose statement below. Qualify your position if necessary, but take a definite stand.

_____

_____

_____

**Step Four: Make Your Plan.**    Before writing an outline, first review the learning notes on the argument essay, especially point 5 on ways to set up an argument paper. Decide what organizing principle you will use for each of the paragraphs. Next, review the learning notes on page 226 on paragraph development. Finally, write an outline showing how you will develop each paragraph.

**Step Five: Write.**    As you write, keep reminding yourself of who your audience is and of the purpose of an argument essay, which is to convince your readers of the validity of your point of view. Would you yourself be convinced by what you are writing? Make use of quotations, statistics, and other facts from your research to back up your points.

**Step Six: Evaluate and Edit.**    Using the revision checklist on the front inside cover, evaluate your paper. Write a paragraph commenting on the organization and style of the essay.

Edit your paper, making use of the checklist on the back inside cover.

**Writing Assignment #2**    A first year English student wrote the letter below to the editor of her college newspaper. In it she called on her fellow students to support the Equal Rights Amendment (ERA). (If the ERA had gone into effect, this statement would have been added to the Constitution: "Equality of rights under the law shall not be denied or abridged by the United States or by any state on account of sex." For the Equal Rights Amendment to become law, however, it had to receive the support of three-fourths of the state legislatures. It did not, but the ERA movement is building once again.)

Your assignment is to write a letter of 200 to 300 words to the same newspaper agreeing or disagreeing with the student's letter. Make use of the resources in the library and carefully support your arguments. The student is arguing for the Equal Rights Amendment from her experience. Your task is to agree or disagree with her both on the basis of your experience and also on the basis of what you have read on the subject. Think of the readers of your school newspaper as the audience.

Dear Editor:

As you know our state legislature will soon vote on ratification of the Equal Rights Amendment. I urge the readers of this newspaper to write their state representatives asking them to vote for ERA. Women are oppressed in our society, and the ERA by providing "equality under the law" will help us to gain our rights.

We are victims of job segregation. Many people say that women should stay home and do domestic chores, but I believe women should have the same rights in choosing an occupation as men have. We often feel useless being traditional housewives, and some of us have to work in order to support our families.

Women want challenges. We want to work and use our minds. Unfortunately, no matter where we work, we still get paid less than men do for doing the same job. I have heard that women get paid only 69¢ for every dollar men get paid. But we have the same abilities as men and can do any job they can. There are even women welders and electricians. The ERA will help us receive the same salaries as men.

Women are also deprived of political importance in this society. Many people say that women can not think for themselves and men should talk about politics to other men because it would bore women. I disagree. Women are very intelligent and have the same mental ability to work in politics as men. Many of us have gone to college and have vast amounts of knowledge to contribute to the rest of society. While the ERA can not guarantee us more political power, it can help us to gain more respect in the community, and then we will be able to demand political power.

Women have progressed a great deal, but we have a long way to go. Please ask your representative to vote "yes" on ERA.

Reina Bougere

**Writing Assignment #3**

Write an essay of 300 words or more defending a view that is different from what practically everyone else thinks. Make use of the learning notes on writing an argument essay and the step-by-step procedure given for the first writing assignment, and study the student samples on pp. 236–237.

Choose one of the following purpose statements, or make up your own:

1. Millions of people in this country are trying to lose weight, but I think fat is beautiful.
2. Most people think _____ is outstanding, but I
   (name the person)

   think (he or she) is _____.
3. Millions of people watch television every chance they get, but I think TV should be banned.
4. Almost everyone in our state believes we should build more prisons and send more people to them, but I say the only way we can really stop people from being criminals is to tear down the prisons.
5. Most colleges and professions require that you write in standard English, but I say standard English is for the birds.
6. Most people in this country argue over whether or not we should elect a Democrat or Republican as president, but I think we should have a king.

## TONS OF FUN

One of America's most deadly diseases is obesity. More than half  1
of our population has this problem, and millions are trying to lose weight.  2
But we forget that being fat has many good points as well.  3

When you finally accept the fact that you are fat and likely to  4
remain so, the fun begins. From this time on you don't have to worry about  5
starving yourself with all those new diets. You can live by the old saying:  6
"Eat, drink, and be merry." At night you can sit back and enjoy television  7
and not have to worry about all the calories you consumed during the day.  8

When you learn to live with yourself and your size, you can also  9
start to put a little more money towards your food bill. Now you don't have  10
to worry about what is in style because you can't fit into most of the modern  11
clothes anyway. You don't have to pay $40.00 for a pair of tight jeans  12
because all of your jeans are tight. Being fat will even help you learn a  13
very important skill. Since not many clothes in the store will fit you, you will  14
most probably have to learn to sew.  15

And then comes the day when love enters the heart. When Mr.  16
Right comes into your life, you will not have to ask the question: Why did  17
he ask me to marry him? You will know it wasn't because of your body.  18
And when that wonderful day comes when you find that the stork is going  19
to visit, you can keep it a secret for as long as you like.  20

One last point. The government will be very happy with you be-  21
cause you will be well-insulated and will not need to keep the heater so  22
high and contribute to the energy crisis. Obesity may be bad for your  23
health, but if you find you can't lose weight, cheer up. You will discover  24
that fat is beautiful.  25

## THE BIGGEST LOUDMOUTH

Many people think Howard Cosell is outstanding, but I think he is  1
the biggest loudmouth of the twentieth century. For over two decades  2
Americans have been listening to Howard Cosell make a fool of himself on  3
national television. He's on one channel one day and on another the next.  4
He will bore you while you are watching football, basketball, boxing, and  5
baseball. Cosell can be seen in Germany one day and in Cuba the next,  6
but he's always the same.  7

Cosell lets viewers know how much he knows about sports by tell-  8
ing them about sports heroes of the past and present. This can be very  9
aggravating. Cosell will talk about the great Bart Starr, the former quarter-  10
back of the Green Bay Packers, while an important play is going on. If he  11
doesn't bore you while talking about Starr, he will certainly bore you when  12
he starts off on Muhammad Ali. Cosell must either be afraid of Ali or be  13
paid by him to build him up. I used to like Ali before I started listening to  14

Howard Cosell. A person can be watching a football game and Cosell will    15
start talking about the "late, great Babe Ruth." What does Babe Ruth, a    16
baseball player, have to do with football?    17

Howard Cosell must use words that he borrows out of *Webster's Dic-*    18
*tionary.* He loves to use such words as *idiosyncrasy* and *idolatry.* By the time    19
a person realizes the meaning of a word used by Cosell, the game the    20
person was watching is over. For some reason, Cosell likes to let everyone    21
know that he is an educated man. Though he is very intelligent, he doesn't    22
have to brag about it.    23

The worst thing about Cosell is that he has a way of insulting his    24
audience. I've actually heard him say, when he was in New Orleans, that    25
New Orleans has the worst sports fans he has ever seen. I think he said this    26
because every time he is in New Orleans a few people like me boo him    27
and call him all sorts of names.    28

So, next time you're thinking about watching a game on television    29
and Howard Cosell is the announcer, take my advice and have a bottle    30
of aspirin nearby.    31

I was sitting at my desk with only my desk lamp on; my fingers were racing across the typewriter keys. Thoughts were coming to me so quickly that I could hardly type fast enough to write them all down. It was well into the middle of the night when she made herself known

# Part Two

## Writing in Standard English

Part One of this text deals with the process of writing: how to express your thoughts in a single paragraph or a short essay consisting of several paragraphs. The emphasis is on communication—saying what you want to say, and saying it with style and with clarity. Part Two deals with the mechanics of writing—how to express your thoughts in standard English, with proper spelling and correct punctuation. The emphasis here is on the single sentence, its parts, and its various uses.

Each chapter is divided into sections designated by decimals to help you find your way around. Chapter 5, on the parts of speech, for example, consists of eight sections:

5.0   Introduction
5.1   Nouns
5.2   Nouns (Used as Subjects) and Verbs
5.3   Subjects and Verbs Reversed
5.4   Objects and Prepositions
5.5   Pronouns
5.6   Adjectives
5.7   Adverbs
5.8   Conjunctions and Interjections

# Chapter 5
## Parts of Speech

## 5.0 Introduction

Grammatical units in this part of the text will be described as words (simple and compound), phrases, clauses, and sentences. *Simple* means one; *compound* means two or more. A simple verb, therefore, is a one-word verb, like "I love"; a compound verb is a verb consisting of two or more parts, like "I <u>love</u> and <u>hate</u>." Note the difference between a phrase and a clause and a clause and a sentence:

**Phrase** ▸ A group of closely related words (two or more) that does not have both a subject and a verb:
<u>into the house</u>, <u>singing in the rain</u>, <u>never too much</u>

**Clause** ▸ A group of words with a subject and a verb that makes up part of a sentence:

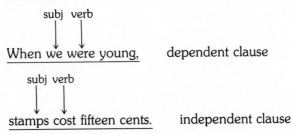

**Sentence** ▸ A group of words with a subject and a verb that can stand by itself:

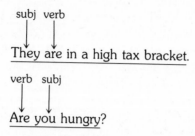

subj  verb

They are in a high tax bracket.

verb  subj

Are you hungry?

The subject of this chapter is the eight parts of speech that make up all sentences: nouns, pronouns, verbs, prepositions, adjectives, adverbs, conjunctions, interjections. As you study the various parts of speech, remember that many words can be used as different parts of speech in different contexts; for example, the word *hate* can be used in these three different ways:

▶ I <u>hate</u> pain.   (verb).

▶ His expression revealed <u>hate</u>.   (noun)

▶ The Senator received many <u>hate</u> letters.   (noun used as an adjective)

Learning the parts of speech is not an end in itself but rather a means to help you learn the conventions of standard English. Here are just three examples:

▶ When you study how to write titles, you will learn that you do not capitalize articles, short conjunctions, and short prepositions, unless they come at the beginning or end of the title. Look at the following title, for example:

The Beginning and the End of the Road

You will learn that *and* is not capitalized because it is a conjunction, *the* is not capitalized because it is an article (a kind of adjective), and *of* is not capitalized because it is a preposition.

▶ When you study verb agreement, you will learn that the third-person singular verb takes an -*s* ending in the present tense, but not in the past tense. For example:

An apple costs more this year than it cost last year.

You will learn that the first form of *cost (costs)* takes an *s* because it is a present-tense verb and its subject is the noun *apple,* which is singular in number. The second form of *cost,* on the other hand, does not take an *-s* ending because it is a past-tense verb.

▶ When you study pronoun case, you will learn that you must use the object form of the pronoun when it follows a preposition. You have to say:

Just between you and <u>me</u> . . .

You cannot say, in standard English:

Just between you and <u>I</u> . . .

You will learn that *between* is a preposition and *me* is the object form of the personal pronoun *I.*

## 5.1 Nouns

**Explanation: Nouns Defined**   A *noun* is a part of speech that names a person, place, thing or idea. Nouns are often preceded by *a, an, the, this* (or *these*), *that* (or *those*). The underlined words in the following are nouns:

▶ a <u>dog</u>     the giant <u>tree</u>     this lovely <u>sample</u>     that <u>noun</u>

a brilliant <u>idea</u>     the perfect <u>plan</u>     an <u>outrage</u>

Possessive pronouns, such as *her, his, our, their,* and *my,* and prepositions, such as *in, of, on,* and *by,* may also point to nouns:

▶ our <u>house</u>     my leaky <u>pen</u>     their great <u>victory</u>     of <u>neces-</u>

<u>sity</u>     in the first <u>place</u>     in <u>1984</u>

**Practice**   Underline each of the nouns in the following sentences. (There are eleven of them altogether. The words *they* and *you* are not nouns but pronouns.)

1. An *essay* on a test need not be a difficult task.   (3 nouns)
2. First, students should gather their thoughts and, if time permits, write an outline.   (4)

3. Next, they should put all their ideas down in the best possible order.   (2)
4. Be sure your sentences are clear and complete.   (1)
5. If you have the time, proofread.   (1)

**Explanation: Proper Nouns**

Some nouns are *proper;* that is, they refer to particular people, places, or things and, therefore, are capitalized. The underlined words in this sentence are all proper nouns:

▸ Edgar Allan Poe, who lived in both England and the United States, is the author of many short stories, including "The Gold Bug" and "The Tell-Tale Heart."

**Practice**

Underline each of the nouns in the following student essay. (Words like *it, he, him, himself* are not nouns but pronouns.)

In 1937, Richard Wright wrote his great book, *Black Boy.* It is the  1
story of the experience of an Afro-American growing up in the Deep South.  2
It takes place between 1905 and 1925, and most of the story is set in the  3
cities of Memphis and Jackson. The book is about how Richard freed him-  4
self from the bondage of his early years.  5
Richard Wright had many obstacles to overcome. It was espe-  6
cially hard for him to obtain a good education because the schools for  7
blacks were inferior in those days. His family was so poor that Richard often  8
went to bed hungry. Richard had to buy his own clothes, books, and much  9
of his food.  10
But Richard did free himself. Many things enabled him to break  11
free, for example: his reading, his courage, his defiance, his learning to  12
cope, and his determination. He took all sorts of prejudices against him in  13
stride. He always found a way to get hold of magazines and books to  14
read. Finally, he saved up the necessary money to get away.  15
After the long, hard struggles of his youth, Richard entered the  16
adult world a free man. But the South had left him with feelings that he  17
would never forget.  18

**Explanation: Nouns as Subjects and Objects**

Nouns can function in different ways in sentences. First, a noun can function as a *subject,* that is, as what the sentence is about. For example:

▸ Richard Wright had many obstacles to overcome.

The noun *Richard Wright* is a subject; *he* is what the sentence is about. Subjects and their verbs will be explained in Sections 2 and 3 of this chapter. A noun can also function as an *object of a verb* or as an *object of a preposition*. Here is an example of each:

▸ Richard bought his own <u>clothes</u> and <u>books</u>.  (objects of the verb *bought*)

▸ The book is about how he freed himself from his <u>bondage</u>.  (object of the preposition *from*)

Nouns used as objects will be explained in Section 4 of this chapter.

## 5.2 Nouns (Used as Subjects) and Verbs

**Explanation: Subjects**

A sentence is a group of words expressing a thought that can stand on its own and containing a subject and a verb. The *subject* is what the rest of the sentence is about. All sentences must have a subject, and all subjects are either nouns or pronouns. (Pronouns, discussed in Section 5, are words that can replace nouns, like *they, it, I, you, he, she, we, who,* and the like.) In the examples that follow, the underlined words are subjects; they are what each sentence is about:

▸ My ninety-year-old <u>grandmother</u> is a spunky lady.

▸ The <u>baby</u> cried half the night.

**Practice**

What are the subjects in the following sentences? (What noun or pronoun best indicates what each sentence is about?) Underline the subjects.

1. Since the beginning of time, men have been using and abusing women.
2. Cavemen dragged, pulled, and beat women all the time.
3. Today, women are striking back on behalf of their cavewomen ancestors!
4. I have developed my own ways of getting even with men.
5. They had better watch out.

**Explanation: Verbs Defined**

A *verb* is a part of speech that says what a subject *is (was, will be)* or *does (did, will do)*. Here is an example of a verb that says what a subject *is*:

     subject    verb

▸ My <u>grandmother</u> <u>is</u> ninety years old.

If you are speaking of the past, the verb says what a subject *was:*

subject  verb

▸ Granny was a ball of fire in her day.

If you are speaking of the future, the verb says what the subject *will be:*

subject                          verb

▸ Miss Jean, as she is known, will be ninety-one next month.

Here is an example of a verb that says what a subject *does:*

subject verb

▸ The deer leaps over the fence escaping from the hunters.

If you are speaking of the past, the verb says what a subject *did:*

subject  verb

▸ Unfortunately, our cat caught not a rat but a squirrel.

If you are speaking of the future, the verb says what a subject *will do:*

subject verb      verb

▸ The wolf will only kill what the pack will eat.

Subjects of sentences that command are often not expressed, but implied:

verb

▸ Come here. (The subject is *you.*)

verb

▸ Don't forget your overcoat. (Again, the subject is *you.*)

**Practice**    Write sentences (thoughts that will stand on their own with the following subjects and verbs):

1. (criminals, are) _____

2. (president, was) _____

3. (looks, tell) _____

4. (architect, designed) _____

5. (smoking, will) _____

6. (high school bands, _____) _____
   <sub>supply verb</sub>

   _____

7. (police officers, _____) _____
   <sub>supply verb</sub>

   _____

8. (_____, swam) _____
   <sub>supply subject</sub>

   _____

9. (_____, kissed) _____
   <sub>supply subject</sub>

   _____

10. (Express a command with the verb *get*.) _____

    _____

**Explanation: Simple Verbs and Verb Phrases**

If verbs consist of one word, they are called *simple verbs*; if they consist of more than one word, they are called *verb phrases*. Chapters 7 and 8 are devoted to various verbs and their uses. For now, note the following examples of verb phrases. (The *helping verbs* that go with the main verb *love* are underlined.)

| | |
|---|---|
| <u>do</u> love | <u>were</u> loved |
| <u>does</u> love | <u>have been</u> loved |
| <u>did</u> love | <u>would have</u> loved |
| <u>might</u> love | <u>could have</u> loved |
| <u>can</u> love | <u>am</u> loved |
| <u>could</u> love | <u>will be</u> loved |
| <u>should</u> love | <u>might be</u> loved |
| <u>may</u> love | <u>is</u> loving |

have loved      am loving

has loved      was loving

had loved      were loving

is loved      will have been loving

was loved      should have been loving

If you are ever confused about where the verb is in a sentence, change the tense (the time) of the sentence and see which word or words change. (From this point on, the *time* of the verb will be referred to as the *tense*.)

*Present tense*                *Past tense*

Today, I want to compare     Yesterday, I wanted to com-
   answers.                      pare answers.

They can't get themselves     Yesterday, they couldn't get
   together.                     themselves together.

In the first sentence, *want* changes and is, therefore, the verb. In the second sentence, *can't* changes and is thus part of the verb. The full verb is *can't get*. Here is an example of a sentence that has a compound verb. (In grammar usage, *compound* means two or more.)

*Present tense*                *Past tense*

Fall cools the city and     Fall cooled the city and
   calms tempers.              calmed tempers.

## Practice

A ▸ Rewrite the following sentences, changing the tense as indicated. Underline the subject once and verb twice in the first sentence of each pair.

1. Every day the teacher complains about our behavior.

   (past) Yesterday, *the teacher complained about our behavior.*

2. We are mighty scared and do not know what to say.   (2 verb changes)

   (past) Yesterday, _____

3. She signals to us to come out of the classroom.

   (past) Yesterday, _____

4. When we are outside in the hall, she starts to question us.  (2 verb changes)

   (past) Yesterday, _____

5. We denied that we were cheating and made up a magnificent lie.  (3 verb changes)

   (present) Every day, _____

   _____

6. But she didn't believe us and sent us to the office.  (2 verb changes)

   (present) _____

7. I told my mother that I would never cheat again.  (2 verb changes)

   (present) Every day, _____

B ► Underline the subjects once and the verbs twice in the following sentences. Be sure to underline the helping verbs as well as the main verbs. (See the list of helping verbs on page 247.)

1. I do believe the testimony.
2. The testimony could hurt the defendant.
3. The troop will have been hiking for three hours.
4. That extra five minutes could have made the difference.
5. The choir members were greeting everyone at the door.
6. The Marines want a few good people.
7. Their affair is known all over town.
8. The stereo is turned up too loud.
9. My wallet is empty.
10. David should have been chosen.
11. Marie doesn't think she will register.

**Explanation:**
**Linking Verbs**

Linking verbs always tell what a subject *is, was,* or *will be.* Thus, they can be any form of the *be* verbs, such as *am, is, are, was, were, has been, will be.* Other linking verbs are *become, feel, seem, look, appear. Predicate nominatives* are nouns that are closely related in meaning to the subject and are joined (or linked) to the subject by a linking verb, for example:

▸ My ninety-year-old <u>grandmother</u> <u>is</u> a spunky <u>lady</u>.

*Grandmother* is the subject of the sentence; *she* is what the sentence is about. The word *lady* is a predicate nominative: it refers to the same person as the subject—it renames the subject—and is linked to the subject by the verb *is.* Think of the linking verb as an equals sign in an equation:

▸ <u>grandmother</u> = <u>lady</u>

In the following two examples the subjects and predicate nominatives are underlined once, the linking verbs twice:

▸ <u>Joe</u> <u>is</u> the best long-distance <u>runner</u> on the team.

▸ The <u>recruits</u> at the police academy <u>will become</u> <u>officers</u> soon.

**Practice**

In the following sentences, underline the subjects and the predicate nominatives once and the linking verbs twice:

1. Yesterday was the last day of the concert series.
2. Many popular movies of the early 1970s were disaster films.
3. Mr. Reynolds has been the chairman of the department for years.
4. Under the circumstances, that solution seems the best one.
5. This painting is an example of impressionistic work.
6. Tom was the best-dressed member of the wedding party.

## 5.3 Subjects and Verbs Reversed

**Explanation: Sentences That Ask Questions**

Sometimes sentences are inverted, that is, out of their natural order. In such cases, the subject comes not at the beginning of the sentence but after the verb. One common type of inverted sentence is a question, such as:

▶ Did the instructor say that?

The sentence is about the instructor, so you know *instructor* is the subject. You can identify the verb by putting the sentence back in its natural order:

▶ The instructor did say that.

Now you can see that the verb is *did say*.

**Practice**    Change the following questions to statements in the spaces provided. Then underline the subjects once and the verbs twice in the questions themselves. Be sure to underline the helping verbs as well as the main verbs.

1. Will the teller cash our check?

   *The teller will cash our check.*

2. Is it a long way to Tipperary?

   _____

3. Were Mary and Martha the sisters Jesus loved?

   _____

4. Should the employees insist on collective bargaining?

   _____

5. Is physics the most difficult freshman course?

   _____

6. Should we have listened to Einstein when he warned us against atomic power? _____

   _____

**Explanation: Expletive Expressions**    Another common type of inverted sentence is one that begins with an *expletive expression (there is, there are, here is, here are,* and *it is),* for example:

▶ There are three possible answers to that question.

Expletives like *there* point to subjects—introduce subjects—but are not subjects themselves. The subject in the above sentence is *answers*.

## Practice

A ► Underline the subjects in the following sentences once and the verbs twice, and draw an arrow from the expletive to the subject.

1. There is a bug in my Coke.
2. There are five volunteers for the job.
3. Here is all my change.
4. Here are four examples of prejudice in our newspaper.
5. There is still one of us left.
6. There are still three of us left.
7. It was a bad day at Black Rock.

B ► Underline the subjects once and the verbs twice. Be sure to underline helping verbs as well as main verbs.

1. Will television ever replace classrooms and teachers?
2. Many children watch "Sesame Street" and other educational programs.
3. Perhaps in the future, such programs will occupy more and more of our children's time.
4. What did Neil Armstrong say when setting foot on the moon?
5. There are two main advantages to such a computerized system.
6. Students learn in a nonthreatening environment.
7. In her class, no one feels embarrassed by mistakes.
8. Second, a person can progress at his or her own speed.
9. One drawback, however, is the isolation of television viewing.
10. Will the space program survive the budget cutbacks?
11. There are no opportunities for a person to relate to others.
12. The team should have chosen her as captain.
13. A young couple often has difficulty establishing credit.
14. Haven't those young mothers listened to their doctors?

15. Teaching techniques should combine both traditional and inno-
    vative approaches.

16. Study hard, and you will succeed.

## 5.4 Objects and Prepositions

**Explanation:** The types of nouns you have studied so far—subjects and predicate
**Direct Objects** nominatives—have *nominative functions*. Nominative means referring to the subject—the person, place, thing, or idea the sentence is
about. In addition, nouns may have three *objective functions*: they
may serve as direct objects, indirect objects, and objects of prepositions.

A *direct object* is a noun that receives the action of a verb. It answers *what* or *whom* after a verb that expresses action. Here are two
examples:

▸ John threw the javelin.

*Javelin* is the direct object of the action verb *threw*. You can check its
function by asking the question, "John threw *what?*"

▸ Mark invited his girlfriend.

*Girlfriend* is the direct object of the action verb *invite*. You can check
its function by asking, "Mark invited *whom?*"

**Practice** In the sentences that follow, underline the subject once, the verb
twice, and circle the direct object. Say whether the object tells *what*
or *whom*.

1. We watched television on Thursday evening. *tells what*

2. The girls baked peanut butter cookies.

3. Andy asked Melissa for a date.

4. Andy ate two dozen cookies and drank a quart of apple cider.

5. Andy had a stomachache on Friday.

6. The math instructor assigned several chapters for homework.

7. Karen defeated Janice in the tennis tournament.

8. She worked the problems in an hour.

9. She passed the test easily on the next class day.

10. The instructor returned the paper with an *A* at the top.

11. Dr. Laska gave me laughing gas.

**Explanation:**
**Indirect Objects**

An *indirect object* is a noun that tells *for whom* or *to whom* something is done. It usually comes between an action verb and its direct object, for example:

▸ Tony gave his younger <u>sister</u> a (quarter)

*What* Tony gave her was a quarter; therefore, *quarter* is the direct object. The person *to whom* he gave the quarter was his sister; therefore *sister* is the indirect object.

▸ The worried mother sent her <u>son</u> a care (package) during his first week of college.

*What* the mother sent was a package. The person *to whom* she sent it was the son. *Son* is therefore the indirect object. Notice that it comes between the verb *sent* and the direct object *package*.

**Practice**

In the sentences below, circle the direct object and underline the indirect object.

1. Tom brought his <u>friend</u> a (basket) of fruit.

2. Elizabeth gave her instructor some free advice.

3. The news gave the family quite a shock.

4. Doug offered his neighbor a lift to school.

5. The real estate agent offered his clients a special deal.

6. That thief sold my wife a fake diamond.

**Explanation:**
**Objects of**
**Prepositions**

The third objective function of a noun is when it serves as an *object of a preposition*. A *preposition* is a part of speech that connects a noun or pronoun (the object of the preposition) to the rest of the sentence, for example:

▸ It is difficult <u>for</u> a hard-working person to stay awake.

*For* is the preposition and it connects *hard-working person* to the sentence. In this sentence *person* is the object of the preposition and *hard-working* is the modifier. Here is an example of two prepositional phrases next to each other:

▶ Between the hours of 8 P.M. and midnight, my brain becomes increasingly tired.

*Between* is the first preposition; *hours* is its object. *Of* is the second preposition; *8 P.M.* and *midnight* are its objects.

Most prepositions are short single words. Here are the most common. The underlined words are objects of the prepositions.

| | | | |
|---|---|---|---|
| above | (above the city) | from | (from John and me) |
| across | (across the river) | in | (in those days) |
| after | (after his death) | into | (into the unknown) |
| among | (among his strengths) | like | (like King Kong) |
| at | (at the crossroads) | of | (of human bondage) |
| before | (before breakfast) | on | (on the mountain) |
| behind | (behind the door) | onto | (onto the roof) |
| below | (below sea level) | over | (over hill and dale) |
| between | (between you and me) | through | (through the woods) |
| by | (by train) | to | (to grandmother's house) |
| down | (down the street) | up | (up the stairs) |
| during | (during class) | upon | (upon this rock) |
| for | (for whom) | with | (with your personality) |
| | | without | (without me) |

Groups of words may also serve as prepositions, for example:

| | |
|---|---|
| along with | (along with your exercises) |
| according to | (according to our source) |
| in spite of | (in spite of our differences) |
| on account of | (on account of the war) |
| such as | (such as those children) |

## Practice

A ► For each of the thirty-two prepositions listed above, make up your own prepositional phrases.

B ► In the following, put the prepositional phrases in parentheses.

1. (During the <u>sixties</u>) many people became interested (in <u>drugs</u>.)
2. You could hear the names of particular drugs, such as LSD and marijuana, on the news every day.   (3 prepositional phrases)
3. Incidences of experimentation with drugs increased dramatically at this time.   (3)
4. With the increase in drug use came the danger of drug abuse.   (3)
5. Unfortunately, for some, drugs led to an early death.   (2)
6. Others were not harmed by drugs.   (1)

## 5.5 Pronouns

**Explanation: The Subjective Case**

A *pronoun* is a part of speech that substitutes for a noun, serving in any of the noun functions: as a subject, a predicate nominative, a direct object, an indirect object, or an object of a preposition. Here are two examples:

► Dr. Lawson gets a gleam in his eye when he goes to pull a tooth. (The pronoun *he* takes the place of Dr. Lawson.)

► Representative Taylor was delighted when the Governor gave the award to her. (The pronoun *her* replaces Representative Taylor.)

Unlike nouns, some pronouns change their form according to their use in the sentence. For example, the pronoun *he* becomes *him* when used as an object and *his* when used to show ownership. *Pronoun case* is the designation used to show the different uses of pronouns in a sentence. Learn the three cases for *personal pronouns,* which are shown below. (A personal pronoun usually refers to a person but sometimes to a thing.)

| | *Subjective case* | | *Objective case* | | *Possessive case* | |
|---|---|---|---|---|---|---|
| | S | P | S | P | S | P |
| First person ► | I | we | me | us | my, mine | our, ours |
| Second person ► | you | you | you | you | your, yours | your, yours |
| Third person ► | he, she, it | they | him, her, it | them | his, her, hers, its | their theirs |

In the illustration above S stands for singular, which means one; P stands for plural, which means more than one. Read *first person, second person, third person* forms across. (For example, the first person forms are *I, we, me, us, my, mine, our, ours.*) Notice that in the third-person singular there are three genders: masculine *(he, him, his),* feminine *(she, her, hers),* and neuter (*it* and *its*).

Two other pronouns (*who* and *whoever*) change in form:

| *Subjective Case* | *Objective Case* | *Possessive Case* |
|---|---|---|
| who | whom | whose |
| whoever | whomever | |

Because of the complexities of pronoun use, a separate chapter of this text, Chapter 10, is devoted to pronouns: when to use them, how to make them agree with the words they stand for, when to use masculine and when to use feminine pronouns, and so forth. The rest of this section is devoted to pronoun case and identifying various kinds of pronouns in a sentence.

The *subjective case* is used when the pronoun functions as the subject of a verb or as a predicate nominative:

Subject ▸ She said, "Don't count your chickens before they hatch." (*She* is the subject of the verb *said*.)

Subject ▸ He runs as fast as I. (The pronoun *I* is used instead of *me* because the sense of the sentence is actually "He runs as fast I run." *I* is thus the subject of the verb *run,* which is understood.)

Predicate nominative ▸ This is she. (*She* is linked to the subject *this* by the verb *is*.)

Predicate nominative ▸ The winners were we freshmen. (*We* is linked to the subject *winners* by the verb *were*.)

Practice    Using the diagram on page 256, supply the designated subjective pronoun for each of the following:

1. (third-person singular, masculine gender) Kathleen is taller than ___*he*___.
2. (first-person singular) John and _____ are studying together.
3. (third-person singular, feminine gender) _____ is her own worst enemy.
4. (first-person singular) Clarence and _____ are the best of friends.

5. (first-person plural) They are no better than _____.
6. (third-person plural) "Are these _____?" I asked. "Yep, that's them," he replied.

**Explanation: The Objective Case**

The objective case is used when the pronoun functions as a direct object, an indirect object, or the object of a preposition. Here are some examples:

Direct Object ▶ I told her so. (*Her* is the object of the verb *told*.)

Indirect Object ▶ Aunt Nanny sent me a present. (*Me* is the one *to whom* Aunt Nanny sent the present.)

Object of the Preposition ▶ This secret is between you and me. (*Me* is the object of the preposition *between*.)

*Note:* Watch out for pronouns used in compound constructions. They should be treated according to their function, just as single pronouns are:

▶ My friend and I ate cereal for breakfast. (Choose *I* over *me*. You wouldn't say "Me ate cereal for breakfast.")

▶ She bought the present for Jim and me. (Choose *me* over *I*. You wouldn't say: "She bought the present for I.")

An error in pronoun case is designated PC in the editing checklist on the back inside cover.

**Practice**

First, determine the function of each pronoun in the sentences below and write it in the blank. It will be either subject (subj), predicate nominative (pn), direct object (do), indirect object (io), or object of the preposition (op). Then circle the correct pronoun choice.

1. _subj_ (I, me) took the test before John took it.
2. _____ Rachel brought Mary and (I, me) the notes to study.
3. _____ John saw (we, us) players on the practice field.
4. _____ David can't type as fast as (she, her).
5. _____ Was it really (she, her) that you saw?
6. _____ The near-crash did not alarm Maria or (I, me).
7. _____ The answer was apparent to both (he and I, him and me).

8. _____ Dad gave (I, me) the stereo as a birthday present.
9. _____ Harry and (I, me) have three children.
10. _____ Just between you and (I, me), Mr. Norton has been acting mighty strange lately.
11. _____ José doesn't jog as often as (I, me).
12. _____ (Who, Whom) is your advisor?
13. _____ (Whoever, Whomever) wants this day-old sandwich may have it.
14. _____ Give the invitation to (whoever, whomever) you can find.
15. _____ For (who, whom) does the bell toll?
16. _____ This is (she, her).

**Explanation: Seven Classes of Pronouns**

There are seven classes of pronouns altogether. Study the function of each.

a. *Personal pronouns* distinguish between the person speaking (first person), the person spoken to (second person), and the person spoken about (third person):

**First Person ▶**   I, me, we, us, my, mine, our, ours

**Second Person ▶**   you, your, yours

**Third Person ▶**   he, she, it, him, his, her, hers, its, they, them, their, theirs

b. *Demonstrative pronouns* point to persons or things. The demonstrative pronouns are *this, that, these, those.* They are often subjects.

**Examples ▶**   This is my problem.     These are the facts.

That is your belief.     Those should make the difference.

You may do this but not that. (Here this and that are objects.)

c. *Indefinite pronouns* refer to certain individuals or things without specifying which ones:

| | | | | |
|---|---|---|---|---|
| any | either | many | neither | some |
| anybody | everybody | more | nobody | somebody |
| anyone | everyone | most | no one | someone |
| anything | everything | much | none | something |
| each | | | | |

Examples ► Somebody is missing a pen.

Everyone misses you.

See Chapter 7.8 and page 346 for a discussion of when indefinite pronouns function as singular pronouns and when they function as plural pronouns.

d. *Intensive pronouns* emphasize a particular noun or pronoun:

| Singular | Plural | |
|----------|--------|---|
| myself | ourselves | Note that the plural |
| yourself | yourselves | of *self* is always |
| herself | themselves | *selves*. Also, there |
| himself | " | are no such |
| itself | " | words as *hisself* |
| | | or *theirselves*. |

Examples ► The players themselves refused to cheat.

I myself will take the blame.

(*Players* is emphasized in the first sentence; *I* is emphasized in the second.)

e. *Reflexive pronouns* show that the subject acts upon itself. (They are formed like intensive pronouns.)

Examples ► I hurt myself in the game.

You can fool other people, but you can't fool yourself.

(The person *I* hurt was *myself*; the person *you* can't fool is *yourself*.)

f. *Interrogative pronouns* ask questions:

| Who? | Whoever? | Which? |
|------|----------|--------|
| Whom? | Whomever? | What? |
| Whose? | | Whatever? |

Examples ► Who is the best dressed? Whose is that?

g. *Relative pronouns* introduce dependent noun and adjective clauses:

who     whoever     whose     that

whom    whomever    what    which

Examples  ▸  The company makes pens that don't write.

The tree, which is outside my window, was hit by lightning.

The people who live on our block are no neighbors.

(Use *who* to refer to people, *that* and *which* to refer to things.) See Chapters 6.3 and 7.8 for a more complete discussion of how relative pronouns function in a sentence.

## Practice

A ▸ The pronouns in the following paragraph are underlined. Identify each pronoun by type, using the following abbreviations: personal (per), demonstrative (dem), indefinite (ind), intensive (int), interrogative (inter), reflexive (reflex), relative (rel). Note that the word *that* can be used as a demonstrative or relative pronoun.

              *rel*
    My Aunt Birdie is a rare species of aunt who will soon become 1

     *per*
extinct. She is so considerate of other people that sometimes you can ac- 2

tually see a halo over her head. My aunt is seventy-nine years old, five feet 3

tall, and shaped like a loosely-rolled sleeping bag. She talks to herself all 4

the time about her old boyfriends. Her hair is snow-white, which matches 5

her teeth that sit upon her bureau every night. She has a huge hernia that 6

forces her to tilt to the left when she walks. Though Aunt Birdie has a hard 7

time getting around, she won't let anyone help her. She does everything for 8

herself. That is how she likes it. 9

B ▸ In this paragraph, underline the pronouns and identify them using the above abbreviations.

    Aunt Birdie rises with the Mississippi sun every morning and fixes a 1

full breakfast for Uncle Buddy and herself. This is what she likes to do most, 2

cook for Uncle Buddy. She then goes about the business of cleaning her 3

small wood-frame house, which is just like the other houses in the area. 4

What do you suppose she does next? She does what all other housewives 5 do; she watches her favorite soap opera. When she finishes that, she   6

washes the clothes. Since she doesn't trust washing machines, she washes   7

her clothes by hand. In the afternoon, Aunt Birdie babysits for her many   8

grandchildren, whom she loves dearly. This is how she spends most of her   9

days. She does everything she can for everyone, and everyone is devoted   10

to her.   11

## 5.6 Adjectives

**Explanation**   An *adjective* is a part of speech that modifies or describes a noun or pronoun. Here are some examples:

▸ the scorching sun      the blinding glare      unfriendly people

a frozen pond      a terrible day      the worst storm

The following are special types of adjectives:

a. *Articles: a, an, the*

▸ a house      a batch      an apple      an image

an image      an hour      the truth      an honest mistake

Note that *an* is used before words beginning with a vowel (*a, e, i, o, u*) or a vowel sound (such as the *o/oh* sound in *hour* or *honest*).

b. *Predicate adjectives:*

▸ My canary is sick.

▸ The trip seemed dangerous to me.

Predicate adjectives function like predicate nominatives in a sentence (see Section 2 of this chapter); they follow a linking verb and refer to the subject of the sentence. In the sentences above, *sick* modifies *canary*, and *dangerous* modifies *trip*.

c. *Demonstrative adjectives: this, that, these, those*

▸ This place is prettier than that place.

▸ These places are prettier than those places.

Demonstrative adjectives have the same form as demonstrative pronouns. Instead of serving as subjects or objects, however, they modify nouns.

d. *Indefinite adjectives: some, few, any, each,* and the like.

▸ some people    a few dollars    any approach
each person

Many adjectives change form when they are used to compare two or more things:

▸ big becomes bigger (two things) or biggest (more than two things)

▸ bad becomes worse (two things) or worst (more than two things)

Longer adjectives require more or most to compare two or more things:

▸ influential becomes more influential or most influential

See page 196 for a more complete description.

**Practice**    Identify the adjectives in the following sentences by underlining them. Draw arrows to the nouns or pronouns they modify. (Remember that the articles *a, an,* and *the* are classified as adjectives.)

1. The Kool Jazz Festival is a mixture of jazz and soul music. (4 adjectives)

2. These concerts bring out different types of people.   (2)

3. They bring out the rowdy ones, the dreamy lovers, the smokers, the ones who stand against the walls the whole night, and the ones who use profane language.   (11)

4. The rowdy ones are young.   (3)

5. They dance, scream, push, and blow those loud whistles.   (2)

6. The dreamy lovers sit through the whole concert watching one another with moony eyes.   (5)

7. The smokers fill the air with the disgusting smell of marijuana.   (4)

8. The wall-standers are unfriendly to everyone, even to one another.   (2)

9. The cursers sit everywhere and do not show any respect for anyone, not even for the older people.   (4)

10. Still, the Kool Jazz Festival is terrific; I never miss it.   (2)

## 5.7 Adverbs

**Explanation**    An *adverb* is a part of speech that modifies or describes a verb, adjective, or other adverb:

▸ He drove wildly.

▸ The child wept quietly.

The adverbs above tell how he *drove* and how the child *wept*: they modify verbs.

▸ The very large man is my father.

▸ She is extremely wet.

These adverbs tell just how *large* the man is and just how *wet* she is: they modify adjectives.

▸ He was running so rapidly that no one could keep up with him.

▸ The car was going quite slowly on the interstate.

These adverbs tell just how *rapidly* he was running and just how *slowly* the car was going: they modify other adverbs.

Adverbs often end in -ly. Here are some examples:

| | | | |
|---|---|---|---|
| beautifully | extremely | poorly | triumphantly |
| bluntly | hardly | prudently | wholly |
| cruelly | immediately | quietly | wisely |
| curiously | incompetently | smoothly | zealously |
| daily | nicely | tactfully | |

Some adverbs, such as the following, do not have -ly endings:

| | | |
|---|---|---|
| almost | more | quite |
| always | most | too |
| even | never | very |
| fast | not | well |

And some adverbs are called *conjunctive adverbs,* such as:

| | | | |
|---|---|---|---|
| also | furthermore | next | then |
| consequently | however | on the other hand | therefore |
| for example | moreover | plus | thus |
| for instance | nevertheless | | |

The use of these conjunctive adverbs in a sentence is discussed in Chapter 6.5.

Adverbs used to compare two things are preceded by *more:*

▶ She drove to work <u>quickly</u>.

▶ She drove to work <u>more quickly</u> than she had before.

See page 197 for a more complete description.

**Practice**  Identify the adverbs in the following sentences by underlining them. Draw arrows to the verbs, adjectives, or other adverbs they modify.

1. It was <u>so</u> dark that I stumbled and fell <u>noisily</u> over the chair.  (2 adverbs)

2. The flowers were so beautifully arranged that all the children noticed them.  (2)

3. Although they conducted the investigation very incompetently, they did catch the thief, who had been quietly stealing from everyone.  (3)

4. My neighborhood is just too noisy to enjoy.  (2)

5. He generously gave his mother a most lovely home.  (2)

6. The lady in the lounge has been waiting for you most impatiently.   (2)

7. With his rag-tag band, he entered the city triumphantly, riding very slowly on the back of a donkey.   (3)

8. It is extremely hard to work forty hours a week, attend school, raise children, and not complain.   (2)

9. Reverend Davis always begins his sermon with an unnecessarily long prayer.   (2)

10. Dr. Nguyen never admits a patient who has not been carefully screened.   (3)

**Explanation: Distinguishing Adjectives and Adverbs**

A common mistake of beginning college students is to confuse adjectives and adverbs. Remember that adjectives must modify nouns or pronouns; adverbs must modify verbs, adjectives, or other adverbs. The following sentence is incorrect:

▸ They prepare you very good at that high school.

If you look up *good* in a dictionary, you will see that it cannot be used as an adverb, though in the sentence above it is used as if it were an adverb modifying the verb *prepare.* The adverb *well* should be substituted, and then the sentence will read "They prepare you very well at that high school."

Likewise, the sentence below is incorrect:

▸ He arrived as quick as he could.

*Quick* is an adjective; the adverb *quickly* must be used instead to modify the verb *arrived:* "He arrived as quickly as he could." A misused adjective or adverb is designated WW (for Wrong Word) in the editing checklist on the back inside cover.

**Practice**

Some of the sentences that follow require adjectives, some adverbs. Choose the correct word and draw an arrow to the word it modifies.

1. Carry those dishes just as (careful, <u>carefully</u>) as you can.

2. The librarian looked at me very (curious, curiously).

3. He has fixed up the room really (nice, nicely) for the children.

4. Her fingers were moving across the keys very (rapid, rapidly).

5. She looks (beautiful, beautifully) in her wedding gown.

6. These dogs bark so (loud, loudly) that they wake the whole neighborhood.

7. They play (good, well) music on radio station WILD.

8. The WILD jazz band plays (good, well).

9. With her new hair style, she certainly looks (good, well).

10. The waiter frowns at me (frequent, frequently).

11. They have been carrying on (crazy, crazily) lately.

## 5.8 Conjunctions and Interjections

**Explanation: Conjunctions**
A *conjunction* joins words, phrases, or clauses in a sentence. There are three types of conjunctions: coordinating conjunctions, subordinating conjunctions, and correlative conjunctions.

A *coordinating conjunction* joins elements that are equal in a grammatical sense. There are seven coordinating conjunctions:

▸ and     but     for     so     yet     or     nor

Here is how they are used:

**To Join Words** ▸ the dog and his bone

the ballot or the bullet

**To Join Phrases** ▸ over the river and through the woods

not into darkness but into light

**To Join Clauses** ▸ He stayed at home, and she went to work.

He stayed at home, but she went to work.

See Chapter 6.4 for a more complete discussion of coordinating conjunctions.

A *subordinating conjunction* introduces a subordinate or dependent clause in a sentence, for example:

sub conj

↓

▶ Although we were tired, we went to work anyway.

*Although* introduces a dependent clause (underlined) and joins the clause to the rest of the sentence. Here are other examples of dependent clauses (underlined) introduced by subordinating conjunctions:

sub conj

↓

▶ He acts that way to his family because he hates himself.

sub conj

↓

▶ Because he hates himself, he acts that way to his family.

sub conj

↓

▶ When he went to the psychiatrist, he found out that he was bored with life.

sub conj

↓

▶ Though they function pretty well day by day, they are a troubled family.

These are some of the most common subordinating conjunctions:

| | | | |
|---|---|---|---|
| after | before | so that | where |
| although | even though | though | wherever |
| as | if | till | whether |
| as if | in order that | unless | while |
| as though | since | until | |
| because | so *(so that)* | when | |

See Chapter 6.2 for a more complete discussion of subordinating conjunctions.

*Correlative conjunctions* are always used in pairs:

| | |
|---|---|
| either/or | both/and also |
| neither/nor | not only/but also |

Here are two examples:

▶ Either you fix the car, or I will take it to the shop.

▶ Not only should you listen, but you should also take notes.

See Chapter 7.4 for a discussion of how subjects and verbs are used in sentences with correlative conjunctions.

**Practice**    Underline and label all conjunctions with the following abbreviations: coordinating conjunctions (cc), subordinating conjunctions (sub), correlative conjunctions (cor).

1. Mama Linda is *both* my aunt *and also* my friend.

2. When the wind is from the south, it blows the hook in the fish's mouth.

3. Many people are walking the streets of London because, while they were playing bridge, they failed to lead out trumps.

4. One door closes, and another door opens.

5. If you look hard, you will discover that a good man or woman is not hard to find.

6. You will bloom where you are planted.

7. You can fool some of the people some of the time, but you can't fool all of the people all of the time, or can you?

8. Every creature in the world either eats or is eaten.

9. Because you love, you will live.

10. He reads to his grandchildren when they ask him to.

11. And he teaches them many old sayings while he has their attention.

**Explanation: Interjections**    An *interjection* is a part of speech used to express either a mild or a strong emotion. Interjections are used more commonly in speech than in writing. An expression of strong emotion is followed by an exclamation point:

▶ Ouch!    Help!    Stop!    Wait!

An expression of mild emotion is followed by a comma and hooked to the sentence:

▶ My, my, you certainly are clever these days.

▶ Well, that's when the fun really started.

# Chapter 6

# Writing Whole Sentences

## 6.0 Introduction

A sentence is a group of words expressing a thought that can stand on its own. Most everything that you write in freshman English should be in the form of a sentence. Exceptions are titles of essays, which usually are not full sentences, and sometimes quotations from conversations. Here are two tests to determine whether a statement is a sentence:

1. If you walked up to someone and made the statement, would it make sense? If someone wrote the statement on a note to you with nothing else on the note, would that make sense?
2. Does the statement have a subject (at least understood) and a verb?

Writing in complete sentences is a natural process because most of what we say, we say in sentence form. To write in complete sentences consistently, the most important thing to remember is to *listen* to what you are writing. Read your writing aloud, sentence by sentence, and ask if each sentence can stand alone.

   In this chapter you will practice writing different kinds of sentences, called simple, complex, and compound; you will learn how to apply six comma rules as you write your sentences (reference will be made to the list of ten comma rules in Chapter 11.4), and finally, you will learn how to detect and prevent errors that keep statements from being correct sentences. The three kinds of sentence errors listed in the editing checklist on the back inside cover are

**Fragments (F)** ► Statements that cannot stand alone and, therefore, are not sentences, for example:

Which is what I wanted to do all along.

Because he did not want to go with us.

First, the arguments for capital punishment.

**Run-On Sentences** ► Statements consisting of two sentences that are run together either
**(RO)** with no punctuation or with a comma. A run-on sentence with no punctuation is also called a *fused sentence*; a run-on sentence with a comma is also called a *comma splice*:

Capital punishment is ethically unacceptable it is against the morals of civilized societies.   (Fused sentence)

Capital punishment is ethically unacceptable, it is against the morals of civilized societies.   (Comma splice)

**Sentence Sense** ► Statements that do not make sense as written but cannot be easily
**Errors (SS)** classified as fragments or run-on sentences.

### Practice

**A** ► Remain silent for ten seconds and then write down exactly what you

are thinking. _____

_____

_____

Did you write a whole sentence: What is the subject and what is the verb? Your instructor may ask several people to read aloud what they wrote down to see if most of the class expressed themselves in whole sentences.

**B** ► From the list below, identify which statements are sentences (mark these S) and which are fragments (mark these F). Apply the test: if you walked up to someone and made the statement, would it make sense? Would it make sense if you received it by itself in a note? Remember that whole sentences can begin with pronoun subjects.

1. ____*S*____ Shut the door.

2. _____ Will you help me with my homework?

3. _____ Because they live on Park Place.

4. _____ When I leave home at seven in order to catch the seven-fifteen bus.

5. _____ It is a story about the best of times and the worst of times.

6. _____ The time I went to see my Aunt Nancy in Philadelphia.

7. _____ Which is a most controversial law.

8. _____ That is what you should do.

9. _____ To dress up my walls with bright colored paintings.

10. _____ First, how my pet and I are alike.

It may seem easy enough to pick out these fragments, but it is just these kinds of fragments that students sometimes write on freshman essays. Make the above fragments into whole sentences by adding whatever information is necessary.

C ▶ Identify the three fragments in the paragraph below. Mark them with an F.

> I too feel sad for the young man in the poem. He was so much an 1
> individual and so creative, but he could not share himself. There was no 2
> one to see his picture, no one to react. No one to care. He had only himself 3
> to hold onto, but that got very lonely. Finally, he threw away his picture, 4
> gave up his old self, and put on a tie. When he could take it no longer. He 5
> was the flower trying to grow in the crack in the sidewalk of society. The 6
> sun still shone. The rain still fell, but there was no one to support him, so he 7
> gave up. And lost himself and was dead before he died. 8

Many fragments, such as the ones in the paragraph above, can be corrected by hooking the fragment onto the sentence that comes before it or the sentence that comes after it. For example, you can correct the first fragment in the following way:

▶ There was no one to see his picture, no one to react, no one to care.

Often when you hook a fragment to the preceding sentence you must use a comma. See Comma Rule #10 in Chapter 11.4 for using commas before afterthoughts. For practice, correct the other two fragments in the above paragraph by hooking them onto the preceding sentences. Use commas if necessary.

D ▶ The following paragraphs together contain three fragments, which are missing a subject or a verb or both. Identify them with an F and correct them by supplying the necessary subjects and verbs.

As you go through the front door of my dream house, you first enter   1
the living room. The room has a huge picture window opening on a gar-   2
den. There two distinct areas within this room. One area contains an over-   3
stuffed, floppy sofa with three pieces that join together. The other area, a   4
60″ television screen and all the component parts of the latest stereo   5
equipment.   6

As you move through the living room, to the right, you come to the   7
dining room and kitchen. There you see the latest appliances, such as a   8
refrigerator-freezer with a drinking fountain, a dishwasher, a microwave   9
oven, a conventional oven, and a garbage disposal. There is a small room   10
to the side of the kitchen. Contains shelves to store food that does not need   11
to be refrigerated. . . .   12

If you haven't found the three fragments, read the paper from the bottom to the top, a sentence at a time. Section 7 of this chapter contains more exercises on preventing fragments.

## 6.1 The Simple Sentence

**Explanation**   The term *simple sentence* does not mean a simple-minded sentence. In a grammatical context, as we have pointed out, *simple* means one, as opposed to *compound,* which means two or more. A simple sentence consists of one independent clause. As defined in Chapter 5.0, a clause is a group of words with a subject and verb. Clauses can be dependent (those that cannot stand alone) as well as independent (those that can stand alone). The following are examples of dependent clauses:

▸ because they are our neighbors     when the test is administered

▸ which she gave us     as the President says

Each has a subject (underlined once), and each has a verb (underlined twice), but none can stand alone; thus, they are called dependent. (If written by themselves, they would be fragments.)

The following clauses, however, are independent:

▸ they are our neighbors     the test is administered each Friday

▸ she gave us a dictionary     the President said it

Each of the above could be written as a simple sentence, as follows:

▸ They are our neighbors.     The test is administered each Friday.

▸ She gave us a dictionary.     The President said it.

They are sentences because each has a subject and verb and can stand alone; they are simple sentences because each consists of one independent clause. Notice that, as sentences, each begins with a capital letter and ends with a period. (Questions end with question marks; exclamations end with exclamation marks. See Chapter 11.2.)

A simple sentence often has two or more subjects (called compound subjects) or two or more verbs (called compound verbs):

▸ Anthony and Alice made A's.    (compound subjects)

▸ They walked and jogged for three hours.    (compound verbs)

## Practice

A ▸ Write simple sentences, using the following as subjects. Underline the subjects once and the verbs twice.

1. (Charlie Brown) _____

_____

2. (the catcher) _____

_____

3. (John Kennedy) _____

_____

4. (Tennis and swimming) _____

_____

5. (Jackie and Susan) _____

_____

**B** ▶ Write simple sentences, using the following as verbs. Underline the subjects once and the verbs twice.

1. (strutted) _____

_____

2. (teased and flirted) _____

_____

3. (loves) _____

_____

4. (comes and goes) _____

_____

5. (devoured) _____

**C** ▶ Identify the four simple sentences (one-clause sentences) in the paragraph below by underlining them:

This story began in 1943 when my mother was a little girl. One day   1
she was in the backyard running and playing in the corn field. A crow flew   2
around the field and suddenly lit on my mother's shoulder, and she gave   3

him an ear of corn. Every day from then on the crow and my mother would    4
meet in the corn field. Mother would feed the crow, and the crow would    5
perch itself on mother's shoulder. They walked together that way all over    6
the field. One day, mother went out into the field to play, and the crow    7
was lying in the dirt, dead. She told her mother, Ms. Betty, and Ms. Betty    8
said, "Baby, the dead crow means that someone very close to you is going    9
to die." That night her uncle, Al Reynolds, died of a heart attack.    10

## 6.2 The Complex Sentence (with Subordinate Conjunctions)

**Explanation: Complex Sentences Defined**

A complex sentence consists of an independent clause and one or more dependent clauses. In the sentence "Because I was sick, I stayed home," there is a dependent clause and an independent clause. Here are two ways to write the same sentence:

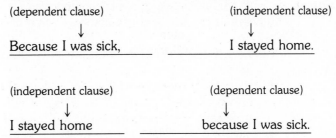

Notice how the independent clause, "I stayed home," functions just like a simple sentence. But if the dependent clause were written by itself, it would be a fragment. Notice also that a comma follows the dependent clause in the first illustration, but in the second illustration, when the dependent clause comes at the end of the sentence, there is no comma. Study Comma Rule #1 in Chapter 11.4.

If you are going to say what you want to say in writing, you will write many complex sentences. There is nothing wrong with writing simple sentences—they can be strong and will give your essays variety—but if you write only in simple sentences, your writing will sound flat and not like you. The following simple sentences are choppy and can be joined together as indicated. (The dependent clauses are underlined.)

**Choppy** ▶ The show was over. The last person had left. We finally went home.

**Joined** ▶ When the show was over and the last person had left, we finally went

home.    (Note that a comma follows the dependent clause.)

Choppy ▸ I was sweeping the rug. I saw a little mouse staring at me.

Joined ▸ <u>While I was sweeping the rug</u>, I saw a little mouse staring at me.    (Note that a comma follows the dependent clause.)

Choppy ▸ I know you will not change your mind. You have shown courage in the past.

Joined ▸ I know you will not change you mind <u>because you have shown courage in the past</u>.    (Note that there is no comma because the dependent clause comes at the end of the sentence.)

**Practice**    Combine the following simple sentences and fragments. Underline the dependent clauses, and use commas when necessary.

1. The president stood by what he said. Because he was a man of conviction.
2. If you really mean what you say and are sure you will not change your mind. I will go with you.
3. I'm leaving. Before I get caught in the rain.
4. Unless he is willing to plead guilty to manslaughter. The state will charge him with first-degree murder.
5. While it is easy to see a glass half empty. It is better to see it half full.

**Explanation: Using Subordinating Conjunctions**    You can usually recognize dependent clauses in complex sentences by the words that make them dependent. There are two classes of these words: *subordinate conjunctions* (words like *when, while, because, if, before, unless*) and *relative pronouns* (words like *who, whom, which, that*). In the next section, you will concentrate on dependent clauses that begin with relative pronouns, but in the rest of this section, you will work with subordinate conjunctions.

The word *subordinate* means "in a lower class, order, or rank." A subordinate in an industrial or military heirarchy is one who is under someone else. A *subordinate conjunction* begins a clause that is "lower" than (not as important as) the main or independent clause. In the sentence "Because I was sick, I stayed home," the information that the speaker stayed home is more important than the reason why he or she stayed home. Here is a list of the most common subordinate conjunctions, arranged by six functions. Try out each of them in the designated sentences.

1. *To show time:*

   as (at the same time)     _____ I ate (was eating) my sup-
   after                             per, the disc-jockey called.
   before
   when
   while

2. *To show cause* (or reason why):

   as                   He will do anything for you _____
   because             you are his best friend.
   since

   in order that         She married a man she hardly knew
   so that              _____ she would not be alone.

3. *To show on what condition:*

   if                     _____ the two countries go to war,
   in the event that     we will have to take sides.

   till                I can't tell you how you are doing _____
   unless            you turn in your essays.
   until

4. *To show a contrasting thought:*

   although          I am still going fishing, _____ it is
   even though      raining.
   even if
   though

   whether           I am still going fishing, _____ it is
                          raining or not.

   while             Shopping with money is frustrating, \_\_\_\_\_
                          shopping without money is fun.

   *Note:* Commas are usually inserted before contrasting-thought clauses. *See* Rule #10 in Chapter 11.4.

5. *To show place:*

   where              _____ Naomi goes, Ruth will go.
   wherever

6. *To show the manner in which* (or how):

   as if              We felt _____ we would never
   as though        make the last mile.

   (*Like* should not be used to replace *as if* or *as though* when introducing a dependent clause. *Like* introduces nouns: "He is big and hairy and looks mean, like King Kong.")

Words that function as subordinating conjunctions often have other functions as well. The following, for example, are used as prepositions and introduce not clauses, but phrases:

▶ <u>after</u> a hard day's work    <u>because</u> of you    <u>before</u> the year 1100

## Practice

A ▶ Combine the pairs of sentences below using each of the following subordinating conjunctions at least once: *when, while, since, because, although.* The dependent clauses may come at the beginning or the end of the sentences. Supply commas as necessary. (See Rules #1 and #10 in Chapter 11.4.)

Example ▶ We moved to a new town. At that time I was five years old.

Combined ▶ We moved to a new town when I was five years old.   (Notice that the phrase *at that time* is now omitted.)

Example ▶ Josh does not have enough money to live comfortably. For that reason he is looking for a new job.

Combined ▶ Because Josh does not have enough money to live comfortably, he is looking for a new job.   (Notice that the phrase *for that reason* is now omitted.)

1. I moved to Jefferson City about five years ago. At that time I was puzzled by certain words I heard people use.

———————————————————————————————————

———————————————————————————————————

2. Some words were very hard to understand. The reason was that people pronounced them in a funny way.

———————————————————————————————————

———————————————————————————————————

3. I frequently had to ask people to repeat themselves. I couldn't understand what they were saying.

_____

_____

4. Some words, like "yat," were clearly pronounced. All the same they were so odd that they sounded foreign.

_____

_____

5. I finally asked someone what "yat" meant. I was told that "yat" comes from the greeting "whereya at."

_____

_____

6. Some people in the city use the word "yat" all the time. For that reason they are called "yats."

_____

_____

7. Most yat mothers call their children by names such as Precious, Sweetheart, and Dawlin'. Angry yat mothers call their children Noodlebrain.

_____

_____

_____

B ► Make *complex sentences* using the following dependent clauses. Circle the subordinate conjunction, and at the end of the sentence say which of the six functions explained above it serves.

1. When the moon comes over the mountain, _____

_____

2. Although candy is dandy _____

_____

3. While Mrs. Toodle was looking out of the window _____

_____

4. If you mail in one Fritzie box top and $2.00 _____

_____

5. Because Mary talks to her plants _____

_____

6. Unless I pass this math test _____

If you did not put a comma after each introductory dependent clause, do so now.

C ► Make *complex sentences* using the following dependent clauses at the end of each sentence. Circle the subordinate conjunction, and say which of the six functions it serves.

1. _____ after you went home.

2. _____ because it is stormy.

3. _____ while we were watching the Saturday night special.

4. _____ before I get really mad.

5. _____ unless you really want me to.

If you put in any commas, go back and take them out.

D ► Make *complex sentences* by using the following subordinate conjunctions to introduce dependent clauses:

1. *You should always check your oil* before *you leave on a long trip.*

2. _____ because

3. _____ since

4. _____ unless

5. _____ while

6. _____ if

E ▶ Now reverse your independent and dependent clauses (as shown in the diagram on page 277) and supply commas.

1. *Before you leave on a long trip, you should always check your oil.*

2. _____

3. _____

4. _____

5. _____

6. _____

_____

_____

_____

**F ▶** In the paragraph below, underline the ten dependent clauses _that begin with subordinate conjunctions_ and supply the four missing commas required by Rule #1 in Chapter 11.4.

As I walked up the gravel road I looked up at the morning sky. It    1
was beginning to turn dark blue in places. Everything was still the same,    2
including the tall pine trees, the wire fences, the houses and even the "you-   3
keep-out" sign posted to a tree. The leaves on the trees were trembling    4
because the wind was blowing slightly. Dew was falling to the ground from   5
the trees. Some even fell on me.    6
I continued walking until I saw a small child with light brown hair.    7
She wore a little rust and blue plaid dress. Barefoot, she was playing in a    8
pile of sand and gravel. She acted as though she did not have a care in    9
the world. I walked closer to the girl, and I noticed her blue eyes. They    10
were the same color as my eyes when I was young. Then I noticed the    11
dress. It looked like the dress my parents bought for me years ago.    12
As she looked up she asked what I was doing there. When she    13
spoke I realized I was seeing myself when I was young. I was stunned. Then,    14
without allowing me to answer, she asked me to sit down and play with    15
her. But I told her that I didn't have the time. While I was turning to leave I    16
changed my mind. But she was gone, just as the past has been gone from    17
my memory, until now.    18

**G ▶** Identify the three fragments (F) in the following paragraph. Correct each by connecting it to the sentence that comes before it. Use commas when you connect afterthoughts. _See_ Rule #10 in Chapter 11.4.

A salesman must have the ability to handle customers in the right    1
manner. Even if they are hard to handle. I work as a salesman at Danny's    2
Men's Store. Some of the wildest people in the world shop at Danny's. Men    3
don't know what they want to buy, and women don't know what size their    4
husbands wear. A salesman has to try to fit a certain type of garment to a    5
certain type of person. Whether that person is a sportsman, a swinger, or    6
a conservative. I have been working at Danny's for three years now and    7
still haven't learned how to deal with all the customers. Because some of    8
them are crazy. It is especially hard to serve the ones who come in bare-    9
footed.    10

## 6.3 The Complex Sentence (with Relative Pronouns)

**Explanation:**
**Noun Clauses**

Dependent clauses within complex sentences often begin with one of a small group of words called *relative pronouns:*

who, whom, whose    whoever, whomever

that, which, what    whichever, whatever

These words introduce *noun clauses* and *adjective clauses,* so called because they function as nouns and adjectives in sentences. Noun clauses name a person, place, thing, or idea; adjective clauses describe a noun or pronoun.

Here are several examples of how noun clauses can be used in a sentence:

▶ *As a subject:*

Whoever comes late may not get any lunch.

▶ *As a direct object:*

I think that it might rain.
              *or*
I think it might rain.    (Here *that* is omitted but nevertheless understood.)

▶ *As an indirect object:*

I am going to give whoever stole my orange tennis shoe a piece of my mind.

▶ *As the object of a preposition:*

Take the advice for whatever it is worth.

▶ *With a linking verb:*

This is just what the doctor ordered.

An important thing to remember about noun clauses is that you do not use commas with them. Just as you do not separate a subject from a verb or a verb from its object with a comma, you should not use a comma to separate a noun clause from the rest of the sentence.

**Practice**    Underline the noun clauses in the following sentences:

1. <u>Whoever laughs last</u> laughs best.
2. Whoever understands noun clauses should be able to do this exercise.
3. I plan to say whatever comes to mind.
4. Is this what you wanted?
5. Jerry understands that his answers to this test are crucial.
6. He said it was too good to be true.
7. What you see is what you get.

**Explanation:**    Adjective clauses function as adjectives in sentences; that is, they de-
**Adjective Clauses**    scribe nouns or pronouns, for example:

▶ Marcia, <u>who is quite talented as a musician</u>, is coming for a visit.

The dependent clause *who is quite talented as a musician* describes the proper noun *Marcia*. Adjective clauses are usually introduced by relative pronouns but can be introduced by *where* and *when*, for example:

▶ I am planning to make a trip to Israel, <u>where three of the world's great religions were born.</u>

Sometimes the relative pronoun in an adjective clause is omitted but nevertheless understood:

▶ Kurt Vonnegut is a writer <u>I admire.</u>

The relative pronoun *whom* has been omitted. Compare "Kurt Vonnegut is a writer whom I admire."

**Practice**    Underline the adjective clauses in the following sentences. Draw arrows to the nouns or pronouns they describe.

1. Everybody wants a life <u>that is filled with good friends and good times.</u>

2. Joe, who is usually the last to leave a party, didn't tire until almost dawn.

3. My car, which hasn't been washed in two years, looks rather battered.

4. The town where I grew up has changed dramatically in the last few years.

5. Anita, who was very tall for her age, took a lot of teasing from her friends.

6. I gave my bike to Karen, who didn't have a way to get to school.

7. He is the one I would like to see run for office.

8. The year 1963, when President Kennedy was assassinated, was a turning point in my life.

**Explanation: Using Commas with Adjective Clauses**

You probably noticed that some adjective clauses in the sentences above were set off by commas; others were not. If the adjective clause is essential to the meaning of the sentence, do *not* use commas, for example:

▸ People who need people are the luckiest people in the world.   (If you omitted *who need people,* the sentence would not make sense. Therefore, you do not use a commas.)

If, however, the adjective clause is not essential to the meaning of the sentence, you set it off with a comma or commas, for example:

▸ Mother, who is nearly eighty, is still in excellent health.   (If you omitted *who is nearly eighty,* the sentence would still make sense. Therefore, you need commas.)

Study Comma Rule #2 in Chapter 11.4.

**Practice**

Underline the adjective clauses in the following sentences. Then decide whether commas are needed to set off the clauses. (*Hint:* Clauses beginning with *which* are usually set off by commas; clauses beginning with *that* are usually not set off by commas.)

1. Jennifer, <u>who is a very neurotic person</u>, still sleeps with a teddy bear.
2. Rafting down the Colorado River is the one experience that he will never forget.

3. The plan that we finally decided upon was our best alternative.
4. My typewriter which hasn't been cleaned in eight years is in poor condition.
5. Everybody rushed to meet the celebrity who was doing his best to avoid the crowd.
6. The film that Altman directed was the best.
7. Friends who talk behind your back are no friends.
8. I moved to California where the grass was not greener but brown.

**Explanation: When to Use *Who, Whom, That, Which***

In writing adjective clauses, use *who, whose, whom,* and occasionally *that* to refer to people, not *which* or *of which.*

▸ The person <u>who</u> does the work will be the one to succeed.

Note that *who* is used instead of *whom* because within the adjective clause *who* is the subject of the verb *does.*

▸ He is the player <u>whom</u> we talked about earlier.

Here *whom* is used instead of *who* because within the adjective clause *whom* is the object of the preposition *about.*
Use *which, of which,* or *that* to refer to things.

▸ The car <u>which</u> (or <u>that</u>) I bought is a beauty.

You will want to use many relative clauses in your writing in order to give your sentences variety and to make them sound like you talking.

**Practice**

A ▸ Combine the following pairs of sentences using *who, which,* or *that* as you make one clause dependent on the other. Be sure to place the adjective clause after the noun it modifies. Use commas as necessary.

Example ▸ The car trip was an unforgettable experience. I took the trip with my brother Tom.

Combined ▸ The car trip that I took with my brother Tom was an unforgettable experience.  (The adjective clause beginning with the word *that* comes after *trip,* which is the noun it modifies.)

**Example** ▶ Tom and I had been looking forward to the trip for a long time. We both like the out-of-doors.

**Combined** ▶ Tom and I, who both like the out-of-doors, had been looking forward to the trip for a long time.    (The adjective clause beginning with the word *who* comes after *Tom and I,* which are the nouns it modifies.)

1. The hillsides were covered with trees of fiery red and orange. They extended as far as the eye could see.

_____

_____

2. My parents would love to see a mountainside with trees turning red and gold. They have never been to New England.

_____

_____

3. Our decrepit Volkswagen did its best on the mountain roads. It was loaded down with luggage.

_____

_____

4. We finally arrived at the ski lodge. It was to be our home for the next few weeks.

_____

_____

5. The owner of the lodge helped us unload. He looked like an aging Woody Allen.

_____

_____

6. I remember watching the first snowfall. It was a sight worth traveling four days to see.

_____

_____

7. The local people probably wouldn't share my enthusiasm over snow. They have experienced icy roads and snow-shoveling all their lives.

_____

_____

B ▸ Make whole sentences with the following adjective clauses using commas as necessary. Use the clauses in the middle or at the end of sentences. Be sure you do not write a fragment.

1. (which is something I have always wanted to do) *Skiing,* *which is something I have always wanted to do, is very expensive.*

2. (who are the nicest people you will ever meet) _____

_____

3. (where I plan to live) _____

_____

4. (which is the best thing that could have happened to her)

_____

_____

Go back and draw an arrow to the noun each adjective clause describes. If you cannot find such a noun, perhaps you have not written the clause as an adjective clause.

## 6.4 The Compound Sentence

**Explanation: Compound Sentences Defined**

A *compound sentence* consists of two or more independent clauses, each with its own subject and verb, each able to stand alone, for example:

▸ The slender girl pushed the big car, and her father gave her encouragement.

Both underlined clauses are independent: they could be written as simple sentences. The joining word *and* is called a coordinating conjunction because it joins equals, in this case two equal or independent clauses. (The subordinating conjunction, recall, joins two unequals—an independent and a dependent clause.) There are seven coordinating conjunctions. Memorize them.

▸ <u>and</u>    <u>but</u>    <u>for</u>    <u>or</u>    <u>nor</u>    <u>yet</u>    <u>so</u>

Here are some more examples of compound sentences with coordinating conjunctions:

▸ <u>He really didn't mean to do it</u>, but <u>he could not help himself.</u>

▸ <u>The faces of the jurors were tense</u>, for <u>they were about to sentence a man to die.</u>

▸ <u>He could rush into battle and get killed</u>, or <u>he could desert and be executed.</u>

Notice that a comma is used before each coordinating conjunction in the above compound sentences. Study Comma Rule #3 in Chapter 11.4.

**Practice**    In the paragraph below, underline the compound sentences and insert the necessary commas.

> This past Tuesday night, my husband and I were shopping at Maison Blanche and we were about to call it a night. Just before we left, we met Ed, an old friend from high school days. I asked the usual question about how his family was. To our shock, we discovered that Ed and his wife had gotten a divorce. I have come across this unhappy situation many times but each time it shocks and saddens me. The rising divorce rate is especially distressing for many of the marriages could have been saved. Since Tuesday night I have been depressed and have been wondering how secure my own marriage is.

1
2
3
4
5
6
7
8
9

**Explanation: Using Coordinating Conjunctions**    As pointed out above, compound sentences consist of two or more independent clauses. If you leave out the coordinating conjunction, each clause can function as a simple sentence, for example:

▸ Our club sponsored a car wash on Saturday, <u>and</u> we were quite successful.

▶ I like strawberry ice cream, <u>but</u> Sal prefers chocolate chip.

If you left out *and* in the first sentence, you would have two separate sentences. By using *and,* however, you show a close relationship of two ideas. In the second sentence *but* shows a contrast, the opposition of two ideas. Each of the seven coordinating conjunctions has a special function:

a. *And* means addition:

▶ The Bernados sisters are planning a big party Saturday night,
   <u>and</u>
   everyone is invited.

b. *But* means contrast:

▶ The Bernados sisters are having a big party Saturday night,
   <u>but</u>
   their parents don't know it.

c. *For* shows reason and thus means roughly the same as *because:*

▶ The Bernados sisters are having their big party Saturday night,
   <u>for</u>
   it is the only time everyone can come.

d. *Or* shows choice:

▶ The Bernados sisters will have their party Saturday night,
   <u>or</u>
   they may choose to have it Friday night instead.

e. *Nor* (like *or*) shows choice, but *nor* shows negative choice:

▶ Tony does not plan to come,
   <u>nor</u>
   will he encourage his friends to come.
   (Notice that when *nor* joins sentences, the second clause has an
   inverted order, like a question.)

f. *Yet* (like *but*) shows contrast:

▸ Tony does not plan to attend the party,
        <u>yet</u>
he admits it will probably be fun.

g. *So* shows results and thus means roughly the same as *therefore:*

▸ Tony does not plan to attend the party,
        <u>so</u>
he will be free on Saturday night.

## Practice

A ▸ Combine the following pairs of sentences using *and, but, for,* and *or* at least once:

1. It is best not to thrash around in shark-infested waters. The movement and the sound might attract the sharks.
2. My family is planning to leave town on the tenth. We will be gone about two weeks.
3. Our house is small and dark. I like it.
4. You need to make a decision quickly. Time is running out.
5. We may go to a movie tonight. We may stay home and watch TV.
6. I am usually in bed by 10:00 P.M. My roommate is a night owl.
7. Our tennis match is scheduled for late afternoon. We plan to have dinner afterward.
8. I may decide to continue my subscription to *Time* for another year. I may cancel it now.

Did you insert commas as required by Rule #3 in Chapter 11.4?

B ▸ Combine the pairs of sentences below using *nor, yet* and *so* at least once. (You must change the wording of the sentence when you use *nor.* See the explanation on p. 292.)

1. My sister isn't fond of raw oysters. She doesn't like any other shellfish.

2. This movie is rated PG. We probably should not take your four-year-old niece.

3. Julio is rather an odd looking character. Many women find him attractive.

4. Amy will enter an ice-skating competition next month. She practices several hours a day.

5. In buying his clothes, George doesn't listen to his friends' advice. He doesn't pay attention to current fashion either.

6. Marcus Duffy is in his sixties. He still jogs several miles a day.

Did you insert commas as required by Rule #3?

C ▸ Write your own *compound* sentences with each of the seven coordinating conjunctions: *and, but, for, so, yet, or, nor.* Don't forget to insert the commas.

_____

_____

_____

_____

_____

_____

**Explanation: Using the Semicolon**

Another way to make a compound sentence is to combine the independent clauses with a semicolon (;), as follows:

▸ The slender girl pushed the big car; her father gave her encouragement.

▸ The weather was stormy; it was a terrible night.

Use semicolons sparingly in making compound sentences, and only if the following two conditions exist:

▸ The thoughts of the two independent clauses are closely related.

▸ A period could be substituted for the semicolon to make two sentences. (In the examples above a period could be substituted for each semicolon to make two sentences.)

See Chapter 11.5 for more on the semicolon.

**Practice**    Combine the following sentences with semicolons.

**Example** ▸ Spring is my favorite time of year. It is the season for canoe trips and long walks in the valley.

**Combined** ▸ Spring is my favorite time of year; it is the season for canoe trips and long walks in the valley.

(Notice that a lower case letter, *i*, follows the semicolon.)

1. Gina wants to go into nursing. She is attracted by the salary and the opportunity to help others.
2. Bridge is more than a game of cards. It is a science.
3. Vacations are not a luxury these days. They are a necessity.
4. Sal is addicted to jogging. He feels sleepy if he doesn't jog every morning.
5. I wish everyone could hike in the Smoky Mountains. They are spectacular.

**Explanation: Preventing Run-on Sentences**    For your writing to sound like you, you will want to write many compound sentences, as well as complex and simple ones. By learning the structure of compound sentences you will be able to use them often without making run-on-sentence errors. A run-on sentence, recall, occurs when you attempt to join two independent clauses with a comma (a comma splice) or with no punctuation (a fused sentence), for example:

**Comma Splice** ▸ I came to an open field, it was just like the one next to our house.

**Fused Sentence** ▸ I came to an open field it was just like the one next to our house.

Here are four ways you can prevent (or correct) run-on sentences:

▸ *By making two sentences:*

I came to an open field. It was just like the one next to our house.

▸ *By inserting one of the seven coordinating conjunctions (with a comma):*

I came to an open field, and it was just like the one next to our house.

▸ *By inserting a semicolon:*

I came to an open field; it was just like the one next to our house.

▸ *By making one of the clauses dependent.* (Sometimes you must change the wording of the sentence if you choose this method. See Section 2 and 3 of this chapter.)

I came to an open field, which was just like the one next to our house.

*or*

When I came to an open field, I discovered that it was just like the one next to our house.

Beware of writing too many short simple sentences, and beware also of using too many semicolons. Section 8 of this chapter gives more exercises on preventing run-on errors.

## Practice

A ▸ Correct the following run-on sentences by using the designated coordinating conjunctions. Insert commas as necessary.

1. (and)   I just bought a new dress I know you will like it.
2. (but)   He enjoyed the camp last summer he is not going again.
3. (for)   There is no need to worry we will get there on time.
4. (yet)   I didn't like what she was telling me, I knew she was right.
5. (so)    It began to rain outside we had to call off our picnic.

6. (or)    I'm driving to Seattle, I'm not going anywhere.

7. (nor)    He won't go to school, he won't look for a job. (As pointed out above, when you use *nor* you will have to change the wording of the sentence, for example: <u>He isn't too young, he isn't too old</u> becomes <u>He isn't too young, nor is he too old.</u>)

B ▸ Using each of the seven coordinating conjunctions at least once, correct the following run-on sentences. Insert commas as necessary.

1. The cabin was cold there was no more firewood.

2. He was a strange young man, I liked him.

3. She gave me a big shove I fell in the fishpond.

4. Dorm life is unpleasant sometimes, it has been all right on the whole.

5. Cynthia said, "Marry me, I will not see you again."

6. My cat is fed well still she is skinny.

7. Let me go I have to be in class in two minutes.

8. He brought this date home she had not met his parents.

9. I finished high school at St. Joseph's Academy, now here I am at the university.

10. He will not sleep, he will not eat.

C ▸ Correct the following run-on sentences by using a semicolon or by making two sentences. If you use a semicolon, make sure the thoughts of the two independent clauses are closely related.

**Examples**

Run-On ▸ You are right this can't go on.

Corrected ▸ You are right; this can't go on.

Run-On ▸ The early morning sounds brought back childhood memories, as I listened I recalled the summer I lived on my grandfather's farm.

Corrected ▶ The early morning sounds brought back childhood memories. As I listened, I recalled the summer I lived on my grandfather's farm.

1. Nowadays, many people are completely dependent on their watches, they would be nervous wrecks without them.

2. Go ahead and check out the water it looks good to me.

3. Shut the door it's cold in there.

4. It does not make a lot of difference which one you take both roads will get you there.

5. You are a changed woman your past doesn't matter to me now.

6. It was not my imagination, it was a little girl.

7. Look at all of those people someone will surely help us.

8. Where I live is only about five blocks from the university, the blocks aren't long each one of them has only four or five houses on it.

9. Take me, for instance, I'm not your average success story.

10. In the film Anthony Quinn said, "I like my women fat, I like my women mean."

D ▶ Correct the following run-on sentences by using a subordinate conjunction to introduce either the first or second clause. Use one of the following subordinate conjunctions: *if, when, since, although, while, because.* Insert commas as necessary.

1. I hate to go shopping with Joyce~~,~~ *because* she takes so long.

2. He graduates this May, I am going to miss him.

3. You study in our room, I'll go study in the library.

4. The states of our nation are different in most ways, they do have one thing in common.

5. The Equal Rights Amendment will be proposed again and will eventually pass, it will take many years.

6. Kids are playful, joyful, and bright that's why I decided to write about my little sister.

E ► Correct the following run-on sentences by using any one of the four methods described on page 296. Two sentences are correct.

1. I couldn't believe my eyes the car was just what I needed.

2. Shut the door, let's keep as warm as possible.

3. The rock hit him beneath his eye that taught him a lesson.

4. "Are you my husband, are you my man?" she asked.

5. I need those notes, please give them to me.

6. Give me your tired and your poor I will make them into a great nation.

7. The students at this university are not very friendly, in fact they are sometimes hostile.

8. I started college in the fall of 1981 in so doing, I jumped from the frying pan into the fire.

9. Russell is 6'5" he weighs 175 pounds.

10. Usually, I work eight to five, but sometimes I must work long overtime hours.

11. I really enjoy going out with college men, I know they will not be jerks.

12. She had a demanding style of teaching, she expected perfection.

13. Try harder you say to yourself there is one more ball left to play.

14. The noise has stopped, and the lights are out, all except the one that says "tilt."

15. That is how the machine really wins it eats your money.

F ► Edit the following essay, correcting the run-on sentences by whatever method seems best. Make sure that you use commas correctly.

### BACK TO NATURE

If anyone had told me three years ago that I would be spending most of my weekends camping, I would have laughed heartily. Campers, in my eyes, were nothing but masochists who enjoyed insect bites, ill-cooked meals, and damp sleeping bags, they had nothing in common

with me. I was to learn a lot about camping since then, however. (1 run-on  5
sentence, RO)  6

The friends who introduced me to camping thought that it meant  7
being a pioneer. The first trip they took me on, we roughed it, we slept in  8
a tent, cooked over an open fire, and hiked to the shower and bathroom  9
facilities. This brief visit with Mother Nature cost me two days home from  10
work recovering from a bad case of sunburn. There was no shade, the  11
tallest tree on our campsite was three feet tall. Another momento from the  12
trip was the doctor's bill for my son's poison ivy. (2 RO)  13

I was, nevertheless, talked into going on another fun-filled holiday  14
in the wilderness, this time we camped with friends who believed that Dan-  15
iel Boone would have been proud to use the light bulb if he had known  16
about it. There was no tent, we had a pop-up camper with comfortable  17
beds and an air conditioner. These nature lovers had remembered to bring  18
all the necessities of life they brought lounge chairs, a screened porch, the  19
TV, and even a blender. I can still taste those Piña Coladas. (3 RO)  20

After that trip, my husband and I became quite interested in  21
camping, we have done a lot of it since. Recently, we purchased a  22
twenty-eight foot travel trailer complete with bathroom and built-in TV an-  23
tenna. There is a separate bedroom, a modern kitchen with refrigerator  24
and a roll-out pantry, the trailer even has carpet and draperies to match.  25
(2 RO)  26

I must say that I have certainly come to enjoy camping. It must be  27
true that, sooner or later, everyone finds his or her way back to nature, I  28
recommend that you find your way in style. (1 RO)  29

## 6.5 The Compound Sentence (with Conjunctive Adverbs)

**Explanation**   A *conjunctive adverb* is an adverb used to show a special relationship between two independent clauses that are joined together with a co-ordinating conjunction or a semicolon, for example:

▸ He threw a touchdown pass, and <u>then</u> he kicked the extra point.

▸ It is a good day for catching pompano; <u>however</u>, with my luck we will probably catch toad fish instead.

In the first sentence the conjunctive adverb *then* shows a time relationship between the first clause and the second. In the second sentence the conjunctive adverb *however* shows a relationship of contrast between the two clauses. In the first sentence, *and* joins the two clauses and in the second sentence, a semicolon joins the two clauses.

A conjunctive adverb can also begin a new sentence, as follows:

▶ Their favorite novels were about the sea. <u>For example</u>, they really enjoyed *Moby Dick* and *The Old Man and the Sea.*

While *For example* begins a new sentence in this example, it nevertheless relates back to the preceding sentence and illustrates it.

Here are the most common conjunctive adverbs, according to function:

1. *Time:* then, next

   ▶ First, we visited the Washington Monument, and <u>then</u> we toured the White House.

2. *Addition:* also, moreover, furthermore

   ▶ We saw St. John's Church, and <u>also</u> we got to see some of the exhibits in the Smithsonian.

   ▶ We saw St. John's Church; <u>moreover</u>, we got to see some of the exhibits in the Smithsonian as well.

3. *Results:* consequently, thus, therefore

   ▶ Summer vacation begins on the first of June; <u>consequently</u>, I cannot begin to work until then.

4. *Contrast:* however, nevertheless, on the other hand

   ▶ Rudolfo originally planned to join us; <u>however</u>, he later changed his mind.

5. *Illustration:* for example, for instance

   ▶ We have many privileges in this country that we take for granted; <u>for example</u>, almost everyone has easy access to a public library.

Note that a comma follows most conjunctive adverbs, as shown in four of the examples above. However, a comma does not usually follow *then* or *also*. For further reference, study Comma Rule #4 in Chapter 11.4.

## Practice

A ▸ Combine the following pairs of sentences with *and* or *but* and a conjunctive adverb or with a semicolon and a conjunctive adverb. Use at least one conjunctive adverb from each of the five groups noted above. Supply commas as needed.

Examples ▸ I have got to study first. After that I may go to the movies with you.

Combined ▸ I have got to study first, and then I may go to the movies with you. (Notice that *after that* is omitted.)

Example ▸ I wasn't sick after eating the pizza and marshmallows. Helen and Tom missed two days of school.

Combined ▸ I wasn't sick after eating the pizza and marshmallows; however, Helen and Tom missed two days of school.

1. We had many things to talk about. The time passed quickly.

2. The poet Keats died in his midtwenties. His poetry is more valued than that of many a writer who lived to a ripe old age.

3. The barbeque restaurant will probably be more successful now that it is in a better location. Its new management is first-rate.

4. Paula knows how to fix anything. She even fixed her grandfather's cuckoo clock.

5. It was only a small inexpensive gift. It was a well-chosen one.

6. I enjoy working in the early morning because I feel rested then. It's the only time the house is quiet.

7. Every day Mrs. Carr picks whatever is ripe. After that she feeds the chickens.

8. Christy Brown was an Irish writer who was severely brain damaged from birth. He published several extraordinary books in his lifetime.

9. The day was clear and sunny. We decided to move the party out-of-doors.

10. Thousands of people greet each other every day in the Los Angeles airport. It is not the place to form a lasting relationship.

B ▶ Write your own *compound* sentences using the following conjunctive adverbs to relate the two independent clauses: *then, however, for example, also, nevertheless, therefore, moreover.* Use commas as necessary.

**Explanation: Run-on sentences with Conjunctive Adverbs**    Some conjunctive adverbs seem to function like the seven coordinating conjunctions, but they are not conjunctions and they cannot join independent clauses. The following are typical run-on sentences caused by this confusion:

Fused sentence ▶ He threw the touchdown pass then he kicked the extra point.

Comma splice ▶ It is a good day for catching pompano, however, with my luck we will probably catch toad fish instead.

Comma splice ▶ Their favorite novels were about the sea, for example, they really enjoyed *Moby Dick* and *The Old Man and the Sea.*

See pp. 300–301 for ways of writing these sentences correctly.

## Practice

A ▶ Correct the following run-on sentences by using semicolons before the conjunctive adverbs. Insert commas as necessary, using Rule #4 in Chapter 11.4.

1. First, he ruined his health ; then he ruined his marriage.
2. She is the most considerate person I know also she is the most intelligent.
3. The president is correct about inflation, however he does not seem to know what to do about it.
4. A few items are still inexpensive, for example you can still buy water for almost nothing.
5. High school was too strict, on the other hand college is not strict enough.

6. You first make a cream sauce then you brown your shrimp in another pan.

B ▸ Correct the following run-on sentences by inserting either *and* or *but* before the conjunctive adverb. Commas are needed in two sentences. Insert them.

1. We are driving from here to Nebraska, then we will drive to San Francisco.

2. He was the most popular president we ever had, also he was the most courageous.

3. The whale turned over on its back as though it were dead, then it started breathing again.

4. The Surgeon General issued a stern warning against cigarette smoking, consequently 30 percent of the nation's smokers stopped.

5. If sex education were taught in high school, the number of pregnancies would be reduced, moreover young people would protect themselves more effectively against venereal disease.

## 6.6 Sentences with Appositives

**Explanation: Using Appositives**  An *appositive* is a word, phrase, or clause that further identifies or gives more information about a noun, a noun phrase, or a pronoun. Here are several examples:

▸ This is Tom, my brother.   (The word *brother* further identifies the proper noun *Tom.*)

▸ She is going to Texas, the second largest state, and then to California. (The phrase *the second largest state* further identifies the proper noun *Texas.*)

▸ Al found a cushion, the only thing left to sit on.   (The phrase *the only thing left to sit on* further identifies the noun *cushion.*)

Notice that the above appositives are set off by commas. Study Comma Rule #5 in Chapter 11.4.

Make frequent use of appositives in your writing. They will help your writing sound smooth and will give it variety. These two sentences are choppy:

▸ John watches television twelve hours a day. He is a near-sighted person.

To combine them, you take the "meat," or the substance, of the second sentence and you place it next to *John.*

▸ John, a near-sighted person, watches television twelve hours a day.

Here are two more choppy sentences:

▸ He will sell you almost anything. For example, he will sell you jewelry, an old bicycle, a new pocketbook, and yesterday's newspaper.

Why repeat *He will sell you?* Simply write

▸ He will sell you almost anything, for example, jewelry, an old bicycle, a new pocketbook, and yesterday's newspaper.

## Practice

A ▸ Complete the following sentences by adding the appositives.

1. She plays four sports, tennis, _____,

   _____, and _____.

2. The United States, a nation of _____, is the home of 225 million people.

3. *ET* (or supply your own title _____), a movie about

   _____, was a huge success.

4. The Steelers are happy about their new quarterback, a man who

   _____.

5. Sabrina, a _____, gives me a ride to school every day.

B ▸ Combine the following pairs of sentences so that one becomes an appositive. Use the above sentences as models. Insert commas as necessary, making use of Comma Rule #5 in Chapter 11.4.

1. The puppy chewed up everything in sight. He chewed up shoes, newspapers, and even the corner of the couch.

_____

_____

2. Greece is a popular vacation spot for Europeans. It is a land of blue skies and whitewashed houses.

_____

_____

3. Updike's latest novel is supposedly his best. It is a book about failing relationships. _____

_____

4. The defensive-driving coach was a little nervous about his new pupil. His pupil was a man convicted three times for driving while intoxicated. _____

_____

_____

5. Maria decided not to join the neighborhood softball team. She is now eight months pregnant. _____

_____

C ▸ Complete the following sentences by adding the appositives.

1. Sharon, _____, is endangering her health by eating only raisins, nuts, and lettuce leaves.

2. Many freshman courses at our college are difficult, especially
   _____, _____, and _____.

3. She bought everything in sight, everything from _____ to
   _____.

4. I have three favorite movie stars, _____,
   _____, and _____.

5. We have discussed several controversial issues in class, for example,
   _____, _____, and _____.

6. And then I took Algebra 102, a course _____
   _____.

D ► Combine the following pairs of sentences so that one becomes an appositive. Use the sentences above as models and insert commas as necessary.

1. Paco brought everything he thought he might need for a weekend visit. He brought everything from five outfits to a video tape recorder.
   _____
   _____

2. I have three favorite politicians. They are Ted Kennedy, Barry Goldwater, and Howard Baker. _____
   _____

3. Movies rated *R* may include controversial material. There may be both sex and violence. _____
   _____

4. Choon Jai likes horror films. He especially likes the old-fashioned ghost stories with creaking doors and rattling chairs. _____
   _____

5. Joan gave me a Christmas present that I really needed. It was a heavy wool sweater. _____

6. He reads magazines every chance he gets. He reads everything from *The Reader's Digest* to *Sports Illustrated*. _____

_____

**Explanation: Preventing Fragments**    Appositives written by themselves are fragments. While appositive fragments are easy to write, they are even more easy to correct: you simply hook them onto the preceding sentence and set them off with a comma.

**Practice**    Make whole sentences out of the following and draw an arrow from the appositive to the noun it further identifies. Apply the comma rule.

1. I found excitement in Boston, Massachusetts, A unique place in culture and atmosphere.

2. I would love to see some trees in front of the Student Center. Like pines and oaks.

3. For a meal to be nourishing, it should consist of several types of food. Such as milk, fruit, starches, and poultry or meat.

4. I like this gadget. Whatever it is.

5. The lottery seems to be a tradition of the older generation. A tradition handed down through the village's history.

6. I have found some evidence in the story that the ritual was changed. Evidence that the wooden box was no longer filled with scraps of wood.

7. The perfect place to live would have to include many natural features. Especially flowers, wild animals, and a clear-running stream.

## 6.7 Preventing Fragments (Additional Practice)

**Explanation**    So far in this chapter, the following kinds of fragments have been pointed out:

▶ *The dependent clause fragment:*

<u>Which is what we should have done.</u>   (Never start a sentence with *which* unless you are asking a question.)

<u>Because it is too late.</u>   (A *because* clause must be accompanied by an independent clause.)

▶ *The fragment with an omitted subject or verb or both:*

<u>First, sex education, a way to prevent early pregnancies.</u>   (When you introduce a new topic in a paper, you must write a complete sentence.)

<u>There many points of view on the subject.</u>   (The verb has been omitted.)

▶ *The appositive fragment:*

The chief made an unpopular decision. <u>One that the men on board ship are still complaining about.</u>   (Hook an appositive fragment onto the preceding sentence with a comma.)

The officers often got more seasick than the enlisted personnel. <u>Particularly, Ensign Tomilinson and Lieutenant Dombroski.</u>

▶ *The afterthought fragment:*

She called all her children to her bedside. <u>Knowing that the end was near.</u>   (Usually, you hook an afterthought to the preceding sentence with a comma. See Comma Rule #10 in Chapter 11.4.)

The *Chilula* was a fine ship to serve on. <u>Although we did not get out to sea very much.</u> (Use commas before *although* clauses.)

The Coast Guard officers and enlisted personnel are the best. <u>Not "Holligans," as they are called by the Navy.</u>   (Use commas before afterthoughts beginning with *not.*)

**Practice**   Before completing the exercises, review Comma Rules #1, #2, #5, and #10 in Chapter 11.4. In the exercises, insert commas as needed.

**A ▸** Make sentences out of the sample fragments above.

**B ▸** This paragraph has three fragments. Correct them.

Americans take pride in the wide variety of goods that are avail- 1
able to the public. Thousands of companies, factories, and stores supply 2
us with millions of different products very neatly packaged in colorful, 3
"easy to open" boxes. All tagged with labels saying "new and improved." 4
Many show glossy photos of happy folk enjoying the product. They suggest 5
the image of an ideal, simple way of life. While in reality our lives are 6
growing more complicated all the time. An overabundance of material 7
goods creates many problems. Such as how to operate self-propelled 8
lawn mowers, sensor-touch ovens and ribbonless typewriters. I ask you, is 9
this progress? 10

**C ▸** This paragraph has five fragments. Correct them.

Television has been around for almost half a century. It was first 1
introduced to the public at the World's Fair back in 1939. But did not 2
achieve widespread popularity until the decade of the 1950's. Which was 3
considered television's golden era. A time of continual experiments, all of 4
which were done live. Entertainment shows such as "I Love Lucy" and "The 5
Life of Riley" made their appearance. There were also quite a few excel- 6
lent children's shows. "Howdy Doody," "Lassie," "The Wonderful World of 7
Disney," to name only a few. Through the years, television has expanded 8
its scope. And added bigger and better variety shows along with dramas 9
and soap operas. People will always turn to television as a source of en- 10
tertainment and relaxation. 11

**D ▸** The paragraph below has seven fragments. Correct them.

Registration day totally changed my views about college life. I 1
had thought college would be a well-ordered, calm, relaxing place. I had 2
my schedule all prepared, and everything seemed perfect. The hours and 3

instructors I wanted and the classes I needed. Everything was arranged in   4

the proper order. I was even early that day. Because I knew registration   5

would be crowded. However, I was not prepared for the sight before me   6

when I walked into the University Center. People running around like chick-   7

ens with their heads cut off. Frantically searching for answers. Some lying   8

on the floor in a daze, others leaning against walls to write in changes on   9

their schedule cards. A few even looked near tears. For a moment I thought   10

about forgetting college and going back to work at McDonald's. However,   11

I eventually pulled myself together and sprinted across the floor. An area   12

littered with bodies and schedule cards. After thirty minutes of grabbing,   13

kicking, and running, I was a registered college student. Not a happy one,   14

but registered, nevertheless.   15

## 6.8 Preventing Run-On Errors (Additional Practice)

**Explanation**   The following kinds of run-on sentences are common:

▸ *Run-on sentences with pronoun subjects in the second clause:*

Boot camp was just what I had expected, it was terrible.   (It is very easy to run these two independent clauses together when writing them because when we say them, we say them in one breath. The comma before the pronoun *it* does not correct the run-on. What noun in the first clause is the antecedent of *it*?)

My drill instructor at Parris Island surprised me, he was actually very nice.   (The comma before *he* does not correct the run-on. What noun in the first clause is the antecedent of *he*?)

▸ *Run-on sentences with conjunctive adverbs:*

First you knead the dough, then you smooth it out with a rolling pin.   (You cannot join two independent clauses with conjunctive adverbs, like *then, also, however, consequently, moreover, for example,* or *therefore.*)

Bake the cookies for about half an hour, however, if you have a slow oven, bake them a little longer.   (When *however* introduces an independent clause, either use a semicolon before it or make two sentences.)

► *Run-on sentences in narratives:*

I looked across the field and saw a little boy, the child reminded me of someone I knew.   (In telling stories aloud, you probably run sentences together, but in writing you must write them separately or join them correctly.)

► *Run-on sentences in quoted speech:*

The drill sergeant made me say, "This is my rifle, it is never a gun."   (Always watch out for run-on sentences inside of quoted speech. Many instructors will ask you to correct run-on sentences within such quotations by making two sentences instead of by using a semicolon.)

**Practice**   Before doing these exercises, review Chapter 11.4, Comma Rule #3, and the four ways of correcting run-on sentences found on page 296.

A ► Correct the sentences in the sample run-ons above.

B ► Correct the following run-ons, using one of the four methods.

1. My sister Marie enlisted in the Air Force two years ago, she is stationed in England now.

2. She took a special liking to one elderly couple they accepted her as a member of the family.

3. They gave Marie a standing invitation to stop by on holidays she had only to give them a phone call.

4. Marie was also invited to several dart tournaments darts is a game the British especially love.

5. The beautiful English countryside impressed her as much as the

warmth of the people it is a land whose rolling hills remain green year round.

6. Many of these hills are dotted with small farms, one can often see small herds of sheep grazing leisurely on them.

7. Marie also visited France and Italy, she loved the beautiful beaches in the South.

8. She found the French people very friendly, too, they are especially hospitable to those who make an effort to speak their language.

9. However, her favorite European country is Switzerland, it has breathtaking scenery and a brisk, cool climate.

10. The city of Geneva is especially lovely, it is located on a clear, blue lake.

11. On one occasion she went mountain climbing in the Alps, however, the snow forced her to turn back before she got to the top of the Matterhorn.

12. They rode the lift to the lodge, then they set out across a sky-high glacier on foot.

13. The snow was fresh on the glacier, also the sun was blinding.

14. She and her party were tied together by ropes, however, no one slipped.

15. On one occasion, the guide said, "Marie, be careful, it's a three-thousand-foot drop."

16. "Don't worry, I will," she answered.

C ▸ Correct the run-ons in the following student essay, their using one of the four methods described on page 296.

It was a calm peaceful morning as I walked down the main street    1
of Atlanta. Everything was so quiet because it was Sunday morning, peo-    2
ple were still in church. When I arrived at Main and Broad, near the Liberty    3

Monument, I saw seventy-five Knights of the Ku Klux Klan marching up  4
Broad to Main Street. They were robed in their usual attire, however, the  5
faces of their hoods were open. (2 run-ons)  6

My name is Tyronne Pellisier, and I am the president of the Atlanta  7
NAACP Youth Council. I had gone downtown this particular Sunday morn-  8
ing because I had never seen the Klan before, I wanted to see what many  9
black folks fear most in the world. The Klan was not at all what I expected.  10
As they approached Main Street, they were shouting, "White power," it  11
struck me funny to see white people hollering about white power in a city  12
that is owned mostly by whites. (2 RO)  13

The group was composed of people who were too young to know  14
what hate is and others who were too old to do anything about it. They  15
stopped their march in front of the Liberty Monument, their leader got ev-  16
eryone's attention and began to make a noisy speech. "We must organize  17
and unify ourselves, next year will be too late," he said. Huh, too late for  18
what? I asked myself. I got up close so that they could see my NAACP  19
button, every now and then I shouted out, "Black power." But they didn't  20
seem to mind. (3 RO)  21

I came to the conclusion that the Klan simply was not as powerful  22
and violent as they used to be. I had thought we would lead a protest  23
against them, however, after seeing what I saw, I don't think it would be  24
worth the time. Don't get me wrong though, I haven't let them off the hook.  25
It's just that I don't see them as such a threat. I hope that some day the  26
Klan and their silent followers will see the light and realize that poor people  27
of all colors need to band together. (2 RO)  28

# Chapter 7

## Verbs (Agreement with Subjects)

## 7.0 Introduction

**An Overview**   In Chapter 5 a verb is defined as a word or words that say what a subject *is, was,* or *will be,* or what a subject *does, did,* or *will do.* You may want to review Chapter 5, Sections 2 and 3, before proceeding.

Verbs become the enemy of many students in their early college writing. "You are asking me to write something that doesn't sound right," many students will say. Why should you have to write, "It doesn't hurt anymore" instead of the familiar "It don't hurt anymore"? Why must you write, "There are three reasons" instead of "There's three reasons"? What difference does it make? And why does it matter if you leave the -*d* off of *used,* as in "He used to be my friend"? Certainly you cannot *hear* the -*d* in normal conversation.

Students who speak dialects such as those described on page 56 often have more difficulty with verbs than with other parts of speech. These kinds of verb constructions frequently show up on papers.

▶ -d *or* -ed *ending omitted:* "They look fine when I saw them."

   *Instead of the standard:* "They <u>looked</u> fine when I saw them."

▶ -s *ending omitted:* "Gasoline cost a lot these days."

*Instead of the standard:* "Gasoline <u>costs</u> a lot these days."

▶ *-s suffix added:* "Paula and Tina often studies together."

*Instead of the standard:* "Paula and Tina often <u>study</u> together."

▶ *The verb* be *used in place of* is: "Roberta always be telling her son that he must find a job."

*Instead of the standard:* "Roberta <u>is</u> always telling her son that he must find a job."

▶ *The verb* have *used with a singular subject:* "Cyril have night duty."

*Instead of the standard:* "Cyril <u>has</u> night duty."

▶ *The whole verb or part of the verb omitted:* "There only two of them left."

*Instead of the standard:* "There <u>are</u> only two of them left."
   Or: "Sue Ellen going to have a hard time explaining that to J. R."

*Instead of the standard:* "Sue Ellen <u>is going</u> to have a hard time explaining that to J. R."

Students who write nonstandard constructions such as the above are mirroring the kind of language they use in their speech. The author of this text grew up in a community where *-ed* was often dropped from verbs in the past tense. As a boy, I would constantly hear such statements as "Aunt Emmy ask Papoo to bring her some of those shrimp he caught," and "Mamoo help Petie with her homework last night." After all these years, these statements still sound right to me, and if I don't concentrate, I will leave off the *-ed* in *asked* and *helped* in my writing.

Throughout this text you have been asked to write your thoughts the way you would express them in speech. But to master correct standard English, you may need to change *some* of your words and expressions in your writing. Besides verbs, you may find that other parts of speech are a problem as well. Many students, for example, leave the *-s* or *-es* off plural nouns ("We had three test this week"). Others use pronouns in a nonstandard way ("just between you and I" *instead of* "just between you and <u>me</u>").

But verbs seem to cause the greatest problem for students accustomed to speaking any of several community dialects. And the problem sometimes gets worse before it gets better. When students learn they cannot always trust their ear—that they cannot just write the verb that sounds correct—they often start making verb errors they would not have made before.

Here is a fairly typical situation. A student learns that the following is not acceptable when standard English is required:

▶ Robin Hood rob the rich to help the poor.

That student must write either "Robin Hood robs the rich to help the poor," or "Robin Hood robbed the rich to help the poor." So, on the next paper the student writes:

▶ Robin Hood robbed the rich to helped the poor.

The instructor then says, "You know that *to helped* doesn't sound right."

The student replies, "But *Robin Hood robs* and *Robin Hood robbed* don't sound right either, and *help* is a verb, isn't it? And the sentence is in past time, isn't it?" The instructor will then have to explain that infinitives like *to love* and *to help* do not take *-d* or *-ed* endings.

The same student may not understand why you do not add *-s* to *rob* in constructions like the following:

▶ Robin Hood will rob the rich.

▶ Robin Hood does rob the rich.

Why not *Robin Hood will robs* and *Robin Hood does robs?* These verbs won't sound right to the student, but neither do certain other verbs.

This text contains two full chapters on verbs. The goal is to teach you virtually all of the rules for forming various verb constructions so that if you can't rely on your ear—on what "sounds right"—you will know from the rules how the verb should be written. If you and your instructor agree that you already use standard verbs consistently in your writing, you may be able to skip some of the exercises that follow in this and the next chapter. But read through all of the explanations carefully and complete the exercises labeled with an asterisk (*).

**Explanation:**
**Verb Agreement**
**Introduced**

In this chapter you will study verb agreement, that is, how to write verbs in the present time (or *tense*) correctly. Present-tense verbs, remember, are verbs that show what a subject *is* or *does* now. In Chapter 8 you will study all of the other verb forms, including past- and future-tense verbs—what a subject *was* or *did* and what a subject *will be* or *will do*.

The following are examples of present-tense verbs. (Subjects are underlined once, verbs twice.)

▶ This year gasoline costs twice as much as it did five years ago.

▶ Every day their colds get worse.

▶ I like swimming but love camping.

▶ Rudy and Mary do everything together.

▶ Nowadays either Rudy or Mary drives the carpool.

In all of these examples the subjects and verbs agree: the *-s* has been added to the verb only when necessary. In the next two examples, however, the verbs do not agree with their subjects:

▶ This year gasoline cost twice as much as it did five years ago.    (The *-s* has been omitted.)

▶ Every day their colds gets worse.    (The *-s* has been added to the verb incorrectly.)

Here is how the present tense of a regular verb looks when *conjugated,* or illustrated. (With regard to verb agreement, all verbs are regular except the *be* verbs and the *have* verbs.) S means singular or one; P means plural or more than one:

|  | **S** | **P** |
|---|---|---|
| First Person ▶ | I love | we love |
| Second Person ▶ | you love | you love |
| Third Person ▶ | he, she, it loves | they love |
|  | (or Rudy loves, Mary loves, or the dog loves) | (or Rudy and Mary love, or the dogs love) |

Notice that the *-s* is added only in the third-person singular form. Regular verbs with *-s* endings are discussed in Section 1 of this chapter.

Many regular verbs take an *-es* ending in the third-person singular instead of an *-s* ending. Regular verbs with *-es* endings are discussed in Section 2 of this chapter. Here is an example:

|  | **S** | **P** |
|---|---|---|
| First Person ▶ | I reach | we reach |
| Second Person ▶ | you reach | you reach |
| Third Person ▶ | he, she, it reaches | they reach |
|  | (or Paco reaches, Lydia reaches, or the bird reaches) | (or Lydia and Paco reach, or the birds reach) |

In using the correct form of *have*, you must change the verb to *has* when its subject is *he, she,* or *it,* or a single person or thing. Here is how the *have* verb is conjugated in the present tense:

|  | **S** | **P** |
|---|---|---|
| First Person ▶ | I have | we have |
| Second Person ▶ | you have | you have |
| Third Person ▶ | he, she, it has | they have |
|  | (or Tony has, Pia has, or the horse has) | (or Tony and Pia have, or the horses have) |

The *be* verbs are highly irregular. In making subjects agree with these verbs, you must be concerned with the simple past tense as well as the present tense. (*Be* verbs and *have* verbs are discussed in Section 3 of this chapter.) Here is how the present and simple past tenses of *be* verbs are conjugated:

*Present Tense*

|  | **S** | **P** |
|---|---|---|
| First Person ▶ | I am | we are |
| Second Person ▶ | you are | you are |
| Third Person ▶ | he, she, it is | they are |
|  | (or John is, Sue is, or the dog is) | (or John and Sue are, or the dogs are) |

*Simple Past*

|  | **S** | **P** |
|---|---|---|
| First Person ▶ | I was | we were |
| Second Person ▶ | you were | you were |
| Third Person ▶ | he, she, it was | they were |
|  | (or John was, Sue was, or the dog was) | (or John and Sue were, or the dogs were) |

Notice that the subject *I* takes *am* in the present tense and *was* in the past tense, and the subjects *he, she,* or *it* (or nouns that could be substituted for *he, she,* or *it*) take *is* in the present tense and *was* in the past tense.

**\*Practice**    Complete the sentences below using the appropriate verb forms for each one.

1.  Students *just love studying verbs.*
    (third-person plural, present tense of *love*)

2.  The student _____
    (third-person singular, present tense of *love*)

3.  Chicago _____
    (third-person singular, present tense of *have*)

4.  Chicago and New York _____
    (third-person plural, present tense of *have*)

5.  A police officer _____
    (third-person singular, present tense of *be*)

6.  The police _____
    (third-person plural, present tense of *be*)

7.  A person _____
    (third-person singular, simple past of *be*)

8.  The people _____
    (third-person plural, simple past of *be*)

9.  Maria _____
    (third-person singular, present tense of *reach*)

10. His pants _____
    (third-person plural, present tense of *reach*)

11. Maria and Dan _____
    (third-person plural, present tense of *love*)

## 7.1 Regular Verbs and Their Subjects

**Explanation**    All verbs except *have* and *be* verbs are regular when it comes to making them agree with their subjects. What makes them regular is that you add an *-s* or *-es* to the third-person singular endings. In this section you will study *-s* endings, in the next, *-es* endings. The most important thing to remember is never to add an *-s* (or an *-es*) to present-tense forms with first-person, second-person, or third-person plural subjects.

|  | Standard | Nonstandard |
|---|---|---|
| **First Person** ► | I love | I loves |
| **Second Person** ► | you say | you says |
| **Third Person** ► | Will and Jan love | Will and Jan loves |
| **(Plural)** ► | foxes live | foxes lives |
| ► | people seem | people seems |

The next most important thing to remember is that you *always* add an *-s* or an *-es* to regular verbs when they do have third-person singular subjects:

|  | Standard | Nonstandard |
|---|---|---|
| **Third Person** ► | our apartment consists | our apartment consist |
| **(Singular)** ► | Washington, D.C., surprises | Washington, D.C., surprise |
| ► | Cassandra fixes | Cassandra fix |
| ► | he robs | he rob |
| ► | she likes | she like |
| ► | it makes | it make |

**Practice**   In the following exercises make use of the present-tense conjugation of the verb *love*.

|  | **S** | **P** |
|---|---|---|
| **First Person** ► | I love | we love |
| **Second Person** ► | you love | you love |
| **Third Person** ► | he, she, it loves | they love |

*A ► Fill in the correct present-tense form for each of the following verbs:

1. (consist)  It _Consists_ The schools _consist_

2. (pledge)  The instructor _____ They _____

3. (cost)  The apple _____ The apples _____

4. (sew)  Mary and Sal _____ Sal _____

5. (involve)  They _____ It _____

6. (seem)  We _____ Antonio _____

7. (reconcile)  I _____ The baker _____

8. (resist)  They _____ You _____

B ▸ Write your own sentences, using the following verbs in the present tense:

1. (hope: first-person plural) _We hope this year will be another year of peace._

2. (involve: third-person singular) _____

_____

3. (practice: second-person singular) _____

_____

4. (spend: second-person plural) _____

_____

5. (sew: third-person plural) _____

_____

6. (consist: third-person singular) _____

_____

7. (give: first-person singular) _____

_____

8. (become: third-person singular) _____

_____

9. (say: third-person plural) _____

_____

10. (use: third-person plural) _____

_____

11. (seem: third-person singular) _____

_____

C ▶ What confuses many students is that you add an -s or -es to make a *plural* noun (*house* becomes *houses*), but you seem to do the opposite with regular verbs in the third person. Make plurals for the following nouns and verbs:

| *Nouns* | | *Verbs* | |
|---|---|---|---|
| **S** | **P** | **S** | **P** |

1. A <u>cabin</u> becomes _Cabins_____, but <u>he lives</u> becomes <u>they</u> _live____.

2. A <u>boy</u> becomes two _____, but <u>Mia sews</u> becomes <u>they</u> _____.

3. A <u>sister</u> becomes two _____, but <u>Chris runs</u> becomes <u>they</u> _____.

4. One <u>fist</u> becomes two _____, but <u>she asks</u> becomes <u>they</u> _____.

5. A <u>risk</u> becomes two _____, but <u>Tom risks</u> becomes <u>they</u> _____.

6. A <u>play</u> becomes two _____, but <u>Sue plays</u> becomes <u>they</u> _____.

7. One <u>dream</u> becomes two _____, but <u>Gina dreams</u> becomes <u>they</u> _____.

D ▶ This exercise is designed to help you see that present-tense singular subjects take verbs with an -s or -es ending, and that present-tense plural subjects take verbs *without* an -s or -es ending. Write your own sentences in the present tense with the following subjects and verbs. Do not use *be* or *have* verbs.

1. (musicians—subject) _Musicians play at the club every night.___

2. (involves—verb) _Our economics instructor involves us in his class.___

3. (whacks—verb) _____

_____

4. (sisters—subject) _____

_____

5. (dances—subject) _____

_____

6. (costs—verb) _____

_____

7. (fans—subject) _____

_____

8. (fans—verb) _____

_____

9. (dresses—subject) _____

_____

10. (dresses—verb) _____

_____

11. (seems—verb) _____

_____

E ▸ In the following sentences underline all subjects once and verbs twice. Rewrite all nonstandard verbs in standard English. (One sentence is correct.)

1. She sleeps very late, but when she get up she like to watch TV.  *(gets, likes)*
2. We get together and talks about interesting and difficult topics.  *(talk)*
3. She weighs about 220 pounds, and she stand about 5'11''.

4. I go by to see Rev. Miller in the hospital and keeps him company.

5. All his emotions comes to the surface when he drinks.

6. When my boss become hot, she control him.

7. If you gives me a description of her and the things she does, you will be my friend.

8. I hope the police arrest the person who stole my car.

9. He always seem to find work when no one else can.

10. When Sundays comes around, he keep his Bible close by.

11. Theresa pitch a fine game every time the manager puts her on the mound.

12. In a referendum the people expresses their opinion when they vote.

**Explanation: Tricky Third-Person Subjects**   The following types of third-person subjects are tricky and deserve special attention:

A ▸ A collective subject, such as *family, class, team* or *union,* takes a singular verb when the subject is considered as one unit:

  ▸ Her <u>family</u> <u>meets</u> all her needs.   (One family meets her needs.)

  ▸ The <u>class</u> <u>seems</u> to like the new instructor.   (One class likes the instructor.)

B ▸ Some collective subjects, such as *jury,* can take either a singular or plural verb depending on the meaning:

  ▸ The <u>jury</u> <u>seems</u> deadlocked.   (Here the word *jury* is considered as one unit.)

  ▸ The <u>jury</u> <u>disagree</u> and cannot reach a verdict. (Here *jury* is considered as individuals.)

C ▸ If the word *people* is understood—but not written—as part of a subject, it takes a plural verb.

▶ The rich get richer, and the poor get poorer.   (The writer is saying that the rich people get richer and the poor people get poorer.)

▶ The courageous die, but the cowards live.   (The writer is speaking of courageous people.)

D ▶ A noun that is plural in form (with an -s ending) but singular in meaning usually takes a singular verb:

▶ The United States gives some of its money to Third World countries.   (The United States is one nation.)

▶ Some think that politics corrupts.   (Politics is one activity.)

But note the following two exceptions:

▶ The scissors turn up each time I lose them.

▶ My son's pants tear each time he goes fishing.

**\*Practice**   Choose the correct verb.

1. The police (raids, raid) a different bar every night.
2. The United States (experiences, experience) hard times as well as prosperous times.
3. The jury (eats, eat) fine meals at the government's expense.
4. The poor (pays, pay) the taxes, and the rich (pays, pay) the tax lawyers.
5. Each graduating class (gives, give) the school a nice present.
6. The family (meets, meet) every Christmas.
7. Politics (makes, make) the world go round.
8. Even the experienced (makes, make) mistakes when they are not careful.
9. The people of the world (needs, need) to unite against nuclear destruction.
10. His pants (shows, show) a lot of wear.
11. The handicapped (demands, demand) equal access to public facilities.

## 7.2 Regular Verbs with -es Endings

**Explanation**   For verbs that end in -ch, -sh, -ss, -x, -z, or -o, add -es in the third-person singular, present tense:

▸ I, you, we, they reach, but he reaches.

▸ I, you, we, they boss, but she bosses.

▸ I, you, we, they push, but she pushes.

▸ I, you, we, they box, but Ali boxes.

You add *-es* to these verbs simply because they would be hard to pronounce if you added only an *-s*. The *-es* adds an extra syllable to the words and makes pronunciation easier. Note, however, that *ask* and *cost* take an *-s*, not an *-es*, ending: *she asks, it costs.*

Particularly troublesome to many students are verbs that end in *-o*.

▸ I, you, we, they do, but it does.

▸ I, you, we, they go, but he goes.

Here, a syllable is not added, but for *do* the pronunciation changes.
   To make *do* or *does* negative, you add the adverb *not* or, in a contraction, the suffix *-n't*. (A *suffix* is a letter or letters that are added to a word.)

▸ I do not (or I don't)

▸ It does not (or It doesn't)

The more formal the writing, however, the less you should use contractions.

**\*Practice**   Use either *do, does, don't* or *doesn't* in the following:

1. Dr. Greenway *doesn't* want to be bothered by his children.

2. Our instructor ＿＿＿＿＿＿ care about her students.

3. This city ＿＿＿＿＿＿ not have many dry days.

4. Only on the weekends ＿＿＿＿＿＿ the noise become unbearable.

5. Why make a young lady keep a man she ＿＿＿＿＿＿ want?

6. They _____ have a lot of money; in fact, you could call them rich.

7. I had to tell her that Santa _____ come to our neighborhood.

8. It _____ hurt anymore; all my tears are shed.

9. The English _____ seem to cherish the Queen.

10. She, in turn, _____ care about her people.

11. _____ it seem strange that our allies go to war with each other?

**Explanation: Verbs That End in y**

If a verb ends in -y and is preceded by a consonant, change the -y to -i and add -es. (A *consonant* is any letter other than one of the five vowels: a, e, i, o, u.) I cry becomes she cries because the -y is preceded by the consonant -r.

I, you, we, they spy, but she spies.

I, you, we, they carry, but it carries.

I, you, we, they bury, but he buries.

I, you, we, they dry, but she dries.

If, however, a verb ends in -y and is preceded by a vowel, simply add an -s to the verb. *They enjoy* becomes *he enjoys* because the -y is preceded by the vowel -o.

I, you, we, they play, but it plays.

I, you, we, they say, but she says.

I, you, we, they enjoy, but he enjoys.

I, you, we, they journey, but it journeys.

(Note that when you add an -ing to a verb ending in -y, you do not change the -y: cry becomes crying; enjoy becomes enjoying; journey becomes journeying.)

## Practice

*A ▸ Fill in the blanks for the designated verbs, keeping them in the present tense.

1. (teach)  Mary *teaches*          9.  (employ)  She _____
2. (defy)  Ben _____          10. (box)  Choon Jai _____
3. (rush)  George Rogers ____      11. (whizz)  The arrow _____
4. (try)  She _____          12. (say)  It _____
5. (do)  It _____            13. (ask)  The judge _____
6. (do + not)  It _____        14. (do)  People _____
7. (do + -*n't* suffix)  It _____    15. (cost)  It _____
8. (go)  The van _____        16. (carry)  He _____

B ▸ List all the present tense forms of the following verbs.

*Cry*                                          *Ask*

First Person ▸ *I cry*      *we cry*      _____  _____

Second Person ▸ *you cry*   *you cry*     _____  _____

Third Person ▸ *he cries*   *they cry*    _____  _____

*Reach*                                        *Enjoy*

First Person ▸ _____  _____      _____  _____

Second Person ▸ _____  _____      _____  _____

Third Person ▸ _____  _____      _____  _____

*Do*                                          *Do + -n't suffix*

First Person ▸ _____  _____      *I don't*     _____

Second Person ▸ _____   _____     _____   _____

Third Person ▸ _____   _____     _____   _____

C ▸ Rewrite the following nonstandard verbs in standard English, keeping them in the present tense. One sentence is correct.

1. The police ~~asks~~ *ask* him for his license, and he ~~give~~ *gives* it to them.

2. But she don't like to discipline her mischievous little boy.

3. Her husband always try out the merchandise before he buys it.

4. What interest me most about New York is Central Park.

5. She clean her house while her daughters just sits around.

6. It don't cost as much this year as it did last year.

7. She fix her van just as good as new.

8. Let me tell you about all the things she do for me.

9. The government employs a lot of people at the Navy Yard.

10. If he push me again, he is going to regret it.

11. In the summer Ferdinand sleeps, eats, and watch a lot of television.

12. Each time the class sings, the music teacher ask me please not to sing.

13. The people comes running and climb down the bank toward me.

14. Mama Linda is very loving and care a lot for lonely children.

15. If the recipe don't come out the way it should, try, try again.

16. It seem that we have a war on our hands.

D ▸ In each of the following sentences first locate the subject of the verb. Underline the subject once and its verb twice. If the subject is a noun, write its pronoun substitute (*he, she, it,* or *they*) above it. If the verb is correct, put a check mark above the verb. If it is incorrect, write in the correct verb.

Example ▸ (They) ✓   (they) *lead*
<u>Children</u> <u><u>do</u></u> anything their <u>minds</u> <u><u>leads</u></u> them to.   (*They* is the pronoun that you would substitute for *children* and *minds. Do* is thus

correct because you would say *they do. Leads,* however, is incorrect because you would not say *they leads* in standard English.)

1. A child believe what she sees.
2. If a child watch certain television programs, he learns many useful things.
3. My Aunt Kathleen always say she is going to live forever.
4. Best of all, television informs its viewers of the local and national news.
5. As far as snacks goes, no one needs them.
6. It seems to me that the president try to do the right thing.
7. When the sauce starts to boil, reduce the heat and simmer it for ten minutes.
8. If Mrs. Frances ask me to stop, I do what she ask.
9. Sal knows better than to call me that name again.
10. Marlene always hurt the man she love.

## 7.3 Irregular Verbs

**Explanation: Have and Has**

Only two verbs do not follow the *-s, -es* ending rule in the present tense: *have* and *be* verbs. Here again is the present tense of *have:*

| | **S** | **P** |
|---|---|---|
| First Person ▶ | I have | we have |
| Second Person ▶ | you have | you have |
| Third Person ▶ | he, she, it has | they have |

Note that the only variation from regular verbs is in the third-person singular form: *Has* is used instead of *haves.* In all other forms the verb is *have.* Knowing the present-tense forms of *have* will enable you to write correctly such verb phrases as the following:

▶ The <u>Dolphins</u> <u>have won</u> many games this year.

▶ <u>Becky</u> <u>has broken</u> her arm again.

▶ <u>She</u> <u>has loved</u> many men in her day.

These verb phrases are discussed in the next chapter.

**Practice**  In the sentences below write the correct form of the verb *have*.

1. The City of Detroit *has*_____ many industries.

2. Everyone just gathers and _____ a good time.

3. You _____ been lying to me all along.

4. China _____ more people than the United States.

5. They _____ done what they could to save her.

6. A soldier these days _____ a pretty nice life.

7. The United States _____ offered them a compromise solution.

8. The scissors _____ not cut him so far.

9. The police _____ a difficult job to do.

10. People in Latin America _____ close ties with us.

11. The class _____ elected its representative.

**Explanation: The Be Group of Verbs**  Unlike all other verbs, *be* verbs are highly irregular. Here again is the present tense and the simple past of the *be* verbs:

*Present*

| | **S** | **P** |
|---|---|---|
| First Person ▶ | I am | we are |
| Second Person ▶ | you are | you are |
| Third Person ▶ | he, she, it is | they are |

*Simple past*

| | **S** | **P** |
|---|---|---|
| First Person ▶ | I was | we were |
| Second Person ▶ | you were | you were |
| Third Person ▶ | he, she, it was | they were |

*Be* is the only verb that has a subject-verb agreement change in the first person and in the simple past. Knowing the present tense and simple past of *be* will enable you to write correctly such verb phrases as the following:

▸ Life is given, and life is taken away.

▸ We are living each day to its fullest.

▸ They weren't having any luck until they played the Saints.

Note that it is normally not correct to write the word *be* after a personal pronoun:

| Standard | Nonstandard |
| --- | --- |
| You are going. | You be going. |
| She is a close friend. | She be a close friend. |
| I am working hard. | I be working hard. |

**\*Practice**   *In the sentences below write the correct form of the* be *verb.*

1. (present)   The people __*are*__ what make any place.

2. (past + -*n't* suffix)   Uncle Mac __*wasn't*__ the same after his stroke.

3. (present)   We _____ going to regret a premature decision.

4. (present + -*n't* suffix)   They _____ my kind of people.

5. (present + *not*)   The president _____ going to bow to pressure.

6. (present)   The jury _____ making its decision now.

7. (simple past)   My husband and brother-in-law _____

   steering the boat into high winds. I _____ terrified.

8. (simple past + -*n't*)   They _____ sure whether or not they would make it through the storm.

9. (simple past)   Congress _____ in session when we

   _____ attacked.

10. (simple past)  The scissors you gave me _____ the best I ever had. You _____ very thoughtful.

11. (simple past + *not*)  The Cubs _____ nearly so bad as everyone said.

12. (simple past)  One of my legs _____ broken.

**Explanation: Using Expletives**

As defined in Chapter 5.3, an *expletive* is a word that points to a subject but is not itself a subject. Here are two examples:

▸ There is constant trouble between the two families.   (*Trouble* is the subject and takes the singular verb *is*).

▸ There were only a few survivors from the crash.   (*Survivors* is the subject and takes the plural verb *were*.)

Avoid the contraction *there's;* instead write out *there is*. And don't even attempt the contraction *there're*. See page 344 for more on expletives.

**Practice**

* ▸ Underline the subjects and write in the correct form of the verb *be*.

1. (simple past)  There _*were*_ <u>deer</u> everywhere.

2. (present)  There _____ something I have been meaning to tell you.

3. (present)  There _____ often street fighting on the next block.

4. (simple past)  _____ there many survivors from the crash?

5. (present + *not*)  There _____ any use in saying it again; the dean has made up her mind.

6. (simple past + *not*)  There _____ a thing the doctors could do for him.

Rewrite the following sentences in standard English. Where the verb has been left out, add it. Two sentences are correct.

1. Uncle Sam ~~have~~ *has* a good job waiting for you.

2. Those teen-agers the ones that has been causing the problem.

3. Althea be looking for trouble.

4. There hasn't been any more problems since you spoke to her.

5. The winos on the corner is called "the Birds" because they on the corner before the birds get up.

6. Junkyard Sam the nicest man in the whole downtown.

7. He the last one I would go to for advice.

8. You always be telling me to study, so I study but still is behind.

9. The people in Little Rock are the nicest people you will meet anywhere.

10. They the same ones that got me in trouble before.

11. There weren't anyone left that I could trust.

12. Beatrice don't mean what she say.

13. We was telling the truth, but she did not believe us.

14. You be bothering me, girl!

15. He be running his mouth off again.

16. Was they listening to what I said?

17. Doesn't it make sense to look at all the possibilities?

18. New Orleans have many streets with French and Italian names.

## 7.4 Verbs with Two or More Subjects

**Explanation: Subjects Joined by *and*** Many of your verbs will have two or more subjects (often called *compound subjects*). They usually are joined by the coordinating conjunction *and*.

▶ Ron and Don are twin brothers. Sally and Julius study together. (Because Ron and Don together are the subject of the sentence and represent more than one person, they take the plural verb *are*. The same is true of Sally and Julius.)

▸ What I <u>say</u> and <u>what I do</u> <u><u>are</u></u> not always the same. (*What I say* and *what I do* both function as individual nouns, as explained in Chapter 6.3, but together take the plural verb *are*.)

▸ <u>Appointing officials</u> and <u>initiating legislation</u> <u><u>are</u></u> the governor's primary responsibilities. (*Appointing officials* and *initiating legislation* both function as individual nouns, as explained in Chapter 8.8, but together take the plural verb *are*.)

**\*Practice**  In the following sentences underline the subjects and supply the correct verbs.

1. (sew, sews)  <u>Mother</u> and <u>I</u> often _____*sew*_____ together.

2. (cost, costs)  Gas and oil both _____ more this year.

3. (aren't, isn't)  What I want and what she wants _____ always the same.

4. (are, is)  But what I want _____ the same as what my other friend wants.

5. (give, gives)  This man and this woman _____ themselves to each other in marriage.

6. (are, is)  Getting better grades _____ my chief goal this year.

7. (are, is)  Getting better grades and playing more tennis _____ my chief goals this year.

8. (buy, buys)  My aunt and uncle sometimes _____ more than they need.

9. (seem, seems)  The potatoes, corn, and spinich all _____ fresh.

10. (protect, protects)  The Bill of Rights and the Constitution both _____ our rights.

11. (are, is)  Making clothes for her children _____ what she enjoys most.

**Explanation: Other Ways of Joining Subjects**

A ▸ Some of your sentences will have subjects that are connected by the coordinating conjunction *or* or the correlative conjunctions *either/or:*

▸ Either <u>Ron</u> or <u>Don</u> <u>is going</u> to medical school.   (A singular verb is used; one of them will go to medical school, but not both.)

However, if one of the subjects joined by *or* is plural, use a plural verb *when the subject closer to the verb is plural:*

▸ Either <u>Tina</u> or her <u>parents</u> <u>are</u> mistaken.   (The verb *are* is used to agree with the plural subject *parents.*)

But use a singular verb when the subject closer to the verb is singular:

▸ Either the <u>eggs</u> or the <u>bacon</u> <u>is</u> burning.   (Even though *eggs* is plural, *bacon* is closer to the verb and thus determines that it is singular.)

B ▸ The coordinating conjunction *nor* and the correlative conjunctions *neither/nor* and *not only/but also* function in a sentence the same way *or* and *either/or* function:

▸ Neither <u>mother</u> nor <u>father</u> <u>lets</u> me use the car.

▸ Not only my <u>hotel accommodations</u> but also my <u>airplane ticket</u> <u>costs</u> more this year.

▸ Not only my <u>airplane ticket</u> but also my <u>hotel accommodations</u> <u>cost</u> more this year.

**\*Practice**  In the following sentences underline the subjects and supply the correct verbs.

1. (come, comes)  Every day either <u>Mrs. Appleby</u> or <u>Mrs. St. John</u>

_____*comes*_____ by and brings me supper.

2. (are, is)   Neither you nor they _____ going to do well in the match on Saturday.

3. (are, is)   Abraham and his son, Isaac, _____ walking toward a place called Moriah.

4. (are, is)   Either Abraham or his servants _____ going to sacrifice Isaac upon an altar.

5. (appear, appears)   But then suddenly a ram or some other kind of animal _____ in a thicket and serves instead as the sacrifice.

6. (are, is)   Not only Isaac but also Abraham _____ thus spared.

7. (jog, jogs)   Not only the grandfather but also the children _____ each morning.

8. (jog, jogs)   Not only the children but also the grandfather _____ each morning.

9. (have, has)   Either Sophia or you _____ misunderstood.

10. (sleep, sleeps)   Both the cat and the dog _____ in the house at night.

11. (experience, experiences)   Neither Russia nor the United States _____ severe poverty.

## 7.5 Subjects with Two or More Verbs

**Explanation**   When you use two or more verbs with one subject, be sure that all verbs agree with the subject:

▶ Ron and Don are twin brothers and look exactly alike.

▸ Every night, Julius <u>studies</u> his notes and <u>reads</u> the assigned chapters but <u>seems</u> to get nowhere.

In the first sentence the plural subject *Ron and Don* takes the plural verbs *are* and *look*. In the second sentence the singular subject *Julius* takes the singular verbs *studies, reads,* and *seems*. Note that commas are not used. See Rule #3 in Chapter 11.4.

## Practice

*A ▸ Underline the subjects in these sentences and supply appropriate present-tense verbs.

1. She gives her check to her parents and *does* most of the housework as well.

2. I clean the dishes, scrub the floors, work in the yard, and much of the time _____ like Cinderella.

3. She is selfish with her possessions and also _____ a bad temper.

4. The radio and television are on all the time and _____ so much noise that I can't think.

5. The people on my street sometimes yell at their children and _____ things I don't want to repeat.

6. My husband doesn't drive himself but _____ everyone else how to drive.

Why are commas used in #2?

B ▸ Make sentences using each pair of verbs *with the same subject.*

1. (loves, hates) *Our dog loves winter but hates summer.*

2. (sings, dances) *Liza goes off by herself and sings and dances for hours at a time.*

3. (defends, accuses) _____

_____

4. (lives, dies) _____

_____

5. (is, is not) _____

_____

6. (does, does not) _____

_____

7. (has, hasn't) _____

_____

Did you use any commas incorrectly? If you are in doubt, see Rule #3 in Chapter 11.4.

C ▸ Rewrite the nonstandard verbs in standard English. (*Note:* Some sentences are correct.)

1. She and I *were* ~~was~~ the smartest in the kindergarten.

2. I hope this paper gives you some ideas for what to do on a rainy weekend and help make your rainy weekends more pleasant.

3. When we got there, they had stopped serving dinner and was now serving breakfast.

4. A good newspaper reporter goes out and hit the world head-on to get a story.

5. On weekends, she usually goes to parties or attends school events.

6. Every evening about six o'clock she sits on the front porch and gossips with the neighbors.

7. Sometimes he catch himself before things get too rough and makes a joke out of what has been happening.

8. I think the way I was brought up and the schools I attended have a lot to do with the problems I'm having now.

9. April drives the car pool five days a week and take the children to swimming class twice a week.

10. When the night falls, the young people in the neighborhood come out and play their radios.

11. They love each other and plans to get married soon.

## 7.6 Subjects and Verbs Separated

**Explanation: Sub-jects Separated by Prepositional Phrases**

Many times in your writing, your verbs will not come immediately after your subjects but will be separated by words, phrases, and clauses. Here are two such examples:

▶ I always take the easy way out.

▶ The programs that I've mentioned teach children quite a lot.

Prepositional phrases often separate subjects from verbs, as in these examples:

▶ One of us is crazy.

▶ The people in my neighborhood are nice.

In the first example the prepositional phrase *of us* separates the subject *one* from the verb *is*. In the second the prepositional phrase *in my neighborhood* separates the subject *people* from the verb *are*. Many prepositional phrases that separate subjects from verbs begin with *of, on,* and *in*. You may want to review prepositions in Chapter 5.4 before proceeding.

**\*Practice**

Underline the subjects in the following sentences once, underline the verbs twice, and put parentheses around the prepositional phrases. If the verb does not agree with its subject, change it so that it does agree. Except for *was* or *were* constructions, keep the verbs in the present tense.

1.  The <u>sounds</u> (of my neighborhood) <u>changes</u> from hour to hour.  *change*
2.  All the houses on my block are brick.
3.  Everybody in my classes are working very hard.
4.  My first few years of school was my most difficult ones.
5.  The sounds in my neighborhood is so loud that they disturb the dogs.
6.  My great-grandmother, in most people's eyes, seem to be just a mean old woman.
7.  Just the thought of her children are quite satisfying to Mother.
8.  The construction work on the houses begin next month.
9.  One of us is able to do the job alone.
10. Harold Muskie of Chase Manhattan Bank recommends the *Wall Street Journal.*
11. Their dreams for a better life was fulfilled that day.

**Explanation: Subjects Separated by Adjective Clauses**

Sometimes your subjects and verbs will be separated by adjective clauses, as follows:

▶ My <u>friends</u>, who saw me get up out of that muddy water and then fall back in again, <u>were laughing</u> at me.

▶ The <u>attempts</u> that she makes to help others sometimes <u>fail</u>.

▶ The <u>book</u> she was reading <u>was stolen</u> from her desk.

Note that in the last sentence the relative pronoun *that* is omitted but understood. You may want to review adjective clauses in Chapter 6.3 before proceeding.

**Practice**

*A ▶ Underline the subjects in the following sentences once, underline the verbs twice, and put parentheses around the adjective clauses. If the verb does not agree with its subject, change it so that it does agree.

1. Small children who are not in school has more time to play.

2. Those who don't have the money gets the long sentences.

3. The things she has left behind means so much to her family.

4. The children who live in my neighborhood play baseball every afternoon.

5. The school where my mother taught for the last seven years is closing down.

6. The gifts he brings to my son comes from his heart.

B ▶ Write five of your own sentences and include the following phrases and clauses. Place them between your subjects and verbs, and keep your verbs in the present tense.

1. (who wears her hair down to her shoulders) *Geraldine, who wears her hair down to her shoulders, washes it every night.*

2. (which is the most difficult course I'm taking) _____

_____

3. (which are the best cars on the market) _____

_____

4. (of the people I will write about) _____

_____

5. (who is hard to control) _____

_____

6. (who eat too much ice cream) _____

_____

Use commas for nonessential adjective clauses. See Rule #2 in Chapter 11.4 if you are in doubt.

## 7.7 Subjects and Verbs Reversed

**Explanation** You reverse subjects and verbs when you ask a question or use an expletive:

▸ *When you ask a question:*

Does your daughter still believe in Santa Claus?

Hasn't that plane left yet?

▸ *When you use an expletive:*

There is one thing you haven't told me.

There have been several explanations for the murder.

### Practice

*A ▸ Turn the following statements into questions. Underline the subjects once and the verbs twice.

1. He does need more money for the trip.

   *Does he need more money for the trip?*

2. She is going to the dance with you.

   _____

3. Those children need heavier jackets.

   _____

4. They were the ones we were looking for.

   _____

5. The leg has healed completely.

   _____

   6.  The senator does not deliver on his promises.

   _____

   7.  We are nearly through with verb agreement exercises.

   _____

   8.  The rain has not stopped.

   _____

   9.  The president has not concentrated on the unemployment
       problem. _____
   10. The president has concentrated on reducing the inflation rate.

   _____

   11. You are almost asleep.

   _____

**B** ▶ In the following sentences underline the subject once and verbs twice.
       If the verb does not agree with the subject, write its correct form
       above the sentence.

   1.  There ~~are~~ *is* one major <u>problem</u> in all large cities: crime.
   2.  There is still hope for you if you do not miss any more classes.
   3.  There is no reason to suspect them of the crimes.
   4.  Here's the essays I've promised, written to the best of my ability.
   5.  There hasn't been many changes since he took over as coach.
   6.  There haven't been anything in my life like that experience.

## 7.8 Verbs with Pronoun Subjects

**Explanation:**   Throughout this chapter you have been writing and correcting sen-
**Indefinite**     tences with personal pronouns as subjects: *I, you, he, she, it, we,*
**Pronouns**       *they.* In this section you will practice using *indefinite, interrogative,*
**as Subjects**    and *relative* pronouns as subjects. Before proceeding you may want
                   to review these pronouns in Chapter 5.5.

Though some are plural in meaning, the following indefinite pronouns always take singular verbs:

| anybody | everybody | nobody | somebody |
| anyone | everyone | no one | someone |
| anything | everything | nothing | something |

Thus, you would write:

▸ <u>Anything</u> she wants to do <u>is</u> fine with us.

▸ <u>Everybody</u> <u>says</u> that this is the hottest summer in history.

▸ <u>Somebody</u> <u>has</u> made a mistake.

The indefinite pronoun *some* can take either a singular or plural verb, for example:

▸ Some of the apple is rotten.    (Some of *one* thing is rotten.)

▸ Some of the apples are rotten.    (Some of *several* things are rotten.)

The following words, like *some,* can take either singular or plural verbs: *half, part, all, a lot, more, and most.* You need to ask yourself if they refer to part of one thing or some of several things, for example:

▸ <u>A lot</u> of your writing <u>is</u> clever.

▸ <u>A lot</u> of the students in this class <u>are</u> good writers.

**\*Practice**    Underline the subjects and fill in the correct verbs in the following sentences.

1. (are, is)   Some of you __*are*__ still my friends.

2. (cost, costs)   Everything _____ so much more these days.

3. (are, is)   Anyone _____ able to do the work in this class.

4. (were, was)  Some of the work _____ done.

5. (are, is)  All of the families on the block _____ sick.

6. (involve, involves)  Everything in this life _____ a lot of work.

7. (tell, tells)  Half of my brain _____ me to do one thing; half _____ me to do the other thing.

8. (Do, Does) _____ everyone agree?

9. (have, has)  They are making a statement to the press that most of the prisoners _____ been badly treated.

10. (are, is)  Much of their problem _____ of their own making.

11. (Do, Does)_____ anyone want to study in the library with me?

**Explanation: Interrogative Pronouns as Subjects**

A second kind of pronoun that can cause difficulty in verb-agreement constructions is the *interrogative* pronoun—a pronoun used in questions:

▶ Who?    What?    Which?

When used as subjects these pronouns can take either singular or plural verbs, depending on the words they stand for:

▶ What is that woman's name? (*What* refers to *one* woman's name.)

▶ What are their names? (*What* refers to *several* people's names.)

Interrogative pronouns that do not refer to particular nouns usually take singular verbs:

▶ What is happening?    Who is going with us?

**\*Practice**   In each of the sentences that follow, draw an arrow from the interrogative pronoun to the noun or pronoun it refers to and then supply the correct verb.

1. (are, is)   What _____is_____ the best choice?

2. (were, was)   What _____ their names before they got married?

3. (are, is)   What _____ your agenda for the meeting?

4. (are, is)   Which one of the insurance plans _____ best for your family?

5. (were, was)   Who _____ the lucky winner?

6. (were, was)   Who _____ the lucky winners?

**Explanation: Relative Pronouns as Subjects**   A third kind of pronoun is the *relative* pronoun—a pronoun that connects an adjective clause to a main clause:

▸ who   whose   which   that

Like interrogative pronouns, relative pronouns can take either singular or plural verbs, depending on the words they stand for:

▸ The person who means the most to me is my husband.

▸ The people who mean the most to me are my parents.

In the first example *who* refers to one person and thus takes the singular verb *means*. In the second, *who* refers to more than one person and takes the plural verb *mean*.

**Practice**

**\*A** ▸ In each of the sentences below underline the pronoun subject of the adjective clause, draw an arrow to the noun or pronoun it refers to, and then supply the correct verb.

1. (were, was)   My friends who _____were_____ with me stood up for me when I was arrested.

2. (break, breaks)  It is hard to remain allies with nations that

_____ our treaties.

3. (mind, minds)  The one who _____ his or her own
business is the one who stays out of trouble.

4. (care, cares)   They are the ones who _____ for you the
most.

5. (turn, turns)   The coins that _____ green are copper.

6. (need, needs)  People who _____ others are my kind
of people.

B ▸ Write ten of your own sentences, using the italicized words as *subjects*
with present tense verbs.

1. (*some*, with a plural verb) *Some of the tenants dislike
the landlord's practices.*

2. (*that* as a relative pronoun, with a singular verb) *A typewriter that skips spaces is maddening.*

3. (*everybody*) _____

4. (*what,* as an interrogative pronoun, with a singular verb) _____

_____

5. (*some,* with a singular verb) _____

_____

6. (*anyone)* _____

7. (*who,* as a relative pronoun, with a singular verb) _____

_____

8. (*who,* as a relative pronoun, with a plural verb) _____

_____

9. _(something)_ _____

_____

10. _(which,_ as a relative pronoun, with a singular verb) _____

_____

11. _(which,_ as a relative pronoun, with a plural verb) _____

_____

12. _(which,_ as an interrogative pronoun, with a singular verb) _____

_____

## 7.9 Review Exercises

**\*A ▸** Edit the following essay correcting all the verb agreement errors by writing the corrections above the line.

### Uptown Versus Downtown

I presently live in Jefferson City East, which is known as the uptown   1
area. I have been living uptown for six years now and has enjoyed every   2
moment. Before that I lived downtown and hated every moment. Mother   3
worked hard, sometimes at two jobs, to make enough money so that we   4
could move. (1 error)   5

    Living uptown is very pleasant. Around my neighborhood there   6
isn't any gang fights. People are friendly and helps one another in time of   7
trouble. I can go to the corner drugstore and not have to worry about   8
being mugged. My mother has peace of mind knowing that neither she   9
nor her children is going to be hurt in the streets. Mother sometimes invite   10
people over to see the house and is not embarrassed by dirty surroundings.   11
(4 errors)   12

My experience living downtown was quite different. In downtown 13

Jefferson City where I used to live there was gang fights every day. Some- 14

times in the fights people would get hurt badly or even killed. You was 15

always scared that you would be the next to get hurt. The people in my 16

neighborhood was not friendly at all. A nice drug store was located on the 17

corner, but we were scared of the drug addicts who gathered there. My 18

mother was always worried about the danger in the streets; she was afraid 19

her children would get mixed up with the wrong crowd. She was also too 20

embarrassed to invite people over to the house because of the crime in 21

the neighborhood. This neighborhood was not the atmosphere my mother 22

wanted for her children. (3 errors) 23

These are my reasons for choosing uptown, a better place to live 24

than downtown. I hope I can do for my children what my mother have 25

done for us and keep them away from downtown. (1 error) 26

*B ▶ Write a three-paragraph paper of 150 or more words describing what your pet (real or imaginary), a member of your family, or your best friend does each day: morning, afternoon, and evening. Tell about the pet or the person in the present tense, third person. Since the main purpose of this paper is to give you practice in using third-person singular verbs correctly, include at least twenty verbs with -s or -es endings. You might begin your paper something like this:

▶ Every morning at six o'clock, <u>Halloween</u>, our cat, <u>jumps</u> up on the window sill and <u>cries</u> to be let out. <u>He</u> always <u>wakes</u> us up when <u>he</u> <u>does</u> this . . . .

C ▶ Rewrite the paper, this time in the third person plural, present tense. You might begin something like this:

▶ Every morning at six o'clock, <u>Halloween #1 and Halloween #2</u>, our cats, <u>jump</u> up on the window sills and <u>cry</u> to be let out. <u>They</u> always <u>wake</u> us up when <u>they</u> <u>do</u> this . . . .

# Chapter 8
## Verbs (Other Forms)

## 8.0 Introduction

**An Overview**　The subject of this chapter is all verb constructions other than verb agreement, the subject of Chapter 7. As an overview of the various verb forms you will be studying, examine the following conjugations (illustrations) of the verbs *love* and *have*. The *be* verbs will be dealt with separately. Following the instructions on page 317, be sure to read all explanations carefully and complete *at least* those exercises marked with an asterisk.

LOVE

**S**　　　　　　　　　　　**P**

*Present tense*

First Person ▶ I love　　　　　we love
Second Person ▶ you love　　　you love
Third Person ▶ he, she, it loves　they love

*Simple past tense*

First Person ▶ I loved　　　　　we loved
Second Person ▶ you loved　　　you loved
Third person ▶ he, she, it loved　they loved

*Past tense with* have *or* has

| | S | P |
|---|---|---|
| First Person ▶ | I have loved | we have loved |
| Second Person ▶ | you have loved | you have loved |
| Third Person ▶ | he, she, it has loved | they have loved |

*Past tense with* had

| | | |
|---|---|---|
| First Person ▶ | I had loved | we had loved |
| Second Person ▶ | you had loved | you had loved |
| Third Person ▶ | he, she, it had loved | they had loved |

*Passive voice with* am, is, are

| | | |
|---|---|---|
| First Person ▶ | I am loved | we are loved |
| Second Person ▶ | you are loved | you are loved |
| Third Person ▶ | he, she, it is loved | they are loved |

*Passive voice with* was, were

| | | |
|---|---|---|
| First Person ▶ | I was loved | we were loved |
| Second Person ▶ | you were loved | you were loved |
| Third Person ▶ | he, she, it was loved | they were loved |

*Progressive tense with* am, is, are

| | | |
|---|---|---|
| First Person ▶ | I am loving | we are loving |
| Second Person ▶ | you are loving | you are loving |
| Third Person ▶ | he, she, it is loving | they are loving |

*Progressive tense with* was, were

| | | |
|---|---|---|
| First Person ▶ | I was loving | we were loving |
| Second Person ▶ | you were loving | you were loving |
| Third Person ▶ | he, she, it was loving | they were loving |

## Have

**S**                **P**

*Present tense*

| | | |
|---|---|---|
| First Person ▶ | I have | we have |
| Second Person ▶ | you have | you have |
| Third Person ▶ | he, she, it has | they have |

*Simple past tense*

| | | |
|---|---|---|
| First Person ▶ | I had | we had |
| Second Person ▶ | you had | you had |
| Third Person ▶ | he, she, it had | they had |

*Past tense with* have, has

| | | |
|---|---|---|
| First Person ► | I have had | we have had |
| Second Person ► | you have had | you have had |
| Third Person ► | he, she, it has had | they have had |

*Past tense with* had

| | | |
|---|---|---|
| First Person ► | I had had | we had had |
| Second Person ► | you had had | you had had |
| Third Person ► | he, she, it had had | they had had |

(No passive voice form for this verb)

*Progressive tense with* am, is, are

| | | |
|---|---|---|
| First Person ► | I am having | we are having |
| Second Person ► | you are having | we are having |
| Third Person ► | he, she, it is having | they are having |

*Progressive tense with* was, were

| | | |
|---|---|---|
| First Person ► | I was having | we were having |
| Second Person ► | you were having | you were having |
| Third Person ► | he, she, it was having | they were having |

Each verb has four parts to it: the *base form* (which is used for the present tense), the *simple past* (which is always a single word), the *past participle* (which often ends in *-d* or *-ed* and is the main verb in certain verb phrases), and the *progressive form* (which always ends in *-ing* and is the main verb in other verb phrases). Here are the principle parts of four verbs:

| **A** | **B** | **C** | **D** |
|---|---|---|---|
| *Base form* | *Simple past* | *Past participle* | *Progressive form* |
| love (loves) | loved | loved | loving |
| do (does) | did | done | doing |
| have (has) | had | had | having |
| begin (begins) | began | begun | beginning |

A ► The *base form* is used in the following ways:

► To serve as the present tense of the verb: <u>I love</u>, <u>I do</u>, <u>I have</u>, <u>I begin</u>. (The third-person singular forms in the present tense take an *-s* or *-es* ending, as indicated in the parentheses above: <u>he loves</u>, <u>she loves</u>, <u>it loves</u>, and so forth. See Chapter 7, Sections 1 and 2.)

▶ To serve as the main verb when used with the helping verbs do, does, and did: *I do love; he, she, it does love; I did love.* (See Section 2 of this chapter.)

▶ To serve as the main verb when used with one of the nine modals. (A *modal* is a helping verb used to show various degrees of possibility or probability. See Section 2 of this chapter.)

I will love     I can love     I shall love

I would love     I could love     I should love

I may love     I must love

I might love

▶ When introduced by *to*, to serve as the infinitive. (See verbals in Section 8 of this chapter.)

I tried to love     I tried to do

I tried to have     I tried to begin

B ▶ The *simple past* is used only to tell of a condition that existed in the past or to express an action that happened in the past:

▶ I loved     I did     I had     I began

The simple past of regular verbs is formed by adding *-d* or *-ed* to the base form: I hated, I walked. (See Section 3 of this chapter.)

C ▶ The *past participle* is the main verb of four verb tenses:

▶ The past tense with *have* and *has* (See Section 4.)

I have loved     he, she, it has loved

I have done     he, she, it has done

I have had     he, she, it has had

I have begun     he, she, it has begun

▶ The past tense with *had.* (See Section 4.)

I had loved     he, she, it had loved

I had done     he, she, it had done

I had <u>had</u>      he, she, it had <u>had</u>

I had <u>begun</u>   he, she, it had <u>begun</u>

► The passive voice with *am, is, are.* (See Section 5.)
I am <u>loved</u>; you, we, they are <u>loved</u>; he, she, it is <u>loved</u> (Many verbs will <u>not</u> work in the passive voice.)

► The passive voice with *was* and *were.* (See Section 5.)
I was <u>loved</u>; you, we, they were <u>loved</u>; he, she, it was <u>loved</u>

The past participle of regular verbs is formed by adding *-ed* or *-d* to the base form (in the same way that you form the simple past).

D ► The *progressive* form of the verb is used in the following ways:

► To serve as the main verb for the present progressive tense. (See Section 6.)

I am <u>loving</u>; you, we, they are <u>loving</u>; he, she, it is <u>loving</u>

I am <u>doing</u>; you, we, they are <u>doing</u>; he, she, it is <u>doing</u>

I am <u>having</u>; you, we, they are <u>having</u>; he, she it is <u>having</u>

I am <u>beginning</u>; you, we, they are <u>beginning</u>; he, she it is <u>beginning</u>

► To serve as the main verb for the past progressive tense. (See Section 6.)

I was <u>loving</u>; you, we, they were <u>loving</u>; he, she, it was <u>loving</u>

I was <u>doing</u>; you, we, they were <u>doing</u>; he, she, it was <u>doing</u>

I was <u>having</u>; you, we, they were <u>having</u>; he, she, it was <u>having</u>

I was <u>beginning</u>; you, we, they were <u>beginning</u>; he, she, it was <u>beginning</u>

► To serve by itself as the *present participle* (a progressive verb used as an adjective): "She is a <u>loving</u> person." (See verbals in Section 8.)

The progressive form of regular verbs is formed by adding *ing* to the base form (*walk* becomes *walking*) or by dropping the final *-e* and adding *-ing* (*love* becomes *loving*).

**Explanation:
Regular and
Irregular Verbs**

In Chapter 7 only two irregular verbs were discussed, the *have* and *be* verbs. In this chapter, however, you will encounter many irregular verbs. In regard to tense, a regular verb is one that is formed when you add *-d* or *-ed* to the base form to construct both the simple past and the past participle. An irregular verb is one that is formed when you construct the simple past or the past participle in any other way:

| | Base form | Simple past | Past participle |
|---|---|---|---|
| Regular ▶ | love(s) | lov*ed* | lov*ed* |
| Regular ▶ | walk(s) | walk*ed* | walk*ed* |
| Regular ▶ | carry(ies) | carri*ed* | carri*ed* |
| Irregular ▶ | have(has) | had | had |
| Irregular ▶ | do(es) | did | done |
| Irregular ▶ | break(s) | broke | broken |
| Irregular ▶ | hit(s) | hit | hit |

A list of irregular verbs (and a few regular verbs sometimes mistaken for irregular verbs) follows. Try to learn all of the forms as soon as possible.

**Principal Parts of Tricky Verbs*** (The underlined words remain the same in each form.)

| Base form | Simple past | Past participle | Base form | Simple past | Past participle |
|---|---|---|---|---|---|
| arise(s) | arose | arisen | bite(s) | bit | bitten |
| awake(s) | awoke | awakened | blow(s) | blew | blown |
| beat(s) | beat | beaten | break(s) | broke | broken |
| become(s) | became | become | bring(s) | brought | brought |
| begin(s) | began | begun | build(s) | built | built |

*The progressive form has been omitted because of its regular pattern. See Section 6.

| Base form | Simple past | Past participle | Base form | Simple past | Past participle |
|---|---|---|---|---|---|
| buy(s) | bought | bought | forget(s) | forgot | forgotten |
| catch(es) | caught | caught | forgive(s) | forgave | forgiven |
| choose(es) | chose | chosen | freeze(s) | froze | frozen |
| come(s) | came | come | get(s) | got | got |
| cut(s) | cut | cut | go(es) | went | gone |
| cost(s) | cost | cost | grow(s) | grew | grown |
| do(es) | did | done | hang(s) | hung | hung |
| dig(s) | dug | dug | have(has) | had | had |
| draw(s) | drew | drawn | hear(s) | heard | heard |
| dream(s) | dreamed | dreamed | hide(s) | hid | hidden |
| drink(s) | drank | drunk | hit(s) | hit | hit |
| drive(s) | drove | driven | hurt(s) | hurt | hurt |
| drown(s) | drowned | drowned | keep(s) | kept | kept |
| eat(s) | ate | eaten | know(s) | knew | known |
| fail(s) | failed | failed | lay(s) | laid | laid |
| fall(s) | fell | fallen | (to put or place something) | | |
| feel(s) | felt | felt | lead(s) | led | led |
| fight(s) | fought | fought | leave(s) | left | left |
| find(s) | found | found | lend(s) | lent | lent |
| fly(ies) | flew | flown | let(s) | let | let |

| Base form | Simple past | Past participle | Base form | Simple past | Past participle |
|---|---|---|---|---|---|
| lie(s) | lay | lain | send(s) | sent | sent |
| (to recline) | | | set(s) | set | set |
| lose(s) | lost | lost | (to put something down) | | |
| make(s) | made | made | shoot(s) | shot | shot |
| meet(s) | met | met | sing(s) | sang | sung |
| pass(es) | passed | passed | sit(s) | sat | sat |
| pay(s) | paid | paid | speak(s) | spoke | spoken |
| plead(s) | pleaded | pleaded | stand(s) | stood | stood |
| prove(s) | proved | proven | steal(s) | stole | stolen |
| put(s) | put | put | stick(s) | stuck | stuck |
| quit(s) | quit | quit | swear(s) | swore | sworn |
| raise(s) | raised | raised | swim(s) | swam | swum |
| read(s) | read | read | take(s) | took | taken |
| ride(s) | rode | ridden | teach(es) | taught | taught |
| ring(s) | rang | rung | tear(s) | tore | torn |
| rise(s) | rose | risen | tell(s) | told | told |
| run(s) | ran | run | think(s) | thought | thought |
| say(s) | said | said | throw(s) | threw | thrown |
| see(s) | saw | seen | wake(s) | woke | wakened |
| seem(s) | seemed | seemed | wear(s) | wore | worn |
| sell(s) | sold | sold | | | |

## Practice

*A ▸ Read through the above list and place a check mark next to all regular verbs.

*B ▸ Insert the main verbs in the following sentences. Check the verbs against the above list.

1. (past participle of *break*)  I have *broken* my hand.

2. (simple past of *lay*)  Yesterday I ＿＿＿＿＿＿ my watch on the desk.

3. (simple past of *lie*)  I was so tired that I ＿＿＿＿＿＿ down.

4. (simple past of *set*)  He ＿＿＿＿＿＿ his watch two hours fast.

5. (past participle of *lie*)  They had just ＿＿＿＿＿＿ down when the alarm sounded.

6. (past participle of *lay*)  The soldier has ＿＿＿＿＿＿ down his sword and shield.

7. (past participle of *set*)  Congress has ＿＿＿＿＿＿ us back twenty years.

8. (simple past of *drown*)  The little girl almost ＿＿＿＿＿＿ in the pool.

9. (past participle of *cost*)  It has ＿＿＿＿＿＿ us a lot to live in the city.

10. (past participle of *go*)  She has ＿＿＿＿＿＿ over that with me many times.

11. (past participle of *begin*)  We have ＿＿＿＿＿＿ to see daylight.

12. (simple past of *see*)  The instructor ＿＿＿＿＿＿ to it that we did our work.

13. (progressive form of *have*)  We are ＿＿＿＿＿＿ a wonderful time.

14. (progressive form of *lay*)   They are _____ their cards on the table.

15. (progressive form of *hurt*)   We were always _____ one another.

16. (present tense of *break*)   That country _____ its treaties whenever it wishes.

**Explanation: The Be Verb**

The irregular *be* verb deserves special attention. The base form is *be,* and it is used with the modals and the infinitive:

▸ I can <u>be</u>    I could <u>be</u>    I like <u>to be</u>

The base form, however, is not used for the present tense and cannot be used with *do, does,* and *did.* (In standard English, you cannot say "They be my friends" or "They do be my friends.") The simple past of *be* is *was* or *were,* the past participle is *been,* and the progressive form is *being.* Thus, the four parts of the *be* verb are:

| Base form | Simple past | Past participle | Progressive form |
|-----------|-------------|-----------------|------------------|
| be | was, were | been | being |

Now examine the *be* verb conjugation:

*Present tense*

| | | |
|---|---|---|
| First Person ▸ | I am | we are |
| Second Person ▸ | you are | you are |
| Third Person ▸ | he, she, it is | they are |

*Simple past tense*

| | | |
|---|---|---|
| First Person ▸ | I was | we were |
| Second Person ▸ | you were | you were |
| Third Person ▸ | he, she, it was | they were |

*Past tense with* have, has

| | | |
|---|---|---|
| First Person ▸ | I have been | we have been |
| Second Person ▸ | you have been | you have been |
| Third Person ▸ | he, she, it has been | they have been |

*Past tense with* had

| | | |
|---|---|---|
| First Person ▸ | I had been | we had been |
| Second Person ▸ | you had been | you had been |
| Third Person ▸ | he, she, it had been | they had been |

(No passive voice for this verb)

*Progressive tense with* am, is, are

First Person ► I am being    we are being
Second Person ► you are being    you are being
Third Person ► he, she, it is being    they are being

*Progressive tense with* was, were

First Person ► I was being    we were being
Second Person ► you were being    you were being
Third Person ► he, she, it was being    they were being

## 8.1 Using the Dictionary

**Explanation**    Any time you are in doubt as to what a particular verb form is, look it up in the dictionary. A dictionary appropriate for college use will give you the parts of irregular and troublesome verbs. Suppose, for example, you look up the verb *break* (the base form). To find the various parts of the verb, first make sure you have located a verb. Verbs are designated *v* or *vb, vt* or *tr* (transitive verbs—those that take objects), or *vi* or *intr* (intransitive verbs—those that do not take objects). Nouns are marked *n.* In a medium-length dictionary, you will probably see the following:

► **break** (brāk) *vt.* **broke, broken, breaking**

*break* is the base form

(brāk) is the pronunciation

*broke* is the simple past

*broken* is the past participle

*breaking* is the progressive form

In a more complete dictionary, you may see an entry like this:

► **break** (brāk) vt. **broke** or *Archaic* **brake, broken, breaking, breaks**

*brake* is an alternative for *broke* but is no longer in use

*breaks* is the third-person singular, present-tense form

If you are given a choice as to whether to use one simple past over another, one past participle over another, or one progressive form over another, always choose the first alternative. Choose *broke*, for example, over *brake*.

In looking up a regular verb, like *love* or *walk*, in a medium-size dictionary, you probably will not see any parts of the verb listed. This means that all constructions are regular: you add *-d* or *-ed* to the base form for both the simple past and the past participle, and you add *-ing* to the base form for the progressive form. (If the verb ends in *-e*, you drop the *-ed* and add *-ing* to construct the progressive form.)

If you look up *bring*, you probably will see the following:

▸ **bring** (brĭng) *vt.* **brought, bringing**

*bring* is the base form

*brought* is both the simple past and the past participle

*bringing* is the progressive form

Here are two other examples:

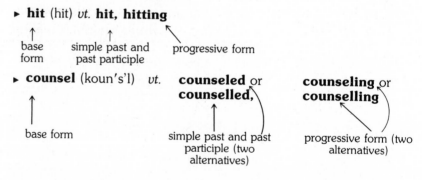

Practice — Look up the base form of the following verbs in a dictionary and write the other three parts of the verb in the designated blanks.

| Base form | Simple past | Past participle | Progressive form |
|---|---|---|---|
| 1. creep | *crept* | *crept* | *creeping* |
| 2. weave | | | |
| 3. mow | | | |

4. bend     _____   _____   _____

5. shine (to give light)     _____   _____   _____

6. forbid     _____   _____   _____

7. shoulder     _____   _____   _____

8. hang (to execute)     _____   _____   _____

9. hearken     _____   _____   _____

10. happen     _____   _____   _____

11. spay     _____   _____   _____

## 8.2 The Base Form

**Explanation: The Base Form with Helping Verbs**

Of the four uses of the base form, two are discussed here: the base form with *do, does,* and *did,* and the base form with the nine modals. (The base form used as the present tense is the subject of Chapter 7; the base form used as the infinitive is discussed in Section 8 of this chapter.)

The helping verbs *do, does, did* have the following functions:

▸ To show emphasis

I, you we, they <u>do love</u>

He, she, it <u>does love</u>

I, you, we, he, she, it <u>did love</u>

▸ To ask a question

<u>Do</u> you <u>love</u>?

<u>Does</u> she <u>love</u>?

<u>Did</u> we <u>love</u>?

Notice that in each of the above examples, present or past, the main verb *love* does not change in form.

Modals are helping verbs that are used to show various degrees of certainty or possibility. Memorize them.

will      can      shall      may      must
would    could    should    might

Unlike the *do* verbs, the modals never change form. But like the *do* verbs, the nine modals *always* take the base form of the verb, so that you say:

I will <u>go</u>            you can <u>explore</u>            we must <u>investigate</u>
she would <u>know</u>    Harry should <u>be</u> aware    the police might <u>arrest</u>

## Practice

\* ▸ Choose a *different* modal verb for each of the sentences that follow.

1. Your friends _____ come if they want to.

2. Jannie _____ ride a rodeo mule.

3. The jacket _____ dry quickly.

4. I really _____ read this text more closely.

5. We _____ adopt a child.

6. If I didn't know Herb so well, I _____ think he was crazy.

7. Antonio _____ have his grades by now.

8. It _____ rain this afternoon.

9. You _____ pass this course!

**Explanation:**
**Modal Verbs and**
**Verb Tense**

While modal verbs can be used in several ways, a good rule to keep in mind is that ordinarily *will, can,* and *may* are used in present-tense constructions (usually with reference to the future) while *would, could,* and *might* are used in past-tense constructions, as follows:

▸ <u>You</u> <u>know</u> <u>you</u> <u>will</u> <u>do</u> well in that class.   (present tense with reference to the future)

▸ You <u>knew</u> <u>you</u> <u>would do</u> well in that class.   (past tense)

▸ He <u>says</u> that <u>I</u> <u>can</u> go to that school.   (present tense with reference to the future)

▸ He <u>said</u> that <u>I</u> <u>could</u> go to that school.   (past tense)

▸ You <u>may be</u> making a mistake.   (present tense)

▸ <u>I</u> <u>told</u> her that <u>she</u> <u>might be</u> making a mistake.   (past tense)

(Note that the modal *may* and the main verb *be* are written as two separate words, *may be. Maybe* is an adverb, as in "<u>Maybe</u> you are right.")

**\*Practice**   Choose the correct verb for each of the following.

1. (can, could)   When I was young, you __*could*__ buy a Coke for a dime.

2. (can, could)   When darkness falls out there, you _____ hear strange sounds in the woods.

3. (can, could)   Once we thought we _____ fly, so we took an umbrella to the top of the roof, and . . .

4. (can, could)   I hope you _____ come with us.

5. (can could)   You _____ have knocked me over with a straw.

6. (will, would)   Leroy knew that he _____ win some day.

7. (will, would)   If we arrive on time, we _____ get the best seats.

8. (will, would)   If they had known we were coming, they _____ have hired a band.

9. (will, would)   Mother said she _____ give the ring to me when I got married.

10. (will, would)   The pants _____ fit when I lose weight.

11. (will, would)  I thought we _____ win.

12. (may, might)  The president _____ be right about in-flation, but many disagree.

13. (may, might)  The president _____ have been right about inflation.

14. (may, might)  Regina told the dean that she _____ be thinking of another career.

15. (may, might)  Students with outside jobs and children to raise

    _____ not find enough hours in the day to do every-thing.

16. (may, might)  Robert said he _____ write the assigned

    essay, but then again he _____ not.

## 8.3 The Simple Past

**Explanation**  When you want to write about something that happened in the past—a moment ago, a year ago, a million years ago—you will often use the *simple past* form of the verb. To make the simple past form for regular verbs, add -*d* or -*ed* to the base form:

▶ I love becomes I loved    I walk becomes I walked

If you are in doubt about how to form the simple past for irregular verbs, look them up in the list on page 358 or consult a dictionary. (See Section 1 of this chapter.) Here are two simple past conjugations:

| *seem* (regular) | | *begin* (irregular) | |
|---|---|---|---|
| I seemed | we seemed | I began | we began |
| you seemed | you seemed | you began | you began |
| he, she, it seemed | they seemed | he, she, it began | they began |

**Practice**

*A ▶ In the first sentence in each of the pairs below, supply the appropriate *present-tense* form of the verb (remembering to add -*s* or -*es* when necessary); in the second sentence supply the *simple past* form. Make use of the list of irregular verbs on page 358.

*Present* →1. (dress)  a. Carlos *dresses* "fit to kill" everyday.

*S. Past* →b. When he was a young man, he *dressed* "fit to kill."

2. (cut)  a. Lee _____ his finger when he chops onions.

b. But yesterday, he nearly _____ his finger off.

3. (begin)  a. Each time I _____ to study, someone interrupts me.

b. The moment I _____ to study, my daughter came in for a chat.

4. (choose)  a. _____ me to represent the class, please.

b. They said that you _____ me. Thanks.

5. (read)  a. My husband _____ to the children every night.

b. Last night, he _____ *Tom Sawyer.*

6. (cost)  a. Gasoline _____ more each year.

b. Ten years ago, it hardly _____ anything.

7. (drown)  a. David _____ her with his love.

b. When she rejected him, he _____ himself in tears.

8. (wake)  a. When she _____ me, the cat awakes also.

b. When she _____ me, the cat awoke also.

9. (have)  a. Dr. Sanders _____ good attendance in her class.

b. Dr. Sanders _____ good attendance in her class until this semester.

10. (feel)  a. I _____ you have been unfair to me.

b. I _____ you were unfair to me.

11. (get)  a. Mrs. Joseph _____ up with the birds.

b. But yesterday, she _____ up before the birds.

B ► Using the instructions for A above, supply the correct verbs in the sentences that follow.

1. (tear)  a. Marlon _____ up his papers without reading the teacher's comments.

b. When he _____ up the last paper, Mr. Hastings got really mad.

2. (lay)  a. When I lie down at night, I _____ my glasses on the window sill.

b. When I lay down last night, I _____ my glasses on the window sill.

3. (say)  a. Grandfather _____ , "Never a borrower or a lender be."

b. Grandfather once _____ , "Never a borrower or a lender be."

4. (ask)  a. I _____ you to marry me.

b. One time I _____ you to marry me.

5. (use)  a. They _____ my umbrella without asking.

b. My sisters _____ to tease me all the time.

6. (look)  a. Cindy _____ pretty in her new dress.

b. Cindy _____ pretty in her new dress.

7. (quit)  a. I _____ ; indeed I do.

b. I _____ ; I did.

8. (hit)  a. Kirby _____ me when I am down.

b. Kirby _____ me when I was down.

9. (begin)  a. When you get older, you _____ to find new strengths.

b. When she got older, she _____ to find new strengths.

10. (plead)  a. The lawyer _____ with the jury to show mercy.

b. Yesterday, the lawyer _____ with the jury to show mercy.

**Explanation: Doubling the Final Consonant**

Often in writing verbs in the simple past it is necessary to double the final letter before adding an *-ed:*

hum becomes hummed    stop becomes stopped

refer becomes referred    commit becomes committed

Before doubling the final letter, make sure the verb meets the following tests:

▸ The final letter is a consonant, not a vowel (not *a, e, i, o, u*) and not *y*. The above verbs end in *m, r, p,* and *t.*

▸ The final letter is preceded by a single vowel (not a double vowel and not a consonant). This is true of all of the above. What are the vowels that precede the final consonants?

▸ The word is either one syllable *or* the accent is on the last syllable. *Hum* and *stop* are both one-syllable words. *Refer* and *commit* are both accented on the last syllable. We say:

comMIT, not COMmit    reFER, not REfer

*Travel,* however, is pronounced TRAvel. Thus, the simple past is *traveled.* Likewise, the simple past of *happen* is *happened.*

**Practice**

*A ▸ Making use of the three rules above, tell why you do *not* double the final letter of the following words:

1. dress _____

2. look _____

3. enjoy _____

4. differ _____

5. return _____

*B ► Write the following verbs in the simple past.

1. (enjoy)   Mary _____ my company those many years.

2. (prefer)   Clarence said that he _____ meat and pota-toes.

3. (gas)   We stopped at the pump and _____ up the car.

4. (step)   They _____ up their passing attack in the third quarter.

5. (suppose)   Chou told me that he _____ he would study medicine.

6. (hum)   Granny _____ me to sleep every night.

7. (counsel)   My advisor _____ me not to take any more subjects.

**Explanation: Verbs That End in *y***

For verbs that end in -*y preceded by a consonant*, change the -*y* to -*i* and add -*ed* to make the simple past:

► cr<u>y</u> becomes <u>cried</u>     app<u>ly</u> becomes <u>applied</u>     marr<u>y</u> becomes <u>married</u>

For verbs that end in -*y* preceded by a vowel, just add -*ed* without changing the -*y*:
enjo<u>y</u> becomes <u>enjoyed</u>    journe<u>y</u> becomes <u>journeyed</u>

obe<u>y</u> becomes <u>obeyed</u>  ·  emplo<u>y</u> becomes <u>employed</u>

(Note that if you add -*ing* to a verb that ends in -*y*, you do not change the -*y*: fr<u>y</u> becomes <u>frying</u>.)

**\*Practice**   Write the following in the simple past, using the verbs shown.

1. (cry)   She _____ a river of tears over me.

2. (fry)   They _____ it in bacon grease.

3. (obey)   Hartford always _____ his mother.

4. (marry)   They _____ when they were much too young.

5. (bury)   Kahn _____ the coin in the yard.

**Explanation:
Avoiding
Unnecessary
Tense Changes**

Ordinarily, you tell something either in the present tense or the past tense, but not in both. You write:

▸ <u>She</u> <u>says</u> <u>she</u> <u>pushes</u> the car while her <u>father</u> <u>watches</u>.

*or*

▸ <u>She</u> <u>said</u> <u>she</u> <u>pushed</u> the car while her <u>father</u> <u>watched</u>.

*but not*

▸ <u>She</u> <u>says</u> <u>she</u> <u>pushed</u> the car while her <u>father</u> <u>watches</u>.

The editing symbol for changing tenses in the same sentence unnecessarily is ST (shift in tense).

**Practice**

**\*A** ▸ In the following sentences, some of the verbs are in the present, some in the simple past. Write them all in the simple past.

1. They surprise us when they came to our school.
   *surprised*

2. When I was young, I use to tear the heads off of my sister's paper dolls.

3. She got so mad that she turns red.

4. They always dress up when they went out to eat.

5. We work, we work, and we work, but we got nowhere.

6. When we return, we freed the prisoners.

7. My wife said you advertise a car in the morning paper.

8. They acted as if they have never seen a young lady before.

9. Maria said that she will study harder this semester.

10. The president told the nation that he can balance the budget.

11. After the war, we come home, just as we said we will.

*B ► The following narrative was written in the present tense. Rewrite the verbs, putting them in the past tense. Do not change verbs inside of quotations, and do not change infinitives (words like *to have, to see,* and so on). In the past tense, *can* becomes *could, will* becomes *would, and have* or *has* becomes *had.*

        *was*

It is a cold, rainy Christmas morning. The year is 1977. For some   1

    *knew*    *got*                   *was*

reason, I know once I get out of bed that this Christmas is going to change   2

my life.   3

       The morning goes by slowly because everybody is complaining   4

about everything. But the fussing really starts when a strange man comes   5

by to see me. I have never seen this man before in all my life. I am so   6

puzzled, but my mother knows him. Everybody thinks he is one of my boy-   7

friends, though he is twice as old as I am. My mother doesn't say one word.   8

       When I go into the kitchen to get away from everyone, my father,   9

Sidney, follows and starts telling me that the man is entirely too old for me   10

and for me to find a boyfriend my own age. That is the last straw. We throw   11

harsh words at each other. I tell him that he is as crazy as he looks, and he   12

tells me that I am headed for trouble. I become very upset.   13

       When I go back out in the living room, Momma and the man are   14

just sitting there looking at each other. Tears roll down my mother's face as   15

she looks at tears rolling down my face. One reason that I am so upset is   16

that this strange man and Momma keep looking at every move I make.   17

Finally, I can take it no longer, and I turn to the strange man and ask who   18

in the world he is. The man who my mother calls Robert turns toward me,   19

gets up slowly, and tells me that he is my real father. The whole family falls   20

out laughing.   21

I am very shocked and can not say a word. My mother cries some   22

more and says, "Don't laugh, because it is true. Robert is Roberta's father."   23

I will never forget that face and those words. I run out of the house and into   24

the carport and weep. My mother then comes out to talk to me, but I have   25

nothing to say to her because I am ashamed and hurt. I can't bring myself   26

to face my brothers and sisters, and I certainly can't bring myself to face   27

Sidney. I love him so much.   28

But things work out just fine after that day. We go on with our lives,   29

although I feel funny for a long time. I tell my mother and Sidney that I   30

never want to see that man again, that Sidney is my father, not Robert.   31

**C ▶** Do the tense conversion exercises on page 46 if you haven't done so already.

**D ▶** The following sentences were written in the present tense. Rewrite the verbs in the simple past. Some sentences will require two or more changes in verb tense.

1. Florence minds *minded* the children while John listens *listened* to the radio.

2. She wants to do everything her father asks her to do.

3. Johnson visits me when I am sick.

4. After they walk away, they just vanish from my life.

5. What I like best about the play is the scenery.

6. They train for months before the season starts.

7. He lies to me about this and that.

8. Mrs. Sanchez snaps at us when we are misbehaving.

9. We forget that communist countries differ a lot from each other.

10. They cherish their children and tend to them gently.

11. The preacher says that God caused scripture to be written.

12. I apply for that job at least once a year.

13. Joe finishes shaving and combs his hair.

14. It suddenly occurs to the senator that he is mistaken.

15. The children on the block use broomsticks for bats when they play that game they call half-rubber.

16. They guess that it is me causing the trouble.

E ▶ Write a three-paragraph paper (150 to 300 words) telling what you did during one particular day of your life: in the morning, afternoon, and evening. You may want to choose either a typical day or an unusual day to write about.

You might begin your paper something like this:

▶ One morning at six o'clock, Halloween, our cat, jumped up on the windowsill and cried to be let out. He always woke us up when he did that. . . .

## 8.4 The Past with *Have, Has, Had*

**Explanation**   If a past-tense verb is written as one word, it is called the *simple past*. Other past tense constructions are formed with *have, has,* or *had*. The main verb in such constructions is called a *past participle*. To form the past participle of regular verbs, add a *-d* or *-ed* to the base form:

▶ love becomes has loved, have loved, or had loved

▶ walk becomes has walked, have walked, or had walked

Note that for regular verbs, the simple past and the past participle are formed in the same way: I loved and I have loved.

If you are in doubt about how to form the past participle for irregular verbs, look them up in the list on page 358 or consult a dictionary. Here are two sample conjugations:
join (regular)

| | |
|---|---|
| I have joined | we have joined |
| you have joined | you have joined |
| he, she, it has joined | they have joined |

| | |
|---|---|
| I had joined | we had joined |
| you had joined | you had joined |
| he, she, it had joined | they had joined |

begin (irregular)

| I have begun | we have begun |
|---|---|
| you have begun | you have begun |
| he, she, it has begun | they have begun |

| I had begun | we had begun |
|---|---|
| you had begun | you had begun |
| he, she, it had begun | they had begun |

**\*Practice**   Fill in the appropriate past participle. (You may look up the verbs on page 358.) Notice how *have* and *has* are used differently from *had*.

1. (teach)  Mother had already ___taught___ me how to read when I began school.

2. (rise)  The sun had _____ before I arose.

3. (begin)  I've _____ to develop a taste for sweets.

4. (choose)  You have _____ well.

5. (sit)  I have _____ in that English class one semester too many.

6. (come)  It has _____ to a show down.

7. (become)  He wanted to know what had _____ of them.

8. (run)  Richard had _____ completely out of money before he got that job.

9. (quit)  He had _____ before he was fired.

10. (put)  Tom has _____ his money where his mouth is.

11. (hit)  Hurricane Gracie has _____ with all her force.

12. (lead)  Debra had _____ a proper life before she met Lewis.

13. (lay)  He has _____ down his sword and shield.

14. (lie)   We have _____ down to rest from our labors.

15. (ring)   They haven't _____ that church bell for ninety years.

16. (begin)   He has _____ to get a little deaf.

17. (seem)   It has _____ that way to me for a long time.

18. (involve)   Marcia hasn't _____ others in her project.

19. (go)   They had _____ before we had a chance to say good-bye.

20. (do)   If you had _____ your project right the first time, you wouldn't be in this difficulty.

21. (see)   Dr. Laska has _____ me before.

**Explanation: When to Use *Have* or *Has* and *Had***

*Have* and *has* are used as helping verbs to show either of the following:

► Action that was begun in the past but continues in the present:

He <u>has begun</u> to get a little deaf.   (The deafness came on him in the past and is still with him.)

<u>Georgia</u> <u>has decided</u> to go to college.   (She made her decision to go to college in the past, and the decision still stands.)

► Action that was completed in the *recent past!*

I <u>have spoken</u> to her about the bill.   (The speaker has just spoken to her about the bill.)

*Had,* however, is used as a helping verb to show action that began in the past and ended in the past:

► <u>He</u> <u>had begun</u> to get a little deaf, but <u>he</u> <u>hears</u> perfectly well now.   (At some point in the past deafness came on him, but it ended in the past.)

▶ Georgia <u>had decided</u> to go to college, but then <u>she</u> <u>met</u> Philip.

(Georgia's decision to go to college was made in the past, but after Philip came into her life she changed her mind.)

*Note:* Many students overuse *had* in their writing. When you do use *had*, be sure you need it to say what you want to say. The simple past will often work just as well.

**\*Practice**   In the first sentence in each of the pairs below, supply either *have* or *has* and the correct past participle. In the second sentence supply *had* and the correct past participle.

1. (love)   a. I *have* *loved* and   lost   many times.

   b. I *had* *loved* and lost many times, but then I met you.

2. (happen)   a. It _____ _____ before and will probably happen again.

   b. It _____ _____ once too often; I called the police.

3. (legalize)   a. They _____ _____ it in some states.

   b. They _____ _____ it, but then they found out that things got worse.

4. (guess)   a. I _____ _____ the   correct   answer.

   b. I thought I _____ _____ the right answer, but, as usual, I was wrong.

5. (finish)   a. I _____ _____ my work.

   b. I thought I _____ _____ my work, but then I found out I had two more assignments.

6. (build)   a. They _____ _____ a ship that will not sink.

b. They said they _____ _____ a ship that would not sink, but when it hit an iceberg, it sank.

**Explanation: *Have, Has,* and *Had* in Stories**

When telling a story in the present tense, use *have* or *has.* When telling a story in the past tense, use *had.* For example:

▸ He <u>says</u> he <u>has</u> lost his way.   (present)

▸ He <u>said</u> he <u>had</u> lost his way.   (past)

**Practice**

The following sentences are written in the present tense. Rewrite them in the past tense, changing not only *have* and *has* but other verbs as well. Remember, infinitives do not change in form.

1. I have been shy most of my life.

2. In college I still stay to myself because I have made no friends.

3. However, I soon get to know Dr. Rosen, a drama instructor, who has taken a liking to me.

4. She has been put in charge of a school play and asks me to play an important role.

5. Before long I have made many friends among the cast.

6. I have a lot to thank her for.

## 8.5 The Passive Voice

**Explanation**

So far you have been studying verbs in the *active voice,* that is, verbs that tell what the subject is or does in the present, past, or future.

      subj           obj
▸ The <u>girl</u> <u>pushed</u> the car.

*Girl* is the subject because she is what the sentence is about, *pushed* is the verb because it tells what the girl did, and *car* is the object because it receives the action. In the *passive voice,* however, the subject and object are reversed:

      subj                obj
▸ The <u>car</u> <u>was pushed</u> by the girl.

Now the subject is *car,* but instead of doing something, the car re-

ceives the action. *Girl* becomes the object of the preposition *by.*
To form the passive voice:

▸ Use some form of the *be* verb as a helper, usually *am, are, is, was,*
or *were.* (On occasion *get* can take the passive voice, as in "She
got married last year.")

▸ Use the past-participle form of the main verb. Consult the list on
page 358 or a dictionary for irregular forms.

Here are two sample conjugations of the passive voice:
suppose (regular)

| | |
|---|---|
| I am supposed | we are supposed |
| you are supposed | you are supposed |
| he, she, it is supposed | they are supposed |

| | |
|---|---|
| I was supposed | we were supposed |
| you were supposed | you were supposed |
| he, she, it was supposed | they were supposed |

understand (irregular)

| | |
|---|---|
| I am understood | we are understood |
| you are understood | you are understood |
| he, she, it is understood | they are understood |

| | |
|---|---|
| I was understood | we were understood |
| you were understood | you were understood |
| he, she it was understood | they were understood |

**\*Practice**   Change the following from the active to the passive voice. The object
will become the subject. Either make the subject the object of the
prepositional phrase beginning with *by* or, in some sentences, omit it
altogether.

                    subj              obj
**Example** ▸ They built the bridge to survive hurricanes.

                    *becomes*

                       subj                    obj
The bridge was built by them to survive hurricanes.

                    *or*

The <u>bridge</u> <u>was built</u> to survive hurricanes.

1. They tear my shirt every time I play football.

_____

2. They tore my shirt every time I played football.

_____

3. The glass split his knee wide open.

_____

4. They built their house upon a rock.

_____

5. The Jackson Five first sang that song.

_____

**Explanation: When to Use the Passive Voice**

Avoid overusing the passive voice in your writing. (In the revision checklist overuse of the passive voice is designated S-6. See page 97.) Ordinarily, your sentences are stronger when your subjects act instead of being acted upon. If you want to tell your reader that Hans read *Julius Caesar*, write:

▸ Hans read *Julius Caesar*.

   *instead of*

▸ *Julius Caesar* was read by Hans.

If you want to tell your reader that the bank cashes your checks, write:

▸ The bank cashes my checks.

   *instead of*

▸ My checks are cashed by the bank.

However, when the receiver of the action is more important than the doer of the action, you may need to use the passive voice, for example:

▸ She was mugged right outside of the grocery store.   (The writer is calling attention to the person who was mugged, not to the un-known mugger.)

▸ Ali was finally beaten in the ring.   (The writer is calling attention to the long-time world boxing champion, not to the person who defeated him.)

## Practice

*A ▸ The passive voice is appropriately used in the following sentences. Supply the correct past participle.

1. (suppose)   You are *supposed* to take no more than an hour on the test.

2. (write)   It is _____ that you should love one another.

3. (use)   They were _____ to his being late all the time.

4. (swear)   I was then _____ in before the judge.

5. (hurt)   My finger got _____ when I fell from the roof.

6. (say)   It is _____ that I am a fine cook.

7. (drive)   Alvina was _____ crazy by the gossip before she left her job.

8. (know)   Nantucket is _____ as "The Gray Lady."

9. (use)   But I will never get _____ to having five children.

10. (freeze)   The lakes were _____ over.

11. (set)   My alarm clock is _____ to go off at five.

*B ▸ The passive voice is inappropriately used in the following sentences. Rewrite them in the active voice.

1. What you have done is greatly appreciated by me.

   *I greatly appreciate what you have done.*

2.  The supplies were really needed by us.

_____

3.  The money will be used by them to buy a car.

_____

4.  Everything was knocked flat by the raging storm.

_____

5.  His lecture was understood by me.

_____

6.  The various verb forms have been carefully learned by you.

_____

**Explanation: The Passive Voice with the Nine Modals**     A fairly common—and appropriate—use of the passive voice is with one of the nine modal verbs, the helping verb *be,* and a past participle, for example:

▸ Anthropology can be defined as . . .

▸ College students should be warned . . .

▸ Work might be viewed as . . .

**Practice**     Use the following verb phrases in sentences.

1.  (would be overthrown) *That government would be overthrown if it were not for the United States.*

2.  (might be seen) _____

_____

3.  (will be chosen) _____

_____

4.  (could be viewed) _____

_____

5. (should be stopped) _____

_____

6. (must be changed) _____

_____

## 8.6 The Progressive Form

**Explanation**    You have studied the base form of the verb, the simple past, and the past participle. The fourth part of the verb is the *progressive form,* which is used to show continuing action or state of being either in the present or in the past, for example:

▸ I love becomes I am loving or I was loving

▸ I walk becomes I am walking or I was walking

The general rule to construct the progressive form is to add *-ing* to the base form of the verb or, if the verb ends in *-e,* to drop the *-e* and add *-ing.* Here are two sample conjugations:

walk

| | |
|---|---|
| I am walking | we are walking |
| you are walking | you are walking |
| he, she, it is walking | they are walking |

| | |
|---|---|
| I was walking | we were walking |
| you were walking | you were walking |
| he, she, it was walking | they were walking |

write

| | |
|---|---|
| I am writing | we are writing |
| you are writing | you are writing |
| he, she, it is writing | they are writing |

| | |
|---|---|
| I was writing | we were writing |
| you were writing | you were writing |
| he, she, it was writing | they were writing |

But note the following exceptions to the general rule:

▸ Do not drop the *-e* when the verb ends in double *-e:*

see becomes seeing    flee becomes fleeing

▶ Do not drop the *-e* in *be, singe,* and *dye:*

be becomes being    singe becomes singeing,

dye becomes dyeing

▶ For verbs that end in *ie,* drop the *i* and the *e,* and add *-y* + *-ing.*

lie becomes lying    die becomes dying    vie becomes vying

▶ For one-syllable verbs (or verbs that are accented on the last sylla-ble) that end in a consonant preceded by a single vowel, double the final consonant before adding *-ing:*
hum becomes humming    begin becomes beginning

occur becomes occurring    quiz becomes quizzing
Note that verbs ending in *-y* retain the *-y* when *-ing* is added:

▶ fry becomes frying    say becomes saying

If you are in any doubt as to whether you should drop an *e* or double a letter before adding *-ing,* consult your dictionary.

**\*Practice**   Fill in the blanks with the progressive form of the designated verbs. Be sure to use the right tense.

1. (look)  You *are looking* _____ mighty handsome these days.

2. (begin)  We *were beginning* _____ to wear out our welcome so we left.

3. (help)  She _____ me   when Mrs. Malloy walked in.

4. (ask)  The paper says they _____ $5,000 for their Chevrolet.

5. (quiz)  Dr. Ward _____ us on that material tomorrow.

6. (dye)  I _____ my shoes when I spilled the boiling water on myself.

7. (travel)  We _____ in Europe when we heard the news.

8. (lie)  The old man _____ face down on the sidewalk when they found him.

9. (lay)  I _____ down my sword and shield and will practice war no more.

10. (say)  Now that we are in the second week of the play, she _____ her lines perfectly.

11. (hit)  She became so angry that she _____ everything in sight.

12. (begin)  I _____ to think I couldn't write but then I gained confidence in myself.

## 8.7 Other Verb Forms

**Explanation**   In addition to the verb tenses presented in this chapter so far, there are other verb forms you will be using from time to time. You will see, however, that you already know the rules for forming these verbs. Here are two summary conjugations. You have already studied the forms that are checked.

<u>reject</u> (regular)

√ I reject (he, she, it rejects)
√ I rejected
√ I will reject
√ I have rejected
√ I had rejected
  I will have rejected

*Progressive tenses*

√ I am rejecting
√ I was rejecting
  I have been rejecting

<u>know</u> (irregular)

√ I know (he, she, it knows)

√ I knew
√ I will know
√ I have known
√ I had known
  I will have known

*Progressive tenses*

√ I am knowing
√ I was knowing
  I have been knowing

I had been rejecting
I will have been rejecting

I had been knowing
I will have been knowing

*Passive voice*

√ I am rejected
√ I was rejected
√ I will be rejected
  I have been rejected
  I had been rejected
  I will have been rejected
  I am being rejected
  I was being rejected

*Passive Voice*

√ I am known
√ I was known
√ I will be known
  I have been known
  I had been known
  I will have been known
  I am being known
  I was being known

The following rules will help you to form the above verb phrases. The rules repeat what you have already learned.

▸ After the modal verb *will,* use the base form of the verb:
will <u>reject</u>    will be rejected    will <u>have</u> rejected
will <u>know</u>    will <u>be</u> known    will <u>have</u> known
(*Reject, know, be* and *have* are all base forms.)

▸ Note that other modals can be substituted for *will,* for example:
might <u>reject</u>    may <u>be</u> known    should <u>have</u> rejected

▸ After *have, has, had,* use the past participle:
I had <u>known</u>    I have <u>rejected</u>    I had <u>been</u>

I had <u>been</u> known    I will have <u>been</u> rejected
(*Known, rejected,* and *been* are the past participles of *know, reject,* and *be.*)

▸ Use the progressive form to show continuous action in the present, past, or future:
I am <u>rejecting</u>    I will be <u>knowing</u>
I was <u>rejecting</u>    I will have <u>been</u> <u>knowing</u>

▸ Use the past participle for other forms:
I will have <u>rejected</u>    I will be <u>rejected</u>    I have been <u>rejected</u>
I will have <u>known</u>    I will be <u>known</u>    I have been <u>known</u>

Try to avoid long complicated verbs. Sometimes, though, you will need two or even three helping verbs to say what you mean. If, for example, you want to tell someone how long you will have been hiking when it gets to be twelve o'clock, you might say:

▸ At twelve o'clock we <u>will have been hiking</u> three hours.

In this case, the verb is consistent with the rules you have studied:

▸ You begin with the modal <u>will</u> to indicate future action.

▸ <u>Will</u> takes the base form of the next helping verb, which is <u>have.</u>

▸ .<u>Have</u>, when used as a helping verb, takes the past participle of <u>be</u>, which is <u>been</u>.

▸ Because you want to show ongoing action—you will still be hiking at twelve o'clock—you use the progressive form of the verb *hike*, which is *hiking*.

If you want to tell a friend that her successful new cooking school will be widely known, you might say:

▸ Sarah, your cooking school <u>will be known</u> throughout the city for its excellence.

▸ Again you begin with the modal <u>will</u> to show future action.

▸ <u>Will</u> takes the base form of the next helping verb, which is <u>be.</u>

▸ Because you are using the passive voice, it is necessary to use the past participle of *know*, which is *known*.

**Practice** Label each of the following M for modal, BF for base form, PP for past participle, and PF for progressive form. Then use the verb phrase in a sentence.

1. (must have happened) *M BF PP*    *The accident must have happened between two and three in the morning.*

2. (could be stealing) _____

   _____

3. (will have been living) _____

   _____

4. (might have been) _____

_____

5. (would have known) _____

_____

6. (should not have been playing) _____

_____

## 8.8 Verbals (Infinitives, Participles, Gerunds)

**Explanation:** Verbals are words that come from verbs but are used as adjectives,
**Infinitives** adverbs, and nouns. There are three kinds of verbals: infinitives, participles, and gerunds. Like verbs, verbals sometimes take objects. The symbol for verbal errors in the editing checklist is *Vb1*.

The *infinitive,* which is introduced by *to,* is the same as the base form of the verb. It can be used as a noun, adjective, or adverb:

▸ To live is to grow.    (These two infinitives are used as nouns, one as a subject, the other as a predicate nominative.)

                                       obj

▸ There must be another way to solve that problem.    (This infinitive phrase is used as an adjective modifying *way.* Within the infinitive phrase, *problem* is the object of *to solve.*)

                          obj

▸ Sandra came out to say good-bye.    (This infinitive phrase is used as an adverb modifying *came out.* Within the infinitive phrase *good-bye* is the object of *to say.*)

Keep the following in mind when using infinitives:

▸ The form of the infinitive does not change. Even when writing in the past tense, you do not add a *-d* or *-ed* to the infinitive: "I did not like to walk those long distances when I was in the army."

▸ When you see that an infinitive or an infinitive phrase is the subject in present-tense constructions, use the third-person singular verb:

<u>To jog the entire distance</u> <u>requires</u> months of training.

Of course, if you use two or more infinitives as subjects, you need to use a plural verb:

<u>To live</u> and <u>to love</u> <u>were</u> the two things he asked.

▸ As a general rule, do not split infinitives. Choose:

It is not always easy to like the one you love.

*instead of*

It is not easy to always like the one you love.

**Explanation:**
**Participles**

The *present participle* is the same as the progressive form of the main verb and is constructed with an *-ing* ending. (See Section 6 of this chapter.) The *past participle* used as a verbal is the same past participle you have been studying. (See Section 4.)

| *Present participle* | *Past participle* |
|---|---|
| seeing | seen |
| beginning | begun |
| loving | loved |
| prejudicing | prejudiced |
| handicapping | handicapped |
| shocking | shocked |

Both the present and past participles can be used as adjectives:

▸ It was a <u>disturbing</u> day at the bank.    (The present participle modifies the noun *day*.)

              obj

▸ <u>Seeing what happened</u>, the boy pulled out his cap pistol.    (The present-participle phrase modifies the subject *boy*. *What happened* is the object of the participle *seeing*.)

▸ <u>Shocked</u>, the robber handed over the money to the boy.    (The past participle modifies the subject *robber*.)

► Satisfied, the boy put his pistol back in his pocket.   (The past participle modifies the subject *boy*.)

**Explanation:
Gerunds**   A *gerund* is formed like a present participle, but it is always used as a noun:

► Seeing is not always believing.   (The first gerund is the subject; the second is a predicate nominative.)

► Living the good life was no longer possible for him.   (This gerund phrase is the subject of *was*. *Life* is the object of the gerund *living*.)

► To my way of thinking, he is a fool!   (This gerund is the object of the preposition *of*.)

**Practice**

*A ► Supply the correct verbal in each of the following sentences.

1. (*see*, present participle) *Seeing* Sandra ahead, he walked fast to catch up with her.

2. (*love*, past participle)  Though _____ by her parents, she still turned out to be a problem child.

3. (*begin*, past participle)  Having _____ the climb to Long's Peak, we were determined to finish.

4. (*shock*, gerund)  Dr. Khan enjoys _____ everyone in her biology class.

5. (*begin*, gerund)  In the _____ , God created the heavens and the earth.

6. (*do* and *be*, gerunds)  _____ is _____.

7. (*do* and *be*, infinitives)  _____ is _____.

8. (*give*, gerund)  We reached an agreement without either side's

_____ in.

9. (*wait,* gerund)   They like _____ on us.

10. (*wait,* infinitive)   They liked _____ on us.

11. (*begin,* present participle) _____ again, we picked up our back packs and moved on.

*B ► Underline the subject or subjects and then choose the correct verb.

1. (make, makes) Facing all those dishes *makes* A. J. wish he was not so liberated.

2. (are, is) Seeing the sun rise over the Cumberland Hills

   _____ something that has great meaning for me.

3. (are, is)   To work hard, to play hard, and to have a cooperative

   family _____ what I want most in life.

4. (are, is)   To be or not to be _____ the question.

5. (are, is)   Skating, fishing, and playing tennis _____ my favorite sports.

6. (prepare, prepares) Working hard in English and math

   _____ you for college.

C ► Use the following verbals in sentences of your own.

1. (*handicapped,* as an adjective) *Handicapped students should have a barrier-free campus.*

2. (*prejudiced,* as an adjective) _____

   _____

3. (*beaten,* as an adjective, not a verb) _____

   _____

4. (*trying,* as a noun) _____

   _____

5. (*gossiping,* as a noun) _____

_____

6. (*complaining,* as an adjective, not a verb) _____

_____

## 8.9 Review Exercises

*A ▸ For each of the following sentences, fill in the correct verbs in the following order:
a. Present tense (simple present or present progressive)
b. Simple past
c. Past participle with an appropriate helping verb or verbs.

1. (try) a. The president *is trying* to give the country moral leadership. b. Up until now the president *tried* to give the country moral leadership. c. During his term of office, the president *has tried* to give the country moral leadership.

2. (rob) a. Robin Hood _____ the rich to give to the poor.

   b. Robin Hood _____ the rich. c. Robin Hood _____ the rich on many occasions.

3. (come) a. A new book on jogging _____ out every year. b. A good book on jogging _____ out last year.

   c. A new book on jogging _____ out almost every year.

4. (see) a. Tom _____ only one way out of his dilemma.

   b. Tom _____ only one way out of his dilemma. c. Before you came up with your suggestion, Tom _____ only one way out of his dilemma.

5. (plan) a. How are we progressing on that trip we _____?

   b. How have we progressed on that trip we _____?

   c. The trip will be a good one because it _____ carefully.

6. (break) a. When the bough _____, the cradle will fall.

   b. When the bough _____, the cradle fell. c. When the

   bough _____, the cradle fell.

*B ► Correct the verb errors (V) and the shifts in tense (ST) in the following essay.

I am the mother of two fine children. I have been bless with a child   1
of each sex. My daughter, Corinne, is seventeen years old and thinks she   2
is a woman of the world. William, my son, is fourteen. He has suddenly   3
discover a light brown moustache, deep voice, and girls! Although I love   4
my children dearly, I sometimes wonder how they can be brother and sis-   5
ter; they are so different. (2 verb errors, V)   6

Attitudes about the value of money in our home are most interest-   7
ing. Will is very concern about cash at all times. He keeps his hard-earned   8
money and birthday money in the top drawer of his dresser under lock and   9
key. He is know in our home as one who is "tight with a buck." When you   10
ask him for a loan of perhaps one dollar, he may or may not give it to you.   11
We are wondering when he will start charging us interest on each dollar   12
we borrow. Corinne, on the other hand, still has uncashed checks earned   13
from her job at Walgreen's dating back to July, 1981. She does not realize   14
that she hasn't cash them. When one is walking through Corinne's bed-   15
room, one sees nickles, dimes, and quarters that are spreaded all over the   16
dresser, desk, and night table. One thing about Corinne, though: she   17
cheerfully lends you money and is anything but a miser. (4 verb errors, V)   18

Entering Will's bedroom is a pleasure. Everything has a place. 19
Books are pile neatly on the desk; the bed is rarely unmade. The closet is 20
very well organize with clothes always hung up, and shoes always lined up 21
in a neat row. Will is a systematic and methodical young man, and his 22
room speaks for his neatness. Corinne's room, on the other hand, is mass 23
confusion. Shoes are everywhere. Clothes are hung over chairs and are 24
laying on the bed, which, by the way, is hardly ever made. It wouldn't 25
surprise me to find an old apple core under the bed. That's Corinne for 26
you; she is disorganized but very relaxed. (3 verb errors, V) 27

Their personalities are like the sun and the moon. Will is extremely 28
quiet and basically a loner, with only one or two close friends. Corinne was 29
just the opposite. She always has had an effervescent personality. She felt 30
immediately at ease with strangers and has had many friends. Despite their 31
differences, they have one important thing in common. They really care for 32
each other. It is my hope that they will continue to care for one another for 33
the rest of their lives. (2 shifts in tense, ST) 34

# Chapter 9
## Spelling

## 9.0 Introduction

Some people are born natural spellers; some are not. The writer of this text is not a natural speller. On one occasion I sent off a manuscript to a publisher with a reference to the shepherd in the parable who left the flock of ninety-nine sheep to find the one that had strayed away. In my most solemn voice, I said that in order to seek out the one that was lost, the shepherd left the "nighty and the nine." I still cannot spell *accommodate*—or is it *acommodate* or *acomodate*? Nor am I ever quite sure when to insert a hyphen and when not to. Frankly I don't like hyphens. For example, I always resist using a hyphen with *first class* when it is used as an adjective, as in *first-class restaurant.* And I have just about given up on when to write *awhile* and when to write *a while.* But there is a way out for the likes of me—the dictionary!

Ask your instructor to recommend a dictionary that you can easily carry around with you. Besides making constant use of the dictionary, you can do several other things to improve your spelling:

▶ Concentrate on each syllable of each word as you write. You can usually avoid the following types of mistakes by carefully pronouncing the words as you write them.

*necessry* for *necessary* (ne • ces • sa • ry)

*practicly*   for   *practically* (prac • ti • cal • ly)

*goverment*   or   *govment*   for   *government* (gov • ern • ment)

the *craddle* that rocked   for   the *cradle* that rocked (cra • dle)

▶ Keep a list of *every* word you ever misspell in any course in college. Anyone can misspell a word like *kindergarten* or *sacrilegious* or *shillelagh,* but you do not have to keep misspelling the same words. Before writing each of your essays, review your list.

▶ Learn the rules for noun and verb endings, which are given in Sections 1 and 2 of this chapter.

▶ Learn the rule for contractions and how to distinguish them from the personal pronouns that sound like contractions, how to distinguish *it's* from *its,* for example. (See Section 3 of this chapter.)

▶ Learn to distinguish homonyms or sound-alike words, such as *there* and *their.* (See Section 4.)

▶ Learn the rules on the use of the hyphen that are given in Section 5.

▶ Study the list in Section 6 of the most commonly misspelled words in college writing. Even if you forget how to spell some of these words later, you will probably remember to look them up in your dictionary when you come to them.

▶ Proofread each of your papers carefully.

If you are still having problems, ask your instructor to suggest a spelling workbook. One that has helped many students is *Programmed Spelling Demons* by George Feinstein. The suggested editing symbol for misspelled words, including contractions, is S. The symbols for related errors are V for verb-ending errors, Pl for errors in making plurals, and Hy for errors in the use of the hyphen.

## 9.1 Plurals of Nouns

**Explanation (with Practice)**    Most plurals are made simply by adding an *-s* to the singular form of the noun: *experience* becomes *experiences, American* becomes

*Americans.* Plurals formed in other ways can be tricky. Learn the rules below. As you read them, fill in the blanks.

a. Add *-es* to nouns that end in *x, ss, z, sh,* and *ch:*

box becomes ___*boxes*___ church becomes ___*churches*___

sex becomes _____ business becomes _____

starch becomes _____ rash becomes _____

b. Add *-es* to a few nouns that end in *-o,* the following, for example:

tomato becomes ___*tomatoes*___ veto becomes _____

hero becomes _____ Negro becomes _____

potato becomes _____
Add *-s* to most other nouns ending in *-o,* such as:

ego becomes ___*egos*___ radio becomes _____

zero becomes _____ two becomes _____

zoo becomes _____ tatoo becomes _____

c. Here are the rules for nouns that end in *-y:*

▶ If the *-y* is preceded by a consonant (a letter other than *a, e, i, o,* or *u*), change the *-y* to *-i* and add *-es.*

cry becomes ___*cries*___ library becomes _____

navy becomes _____ berry becomes _____

▶ If the *y* is preceded by a vowel (*a, e, i, o,* or *u*), add only the *-s.*

play becomes _____ journey becomes _____

▶ If the *-y* is the last letter of a name or number, add only an *-s;* otherwise the name or the number would be changed:

Kennedy becomes _____ twenty becomes _____
d. Change *-f* or *-fe* endings of most nouns to *-ves.*

*self* becomes *selves*    *knife* becomes *knives*

*life* becomes _____    *leaf* becomes _____

*elf* becomes _____    *loaf* becomes _____

But note, *roof* becomes *roofs* and *belief* becomes *beliefs.*

e. You may use the same form for both singular and plural for some nouns, especially animals that are hunted and different kinds of fish:

*deer* remains *deer*    *elk* remains _____

*trout* remains _____    *bass* remains _____

f. Change the noun itself to form yet other plurals:

*man* becomes *men*    *ox* becomes _____

*woman* becomes _____    *mouse* becomes _____

g. You may use *-'s* to form the plural of letters, numerals, and symbols. (Many publishers omit the apostrophe.)

▶ the *t* becomes the *t's*    *1980* becomes *the 1980's*    *&* becomes *&'s*

Do *not* use *-'s* to form any other plurals.

If you are in doubt about a plural, look up the noun, designated *n*, in a dictionary, and you will see the plural, designated *pl.* If you look up *alumnus*, for example, you will see something like this:

▶ a • lum • nus (ə-lŭm′nəs) *n., pl.* **-ni** (-nī).

From this you will know that the plural is *alumni.* (The suffix *-ni* replaces the *-nus* ending.) If two plural suffixes are given, always use the first alternative.

## Practice

A ▶ Give the plurals for the following.

1. watch _____ ax _____ first _____

2. candy _____ sash _____ two _____

3. potato _____ Kennedy _____ woman _____

4. leaf   _____ hero   _____ lady   _____

5. life   _____ Negro   _____ honey   _____

6. 1990   _____ deer   _____ I   _____

7. roof   _____ policeman _____ bath   _____

8. self   _____ stereo   _____ Monday _____

9. hippopotamus _____ (Use your dictionary.)

10. analysis _____ (Use your dictionary.)

B ▶ Edit the following. Six plural endings have been omitted; two have been misspelled.

The area where I live is called Graveyard because of the two   1

graveyard located nearby. I've lived in Graveyard for twelve year now and   2

know all the thing that go on. I get tired of seeing the same people stand-   3

ing on the corner talking to each other all day long. They try to get con-   4

versation started with the ladys who pass by, and they try to bum money   5

from you so that they can buy beer, soft drink and various kind of candys   6

from the sweetshop down the street.   7

## 9.2 Verb Endings

**Explanation**   The rules governing verb endings are given at various points in Chapters 7 and 8. Here is a summary of them.

a. Add -*s* to most verbs to form third-person singular constructions in the present tense:

▶ He, she, it loves    He, she, it walks

b. Add -*es* to verbs to form third-person singular constructions in the present tense if the verbs end in -*o, -x, -ss, -z, -sh,* or -*ch.* (See Chapter 7.2)

▶ He, she, it does    He, she, it reaches

c. If the verb ends in -*y* and is preceded by a consonant, change the -*y* to -*i* before adding -*es* or -*ed*. (See Chapters 7.2 and 8.3.)

▸ <u>spy</u> becomes <u>spies</u> or <u>spied</u>      <u>bury</u> becomes <u>buries</u> or <u>buried</u>

*but*

<u>journey</u> becomes <u>journeys</u> or <u>journeyed</u> (The *y* is preceded by a vowel, *e*.)

d. When adding -*ed* or -*ing,* double the final consonant of one-syllable verbs (or verbs accented on the last syllable) if the final consonant is preceded by a single vowel. (See Chapters 7.2 and 8.3.)

▸ <u>drum</u> becomes <u>drummed</u> or <u>drumming</u>

▸ <u>occur</u> becomes <u>occurred</u> or <u>occurring</u>

*but*

<u>happen</u> becomes <u>happened</u> or <u>happening</u> (The accent is on the first syllable.)

e. When adding -*ing* to verbs that end in -*y,* do not change the -*y.*

▸ <u>fly</u> becomes <u>flying</u>      <u>satisfy</u> becomes <u>satisfying</u>

**Practice**   Fill in the blanks.

| Base form | Third-person singular, present | Simple past and past participle | Progressive form |
|---|---|---|---|
| 1. try | *tries* | *tried* | *trying* |
| 2. open | | | |
| 3. jog | | | |
| 4. counsel | | | |
| 5. occupy | | | |
| 6. travel | | | |
| 7. study | | | |
| 8. refer | | | |

## 9.3 Contractions and Personal Pronouns

**Explanation: Using Contractions**

One meaning of *contract* is to reduce in size. Ice contracts when it melts into water. To make a *contraction* in grammar, you join two words together by reducing the number of letters in them:

it is becomes it's          I would becomes I'd

there is becomes there's    let us becomes let's

cannot becomes can't        Linda is going becomes Linda's going.

Notice that in each of the above an *apostrophe* (') replaces the missing letter or letters:

it is becomes it's          I would becomes I'd
    ↑                           ↑
    omit                        omit

cannot becomes can't    Linda is becomes Linda's
    ↑                           ↑
    omit                        omit

Here is the rule: except for will not, which becomes won't, all contractions are formed by using the apostrophe to *replace* the missing letter or letters. (See Chapter 11.3 for other uses of the apostrophe.)

Most of us tend to overuse contractions in our writing. Some are fine, but give your papers variety by writing out *it is, will not, I would,* and the like, most of the time. In writing a paper—such as a research paper—that requires formal writing, use contractions seldom, if at all. Avoid the following contractions in all of your writing:

► there's for there is   (It is too easy to make a verb agreement error, as in "There's two of us left." Write out "There are two of us left.")

► it's for it has   (Save *it's* for *it is.* Write out "It has been a long time.")

► Linda's going for Linda is going   (The contraction is unnecessarily informal.)

And do not try to make a contraction of *there are.* Also note that if you write out *can't,* you write it *cannot,* not *can not.*

**Practice**   Make contractions of the following.

1. who is _____     6. would not _____

2. they are _____     7. they would _____

3. cannot _____     8. John is going _____

4. let us _____     9. do not _____

5. will not _____     10. you are _____

**Explanation: Contractions and Possessive Pronouns**

Some contractions sound like the possessive forms of certain pronouns and are often confused with the pronouns in writing:

Contractions                              Possessive pronouns

It's (it is) raining                      The dog went to its house.

They're (they are) ready.                 Their knowledge is great.

There's (there is) the knife.             The knife is theirs.

Who's (who is) going to pass?             The ones whose papers are
                                          turned in on time are going to
                                          pass.

You're (you are) a pleasant               Your manner is pleasant.
   person.

To determine whether you need a contraction or the possessive pronoun, apply a simple rule: see if you can convert the word in question into two words. If you can, the contraction is correct.

You can say, "It is              You cannot say, "The dog went
   raining." (Thus, it's is          to it is house."
   correct.)

You can say, "They are           You cannot say, "They are
   ready." (Thus, they're is         knowledge is great."
   correct.)

You can say, "Who is going to
pass?"   (Thus, who's is
correct.)

You cannot say, "The ones who
is papers are turned in on time
are going to pass."

**Practice**    Choose either the contraction or the possessive pronoun for each of
the following.

1. I began to work there in 1977. (It's or Its) location was on Tanis
   Drive in Lexington.
2. If (you're or your) lucky, you might find peace.
3. When (you're or your) home, you cannot leave when you want
   to, as you can when (you are) staying in the dorm.
4. You can count on Mama Linda's cooking because you know (it's
   or its) going to be good.
5. Sometimes you can't even tell what (they're or their) talking
   about.
6. (There's or Theirs) is the least costly way.
7. (There's or Theirs) only one of us left.
8. (It's or Its) not a question of whom you are serving: you must
   always be polite. (You're or Your) reputation is at stake.
9. There are so many people that (it's or its) impossible to know
   them all.
10. (Who's or Whose) going to be the first to jump in?
11. Most of the classes are large, although (there's or theirs) at least
    one small one.
12. (Who's or Whose) child was that?
13. She's the one (who's or whose) watch was stolen.
14. Did the parrot say what (it's or its) name was?

## 9.4 Other Sound-Alike Words

**Explanation
(with Practice)**    Besides pronouns and contractions that sound alike, there are a number of other words that sound similar. Such words are called *hom-
onyms*. Read the definition of each of the following and use the word
in a *short* sentence of your own.

1. ▸ a—an article used before a consonant: a house, a boy

   ▸ an—an article used before a vowel (a, e, i, o, u) or a vowel
     sound: an apple, an egg, an hour

▸ and—a conjunction used to join two or more things

(a) _____

(an) _____

(and) _____

2. ▸ affect—a <u>verb</u> that means <u>influence</u>: The storm affected the crop.

   ▸ effect—a <u>noun</u> that means <u>result</u>: an effect of the storm

   *Hint:* Say to yourself, "The <u>a</u>ffair <u>a</u>ffected her." The noun *effect* is usually preceded by *an, the,* or *in.*

   (affect) _____

   (effect) _____

3. ▸ alone—by oneself

   ▸ along—as in: along the way, along with me

   *Hint:* If you are al<u>one</u>, there is just <u>one</u> of you.

   (alone) _____

   (along) _____

4. ▸ choose—decide for: to choose the way, I do choose

   ▸ chose—decide<u>d</u> for: I chose the way

   *Hint:* Say to yourself, "Last night at the circus the clown ch<u>ose</u> a funny n<u>ose</u>."

   (choose) _____

   (chose) _____

5. ▸ clothes—garments

▸ cloths—materials to make clothes

*Hint:* Say to yourself, "those clothes." Notice the <u>e</u> in both.

(clothes) _____

(cloths) _____

6. ▸ does—third-person singular of <u>do</u>

  ▸ dose—an amount of medicine

*Hint:* Instead of adding an *-s* to the verb <u>do</u>, you add *-es* because <u>do</u> ends in *-o*.

(does) _____

(dose) _____

7. ▸ doing—progressive form of <u>do</u>

  ▸ during—at the time of

*Hint:* You make the progressive form by adding <u>-ing</u> to the verb <u>do</u>.

(doing) _____

(during) _____

8. ▸ ever—always (rhymes with its opposite, <u>never</u>)

  ▸ every—as in: each and every one of you

(ever) _____

(every) _____

9. ▸ accept—a verb that means <u>receive</u>

  ▸ except—a preposition that means <u>not including</u>

<u>H</u>int: If everyone is going <u>except</u> you, you are <u>Xed</u> out, poor you.

(accept) _____

(except) _____

10. ▸ feel—a verb that means <u>perceive through touch</u>

   ▸ fell—the past tense of <u>fall</u>

   *Hint*: Say to yourself, "It is a slimy thing to <u>feel</u> an <u>eel</u>."

(feel) _____

(fell) _____

11. ▸ hear—you <u>hear</u> with an <u>ear</u>

   ▸ here—a place nearby <u>where</u> you put something

   *Hint*: <u>Here</u>, <u>there</u>, and <u>where</u> are all place words.

(hear) _____

(here) _____

12. ▸ know—understand

   ▸ no—the common negative (think of <u>not</u>)

   *Hint*: You would not likely spell <u>knowledge</u>, <u>nolege</u>.

(know) _____

(no) _____

13. ▸ loose—not tight (rhymes with <u>goose</u>): The knot is loose.

   ▸ lose—unable to find (rhymes with <u>booze</u>): I might lose my hat.

   *Hint*: To make <u>loose</u>, you loosen up or stretch out <u>lo se</u> to make room for an <u>o</u>. To make <u>lose</u>, you <u>lose</u> an <u>o</u> from <u>loose</u>.

(loose) _____

(lose) _____

14. ▸ may be—a verb: You may be president someday.

    ▸ maybe—an adverb: Maybe you will and maybe you won't be president.

(may be) _____

(maybe) _____

15. ▸ new—the opposite of another three-letter word, <u>old</u>

    ▸ knew—the past tense of <u>know</u>

(new) _____

(knew) _____

16. ▸ of—belonging to

    ▸ off—from, away: It fell off the shelf.

*Hint*: Memorize this: "You leave an <u>f</u> off of <u>off</u> to form <u>of</u>."

(of) _____

(off) _____

17. ▸ or—as in: either/or (rhymes with its opposite, <u>nor</u>)

    ▸ our—the possessive pronoun: our lives.

    ▸ are—the present-tense <u>be</u> verb

(or) _____

(our) _____

(are) _____

18. ▸ pass—present-tense verb: I hope you pass the test.

▶ passed—past-tense verb: I passed it.

▶ past—a noun or adjective meaning at an earlier time: in the past, the past week

*Hint*: Say to yourself, "In the past, I passed, but now I can't seem to pass."

(pass) _____

(passed) _____

(past) _____

19. ▶ quiet—free of noise

  ▶ quit—stop doing something

  ▶ quite—completely, as in: quite alone

*Hints*: It is not quite right to leave the e off of quite; in fact, it is quite wrong. If you are very quiet, you can hear the two syllables in quiet: qui • et.

(quiet) _____

(quit) _____

(quite) _____

20. ▶ right—correct

  ▶ write—what you do with a pen or pencil

*Hint*: Think of the past tense of write, which is wrote. You would not be likely to leave the w off wrote.

(right) _____

(write) _____

21. ▶ sense—as in: good sense

▶ since—(1) because, (2) before: since daybreak

*Hint*: If you can spell exp<u>ense</u>, you've got the sense to spell <u>sense</u>.

(sense) _____

(since) _____

22. ▶ then—afterward (<u>then</u>, like <u>when</u>, is a word that relates to time.)

   ▶ than—a way to compare two things (one thing is bigger than another)

*Hint*: When you use <u>than</u> to compare two things, think of one thing <u>and</u> another. Notice the <u>an</u> in both <u>than</u> and <u>and</u>.

(then) _____

(than) _____

23. ▶ there—(1) an expletive, (2) a place, not so close by, where you put something

   ▶ their—shows ownership: their house

*Hints*: <u>There</u> is used very much like <u>here</u>: Here it is. There it is. Put it here. Put it there. <u>Their</u> is used *only* as a possessive.

(there) _____

(their) _____

24. ▶ think—what you do with your mind

   ▶ thing—a noun you use when you can't <u>think</u> of any<u>thing</u> else

(think) _____

(thing) _____

25. ▸ though—in spite of

   ▸ thought—the past tense of <u>think</u>

   *Hint*: Though the two words may look alike, <u>though</u> does not have a <u>t</u> sound at the end because it doesn't have a <u>t</u>.

   (though) _____

   (thought) _____

26. ▸ threw—past tense of <u>throw</u>

   ▸ through—(1) finished, (2) into and out of: through the forest

   *Hint*: Say to yourself, "My engine threw a screw. I'm through with it."

   (threw) _____

   (through) _____

27. ▸ too—(1) also: I am going too. (2) the extent to which: too sick, too small

   ▸ to—many uses, such as: to love, to the store, in order to

   ▸ two—the written form of the numeral 2

   *Hint*: Say to yourself, "It is <u>too good</u> to be true that I know how to spell these words." Notice the <u>oo</u> in both <u>too</u> and <u>good</u>.

   (too, meaning also) _____

   (too, meaning the extent to which) _____

   (to) _____

   (two) _____

28. ▸ went—past tense of <u>go</u>: I went home.

▸ when—at the time of (a time word, like <u>then</u>)

(went) _____

(when) _____

29. ▸ were—plural of <u>was</u>

   ▸ where—at the place of (a place word, like <u>there</u> and <u>here</u>)

(were) _____

(where) _____

30. ▸ whole—entire: the whole class

   ▸ hold—present tense of <u>held</u>

   ▸ hole—a round opening: a hole in the ground

(whole) _____

(hold) _____

(hole) _____

31. ▸ weather—as in: How is the weather outside?

   ▸ whether—as in: whether you should or whether you shouldn't

*Hint*: You must put an <u>h</u> in <u>whether</u>, <u>whether</u> you hear it or not.

(weather) _____

(whether) _____

32. ▸ which—as in: Which of us is going?

   ▸ witch—a hag on a broomstick

(which) _____

(witch) _____

33. ▸ read—understand printed words (rhymes with <u>bead</u> when used in the present tense, rhymes with <u>bed</u> when used in the past tense)

    ▸ red—a color

(read, present tense) _____

(read, past tense) _____

(red) _____

## 9.5  Using the Hyphen

**Explanation**  One of the trickiest elements in spelling is the use of the hyphen (-). The following rules will help, but if you are in any doubt as to whether a hyphen is necessary, look up the word in your dictionary. Use the hyphen

a. To carry a word over from one line to the next:

                      . . . an unnec-
cessary remark.

You should avoid carrying words over from one line to the next, but if you must, divide them between syllables with a hyphen. Do not divide short words like *also* or *into*. Your dictionary will give you the breakdown of a word by syllables.

b. To write compound numbers: <u>twenty-one</u> to <u>ninety-nine</u>.

c. To write fractions: <u>three-fifths</u>, <u>two-thirds</u>, <u>one and one-half</u>, and so forth.

d. After a prefix that is joined to a proper name: <u>non-European</u>, <u>un-American</u>.

e. After certain other prefixes, such as <u>ex-wife</u>, <u>semi-invalid</u>.

f. To write certain compound nouns, such as <u>secretary-treasurer</u>, <u>a two-year-old</u>, <u>mother-in-law</u>, <u>president-elect</u>. Consult a dictionary.

*If the compound word is not listed, write it as two separate words.*

g. To join two words used as a single adjective: <u>first-place team</u>, horn-rimmed glasses, warm-hearted coach. Some compound adjectives, such as high school (as in high school team), are so familiar that many professional writers omit the hyphen.

## 9.6 Words Often Misspelled in College Composition

**Explanation**  In addition to the words you have already studied, the following are among those most often misspelled by beginning college students. If you are not sure of what any of the words mean, look them up in the dictionary. Try to learn how to spell them all.

### Single and Compound Words

| | | | |
|---|---|---|---|
| almost | everything | something | a lot |
| already | forever | themselves | all right |
| altogether | itself | throughout | each one |
| always | meantime | weekday | each other |
| anyway | meanwhile | weekend | even though |
| anywhere | nevertheless | whenever | every time |
| apart | nowadays | whereas | high school |
| awhile | nowhere | wherever | in order that |
| cannot | someday | without | no one |
| everyone | somehow | whoever | one day |
| | | | post card |

### Numbers, Days, Months

| | | | | |
|---|---|---|---|---|
| one-half | eighth | nineteenth | ninety-one | Saturday |
| fourth | ninth | twentieth | ninetieth | |
| sixth | twelfth | forty | | January |
| eight | thirteenth | ninety | Wednesday | February |

**Others.**  (See the rule below on when to use ie and ei.)

| A | | | B |
|---|---|---|---|
| absence | advice (noun) | apologize | bath (n) |
| academic | advise (verb) | apology | bathe (v) |
| accidentally | agreeable | argument | beautiful |
| accommodate | amateur | ascend | beginning |
| accumulate | analysis | athlete | belief (n) |
| achieve | analyze | attendance | believe (v) |
| across | apparent | average | bookkeeping |
| | appearance | awful | |

boundaries
breath (n)
breathe (v)
Britain
buried
bury
business
businesslike

**C**

calendar
category
ceiling
certain
college
coming
commission
commitment
committed
committee
competent
conceivable
conscience
conscious
council (n)
counsel (v)
counselor
criticize

**D**

deceased
decision
develop
dictionary
difference
dilemma
discussed
disgust
dormitory

**E**

earliest
either
embarrass

emphasis
emphasize (v)
employee
envelope
equip
equipment
equipped
especially
existence
expense
explanation
extraordinary

**F**

familiar
fascinate
fiery
foreign
freight
fulfill

**G**

gauge
generalize
government
grammar
grateful
guess (n, vb)
guest (n)

**H**

handicapped
handkerchief
handsome
height
hoping

**I**

identical
illegible
immediately
incident
incompetent
inconceivable

independence
independent
intelligence
interest

**J, K**

jewelry
judgment
know
knowledge

**L**

later
latter
leisure
library
license
literature
loneliness
lounge

**M**

machinery
maintain
maintenance
marriage
mathematics
miniature
mischief
mischievous
misspell
moderate

**N**

necessary
Negroes
neither
niece
northeast
noticeable
nowadays

**O**

occasion
occur

occurred
occurrence
o'clock
okay (OK)
omitted
organization

**P**

paid
parallel
participant
pastime
peace (opposite
of war)
percent
perceive
permanent
permitted
personal
personnel
physical
piece (part of)
possession
potato
practical
precede
prejudiced
pressure
principal
(one in charge)
principle
(a rule)
privilege
proceed

**R**

realize
receive
recognize
recommend
referred
relieve
rhyme

| | | | |
|---|---|---|---|
| rhythm | supposed to | vice versa | _____ |
| ridiculous | surprise | vein | |

**S**

| | | | |
|---|---|---|---|
| salary | | | _____ |
| secretary | **T** | **W** | |
| seize | taxable | wage | _____ |
| sense | technical | weird | |
| sensible | thorough | while | |
| separate | till (or until) | women | _____ |
| sergeant | traveled | writing | |
| similar | tragedy | written | _____ |
| sophomore | | | |
| succeed | **U,V** | **Y,Z** | _____ |
| successful | useful | yearbook | |
| suppose | used to | yield | _____ |
| | valuable | zealous | |

**The ie, ei Rule.**  Use i before e, except after c, or when sounded as a, as in *neighbor* and *weigh* (nay · bor and way).

▶ *Use* i *before* e:

| | | | |
|---|---|---|---|
| achieve | conscientious | niece | thief |
| believe | earliest | piece | twentieth |
| conscience | mischief | relieve | yield |

▶ *Except after* c:

| | | | |
|---|---|---|---|
| ceiling | conceivable | perceive | receive |

▶ *Or when sounded as* a:

| | | | |
|---|---|---|---|
| freight | neighbor | vein | weigh |

▶ *Memorize these exceptions:*

| | | | |
|---|---|---|---|
| either | height | neither | their |
| foreign | leisure | seize | weird |

**Practice**    In each of the following, there is one misspelled word. Correct it.

1. almost, always, alright, altogether, already
2. apart, awhile, alot, nowhere, no one
3. everything, someday, throughout, weekend, highschool
4. anywhere, mean time, whereas, without, meanwhile
5. when ever, whoever, cannot, post card, somehow
6. one-half, fourth, twelth, ninetieth, ninety
7. January, Febuary, Wednesday, thirteenth, nineteenth
8. appearance, accidentally, accommodate, agreeable, absense
9. achieve, arguement, apology, apologize, analysis
10. attendence, agreeable, accumulate, across, athlete
11. businesslike, buried, Britain, bookeeping, breathe
12. begining, boundaries, beautiful, business, believe
13. committed, commitment, commitee, conceivable, counselor
14. ceiling, commission, counsel, coming, competant
15. develope, dilemma, disgust, dictionary, dormitory
16. existence, equipped, especially, emphasize, earlyest
17. envelope, emphasis, embarrass, explanation, existance
18. fiery, familiar, freight, fulfill, foriegn
19. guest, goverment, grateful, gauge, generalize
20. hoping, height, handsome, handkercheif
21. incompetent, independant, intelligence, illegible, inconceivable
22. judgment, jewelry, know, knowlege
23. leisure, loneliness, license, libary, literature
24. miniature, misspell, mathmatics, mischievous, maintenance
25. northeast, necessary, neither, neice, noticeable
26. o'clock, occurrence, okay, occured, occasion
27. percent, personnel, preceive, parallel, principle
28. potato, physical, possession, pastime, privilige
29. participent, permitted, precede, proceed, piece

30. rhyme, rhythm, relieve, rediculous, realize
31. seize, separate, sergeant, sensable, sophomore
32. suppose, supprise, similar, succeed, successful
33. traveled, tragedy, til, taxable, technical
34. use to, vice versa, useful, vein, valuable
35. yield, weird, writing, writen, wage

# Chapter 10

## Avoiding Pronoun Errors

Because of the various problems they cause, pronouns deserve a special chapter. Before reading on, however, you should review the introduction to pronouns in Chapter 5.5.

## 10.1 Avoiding Errors in Case

**Explanation**   Most pronouns errors are either errors in case or errors in agreement with *antecedents* (nouns or pronouns for which pronouns stand). The following are errors in case:

▸ Marcus and <u>me</u> were always getting into trouble.   (*Marcus and me* is the subject, but the subjective case of *me* is *I.*)

**Correct** ▸ Marcus and <u>I</u> were always getting into trouble.

▸ Are those <u>them</u>?   (The subjective case of the personal pronoun is needed because the sentence calls for a predicate nominative.)

**Correct** ▸ To <u>whom</u> should I address this letter?

▸ Carlos is older than <u>her</u>.   (The sense of the sentence is "Carlos is older than <u>she is.</u>" Thus, the subjective case is needed for the pronoun.)

Correct ▸ Carlos is older than <u>she.</u>

In the editing checklist, the abbreviation for errors in pronoun case is PC.

Correct ▸ Are those <u>they?</u>

▸ The apartment is just right for you and <u>I.</u>   (The preposition *for* takes the objective case, which is *me,* not *I.*)

Correct ▸ The apartment is just right for <u>you and me.</u>

▸ To <u>who</u> should I address this letter?   (The preposition *to* takes the objective case, which is *whom,* not *who.*)

## Practice

A ▸ All but one of the following sentences contain an error in pronoun case. Make the necessary corrections.

1. Mark was very hurt and began spreading many lies about Troy and I.
   *me*

2. Because he was older than me, he graduated before me and went away to college.

3. When me and Michael broke up, Mother knew just how hurt I was.

4. Now I realize that the little girl and I are closer than ever.

5. Just between you and I, that man is crazy.

6. It was her who finally spoke up.

B ▸ In the following paper there are twelve errors in pronoun case. Correct them, and be able to say why you made the corrections.

Students who work at resorts in the summer often have unusual    1

experiences. Last summer, my friend Regina and me traveled a thousand    2

miles to work at Nantucket, which is a resort island twenty miles from the    3

Massachusetts shore. We arrived with very little money in our pockets, and    4

it was still quite cold. We didn't bring enough clothes and were nearly   5
freezing. Someone told Regina and I to go to the Thrift Shop, where we   6
could buy coats cheap. Regina bought a fine old overcoat for $3.00, but   7
I didn't have as much luck as her. I had to huddle up in my blanket to   8
keep warm.   (3 pronoun case errors, PC)   9

Besides being cold, we were also hungry. Our friend Randy from   10
Penn State was working as a dishwasher and brought Regina and I scraps   11
of food every night. Regina and me didn't have any regular place to stay   12
so we stayed with different friends in rooms they had rented, on the floor.   13
We looked and looked for jobs, but no one wanted to give either she or   14
me employment.   (3 pronoun case errors, PC)   15

At this point I was getting desperate. I didn't know to who I could   16
turn for help. I was determined not to ask my parents for money. Just be-   17
tween you and I, they were furious at me for leaving home to go to Nan-   18
tucket. "Whom do you girls think you are?" my dad said, "traveling a thou-   19
sand miles to work at some funny resort island." But us "girls" (I'm nineteen   20
and Regina is twenty) went anyway.   (4 pronoun case errors, PC)   21

Just before starvation set in, I got a job working as a janitor at a   22
hotel, and Regina got a job working as a "bag boy" in a supermarket.   23
When I wrote my father and told him about our jobs, he thought that Re-   24
gina and me were completely crazy. "You mean you traveled a thousand   25
miles to mop floors," he wrote back. My summer in Nantucket was an un-   26
usual experience, and it was also the most fun Regina and me ever had.   27
Whomever said that parents are always right?   (3 pronoun case errors, PC)   28

## 10.2 Avoiding Pronouns with Unclear Antecedents

**Explanation**    The noun or pronoun for which a pronoun stands is called the *ante-cedent* (it goes *before* the pronoun). When you use a pronoun, make sure your reader knows what the antecedent is. Look at the following two sentences, for example:

► April is the worst month of the year. It is the time when they make you pay your taxes.

The antecedent of *It* is clearly April, so there is no problem. But what is the antecedent of *they?* The writer assumes you will think of the federal government, but such an assumption is not enough. Follow this important rule: *If there is no clear antecedent for a pronoun, replace the pronoun with an appropriate noun.* The two sentences could read:

► April is the worst month of the year. It is the time when the federal government makes you pay your taxes.

In the editing checklist, the abbreviation for pronouns with unclear antecedents is PA. (This is also the abbreviation for pronouns that are not in agreement with their antecedents.)

**Practice**    In the following sentences the antecedents of the underlined pronouns are unclear. Replace them with appropriate nouns or pronouns. Also, change verbs as necessary.

1. Sex education should be taught in high school because parents are either too scared or too busy to teach the facts of life to *their children* them.

2. In the final game I was playing defense and went to make a tackle. When I hit him, he fell on his side and on my finger.

3. When I was in the service, they wouldn't let me grow my hair longer than an inch.

4. One thing I don't like about that restaurant is that they are always trying to hurry you up.

5. No one likes living on the brink of nuclear war. There have been many attempts to change this, but so far none has succeeded.

6. I took my automobile to the dealer to be fixed, but they wanted to charge far too much to fix it.

7. My son would like to major in business, but they are a bit too demanding for him.

8. Our unemployment rate continues to rise. I don't know what the president should do about <u>this</u>, but he should do something.

9. My typewriter is broken, but <u>he</u> said that he would fix it for almost nothing.

10. I hope to be out of my apartment soon; <u>they</u> are charging too much rent and don't want to make any repairs.

11. When I went to the hospital, <u>they</u> took very good care of me the whole time I was there.

# 10.3 Avoiding Errors in Agreement

**Explanation**  Personal pronouns (*I, you, she, they,* and the like) must agree with the nouns they replace in *number, person,* and *gender.* Look at the sentence below, for example:

▸ Music is an art form, and it is the principal art form for many young people.

Instead of repeating the word *music,* you naturally substitute the pronoun *it;* otherwise, the sentence would be awkward:

▸ Music is an art form, and music is the principal art form for many young people.

Thus, it is appropriate to use a pronoun to replace the second *music,* but the pronoun must agree with its antecedent (the first *music*) in number, person, and gender.

The following illustration of personal pronouns in the subjective case shows why *it* appropriately replaces music.

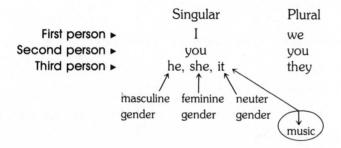

|  | Singular | Plural |
|---|---|---|
| First person ▸ | I | we |
| Second person ▸ | you | you |
| Third person ▸ | he, she, it | they |

masculine   feminine   neuter
gender    gender    gender

music

*It* agrees with *music* in number, person, and gender. *Agreement in number* means that singular pronouns must be used to replace singular antecedents and plural pronouns must be used to replace plural antecedents. It is therefore appropriate to use *it* instead of *they* because *music* is singular.

*Agreement in person* means that first-person pronouns must be used to replace first-person antecedents, second-person pronouns to replace second-person antecedents, and third-person pronouns to replace third-person antecedents. It is therefore appropriate to use the third person *it* to replace *music* because *music,* as a noun, is in the third person.

*Agreement in gender* means that masculine pronouns must be used to replace masculine antecedents, feminine pronouns to replace feminine antecedents, and neuter pronouns to replace neuter antecedents. Since *music* has no sex and is therefore neuter in gender, it is appropriate to use the third-person pronoun *it,* and not *he* or *she,* to replace *music.*

Pronouns used as objects or used to show possession should be written in the objective or possessive case, for example:

▸ <u>Francine</u> was so nice to me that I will never forget <u>her</u>.

*Her* is in agreement with Francine and is the object of the verb *forget.* The abbreviation for errors in pronoun agreement is PA.

## Practice

A ▸ Using the illustration in the explanation above, what personal pronoun (subjective case) would you substitute for each of the following?

1. Charles and I ____*we*____        6. You and he _____

2. The cat (sex unknown) ____        7. The police _____

3. The government _____        8. Geraldine _____

4. The police force _____        9. Mary and Martha _____

5. The Ricos and I _____        10. The people _____

What pronoun in the objective case would you substitute for each of the above? (If in doubt, *see* Chapter 5.5.)

1. ___*us*___   2. _____   3. _____   4. _____   5. _____

6. _____  7. _____  8. _____  9. _____  10. _____

B ► Choose the correct pronoun in each of the following and draw an arrow to the noun or pronoun (the antecedent) that it replaces. In two sentences, you will have to choose the correct verb as well.

1. Movies rated X are for adults only because (it, <u>they</u>) often (contains, contain) pornography and violence.

2. The world would have more crime than (it, they) could handle if everyone saw X-rated movies.

3. Ticket clerks at theaters that show X-rated films often take advantage of my son by selling (him, them) a ticket without asking for proper identification.

4. Hawaii is also known for the many beautiful islands (it, they) (has, have).

5. When I go downtown and see an old lady with a cup begging, I feel sorry for (her, them).

6. *King Tut* is an exciting book; it keeps the reader on (his or her, their) toes all the time.

7. Most mystery stories don't end the way you expect (it, them) to.

8. The government is the worst offender; (it, they) (waste, wastes) more money than anyone else.

C ► In the sentences that follow, correct the pronouns that are not in agreement with their antecedents. Change other words as necessary. (One sentence is correct.)

1. My glasses are very important to me because without it I could not function.

2. Because the United States uses more oil than they can produce, they have to import great quantities from other countries.

3. In conclusion, each state is unique in their own culture, industry, and natural environment.

4. Marge was determined to help her father and brother because she loved him.

5. I have had three jobs since I began working, and each has been rewarding in its own way.

6. My husband gets furious at neighbors who borrow things and never think to return it.

7. When people first met my grandfather, he found him charming.

8. As one got to know my grandfather, however, they found him less charming and more grumpy.

9. The United States is in an oil crisis; they import too much of their oil.

10. These working mothers have more responsibility than they can handle. She needs a lot more help from her husband.

11. When one joins a car pool to get to work, they help save oil.

## 10.4 Avoiding Gender Confusion

**Explanation**   When the antecedent of a pronoun is masculine, use a masculine pronoun (*he, him,* or *his*):

▸ Dr. Carl Regaldo asked me to come see him.

When the antecedent is feminine, use a feminine pronoun (*she, her,* or *hers*):

▸ Prime Minister Thatcher asked her people to trust her new program.

But what do you do when the antecedent is a person, and you don't know the gender, or if it is a word like *lawyer, teacher, parent, someone,* which could refer to both men and women?
   You could say:

▸ A lawyer has to work hard to build up his clients.

But many women, as well as men, are lawyers.
   Or you could say:

▶ A lawyer has to work hard to build up <u>her</u> clients.

But many men, as well as women, are lawyers.
  Or you could say:

▶ A lawyer has to work hard to build up <u>their</u> clients.

The pronoun *their* is clearly wrong because its antecedent is the singular word *lawyer.*

   Up until fairly recently most English texts instructed students to use the masculine form if the antecedent was not clearly feminine. Thus, they taught that you should say, "A lawyer has to work hard to build up <u>his</u> clients." Although this use of the masculine pronoun is still technically correct, more and more textbooks and teachers are turning away from it and suggesting the following alternatives:

▶ If possible, avoid the pronoun altogether. Simply say:

A lawyer has to work hard to build up clients.

▶ Or change the *antecedent* to a plural form.

<u>Lawyers</u> have to work hard to build up <u>their</u> clients.

▶ If the first two alternatives are not possible, use the double pronouns *he or she, him or her,* or *his or her.* If you were announcing to a group of men and women that a car parked outside had its lights on, you would say:

<u>Someone</u> has left <u>his or her</u> lights on.

If you do use *he or she* (or *him or her*) try not to use it more than once in a paragraph, and never use it more than once in a sentence. Never write:

He or she left his or her umbrella in the auditorium.

If you can't figure out another way to say what you mean, just forget about the umbrella.

   Awkward gender constructions are designated P in the editing checklist.

**Practice**   In the following sentences either omit the masculine or feminine pronouns or change the *antecedents* and their verbs to plural forms so that you can use plural pronouns and thus avoid the gender problem.

1. These days a good teacher has a hard time keeping his job.

   *These days a good teacher has a hard time keeping a job.*

2. A doctor must be available to his patients all of the time.

   *Doctors must be available to their patients all of the time.*

3. This type of nurse is always ready to help a patient with any

   problem he may have. _____

   _____

4. Then, there is the nurse who is concerned about her work only

   when someone is watching her. _____

   _____

5. This person is at the bottom; he lives in poverty.

   _____

6. Each of my parents helps me in his own way, and I am grateful

   for what each has done. _____

   _____

7. It is difficult for a parent to relate to his children these days.

   _____

8. A person with a problem should make sure that she sees some-

   body trained to help. _____

   _____

9. To begin with, a teacher should be completely fair to his students.

   _____

10. Secondly, a teacher should plan all her classes carefully.

   _____

**Explanation:
Indefinite
Pronouns
and Gender
Agreement**

A special problem arises in gender agreement when you use a personal pronoun to replace one of the indefinite pronouns, like *each, anyone, someone, everyone, no one,* and so on. (See Chapter 5.5 for a more complete list.) Most indefinite pronouns are singular, which means that you probably will need to use *he or she, him or her,* or *his or her* to agree with them, for example:

► Anyone may turn in his or her paper now.

► No one should go on such a strict diet without his or her doctor's permission.

► You can bet that someone will not do his or her share.

As pointed out above, however, try to limit the use of the double pronoun to a maximum of once a paragraph.

On occasion, when the indefinite pronoun *clearly* refers to a group of people, it is appropriate to use it with a plural pronoun, *they, them,* or *their.* For example:

► Everyone was clapping their hands.

► Everybody worked as hard as they could.

**Practice**

Make up sentences with the indefinite pronouns shown below and use the designated possessive pronouns to refer to them.

1. (Anyone, his or her) *Anyone who wants his or her paper should see me after class.*

2. (Someone, his or her) _____

_____

3. (Anybody, his or her) _____

_____

4. (No one, his or her) _____

_____

5. (Each one, his or her) _____

_____

6. (Everybody, their) _____

_____

## 10.5 Avoiding Pronoun Person Shifts

**Explanation**    A fairly common kind of pronoun-agreement problem is a shift in person within the same sentence, for example:

▶ I came to realize that because <u>you</u> are on earth for only a short time, <u>one</u> should do the things <u>one</u> wants.

The writer began with the second person <u>you</u> and shifted to the third person <u>one</u>. Here are two ways to correct the error:

▶ I came to realize that because <u>you</u> are on earth for only a short time, <u>you</u> should do the things <u>you</u> want.

▶ I came to realize that because <u>one</u> is on earth for only a short time, <u>one</u> should do the things <u>one</u> wants.

In the editing checklist, the pronoun-person-shift error is designated PPS. (Other errors in pronoun agreement are designated PA.)

**Practice**    Correct the pronoun-person-shift errors in the sentences below. One sentence is correct.

1. If you have ever lived as a ''Navy brat'' you know that such a life can be frustrating, especially if <s>one has</s> *you have* moved around as much as I have.

2. When one goes to see her, you should plan on spending the whole day because she always has to bake something for you to eat.

3. Mrs. Lewis passes everyone in her class whether you have good grades or not.

4. One's social class has more to do with your personality than you think.

5. They were always there when I needed them and would always talk to you in a nice tone of voice.

6. Someone has stolen your bicycle.

7. This statement is very strong because it tells me that you should forgive people who have sinned against me.

## 10.6 Other Pronoun Errors

Other pronoun errors are designated P in the editing checklist and include the following:

a. *Reversing the order of pronouns*:

Incorrect ▶    She took <u>me</u> and Robert for a ride.

Correct ▶    She took Robert and <u>me</u> for a ride.

Always put yourself last.
b. *Using the wrong personal pronoun with a gerund*:

Incorrect ▶    She was driven crazy by <u>him</u> nagging.

Correct ▶    She was driven crazy by <u>his</u> nagging.

Use the possessive form of the personal pronoun with a gerund.
c. *Using the incorrect relative pronoun*:

Incorrect ▶    The woman <u>which</u> lived next door was an alcoholic.

Correct ▶    The woman <u>who</u> lived next door was an alcoholic.

Use *who,* and *whose,* with people and *which* and *that* with things. (See Chapter 6.3.)

# Chapter 11
## Capitalization and Punctuation

## 11.0 Introduction

In this chapter the basic rules of capitalization and punctuation will be explained. *Punctuation* is the word that refers to all those marks and signs used in writing: the period, the apostrophe, the comma, the hyphen, and so on. The purpose of using punctuation is to clarify the meaning of writing. In the words of Kurt Vonnegut, the popular novelist, "If I broke all the rules of punctuation, had words mean whatever I wanted them to mean, and strung them together higgledy-piggledy, I would simply not be understood." This chapter is designed to help you be understood as you say what you want to say in writing. It is difficult to learn all of the rules for punctuation in a short time. But you can use punctuation correctly if you will make use of this chapter while you are editing. The more you check your punctuation, the quicker you will master the rules.

## 11.1 Capitalization

**Explanation (with Practice)** Since many of us tend to overuse capital letters, the first rule for capitalization should be: *don't use a capital letter unless you have a particular reason to do so.* Here are twelve reasons for using capital letters. (Errors in capitalization are designated Cap in the editing checklist.)

A. Capitalize the first person pronoun *I,* always.
B. Capitalize the beginning of *every* sentence.
C. Capitalize the first word of a quoted sentence or part of a sentence:

▶ She said, "You are not too young for Geritol."
    ↑

Hamlet said, "To be or not to be?"
    ↑

**Practice** ▶ Capitalize the necessary letters.

▶ then he said, "when you stop crying, i will talk to you."

D. Capitalize proper nouns, but not general nouns:

| *Capitalize* | *Do not capitalize* |
|---|---|
| Kennedy High School | my high school |
| Minneapolis, Minnesota | my home city and state |
| Labor Day | a holiday |
| Edward Manly Royall | my grandfather |
| the Constitution | a treaty |
| Mississippi River | the river |

The Institute of Growth (Capitalize *t* only if *The* is part of the name.)

**Practice** ▶ Capitalize the necessary letters.

▶ If I go into nursing, I hope to go to the columbia school of nursing.

E. Capitalize titles when they are used with proper names:

| *Capitalize* | *Do not capitalize* |
|---|---|
| Dr. Anita Zervigon | our family doctor |
| Senator Barry Goldwater | one of the senators |
| Mr. and Mrs. Johnson | the family next door |
| Peter B. Morial, Ph.D. | a professor of math |

**Practice** ▶ Capitalize the necessary letters.

▶ Our dentist, dr. walter bridges, is excellent.

F. Capitalize the days of the week and the months of the year, but not the seasons:

| Capitalize | Do not capitalize |
|------------|-------------------|
| Sunday | summer |
| Monday | autumn |
| February | weekend |
| January | month |

Practice ▶    Capitalize the necessary letters.

▶ I was strolling in audubon park one day last spring, in april.

G. Capitalize the names of specific courses and language courses:

| Capitalize | Do not capitalize |
|------------|-------------------|
| Mathematics 102 | math |
| English | physics |
| Spanish | political science |

H. Capitalize the names of relatives when used as proper nouns:

▶ My sister calls our mother Mom.

Practice ▶    Capitalize the necessary letters.

▶ Fernando's father, whom he calls pop, wants him to take spanish instead of either economics or history 101.

I. In all titles capitalize the first and last word and all other words except articles (a, an, the), short prepositions, and short conjunctions. (See also page 53.)

▶ Professor Kahn assigned *The Protestant Ethic and the Spirit of Capitalism.*

J. You may, but do not have to, capitalize the titles of heads of nations:

| You may capitalize | Do not capitalize |
|--------------------|-------------------|
| the President of the United States | the president of the college |
| | the chairman of the board |
| | the senators in the United States Congress |

Practice ▶    Capitalize the necessary letters.

▶ Long before he became president, john kennedy wrote a book entitled *why england slept.*

K. Capitalize *north, east, northwest,* and the like, when these words are used to designate recognized geographical areas, but not when used to show direction. Deep South is also capitalized.

▶ You must travel east from Hawaii to reach the West.

L. Capitalize words referring to a particular deity, belief, or religious object:

| *Capitalize* | *Do not capitalize* |
|---|---|
| God | the gods are angry |
| Trinity | divine |
| Ten Commandments | deity |
| Hinduism | holy |
| B.C. (for Before Christ) | a church |
| Bible | religion |
| Torah | |
| Jehovah | |

Pronouns referring to deity are usually capitalized:

▶ Jehovah, as presented in the Bible, sometimes shows His anger.

**Practice** ▶   Capitalize the necessary letters.

▶ The east is the home of many religions, including christianity, hinduism, judaism, islam, and buddhism.

**Practice**   Capitalize the necessary letters in the sentences that follow.

1. The rules that govern our electoral politics need to be changed.
2. President jimmy carter lost his attempt for a second term after wasting time, money, and energy working for his reelection.
3. In an article in *newsweek* entitled "the six year presidency," Jack Valenti wrote, "a president's noblest stirring is toward his place in history."
4. willie morris, who wrote *north toward home,* moved to the north but now lives in oxford, mississippi, the deep south.
5. The torah is the name of the first five books of the bible.
6. One wednesday last fall, i began sitting in on a world history class and found it so interesting that i signed up for history 102.

7. My five-year-old son, ted, asked me, "what makes a car run, dad?"
8. I told him, "gasoline, son."
9. My favorite teacher at carver high school was mr. harry berger, but he is teaching at some junior high school now.
10. She asked us to write an essay entitled "a time I would like to forget."

## 11.2 End Punctuation (., ?, !)

### Explanation

A ▸ Use a period (.), question mark (?), or exclamation point (!) to end all sentences. Errors in end punctuation are designated EP in the editing checklist.

  a. Use a period to end a sentence that makes a statement or expresses a command:

▸ Capital punishment is a controversial issue.

▸ Turn in your papers by Friday.

▸ Instead of saying "I do," the bride said, "I don't."

Note that the period comes inside the quotation marks.

  b. Use a question mark to ask a question:

▸ Will you come with me?

▸ "Will you come with me?" he asked.

Note that the question mark comes inside the quotation marks.

  c. Use an exclamation point after a sentence that expresses strong emotion:

▸ Stop that fighting!

B ▸ A period is also used to indicate most abbreviations:

► Mr. (mister)     M.D. (medical doctor)     M.A. (Master of Arts)
P.M. (post meridian)     B.C. (Before Christ)

An exclamation point is also used to indicate an interjection, which may not be a sentence: Ouch! Nonsense!

**Practice**     Rewrite the following sentences, using periods, question marks, and exclamation points as necessary.

1. Dr. Sosnoski didn't say, "Will you stop smoking"

   *Dr. Sosnoski didn't say, "Will you stop smoking?"*

2. He said, in a quiet voice, "Stop smoking right now"

   _____

3. "Ouch" I said, "That hurts"

   _____

4. I have been smoking twenty years

   _____

5. "May I wait until after Christmas" I asked

   _____

6. "No" he almost shouted "Now"

   _____

7. Are the Surgeon General and Dr. Sosnoski right about smoking

   _____

## 11.3 The Apostrophe (')

**Explanation: Using the Apostrophe**     The apostrophe has varied uses. You use it to mark the omission of one or more letters or numbers, to form plurals of numerals, letters, and symbols, and to show possession or ownership.

► Use the apostrophe to mark the omission of one or more letters in contractions, such as:
cannot becomes can't     that is becomes that's

let us becomes let's     it is becomes it's

See Chapter 9.3 for more examples and practice. The symbol in the editing checklist for errors in contractions is the same as the symbol for spelling errors, S. (Be careful not to overuse contractions.)

▶ Use the apostrophe to mark the omission of letters and numbers in the following:

of the clock becomes o'clock

the class of 1984 becomes the class of '84

▶ Use the apostrophe to mark the omission of letters in quoted dialogue:

He said, "I've just been sittin' and waitin' for my dinner."

▶ Use the apostrophe to form the plurals of letters, numbers, and symbols:

one *t* becomes two *t*'s     one 5 becomes two 5's

one $ becomes two $'s

(Many publishers have dropped the apostrophe in such uses and print the above plurals as two ts, two 5s, two $s.
*Do not use the apostrophe to form any other plurals.*

**Practice**     Supply the necessary apostrophes in the following sentences.

1. Its a long way to Maxine's house, but well go there anyway before it is too late. (2 needed)
2. The women's movement began in about 63 or 64 and is still strong in the 80s. (4 needed)
3. "Havent you ever eaten Mama Linda's chicken? Im tellin you; its better than finger lickin good." (5 needed)
4. Its theirs; you cant have it. (2 needed)
5. My children are sick of my telling them to dot their *i*s and cross their *t*s. (2 needed)

**Explanation (with Practice)**     Use the apostrophe to show ownership, as follows:

A. For a singular noun or indefinite pronoun (*anyone, everyone,* and the like), add an '*s*:

▸ the house of Barry becomes Barry's house

▸ the house of Bess becomes Bess's house

▸ the opinion of everyone becomes everyone's opinion

▸ the trials of today becomes today's trials

**Practice** ▸ Fill in the blanks.

▸ the personality of Hans becomes _____

▸ the norms of society becomes _____

▸ the guess of anyone becomes _____

*Note:* You do *not* use the apostrophe for the possessive case of personal pronouns:

▸ The new car is ours.    The choice is theirs.

The computer can't make up its mind.

B. For a plural noun *that does not end in s,* add *'s:*

▸ the play of the children becomes the children's play

▸ the will of the people becomes the people's will

**Practice** ▸ Fill in the blanks.

▸ the hair styles of the women becomes _____

▸ the ways of the geese becomes _____

▸ the yoke of the oxen becomes _____

C. For a plural noun *that ends in s,* add an apostrophe:

▸ the home of the boys becomes the boys' home

▸ the blades of the propellers becomes the propellers' blades

Practice ▶ Fill in the blanks.

- the grades of the students becomes _____

- the restroom of the ladies becomes _____

- the languages of the nations becomes _____

D. If there is joint ownership, the second noun takes the apostrophe:

- the house of my mother and father becomes my mother and father's house

But notice how you punctuate the following two sentences:

- Rico's and Donna's watches were stolen.   (Here the ownership is not joint because Rico and Donna own their watches separately.)

- Gladys's and my house is up for sale.   (When *my* or *our* is used in such compounds, the apostrophe is added to the noun even though the noun comes first. Note also that *mines* and *my's* are not words.)

E. For a compound word, add *'s* or just the apostrophe to the last word in the compound:

- the demands of a mother-in-law becomes a mother-in-law's demands

The symbol in the editing checklist for all errors related to the apostrophe to show ownership is A.

## Practice

A ▶ Change each of the following to the *'s or s'* form.

1. the room of the men ___*the men's room*___

2. the address of the Smiths _____

3. the address of Charles _____

4. the events of today _____

5. the activities of the ladies _____

6. the husband of a woman _____

7. the relationship of a man and a woman _____

8. the good fortune of a son-in-law _____

9. the attitude of the boy _____

10. the attitude of the boys _____

11. the attitude of the people _____

B ► Correct the errors in the sentences below. Some of the apostrophes are misused; some are omitted. The *s*, as well as the apostrophe, is omitted in three places. One sentence is correct. Remember that you do not use an apostrophe when you are simply adding an *s* to make a plural.

1. President Carter recognized the *People's* ~~Peoples~~ Republic of China.

2. Her sons wives all call her Mother, and she calls them her daughters.

3. His victory was everyones victory.

4. Sandra many boyfriends got together for a reunion.

5. The childrens constant crying is driving me insane.

6. The peoples' fear of crime is increasing.

7. My daughter Marys name for ballet is *ba-leg*.

8. Her two boys' call a window a *win-door*.

9. I like to shop at Natures Way.

10. The Joneses rent is due.

11. Pierre's and Violet's car is in the shop.

12. Uz's and Buzz's names come from the Bible.

13. There is so much smoke from the factories that the air smells as though someone house is on fire.

14. My neighbors lawns have almost been ruined by that garbage truck.

15. In our neighborhood we have different committee's to keep things running smoothly.

16. About seven o'clock you can hear the children mother screaming, "Tommy, Angela, come in. It's time to eat."

17. Next to St. Raymonds Catholic Church is the priests home, where eight of these padres live.

## 11.4 The Comma (,)

**Explanation (with Practice)**

Conventional comma use is perhaps the most difficult punctuation skill to master. Professional writers themselves often disagree about certain uses of the comma. Students tend to overuse commas, perhaps because they were taught to use a comma any time they wanted to indicate a pause in a sentence. To avoid comma errors, it is best to learn the general rules for comma use and to follow the advice of the old saying: *when in doubt, leave the comma out.* As you learn the ten rules given in this text, you can then begin to insert commas. The first five rules and Rule #10 are referred to and put to use in Chapter 6 in connection with writing whole sentences; this section contains an explanation of all ten rules. Make frequent use of them when you are editing your papers. The general abbreviation for comma omission or misuse in the editing checklist is C; the symbols for the individual rules are C-1 to C-10.

**Rule #1.** Use a comma after a subordinate clause when it begins a sentence. (See Chapter 6.2.) Subordinate clauses begin with such conjunctions as *when, if, because, after, although, as, while, since, even though, before,* and *wherever.*

► While the girl pushed the car, her father watched.

But when the dependent clause comes at the end of the sentence, you do not ordinarily need a comma. (See Rule #10 for exceptions.)

► Her father watched while the girl pushed the car.

**Practice** ► Supply the necessary commas.

We were greatly surprised when we found out that Mr. Morales had cancer. But we are not depressed. While there is life there is hope. We know he will get well because he is such a fighter. If Mr. Morales will just do what the doctor says he will live many more years.

**Rule #2.** Use commas to set off an adjective clause if the clause is *not essential* to the meaning of the sentence. (See Chapter 6.3.) Adjective clauses usually begin with *who, which,* or *that.*

► My mother, who likes sardine sandwiches, is an unusual person.

You can omit the clause *who likes sardine sandwiches* and the sentence still makes good sense. Therefore, you need commas. But if the adjective clause is *essential* to the meaning of the sentence, do not use commas:

► My mother is the only one in our family who likes sardine sandwiches.

This time if you omit the clause, the sentence does not make sense. *Hint: Which* clauses usually take commas; *that* clauses seldom do.

**Practice** ► Supply the necessary commas.

Great Britain who was our ally went to war with Argentina who was also our ally. Americans who sided with either Argentina or Britain were criticized. This war which caused many deaths was a tragedy and should never have happened.

**Rule #3.** Use a comma before a coordinating conjunction when it joins two independent clauses. (See Chapter 6.4.) The coordinating conjunctions are *and, but, for, yet, so, or,* and *nor.*

► The weather was stormy, and it was very late.

► The weather was stormy, but I was not cold.

Do not use a comma before a coordinating conjunction when it joins two words, two phrases, or two dependent clauses, such as the following:

- ► <u>Carlos</u> and <u>Lucia</u> are going swimming.   (two nouns)

- ► At lunchtime, we <u>were throwing</u> our food away and <u>were creating</u> quite a disturbance.   (two verb phrases)

- ► When you see those things happen, you will know <u>that the proph-ecy has been fulfilled</u> and <u>that the world is doomed.</u>   (two dependent clauses)

**Practice** ► Supply the necessary commas.

Joseph's brothers took his coat of many colors and then threw him into a pit. Later, they saw a company of Ishmaelites and they lifted Joseph out of the pit and sold him to the Ishmaelites. Joseph was taken to Egypt in slavery but he eventually gained the Pharoah's confidence and became the prime minister. Many years later he saved his brothers from starvation and he told them, ''What you meant for evil, God used for good.''

**Rule #4.**   Use commas to set off most conjunctive adverbs (words like *however, for example, on the other hand, nevertheless, moreover, therefore,* and *consequently.*) (See Chapter 6.5.)

- ► I know I said I would go; however, I have since changed my mind.   (Here *however* follows a semicolon.)

- ► I agree that is what I should do. However, I just cannot bring myself to do it.   (Here *however* begins a new sentence.)

- ► Children learn to read, however, in spite of poor teaching.   (Here *however* comes in the middle of a simple sentence.)

You usually do not use a comma to set off *then* and *also,* although if you want to indicate a significant pause, you may.

**Practice** ► Supply the necessary commas.

Joseph's brothers had sold him into slavery; however he not only forgave them but also extended to them the hand of friendship. When his father Jacob heard the news, he decided to travel to Egypt. Jacob was an old man; nevertheless he was determined to see his son. When his father arrived, Joseph fell at his knees; then he wept.

**Rule #5.**  Use a comma or commas to set off an appositive. An appositive is a word, phrase, or clause used as a noun that identifies or explains another noun or pronoun. (See Chapter 6.6.)

▸ Those were the happiest days in my life, the days when I was young and foolish.  (The noun *days* is repeated and then explained.)

▸ One of their neighbors, Boo Radley, was a very mysterious person.  (The pronoun *one* is identified as Boo Radley.)

Practice ▸ Supply the necessary commas.

She lived her entire life in that house a house that had once been admired by all. When I knew her, however, the building was dilapidated. The porch a beautifully constructed work of art was now rotting. The front door, which had been brought over from England, was nailed shut. Curtains now nothing but rags hung wearily behind cloudy windows. Aunt Kathleen, however, a woman up in her eighties did not change. She was poor but still proud.

**Rule #6.**  Use commas to designate items in a series (words, phrases, dependent and independent clauses). Unless your teacher instructs otherwise, use the comma before the *and* that connects the last item.

▸ She bought <u>apples</u>, <u>oranges</u>, and <u>bananas</u>.   (nouns)

▸ Chitty Chat likes <u>to eat tuna</u>, <u>climb Christmas trees</u>, and <u>chase Hubert</u>.  (infinitive phrases)

▸ <u>We went home</u>, <u>we took a dip in the pool</u>, and <u>then we ate breakfast</u>.  (independent clauses)

Adjectives in a series are more complicated. Here is the rule: use a comma between adjectives in a series *only if* you could replace the comma with the word *and*, for example:

▸ He was a tall, lean man.

The comma is correct because you could say "He was a tall and lean man." But look at the next sentence:

▸ He was a nice old man.

A comma is not correct because you would not be apt to say "He was a nice and old man."

**Practice** ▸ Supply the necessary commas.

You are so civilized so intelligent and so self-possessed that you ought to be *Time*'s "Man of the Year." But *Time* named that determined courageous man from Poland instead.

**Rule #7.**   Use a comma or commas with direct quotations. (See page 69 and Section 7 of this chapter.) Here are various possibilities:

▸ The prophet said, "Go in peace."

▸ "Go in peace," the prophet said.

▸ "Go in peace," the prophet said, "and others will follow you."

▸ The prophet said, "Go in peace," and then he left them.

*Note:* The comma always goes on the inside of the quotation marks. Do not use commas with indirect quotations, such as:

▸ The prophet said to go in peace.

▸ The prophet said that we should go in peace.

**Practice** ▸ Supply the necessary commas.

"If I were you" my dad said "I wouldn't go out in the rain." I told him that I was glad he wasn't me.

**Rule #8.**   Use a comma or commas to set off items in dates and addresses, but not ZIP codes:

► I was born <u>Friday</u>, <u>October 12</u>, <u>1938</u>, in <u>Charleston</u>, <u>South Caro</u>-lina.

► His address is <u>Apt. A</u>, <u>1426 M Street</u>, <u>Washington</u>, <u>D.C.</u> <u>20012</u>.

Do not use commas when prepositions introduce places and dates.

► He was born in Chicago in 1926.

**Practice** ► Supply the necessary commas.

Abraham Lincoln was born in Hardin County Kentucky February 12 1809. He died in 1865.

**Rule #9.**   Use a comma after an introductory phrase if the comma makes the meaning of the sentence clearer:

► After eating, my horse and I set out on our lonesome trip.

► In the still of the night, groans can sometimes be heard from the chest in the attic.

Avoid using commas after short introductory phrases if the meaning of the sentence is clear without the comma.

► Later that day they came to our rescue.

**Practice** ► Supply the necessary commas.

While visiting Mary suddenly became ill. After trying for hours to locate her husband my sister and I took her to the hospital. At about ten o'clock her husband finally arrived.

**Rule #10.**   Use a comma or commas to set off words, phrases, or clauses if they *clearly* break the flow of the sentence. Sometimes the word or words will be at the beginning of the sentence:

► Darren, please drop what you are doing and give me a hand.

Sometimes the word or words will be in the middle of the sentence:

► My grandmother, known for her habit of chewing tobacco, is nearly ninety. (This break in the middle of a sentence is often a nonessential adjective clause, Rule #2, or an appositive, Rule #4.)

Sometimes the word or words will be at the end of the sentence, as an afterthought. It is as though the writer makes a statement, *pauses,* then thinks of something else to add:

▶ Anthony was completely honest about what he had done, not that I would have expected him to act any differently. (You are safe using a comma before all such *not* constructions.)

▶ You do agree with me, don't you?

▶ I think we should do everything possible to find a peaceful solution, although I must say that I am not optimistic. (Even though the dependent clause comes at the end of a sentence, the comma is used because the clause is clearly an afterthought.)

▶ They ended the day in complete silence, knowing that any sound would give them away.

Practice ▶ Supply the necessary commas.

Bob said to me, "Carlos that game was the greatest wasn't it?" I turned to my friend who was grinning at me devilishly and said, "Great for you my friend not for me." One of these days I am going to beat Bob in Scrabble although lately I haven't even come close.

## Practice

A ▶ Supply commas as needed, making use of Rule #1 and Rule #3. When you use a comma, cite the rule that applies.

1. As I have already said job opportunities in my field are not good.
2. My name is Bobby Carter and I'm looking forward to writing this paper.
3. I will know how to handle my clients and will be able to represent them well.
4. If you can survive this college you will do well in your chosen career.
5. I may never become rich but I will be able to acquire the things I want.

6. If I were to study nursing I know I would like it.
7. She wants to complete college but does not know for sure what the future holds for her.
8. My aunt wants to help open the day care center but she doesn't want to work in it.
9. I wanted to be a bank robber when I was small.
10. Although a degree is not needed to open a nursery school it would help.
11. Because you work hard you will succeed.
12. You will succeed because you work hard.
13. It rained forty days and forty nights and the whole world was destroyed.
14. While the earth lasts seedtime and harvest will not cease.
15. Seedtime and harvest will not cease while the earth lasts.
16. When you see those things happening you will know that the end has come and that the world is no more.
17. It is a two-year course and will prepare me for an office management position.
18. I talk to my friends often and I try to help them.
19. I talk to my friends often and try to help them.
20. She would enjoy helping others as a doctor but she can't stand the sight of blood.
21. She would enjoy helping others as a doctor but can't stand the sight of blood.
22. Some social workers specialize in psychiatric social work because they want to become professional counselors.
23. More businesses than ever before are opening up and they will all need to purchase insurance.

B ▶ Supply commas as needed, making use of Rule #2, Rule #4, and Rule #5. Cite the rule or rules that apply. (One sentence does not need a comma.)

1. Edgar Allan Poe  the master writer of horror stories  did not enjoy great popularity during his life time.
2. Joe registered late; consequently he will have to pay a five dollar fine.
3. Sybil  who is a member of the Symphony Club  gave us two tickets for the performance.
4. Only one person a carpenter was injured.
5. My English textbook which had been lost all semester turned up the day classes ended.
6. Luckily our family lives near the coast because we all love fresh seafood especially shrimp, redfish, and crab.

7. Many plants are killed by owners who pay too much attention to them; for example overwatering has killed many a plant.
8. André who had been cramming the whole night slept through the test.
9. We rushed to the theater to see the movie from the beginning; however it had already started when we arrived.
10. Chico our eccentric next-door neighbor is the only person I know who mows his lawn in a bathing suit.
11. Immunization is now available for three of the most dangerous childhood ailments diptheria, typhoid, and measles.
12. My aunt spends most of her free time involved in outdoor activities particularly fishing, hunting, and camping.
13. Any student who has placed all the commas correctly in this exercise deserves a pat on the back.

C ▸ Each of the sentences below needs at least one comma. Insert the commas as necessary and cite the number of the rule or rules that apply (#6–#10). The editing checklist contains a summary of the rules.

1. I told her not to worry but to stay cool, calm, and collected.

   _Rule #6_

2. It was a dark rainy spring day when we first met wasn't it?

   _____

3. Before riding in the automobile with my father my sister always

   takes a tranquilizer. _____
4. The City Council voted yesterday to increase the sales tax al-

   though they know the city will rise up in protest. _____
5. As director you will be responsible for the management of the center the hiring and training of the personnel and the develop-

   ment of new programs. _____
6. "Ask not what your country can do for you" the president said

   "but ask what you can do for your country." _____
7. In the middle of the night time stands still, and you can hear the

   lonely sound of a hoot owl. _____

8. Make love not war. _____

9. "War is not what I want" he said "but peace." _____

10. Then I left home suitcase in hand not knowing what I would do next.

_____

11. Malcolm X, a leader of a movement to unite black people throughout the world, was assassinated in New York City on February 21 1965. _____

D ▸ Some of the sentences that follow need one or more commas; others are correct. Insert commas as necessary and cite the number of the rule or rules that apply (#1–#10). The editing checklist contains a summary of the rules.

1. *Dictionary* spelled backwards is *yranoitcid* but *madam* spelled backwards is *madam*. _____

2. We ended up walking in circles and bumping into the same security officer. _____

3. As the three of us walked outside we argued about which side of the plaza the car was parked on. _____

4. He said that he wanted the choir to sing at his wake and that he wanted to be buried in his choir robes. _____

5. That afternoon we divided into groups and searched the library for the items on the list. _____

6. All the girls wanted the lead because the leading part was that of a glamorous woman. _____

7. After we unloaded the bus our next task was to pitch the tent.

_____

8. I tried to light the stove but I was unsuccessful because the matches were wet. _____

9. I tried to light the stove but was unsuccessful because the matches were wet. _____

10. Finally when we arrived at the Rivergate the people applauded us and the whole effort seemed worthwhile. _____

11. I love seafood especially crab shrimp and oysters. _____

12. I was guarding Tim Owens a 6'6"guard and I am only 6'. _____

13. If you look back you will turn into a pillar of salt. _____

14. You will turn into a pillar of salt if you look back. _____

15. Dwight Eisenhower the thirty-fourth president of the United States was born in Denison Texas on October 14 1890. _____

16. As I continued to walk down the road I noticed a small inviting brown cabin with smoke coming from the chimney. _____

17. We shared some very hard times together but through it all we stuck together and became like sisters. _____

18. "Life is like walking in the snow" Granny used to say "because every step shows." _____

19. In October of 1975 the Navy sent our family to Los Angeles California where I attended Grossmand High School and met Kim Steve and Colleen. _____

20. Honestly I am about ready to scream; these commas are too much.

_____

# 11.5 The Semicolon (;)

## Explanation

A ▸ The semicolon is used to join independent clauses in compound sentences. Here are two types of sentences that require semicolons:

▸ The pronoun subject of the second independent clause refers back to a noun in the first independent clause:

The prisoners at the penitentiary are rioting; they claim that the new warden has been unfair.

After just three days Gina quit her job; it didn't hold her interest, she said.

▶ One independent clause is related to another by a conjunctive adverb, such as *then* or *however,* for example:

We first tried giving money to that country; then we sent in soldiers.

The governor refused to grant the pardon; however, he did say he might consider the case again next year.

Keep in mind the following rule: use the semicolon to make a compound sentence only if the two independent clauses are closely related in content and only if you could substitute a period for the semicolon. This sentence is incorrect:

▶ In those days he tried various drugs; for example, marijuana, LSD, and cocaine.

If you substituted a period for the semicolon, the last part of the sentence would be a fragment:

▶ For example, marijuana, LSD, and cocaine.

See Chapters 6.4 and 6.5 for more on the use of the semicolon as it functions in a compound sentence.

B ▶ The semicolon is also used to set off items in a series if any one of the items has internal punctuation, for example:

▶ For the climb up Long's Peak we took a tent, which only weighed five pounds; two very light goose down sleeping bags; and enough food for a large, hungry army.

**Practice**  Take out the unnecessary semicolons. (No semicolons need to be added.)

1. Chief Donald Sartisky completed twenty years in the Coast Guard; and then decided to go back to college to finish his degree.
2. He found college quite different from the way he remembered it; however, he adjusted quickly to the new atmosphere.
3. He likes to say, "It is even more difficult; than I remember, but I like the challenge."

4. To his surprise, he found that he had much in common with quite a few of the students; many of them were as old as he.
5. The chief was a hospital corpsman in the Coast Guard; and he wants to pursue a career in nursing when he finishes college.

## 11.6 The Colon (:)

The uses of the colon are varied. They include the following:

A. Use a colon after the salutation of a business letter:

▸ Dear Dr. Rittenberg:

B. Use a colon to separate numbers in the time of day and in Biblical passages:

▸ 1:15 A.M.    Exodus 3:15 (chapter 3, verse 15)

C. Use a colon before items in a series when they come after what could be written as a grammatically complete sentence:

▸ Be sure to buy the following: dates, pecans, raisins, and honey.

But do not use a colon when the items are necessary for the sentence to be complete:

▸ As for me, I like sugar, canned foods, and lots of meat.

You could not write "As for me I like" by itself. Therefore, do not use a colon.

D. Use a colon to introduce indented quotations and quotations that are preceded by grammatically complete sentences, such as the one that follows:

▸ Dr. Hume wrote the following in his book, *Doctors East, Doctors West:* "Only those can enter into her life who approach China's citadel by way of friendship."

When you introduce a written quotation with words like *write, says,* and *said,* it is usually appropriate to use only a comma:

> ▶ In his book Dr. Hume writes, "Only those can enter into her life who approach China's citadel by way of friendship."

See page 70 for more examples of using the colon.

## 11.7 Quotation Marks (" ") and Underlining

**Explanation:**
**Direct Quotations**

Quotation marks are always used in pairs. (Don't let your end-quotation marks carry over to the beginning of a new line, and don't end a line with beginning quotation marks.) Quotation marks have several functions. First, they set off direct quotations, which are the exact words someone says or writes. The quoted words are often a sentence within a sentence, for example:

> ▶ The prophet said to his disciples, "Go in peace."

Note the following:

a. The words the prophet said, *Go in peace,* can function as a complete sentence. (The subject *you* is understood.)
b. A comma comes before the direct quote.
c. The quotation begins with a capital letter.
d. The second set of quotation marks comes after the period.

Here are four variations of the above quotation. Notice the position of the quotation marks, commas, and the question mark, and notice how capitalization is used.

> ▶ "Go in peace," the prophet said to his disciples.

> ▶ "Go in peace," the prophet said to his disciples, "and Allah will be with you."

> ▶ "Will you go in peace?" the prophet asked. "Allah will be with you."

> ▶ "Will you go in peace? Allah will be with you," the prophet said.

Notice that in the last example quotation marks are used at the beginning and end of what the prophet said, not at the end of each sentence.

See pages 61 and 69 for more on the use of quotations. The omission or incorrect use of quotation marks is designated by the Q in the editing checklist.

**Practice**     Rewrite the following using quotation marks and other necessary punctuation. Two words need to be capitalized.

1. What's the matter Richard's mother asked. _____

   *"What's the matter?" Richard's mother asked.*

2. It's those same boys he said. They'll beat me. _____

   _____

3. You've got to get over that. Now go on she said. _____

   _____

4. Richard replied but I'm scared. _____

   _____

5. She said how can I let you back down now. _____

   _____

6. Please Momma he said don't make me fight. _____

   _____

**Explanation: In-**    Do not use quotation marks to set off indirect quotations, which are
**direct Quotations**    *not* the exact words that someone says or writes, for example:

▸ She said she would try harder next time.

The words she actually used were these: "I will try harder next time." She did *not* say, "She would try harder next time." The writer used those words to tell what she said. Here are two more examples:

▸ Hume wrote that to enter into the life of China one must approach that nation by way of friendship.

▶ The union members carried signs saying that they would not compromise.

## Practice

A ▶ The following are direct quotations. Rewrite them as indirect quotations. Be sure to write verbs in the past tense as necessary.

1. The School Board said to the union, "You are demanding far too much money." *The School Board said to the union that they were demanding far too much money.*

2. The union replied, "We only want a fair wage." _____

_____

3. The School Board said, "Take your case to the taxpayer." _____

_____

4. The union then said, "The School Board is responsible for the wages of teachers." _____

_____

B ▶ The following sentences are written as indirect quotations. Rewrite them as direct quotations. Change the verbs in the quotations themselves to the present tense.

1. The police chief said that he needed more cooperation from the judges. *The police chief said, "I need more cooperation from the judges."*

2. The judges said that they were already giving out much stiffer sentences. _____

_____

3. The police chief responded that dangerous criminals were still being let out on the streets. _____

4. The judges said that they could not be blamed for the amount of crime in the streets. _____

_____

5. The police chief said that the judges could help. _____

_____

**Explanation: Other Uses of Quotation Marks and Underlining**

Quotations marks have other uses as well.

A. To set off words used as words:

▶ Students often confuse "their" with "there."

It is just as correct, however, to underline such words.

▶ Students often confuse their with there.

Use underlining, not quotations, for foreign words:

▶ coup de grace      femme fatale

(*Note:* In print, italics replace underlining.)

B. To set off the titles of short written works, as follows:

▶ an article in a magazine—"The Power of Islam"

▶ a chapter of a book—"A Time to Laugh"

▶ a poem—"Freedom"

▶ an essay—"The Time I Learned Humility"

Longer works are underlined (italicized in print):

▶ a book—To Kill a Mockingbird

▶ a play—Macbeth

▶ a magazine—Newsweek

Longer works (which are underlined) often contain shorter works (which take quotation marks). A book, for example, contains chapters; a magazine contains articles.

C. To set off the titles of television programs and songs. Underline the titles of movies:

▶ ''Sixty Minutes''      ''White Christmas''      <u>The African Queen</u>

## 11.8 Other Punctuation

**Explanation**  The use of the hyphen (-) is discussed in Chapter 9.5. Although you should generally avoid using the dash (—) and parentheses [( )], here are the rules for the times when you do need them:

A. Use the dash to emphasize certain words, usually at the end of the sentence:

▶ One punctuation mark is misused more than any other—the comma.

▶ There is just one course that I can never seem to pass—Math 1111.

B. Use the dash to indicate an aside to the reader:

▶ She said the ''girls''—they are all over sixty—will play bridge to-night.

▶ The game between Alabama and Michigan—it is sure to be close—will be played in the Superdome.

*Note:* When typing, use a double hyphen for a dash and do not leave a space on either side of it.

C. You may substitute parentheses for the dash when you make an aside to the reader:

▶ She said the ''girls'' (they are all over sixty) will play bridge to-night.

▶ The game between Alabama and Michigan (it is sure to be close) will be played in the Super Dome.

D. Use parentheses to give dates.

▶ Booker T. Washington (1856–1915) was a black American educator.

▶ In her article in the *Atlantic Monthly* (September 1978), she wrote . . .

# Index